sound synthesis with VST INSTRUMENTS

Simon Millward

WITHDRAWN

UNIVERSITY OF CHICHE
AUTHOR:
D1426153
TITLE:
CLASS No:
786.7
MIL
DATE:
8.2006
SUBJECT:
MUS

PC Publishing

PC Publishing
Export House
130 Vale Road
Tonbridge
Kent TN9 1SP
UK

Tel 01732 770893
Fax 01732 770268
email info@pc-publishing.com
web site http://www.pc-publishing.com

First published 2002

© Simon Millward

ISBN 1 870775 73 2

All rights reserved. No part of this publication may be reproduced or transmitted in any form, including photocopying and recording, without the written permission of the copyright holder, application for which should be addressed to the Publishers. Such written permission must also be obtained before any part of this publication is stored in an information retrieval system of any nature.

British Library Cataloguing in Publication Data
A catalogue record for this book is available from the British Library

Cover design by Michelle Raki

Printed in Great Britain by Bell and Bain, Glasgow

Contents

Acknowledgements

My thanks to:

Steinberg – Arbiter Pro Audio UK
Emagic – Sound Technology UK
Paul Beecham – Splash Recording Studio
Véronique Manaut
Risto Sampola
Patrick Stottrop
Music Technology staff and colleagues at the University of York
Applied Acoustics Systems
Bitheadz
GForce
Millenium Music Software
Muon Software
Native Instruments
Sonic Syndicate
Waldorf

and to my friends and family

Dedication

This book is dedicated to my mother and father.

Introduction

VST Instruments (short for Virtual Studio Instruments) are virtual models of sound synthesizers, drum modules, samplers or newly-imagined musical instruments and function within popular VST-compatible host sequencing software such as Steinberg Cubase and Emagic Logic. Most VST Instruments also function in stand-alone form. Through the wonders of advanced software engineering, virtual instruments are now available which match the performance and behaviour of real-world units and, what's more, they are available to anyone with a Mac or PC home computer and can be played in real-time via a conventional MIDI keyboard. VST Instruments offer an unprecedented opportunity for the exploration of sound and musical creativity. Since their introduction, the world of hi-tech music and audio has never been so full of possibilities for experimentation and the creation of new sounds.

'Sound Synthesis with VST Instruments' provides a detailed introduction to sound synthesis and the practical use of VST Instruments. It explores the theoretical aspects of sound and the main sound synthesis techniques, features a comprehensive listing of VST Instruments and provides practical tutorials on synthesizing sounds and using VST Instruments in general. It is relevant to all those who are interested in sound synthesis and particularly those who intend to create their own sounds using VST Instruments and software synthesizers. As well as those VST Instruments which use sound synthesis techniques, the book also covers the operation of sampling instruments, drum and percussion modules and simpler preset and playback units.

The first three chapters of the book provide an introduction to VST Instruments, sound theory and the main sound synthesis and sampling techniques. These include subtractive, additive, FM, physical modelling and granular synthesis, and sampling. If you can understand some of the techniques and terminology involved then you stand a better chance of synthesizing your own sounds with any chosen synthesis instrument.

The remaining chapters go on to link the theoretical aspects of sound and sound synthesis to the practical by describing a collection of VST Instruments, by providing tutorials on synthesizing specific sounds and by describing how to build your own virtual subtractive synthesizer and a virtual electric guitar. The VST Instrument reviews include many of the currently available products; a useful reference for anyone searching for a VST Instrument or software synthesizer. The section on practical projects includes the synthesizing of known real-world musical instruments as well as original sounds. Various techniques with specific VST Instruments are also explored.

Although the VST Instruments described in the book exist in the virtual world inside a computer, the concepts explored can equally be applied to equivalent real-world instruments. The use of VST Instruments in this context makes a practical and convenient solution for the study and exploration of sound synthesis in general. This book is suitable for all levels of musicians, sound synthesists, sound designers and home recordists and also provides a useful reference for professionals in the audio and music industries.

1 Sound synthesis, software synthesizers and VST Instruments

What is sound synthesis?

The word 'synthesis' is most often associated with either the creation of chemical compounds or the creation of sounds. In the music world 'synthesis' is usually associated with the production of 'electronic' sounds using sound synthesizers. In fact, some kind of sound synthesis is involved with the production of all kinds of sounds and so not all synthesized sounds are necessarily 'electronic' in nature. Synthesis is the creation of a composite whole from a number of separate elements. It implies the mixing together of two or more things to create something new.

Sound synthesis involves the creation and processing of sound from a number of building blocks. These include a control interface, such as the parameters found on the front panel of most electronic synthesizers, and a synthesis engine, such as a network of electronic or digital circuits designed to interpret the parameter settings and produce the sound. Sound synthesizers also normally require some method by which the user can initiate sounds and musical events. This is known as the performance interface (or the controller) and usually comes in the form of a piano-type keyboard.

Until recently, most commercially available sound synthesizers were stand-alone units including a keyboard, front panel controls and the sound-making circuitry. These elements came to be the dominant architecture for most sound synthesis instruments (see Figure 1.1). The flow of data through such a system can be summarised as follows: the performance interface transforms raw musical gestures into data which can be understood by the control interface. The control interface defines the effect of this data according to a set of parameters. The synthesis engine interprets the settings of the parameters to produce the sound output.

Figure 1.1
A simplified flowchart for a sound synthesizer

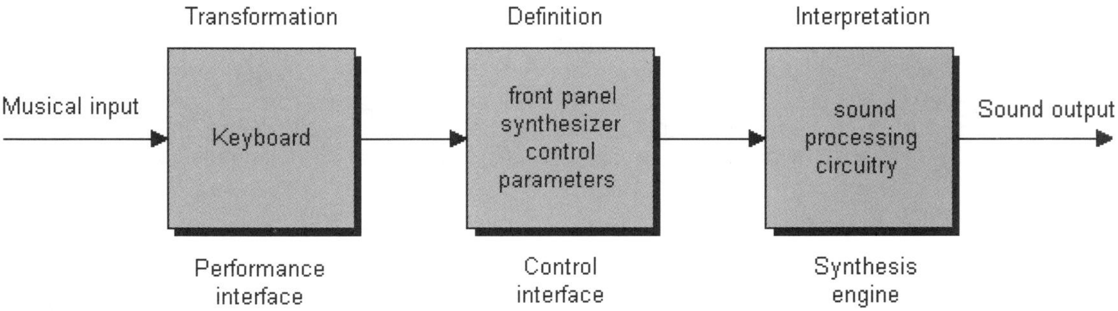

Early synthesizers used what is known as analogue synthesis to produce their sounds. Analogue synthesis is the creation of sound using voltage controlled signals, voltage controlled filters and amplifiers. Analogue synthesis techniques include additive, subtractive and wavetable synthesis. Digital synthesis has since been introduced and is now widely used in almost all synthesizers. Digital synthesis replaces analogue signals with numerical representations, and processes all signals in the digital domain. Digital technology has been responsible for the introduction of many revolutionary new synthesis methods such as FM, sampling, physical modelling and granular techniques. Many of these are outlined in detail in Chapter 3.

What is a software synthesizer?

In addition to the real-world synthesizers described above, further developments in audio hardware and computer processor speed have led to the commercial availability of software synthesizers. A software synthesizer is a special kind of sound synthesizer which exists only in software. Software synthesizers are available as stand-alone programs which you can run in a standard home computer. They use the resources of the host computer's operating environment and hardware to create a fully functional sound synthesizer which exists only in the virtual world of RAM. When you switch off your computer the software synthesizer is no longer available.

Software synthesizers also come in the form of VST Instruments (Virtual Studio Instruments). These operate within VST (Virtual Studio Technology) compatible host software such as Cubase VST, Cubase SX, Nuendo or Logic Audio. Almost all software synthesizers and VST Instruments feature a graphical user interface (GUI) which appears on the computer monitor screen. This is used to adjust the control parameters for the instrument in a similar manner to the front panel controls of a real-world unit. The controller (performance interface) for software synthesizers is usually a MIDI keyboard attached to the computer via a MIDI interface. The sounds of the software synthesizer can thus be triggered live via MIDI allowing the instrument to be played in a similar fashion to a real-world synthesizer (see Figure 1.2).

Software synthesizers are virtual models of imaginary or real-world synthesizers and vary greatly in their design and purpose. The design might be taken from an exisiting real-world instrument, as in the case of the Native Instruments Pro-52, which is a virtual emulation of the original SCI Prophet 5 analogue synthesizer, or it might bear no relation to any particular instrument, as in the case of Native Instruments Reaktor, which is an extremely sophisticated modular software synth, sampler, sequencer and audio processing system.

The types of sound synthesis emulated by software synthesizers vary greatly and might encompass any type of sound synthesis from the worlds of traditional analogue or digital synthesis (although, strictly speaking, all software synthesis is ultimately 'digital' in nature and all references to analogue techniques are virtual emulations of the real thing).

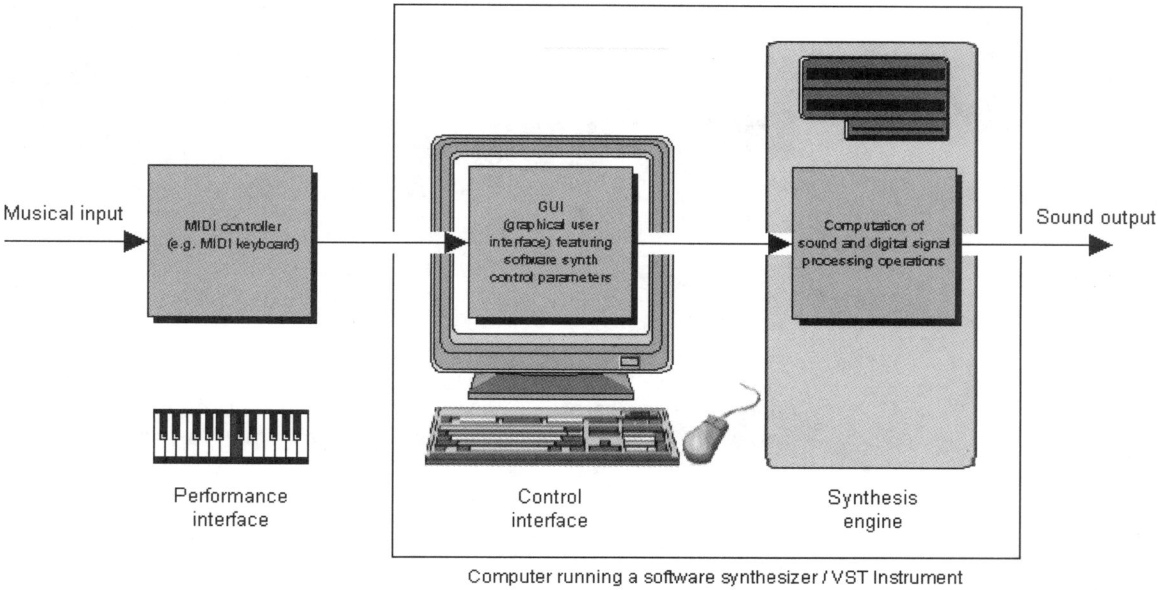

Figure 1.2
A simplified flowchart for a software synthesizer/VST Instrument

What are VST Instruments?

VST is short for 'Virtual Studio Technology' and was introduced by Steinberg in 1996 for their Cubase VST MIDI+Audio sequencing software. Virtual Studio Technology attempts to bring most of the elements of the audio and MIDI recording worlds under the control of a single operating environment. It features such things as a virtual audio mixing console, audio effects and processing units, comprehensive audio routing and multi-tracking capabilities and sophisticated recording and manipulation of MIDI data.

VST compatible audio effects and processing units come in the form of 'plug-ins' which can be added to the host software when required. VST 2.0 technology took this concept one stage further by introducing a special kind of plug-in which allows the transmitting and receiving of MIDI data as well as audio. This encouraged the development of more sophisticated regular plug-ins but, more importantly, it inspired the development of software synthesis and sampling instruments which can operate within the convenient environment of the host software. These became known as VST Instruments (short for Virtual Studio Instruments).

A VST Instrument could be a software synthesizer or sampler, a software drum module or some other virtual sound-making device and, once activated inside the host software, it can be played via MIDI using an external MIDI keyboard or triggered from an existing MIDI Track. In many respects VST Instruments behave in much the same way as their real-world counterparts, the only major difference being that they reside inside your computer.

2 Sound fundamentals

If you intend to create your own synthesized sounds it is helpful to understand the nature of sound itself and some of the common terminology which is used to describe it. It is also helpful to understand how sound is perceived by the human ear. This chapter explores sound from a number of different perspectives including how sound is perceived, how it can be measured and how it can be broken down into its fundamental components. Understanding sound is often a complex issue and this chapter may therefore occasionally require considerable intellectual effort.

The perception of sound

In physical terms, sound can be described as wave motions or vibrations in air (or some other medium). The human sensory response to this phenomenon is an excitation in the hearing mechanism – the ear. What is of particular interest with regard to the human perception of sound is the range of vibrational power and the range of vibrational frequencies within which the human ear is sensitive and how the ear and brain respond to these phenomena. The lower range of frequencies to which we are sensitive can literally be felt in the chest and other parts of the body especially at higher volume levels. However, it is above all the human ear which is responsible for capturing the vibrational information in the air which surrounds us. The brain processes and interprets this information which is perceived as sound. When there are no vibrations (or very few), this is perceived as silence (although anything approaching pure silence is very rare). For most of us, the act of hearing also involves an emotional response, especially when listening to musical sound.

Info

Sound always requires a medium, such as air, through which to travel. It cannot travel through a vacuum.

The perception of sound in all its many forms requires a sensitive piece of equipment, and the human ear is probably the most sensitive of all the apparatus of the human body. It is able to detect sound vibrations over an extremely wide dynamic range from the smallest of vibrations at the threshold of hearing to the most powerful vibrations at the threshold of pain. The difference between these two extremes can be measured at a ratio of approximately 2 million to 1. Sound level is generally measured using the decibel (dB), a relative measure of loudness on a logarithmic scale. The dynamic range of the human hearing system equates to around 120dB SPL (Sound Pressure Level). On this scale, 1dB is roughly equivalent to the ear's perception of a just noticeable difference in sound level (although this depends very much on the precise nature of the sound). A change of approximately 10dB is equivalent to a doubling of the 'perceived loudness'. In other words, the subjective impression of a doubling of sound intensity is equivalent to a raising of the sound pressure level by approximately 10dB.

To appreciate what this means in a real-world example, consider the following. To double the perceived loudness of a single sound source, such as a single violin in an orchestra, we would actually need ten violins (i.e. the change in sound pressure level between one violin and ten violins is around +10dB SPL). The ear, therefore, responds to loudness logarithmically. To get something which sounds twice as loud we need a tenfold increase in signal level. However, all this is further complicated by the fact that, in scientific terms, a real physical doubling in sound pressure level is equivalent to only 6dB. The ear, therefore, requires a greater increase in sound pressure level than would be expected to achieve the subjectively perceived result. This action could be described as a natural form of sound compression i.e. the ear tends to reduce the apparent loudness of sound signals as the sound pressure level is increased.

The ear can also differentiate between minute changes in frequency (referred to as pitch perception in the musical world). Frequency is measured in hertz (Hz), a measure of the number of times that a sound wave oscillates per second. The ear is tuned to a set range of frequencies between approximately 20Hz and 20kHz. It does not have a flat frequency response since it is more sensitive in the middle of this range (between 250Hz and 4kHz with a peak sensitivity between 3.5 and 4kHz). This sensitivity is also influenced by the sound pressure level (loudness) of the sound since, as mentioned above, the ear is a natural compressor. At levels greater than 60dB SPL its variable response to different frequencies flattens out significantly (particularly below 1kHz). However, for low frequencies the pitch is perceived as going down as the loudness is increased, and for high frequencies the pitch is perceived as going up as the loudness is increased.

Similar to loudness perception, pitch is perceived logarithmically. For example, to perceive the successive octaves for any chosen pitch requires that the distance in hertz between one octave and the next is always doubled. In other words, there is not a constant, linear, frequency distance between each octave. Instead, the frequency value of successive octaves must be multiplied by a factor of two to achieve the perceived one octave rise in pitch.

With two ears, our hearing apparatus has the ability to locate the directional source of each sound with a high degree of accuracy. This is important for spatial and panoramic auditory perception and plays a major role in our appreciation of stereo sound. (Note that the accuracy of spatial perception also depends upon the frequency of the sound source, since as the frequency descends into the bass region it becomes progressively more difficult to locate precisely.)

Info

The physical properties of sound are measured using units of amplitude and frequency. These phenomena are perceived by the ear in terms of loudness and pitch. Although there is a link between the physical and perceptual criteria, this link is not always uniform or entirely predictable.

Describing sound with words

Using the remarkable apparatus of the human ear in a musical and sound synthesis context involves the detailed perception of pitch, loudness and timbre. The description of sound using written or verbal language also revolves around these three concepts. The words 'pitch' and 'loudness' are easily understood since they relate directly to the frequency and level intensity of the sound and can be measured and compared on the well-established relative scales mentioned above. Timbre is less obvious. This is derived from the French word meaning 'tone colour' or 'sound texture' and refers to the overall tonal quality of a sound. The primary cue for the recognition of timbre is the harmonic content of the sound. Secondary influences include the attack/decay and vibrato/tremolo characteristics. The attack and decay characteristics describe how the amplitude of the sound evolves over time. Vibrato is a periodic variation in pitch and tremolo is a periodic variation in amplitude, often applied during the steady-state segment of the sound.

Unlike pitch and loudness, timbre has no clearly defined scale and its description usually involves the use of a wide range of adjectives. These give an indication of what the tone 'sounds like' but are not very precise. Common adjectives employed include 'biting', 'breathy', 'bright', 'brittle', 'buzzy', 'clangy', 'coarse', 'cutting', 'dark', 'dry', 'dull', 'fat', 'flat', 'full', 'high', 'hollow', 'mellow', 'metallic', 'nasal', 'piercing', 'pure', 'raspy', 'resonant', 'rich', 'rounded', 'sharp', 'shrill', 'thick', 'thin', 'tinny', 'twangy', 'vibrant', 'warm', 'wet' and so on. It is also commonplace to compare a timbre to an existing instrument using terms like 'brassy', 'reedy', 'string-like' and 'percussive'. While these kinds of words are not very precise they are still useful for attempting to describe the tone colour of any chosen sound. Timbral descriptions of this kind are of particular importance in the world of sound synthesis and are therefore often used throughout the course of this book. However, readers should always bear in mind that describing sound with words is a bit like trying to describe a painting you have never seen. It is better to actually hear the sound just as it is better to actually see the painting.

Vibrations in more detail

As outlined above, sound involves vibrations in air (or some other medium) which are detected by the ear and interpreted by the brain. These vibrations are actually compressions and rarefactions (pressure changes in the air). Compression is the pushing together of air molecules within a given space while rarefaction involves pulling the molecules further apart from each other (the opposite of compression). The characteristics of these compressions and rarefactions produce the particular identity of each sound and these characteristics can be represented graphically as a waveform (see Figure 2.1).

The common analogy for understanding how sound behaves is to imagine vibrations travelling through a stretched spring. This involves the same kind of compressions and rarefactions as sound vibrations. Sound normally has a direction as it travels through the air and generally produces what is known as a longitudinal wave. Sound waves radiate out from the source into three-dimensional space and travel very rapidly (approximately 344 metres per second in air at 20 deg C). The intensity of the sound at different angles and distances from the source varies greatly. The ear actually perceives a mix of the direct sound from the source followed very quickly by the sound waves which are reflected from other nearby surfaces, such as the ground and nearby objects in an outdoor environment, or the walls and floor in an enclosed space.

Sounds from the natural world are often enormously complex, as is the manner in which they behave in different environments. For these reasons they are not immediately useful for gaining an understanding of what is actually taking place. It is more effective to begin with simple sounds which can be easily reproduced, measured and manipulated. One such sound is the sine tone, commonly associated with test signals on electronic equipment and which can be easily produced using a sound synthesizer.

Info

The speed of sound is approximately 344 metres per second in air at 20 deg C (1130 feet per second). This is around 1238 kilometres per hour (770 miles per hour).

Simple waveforms

The sine wave

The pressure changes (compressions and rarefactions) of a sound are commonly represented as a waveform whose shape and amplitude are plotted against time. A sine tone produces a simple waveform which can be easily represented and understood graphically (see Figure 2.1). The central horizontal line is where there is zero energy, (if the waveform itself were to match this line there would be no vibration, i.e. 'silence'). When the waveform rises above the line, there is compression, and when it falls below, there is rarefaction.

Figure 2.1
A sine wave

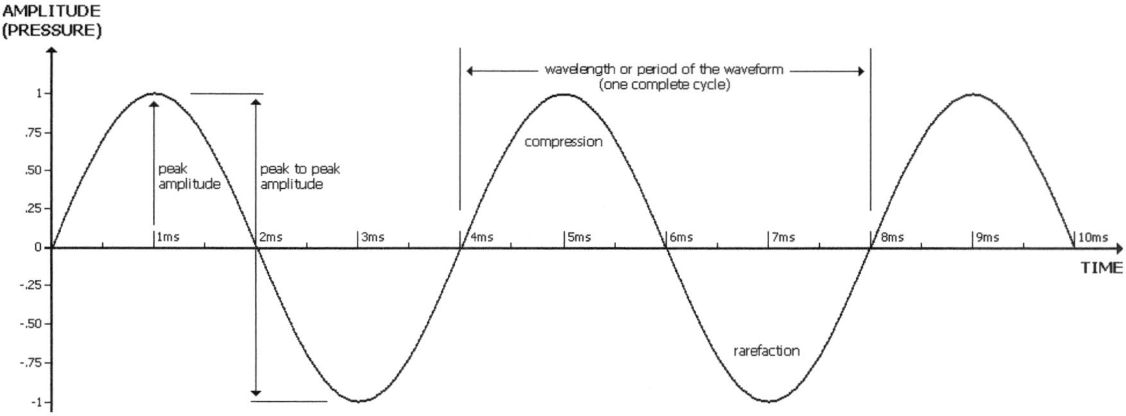

A pure sine tone is based upon the mathematical sine function and produces a uniform, periodic waveform. Uniform means that the shape of the wave is symmetrical and self-similar. Periodic means that the waveform repeats in a continuous cycle at a fixed frequency rate and does not evolve over time. One period is one complete compression and rarefaction cycle (also known as the wavelength). Like all sound waves the sine wave also has an amplitude which is a measure of the depth of the compressions and rarefactions. It contains only one component, which is commonly known as the first harmonic or the fundamental. It is the simplest waveform which can be produced and forms the basic building block for other more complex waveforms.

We can also make some additional observations about the sine wave shown in Figure 2.1. The time ruler reveals that each cycle of this particular waveform has a period of 4ms which means that it repeats at a rate

Info

The most common test tone found in electronic and musical equipment is a pure sine tone at a frequency of 1kHz.

Info

An oscillator is an electronic or digital device designed to produce a regular alternating voltage (or signal) between two values.

of 250 times per second. In other words, its frequency is 250Hz. This is perceived as a pitch just below middle C (C4) on the piano keyboard. In actual physical terms one complete cycle of a sound wave at this frequency is 1.376 metres in length (in air at a temperature of 20 deg C).

We now have an idea of what a pure sine wave looks like and how it behaves but what does it sound like? One real-world source which approximates the sound of a sine wave is that of the sustain segment of a struck tuning fork, but pure sine waves are actually very rare in the natural world. They are, however, easily produced by electronic means using voltage controlled oscillators (VCOs) or digitally controlled oscillators (DCOs).

The alternating signal from the right kind of oscillator produces a perfect sine wave which, when converted into a regular sound wave, can be heard as the characteristic pure tone, as described above. Many readers will have also heard a sine tone in television or radio test transmissions.

So why all this fuss about a simple sine wave? The answer lies in the fact that other more complex periodic wavefoms can be broken down into a number of separate sine waves which oscillate at different frequencies and amplitudes. Understanding simple sine waves therefore helps us understand more complex waveforms. This was first established by Jean Baptiste Fourier (1768 – 1830), who along with Hermann von Helmholtz (1821 – 1894), laid the foundations for the study of timbre at the end of the nineteenth century. Fourier derived a complex mathematical procedure known as the 'Fourier transform' which could calculate the spectrum from a waveform. He also established that there were essentially two ways in which a sound could be represented on a two dimensional graph, amplitude plotted against time (as in Figure 2.1) and amplitude plotted against frequency (as in Figure 2.2). These are also referred to as 'time domain' and 'frequency domain' graphs, respectively. Time domain graphs do not usually show any precise information about the frequency content of the sound. Figure 2.2 shows how a sine wave is represented in the frequency domain.

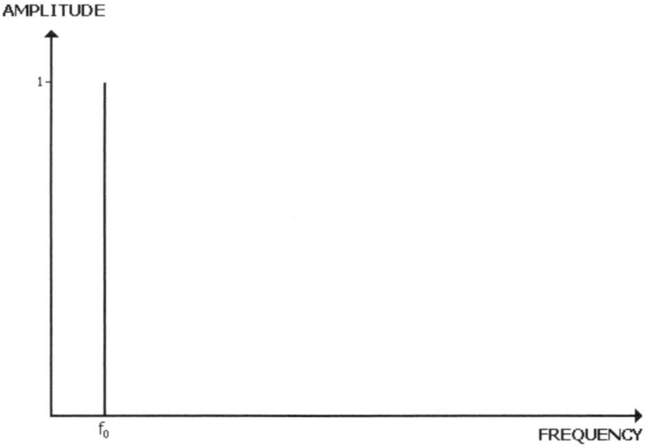

Figure 2.2
A pure sine tone in the frequency domain

As can be seen from the diagram, a pure sine wave contains just one component which oscillates at the frequency which gives the sound its pitch. As mentioned above, this frequency is known as the first harmonic or fundamental. In an amplitude against frequency diagram the fundamental is normally labelled with 'f_0'. (If Figure 2.2 were to represent the same wave as shown in Figure 2.1 then f_0 would equal 250Hz).

Figure 2.3
Adding waveforms a, b and c results in the composite waveform d.

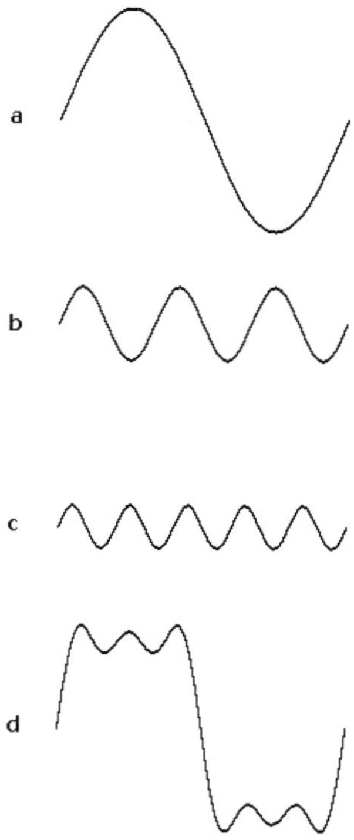

Other simple sound waves

If we take Fourier's discovery that complex waveforms can be broken down into a number of separate sine waves and we reverse the principle i.e. we take, for example, three sine waves oscillating at 220Hz, 660Hz and 1100Hz, where the amplitudes of the second and third waveforms are 1/3 and 1/5 the amplitude of the first wave, and we add them together, then we arrive at a composite waveform whose shape and characteristics we can predict (see Figure 2.3). Adding waves together like this is commonly known as additive synthesis.

The sine waves chosen for Figure 2.3 are related mathematically and harmonically. The 220Hz signal is the lowest frequency with the greatest amplitude and it is usually this component which gives the sound its perceived pitch. The lowest harmonic is usually referred to as the 'fundamental', as described above. In musical terms, 220Hz corresponds with a pitch of A3. A frequency component at double the frequency of the fundamental is known as the second harmonic, three times the frequency of the fundamental is known as the third harmonic, and so on.

This is often referred to as the natural harmonic series. The composite waveform (d) in Figure 2.3 therefore contains the fundamental (f0 at 220Hz) and the third and fifth harmonics (220Hz x 3 and 220Hz x 5). The particular shape of the composite waveform is influenced by the amplitude of each frequency component and choosing 1/3rd the amplitude of the fundamental for the third harmonic and 1/5th the amplitude for the fifth harmonic is not an arbitrary decision. If we were to continue adding all the odd numbered harmonics at similar amplitude ratios (i.e. the seventh harmonic at 1/7th the amplitude of the fundamental, the ninth at 1/9th the amplitude of the fundamental and so on) then we would finish up with a square wave as shown in Figure 2.4. A square wave spends half of its cycle in its most positive position and the other half in its most negative position. Despite its multiple harmonics the square wave shown in Figure 2.4 is still perceived by the ear as a single sound with its pitch at A3 (220Hz).

You may still ask why we would want to create a square wave. As already mentioned, it helps us to understand how a sound can be comprised of a number of sine waves oscillating at different frequencies and with various amplitudes, but there is also another reason. A square wave is more musically interesting and, of course, harmonically richer, than a simple sine wave. It is, therefore, potentially more useful for creating tones in a sound synthesizer. The actual sound of a square wave is a rich, 'hollow' tone and resembles that of a clarinet. Once you are familiar it becomes a recognisable timbre.

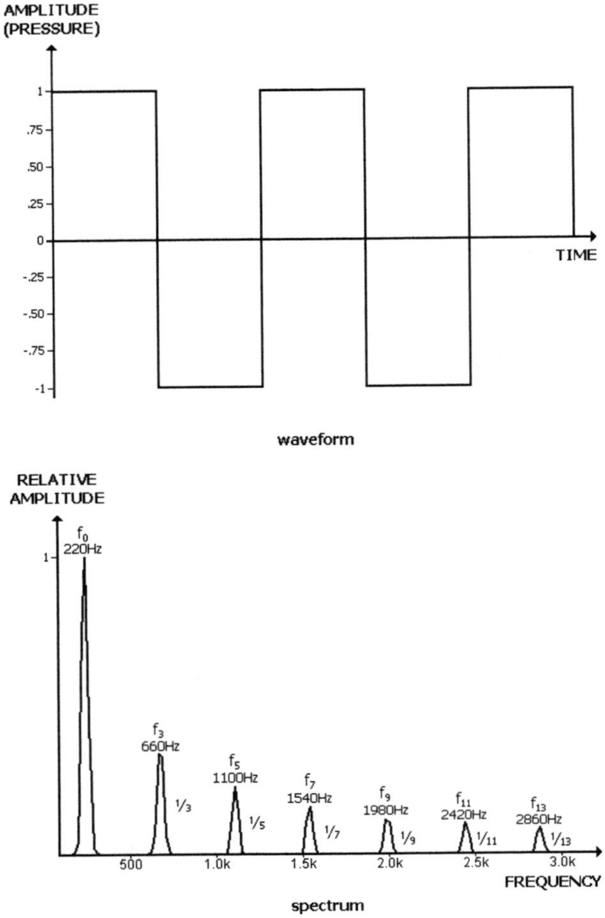

Figure 2.4
Waveform and frequency spectrum of a square wave at 220Hz (A3)

In a similar fashion we can go on to create other composite waveforms which are also musically interesting and useful for the creation of synthesized tones. Figure 2.5 shows three other simple composite waveforms and their spectral components. Like the square wave, these types of waveforms are also commonly found in sound synthesizers.

The sawtooth wave contains all the harmonics in the natural harmonic series with the level of each harmonic at $1/n$ that of the fundamental (where n = the harmonic number). A sawtooth wave produces a sharp 'brass-like' tone.

The triangle wave contains the odd-numbered harmonics at an amplitude of $1/n^2$ that of the fundamental (where n = the harmonic number). A triangular wave produces a simple, 'rounded' tone which resembles that of an organ.

The pulse wave is a variation of the square wave as shown in Figure 2.4. A pulse wave is characterised by its pulse width, the length of time for which the signal is in the compression (or positive) part of its cycle. This is usually expressed as a percentage of one complete cycle. The pulse wave in Figure 2.5 has a pulse width of 25% (it is in its 'high' position 1/4 of the time of each cycle). The spectral components of

Figure 2.5
Some other simple waveforms and their frequency spectra (at 250Hz)

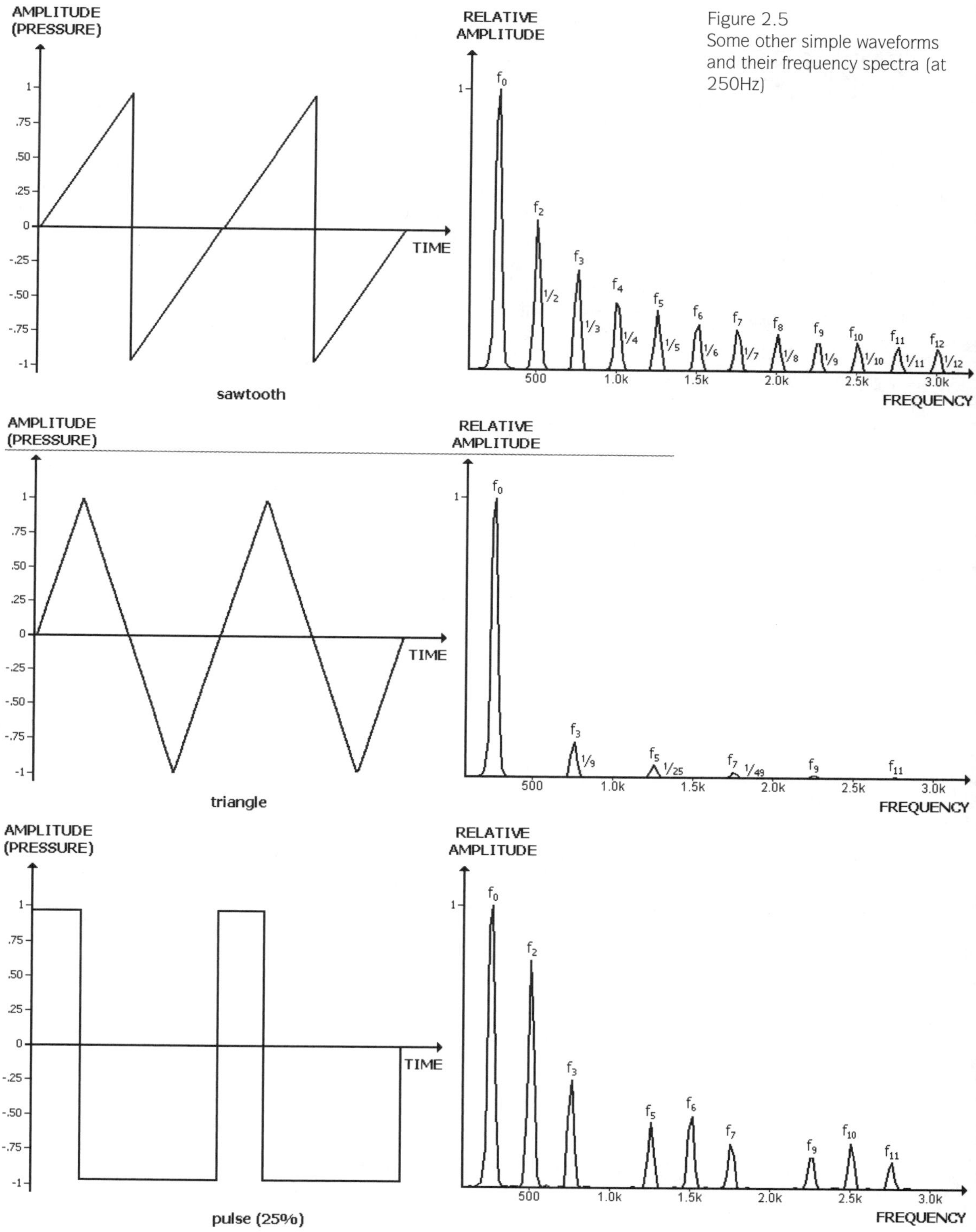

pulse waves can vary greatly but, in general, a pulse wave with a pulse width of 1/n lacks each nth harmonic. Thus the pulse wave shown in Figure 2.5 lacks the fourth, eighth, 12th, 16th ... harmonics.

Info

Pulse waves typically produce rather agressive, 'buzzy' tones which have significantly more high frequency energy than ordinary square waves. As the pulse width is decreased to become very narrow the high frequency energy content increases significantly with a corresponding reduction in lower harmonic energy.

Phase considerations

All the waveforms described so far involve components which are in-phase. Phase refers to the relationships between each component of a complex signal in terms of the time position of the compression and rarefaction parts of each component's waveform. This is usually expressed in terms of the degrees of a circle. Combining two identical waveforms which are perfectly in-phase produces a stronger signal with the same phase as the originals (Figure 2.6, waveforms a and b). Combining two identical waveforms which are, let's say, 90 degrees out-of-phase produces a waveform which is only marginally greater in amplitude and which has a different phase to both of the originals (Figure 2.6, waveforms c and d). Combining two identical waveforms which are 180 degrees out-of-phase results in complete phase cancellation i.e. silence (Figure 2.6, waveforms e and f).

Research has shown that changing the phase of the components of relatively simple waveforms actually has a minimal effect on the perceived timbre. Compared to its sensitivity to the relative amplitudes of the frequency components, the ear is fairly insensitive to the phase relationships. However, with complex sounds, phase changes can play an important role in modifying the timbre.

Figure 2.6
The effects of phase when combining waveforms

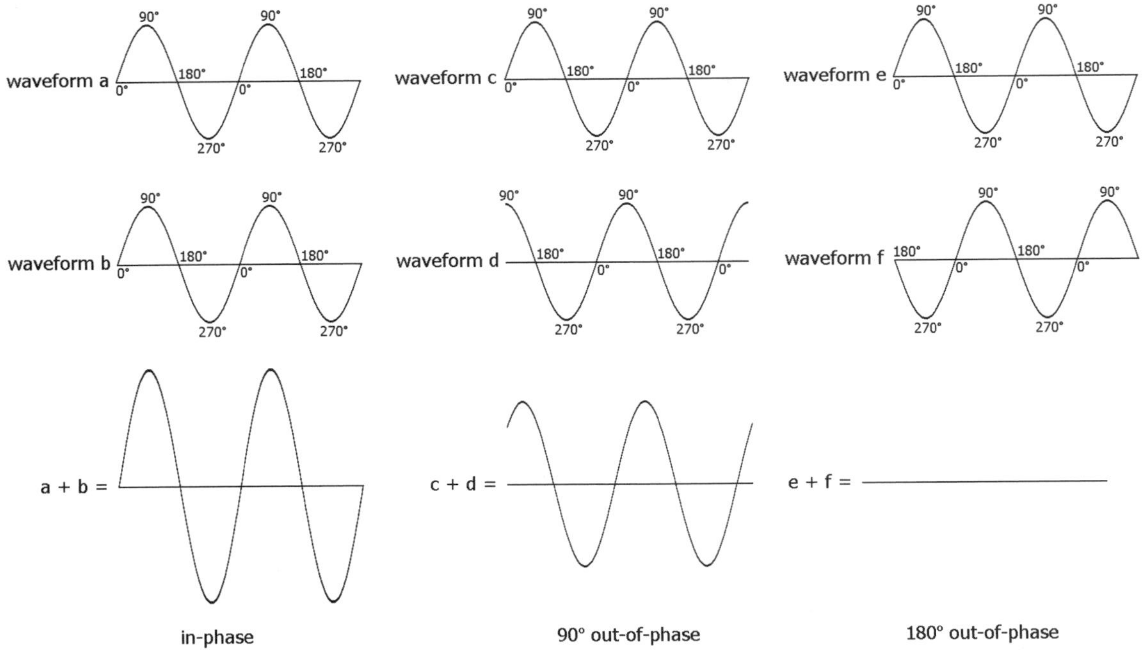

Complex waveforms

All the sounds described above contain only harmonic components and are characterised by a clearly defined periodic waveform, but many sounds contain some or entirely inharmonic spectra with a correspondingly complex waveform. This is particularly true for sounds from the natural world and for acoustic musical instruments. The sounds of acoustic musical instruments are rarely perfectly harmonic and those from the natural world are often entirely inharmonic.

The sound of acoustic musical instruments

The timbral content of acoustic musical instruments can be surprisingly complex. The spectral contents of pitched notes which sound more or less harmonic differ significantly between each instrument and invariably contain no precisely mathematically related amplitude ratios and a number of inharmonic frequency components. These irregularities are often what makes acoustic instruments sound musically alive (too much perfect harmony is actually rather uninteresting to the human ear). For example, bearing in mind that the square wave described above (Figure 2.4) tends to sound like a clarinet, we could conversely take a look at the waveform and spectral components of a clarinet to see if it bears any resemblance to a square wave.

Taking a listen to the timbre of any real clarinet tone reveals that it does, indeed, sound more musically interesting than that of a square wave. Figure 2.7 reveals some of the reasons for this. The figure shows the waveform and 'long term average spectra' (LTAS) for the steady-state segment of a clarinet tone. The clarinet's waveform is periodic but does not resemble that of a square wave. However, looking at its spectral components reveals that it is dominated by the odd-numbered harmonics, a bit like a square wave. The third and fifth harmonics are particularly prominent. The third harmonic even has a higher amplitude than the fundamental but, despite its dominance, the pitch of the sound is still perceived to be A3 (220Hz). The 2nd harmonic is entirely absent in this particular analysis. Comparing the clarinet's spectrum to the square wave shown in Figure 2.4 (which was recorded at the same frequency of 220Hz) reveals that the fifth, seventh, 11th and 13th harmonics in the clarinet tone follow very similar amplitude ratios to the same numbered harmonics in the square wave. However, both the fundamental and ninth harmonics are weaker than might be expected and, as already mentioned, the third is particularly prominent. The spectrum of the clarinet tone is also coloured by several low-level even-numbered harmonics. Unlike the square wave, the actual frequencies of each harmonic are not exact multiples of the fundamental and the amplitude ratios are not precisely related, as would be expected in the spectrum of an acoustic musical instrument.

We can conclude, therefore, that the imperfections in the clarinet tone are what make it sound more interesting and that absolute mathematical precision in the relationship between the harmonics and the ratios of their amplitudes is not necessarily musically desirable. This is valuable information for anyone synthesizing their own timbres (see also Figures 2.13 and 2.14).

For further comparative purposes Figures 2.8 and 2.9 show the waveforms and spectral components of a classical guitar and a piano.

Info

Long term average spectra refers to the process of averaging together the measurements of the spectral components over a period of time to give a single composite reading.

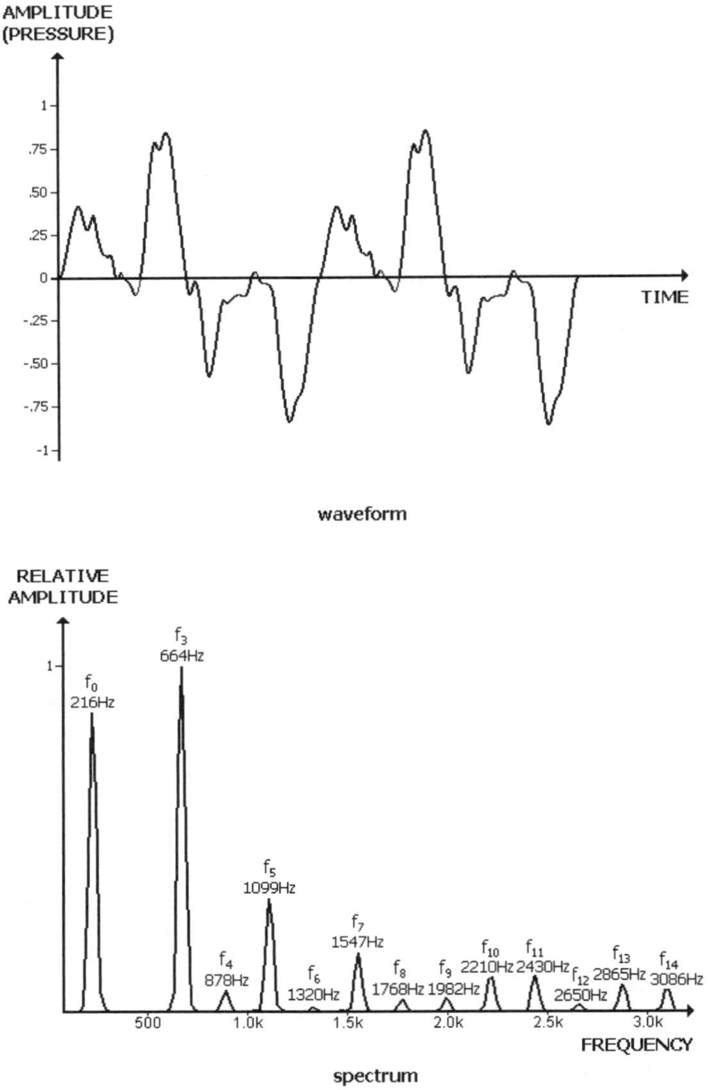

Figure 2.7
The waveform and spectral components of the steady-state segment of a clarinet playing A3 (approximately 220Hz)

Both waveforms are periodic, as would be expected. The guitar has a smooth, rounded and symmetrical waveshape whereas the piano waveshape features lots of angular peaks and irregularities. This behaviour is born out in the frequency spectra for the sounds. The guitar has a comparatively simple set of spectra dominated by the fundamental and the third harmonic in the lower frequencies. The second and fourth harmonics are present at lower amplitudes along with a number of other sporadic low-level components which fade out after the 19th harmonic (at around 2.2k). In contrast, the piano tone is more complex. It is dominated by the fundamental and second harmonic in the lower frequencies followed by two significant concentrated groups of harmonics between the third and seventh and between the ninth and 14th (at a slightly lesser amplitude). The upper harmonics show a continued presence right up to the 27th (almost 3k). These spectral characteristics are typical for a piano tone and produce the rich timbre for which pianos are renowned (see also Figures 2.15 and 2.16).

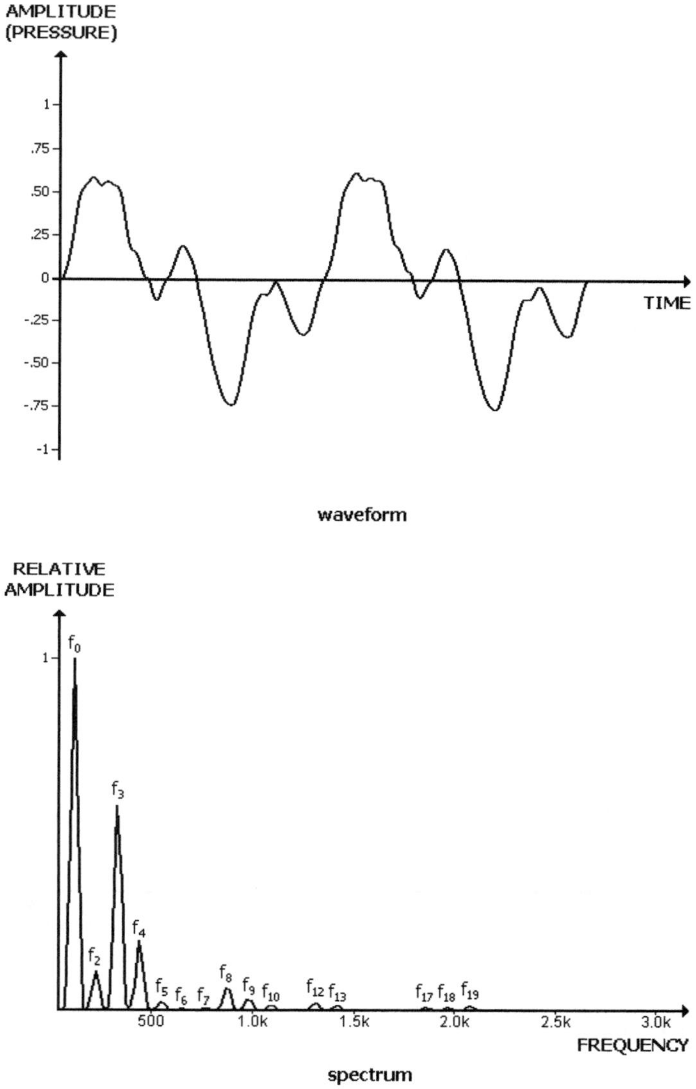

Figure 2.8
The waveform and spectral components of the steady-state segment of a nylon string classical guitar playing A2 (approximately 110Hz)

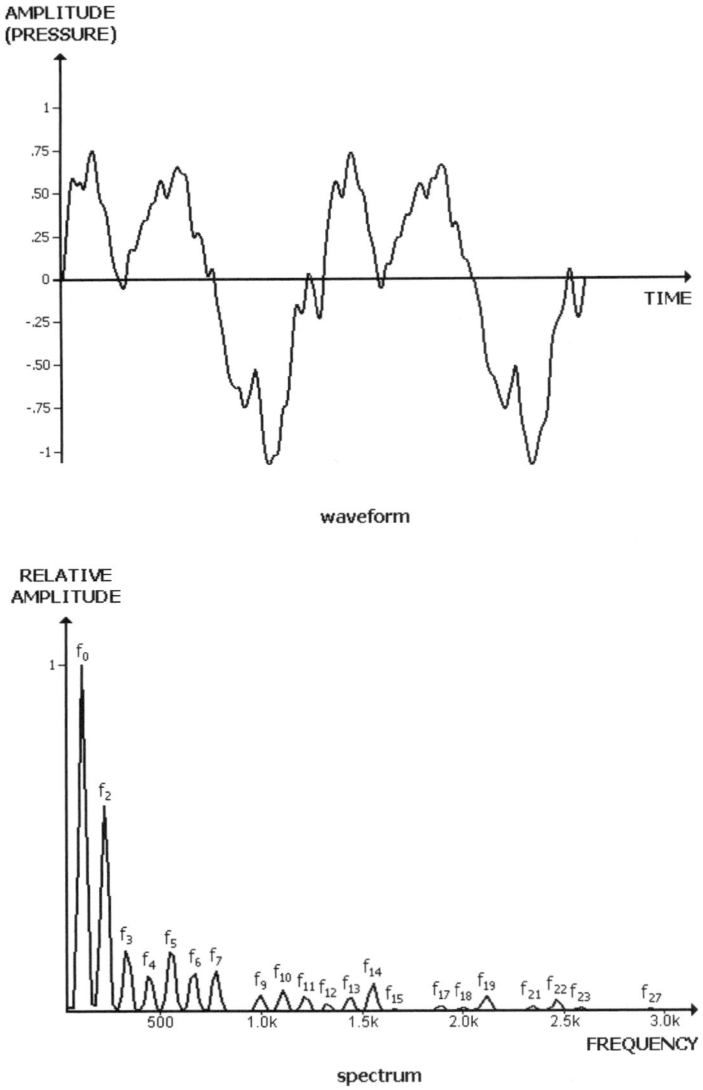

Figure 2.9
The waveform and spectral components of the steady-state segment of a grand piano playing A2 (approximately 110Hz)

Inharmonic sounds

Of course, there are also those sounds which contain only or mainly inharmonic frequency components. These tend to be found in the natural world as various kinds of what might be described as 'noise' and also in percussive musical instruments. Due to their inharmonic nature these kinds of sounds are characterised by aperiodic waveforms i.e. their waveforms contain no clearly defined repeated cycle. They are usually comprised of a large number of spectral components which bear no clear relationship to each other and therefore make it impossible for the ear to perceive any clearly defined pitch. Figure 2.10 shows the waveform and spectral components (long term average spectra) of the steady-state segment of a cymbal crash.

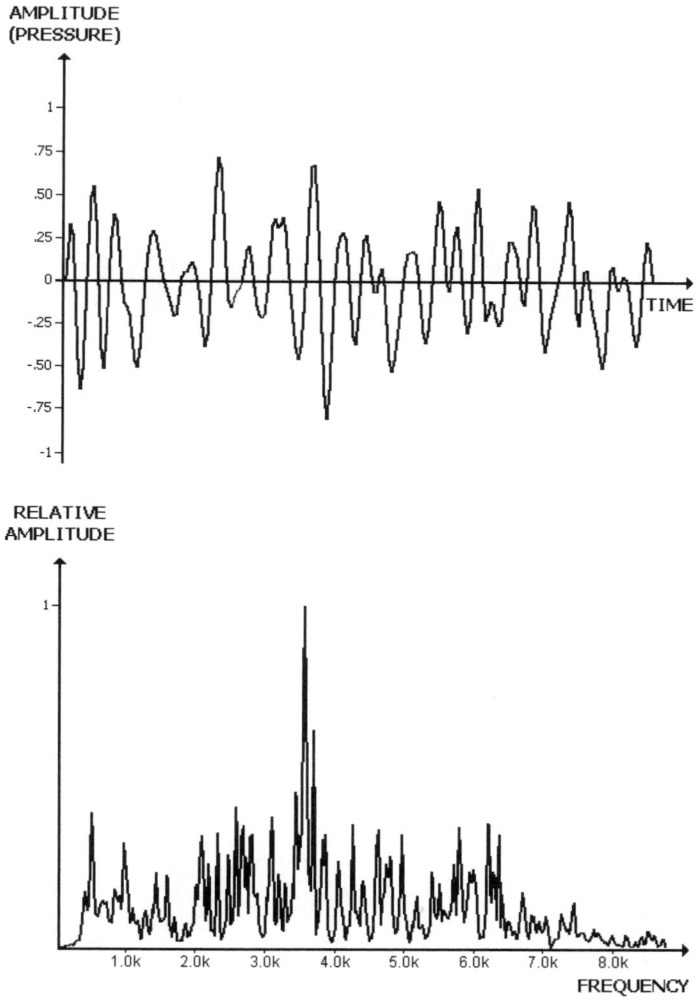

Figure 2.10
The waveform and spectral components of the steady-state segment of a cymbal crash

As can be seen in Figure 2.10 the waveform for the cymbal crash is entirely aperiodic. The frequency components show a widely distributed amount of energy which is particularly prominent in the upper frequencies between 2k and 6.5k with a peak concentration between 3.5 and 3.7k. The high frequency energy is present right up to around 7.5k where the upper frequency amplitudes start to diminish. This kind of high frequency energy is typical of cymbals which by their very nature are bright and explosive.

Another very particular kind of noise which is entirely inharmonic is that of 'white noise'. White noise can be easily produced by digital or electronic means and comprises an aperiodic waveform and (in its ideal form) a uniformly distributed frequency spectrum. This means that for any frequency range within the sound there is the same amount of energy. This might be viewed as the other extreme of the scale to the simple sine wave with its single frequency component. In direct contrast, white noise has an extremely complex, random waveform with a theoretically infinite number of frequency components (see Figure 2.11).

Figure 2.11
The waveform and spectral components of 'ideal' white noise

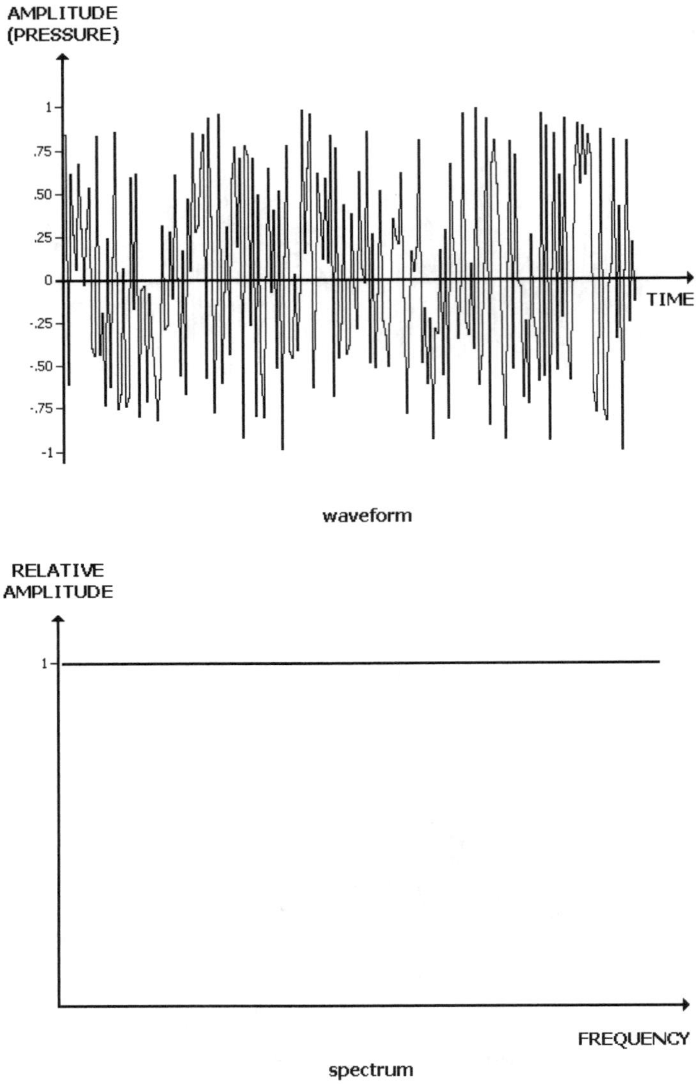

White noise produces a characteristic 'hissing' sound and is often included as a raw signal source in synthesizers since it is useful for the creation of drum, percussive and abstract timbres.

Envelopes

Waveforms and spectral components (as described above) are of paramount importance in any discussion about sound. However, these elements are not the only ones involved. Waveforms generally sit inside what is known as an amplitude envelope and this describes how the overall amplitude of the sound evolves over time. Sounds rarely start and stop instantaneously. They usually take a short while to get started, they then hold their normal operating level for a length of time before fading out naturally at the end of the sound. This is particulary true for musical notes made by acoustic musical instruments. A simple envelope describing this kind of behaviour is typically comprised of the following :

- The 'attack' – the length of time it takes for the amplitude of the sound to rise from zero to its peak level.
- The 'steady-state' segment – a relatively stable and unchanging segment in the sound where it has reached a constant level.
- The 'decay' – the segment where the sound fades away to silence.

In recent times this basic envelope model has been refined to help create the amplitude characteristics of a wider range of sounds, including those which might sustain continuously, such as organ or synth tones. Modern synthesizers, for example, contain a wide range of amplitude envelope generators. Among the most popular is the standard ADSR envelope. This introduces an additional parameter between the attack and steady-state stages of the basic model described above (the terminology for the steady-state and decay stages is also modified). ADSR stands for attack, decay, sustain, release and the four stages function as follows :

- attack – determines the length of time for the amplitude to rise from zero to its peak level.
- decay – determines the length of time for the amplitude to fall from its peak level to its sustain level.
- sustain – determines the level of the sound which continues for as long as the note is being held. (On a keyboard instrument like an organ, for example, the sound remains at this stage for as long as the key continues to be held down. This is equivalent to the 'steady-state' segment, as described above).
- release – determines the time for the amplitude to fall from its sustain level to zero when the sound is terminated (when the key is released on a keyboard instrument, for example)

Envelope generators of this type also feature the idea of a 'gate' time. This is the length of time between the point when the note is activated at the beginning of the attack stage and the point when the note is released just before the release stage. This is usually viewed in terms of a key on a keyboard instrument being held down to produce a note and then released to terminate it (see Figure 2.12).

An amplitude envelope therefore describes how the amplitude of the sound evolves over time. With simple sounds, such as the basic waveforms outlined at the beginning of this chapter, the same timbre is present throughout the entire evolution of the sound. This same timbre varies in amplitude according to the shape of any amplitude envelope which may have been applied. With more complex sounds, such as those produced by acoustic musical instruments, both the overall amplitude and the timbral content of the sound continually evolve throughout

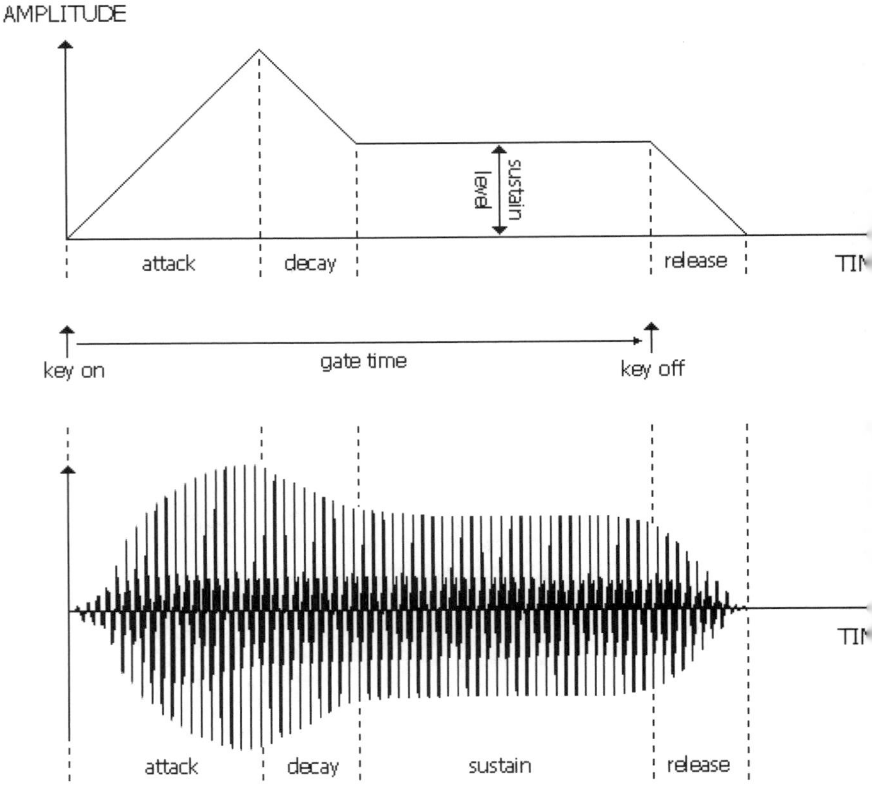

Figure 2.12
ADSR envelope characteristics compared to the amplitude envelope of a real waveform

the course of the sound event. In other words, not only does the overall amplitude envelope evolve over time but the amplitude envelopes of each harmonic within the sound also evolve over time. This kind of behaviour is not easy to visualise on a two-dimensional graph. A time domain graph shows how the overall amplitude of the sound evolves over time and a frequency domain graph shows the frequency contents of one particular time-slice within the sound or, sometimes, the long term average spectra (LTAS) for a particular segment of the sound. This chapter has already explored each perspective in isolation but gaining a better knowledge of the behaviour of sounds from the real world involves the marrying together of these different elements simultaneously.

Real-world sounds are invariably composed of a continuously evolving timbre which sits inside a dynamic amplitude envelope. This amplitude envelope is often intimately linked with the timbral development within the sound, particularly in the case of a note from an acoustic musical instrument. This is particularly important for the attack portion of the note. The attack portion has been shown to be crucial in our perception and recognition of the timbre. Overall, an acoustic musical instrument tone involves inter-related dynamic changes in pitch, loudness and spectral content (timbre). It is anything but static. This dynamic evolution is the essence of what makes many sounds and instrument tones interesting. Such information is extremely useful if you wish to avoid static, dull tones when creating your own sounds using a sound synthesizer.

The best way of actually visualising this kind of dynamic behaviour is to plot the sound's evolution on a three-dimensional graph.

Viewing sound in three dimensions

Representations of sound on a three-dimensional graph are commonly calculated using a computer-based mathematical technique known as a Fast Fourier Transform (FFT). This is a variation on the Fourier transform mentioned earlier in this chapter. An FFT allows an otherwise computationally intensive operation to be achieved with less calculations (developed by J.W. Cooley and J.W. Tookey, 1965).

Three-dimensional graphs help us gain a better understanding of the real nature of how a sound evolves over time. They feature a measurement of the spectral components for each successive point in time. The resolution of the display depends upon the number of frequencies on the frequency axis and how many times the frequencies are measured within a given time period. With an FFT three-dimensional analysis we are essentially viewing how the amplitudes of the harmonics within the sound evolve over time, which is the real essence of what gives sounds their timbral and overall envelope characteristics. FFT three dimensional graphs are also referred to as 'mountain graphs'.

Figure 2.13 shows the FFT analysis for a clarinet tone at Bb3. The complete duration of the note (253ms) is shown. As can be seen from the display, this particular note is uneventful but by no means static. The attack is gentle but the onset time varies for each harmonic. All of the harmonics undergo subtle change as the note progresses so there is always a difference between each successive time-slice. In direct contrast the square wave shown in Figure 2.14 is entirely static and unchanging throughout its course. It exhibits no spectral evolution and for the human ear it is therefore less interesting than the clarinet tone. Although the FFT displays of this particular clarinet tone and the square wave bear a strong resemblance it is by no means the case that all clarinet tones will show the same tendency.

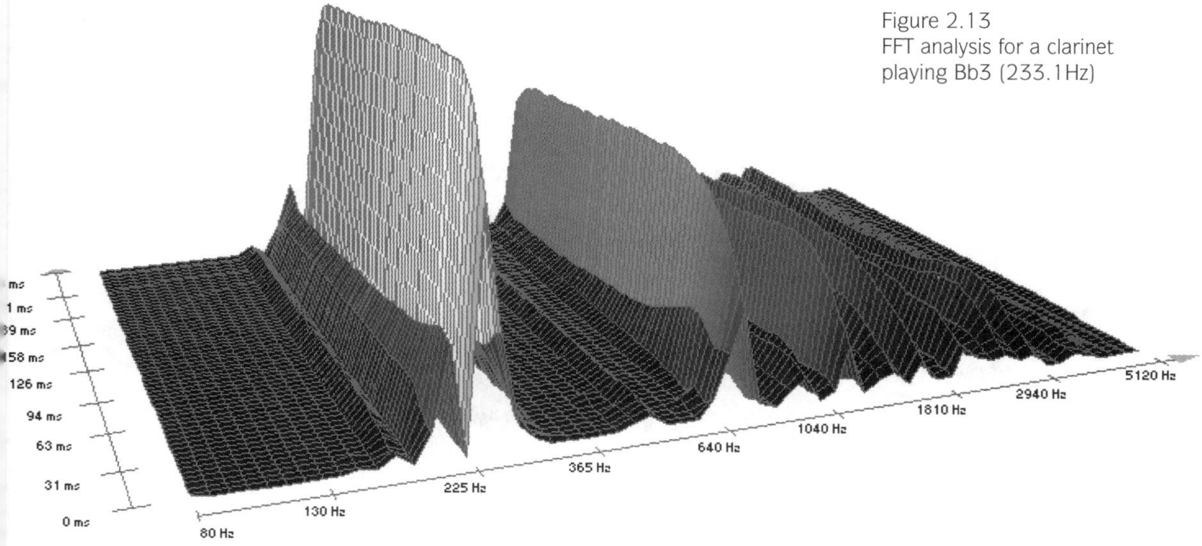

Figure 2.13
FFT analysis for a clarinet playing Bb3 (233.1Hz)

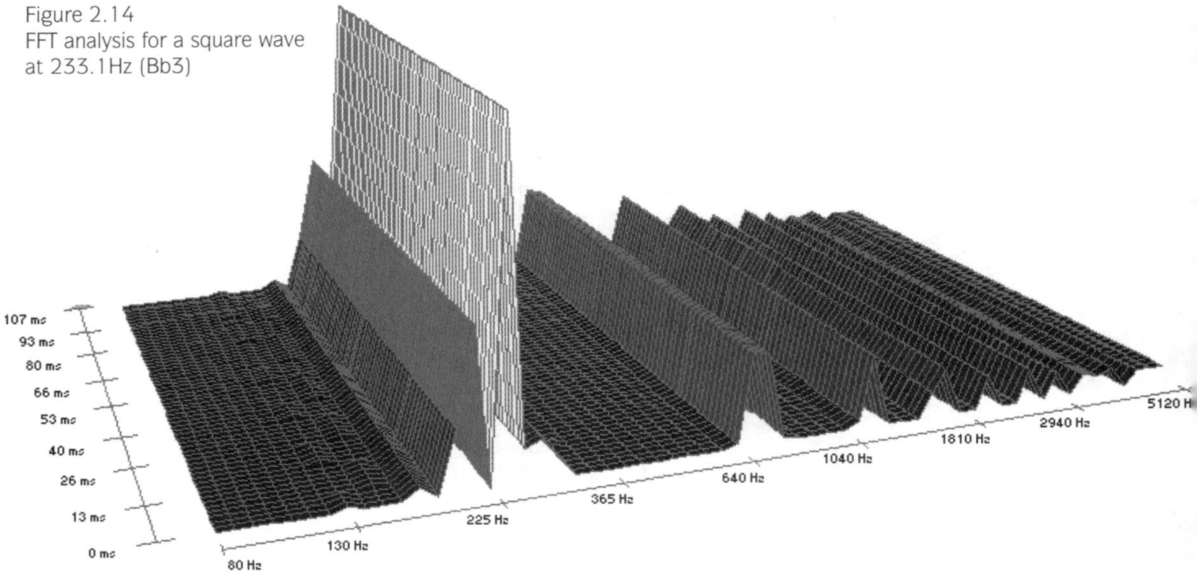

Figure 2.14
FFT analysis for a square wave at 233.1Hz (Bb3)

Figures 2.15 and 2.16 show the FFT analyses for the classical guitar and piano waveforms displayed in Figures 2.8 and 2.9 (both playing A2, 110Hz). The complete durations of the notes are shown (approximately 2.5s and 1.5s respectively). The guitar features a number of very sharp peaks in the attack phase particularly at the fundamental and second harmonic. These peaks are typical for a plucked instrument. The second harmonic features a dramatic reduction in amplitude just after the attack and the rest of the sound is dominated by the fundamental and third harmonic. A number of other low-level harmonic and inharmonic spectra characterise the first half of the sound and the fundamental and third harmonic dominate the decay phase almost exclusively. In contrast to the guitar, the piano tone features a slightly more rounded attack phase dominated by the fundamental and second harmonic (typical for a hammered instrument). Unlike the guitar, the dominant attack

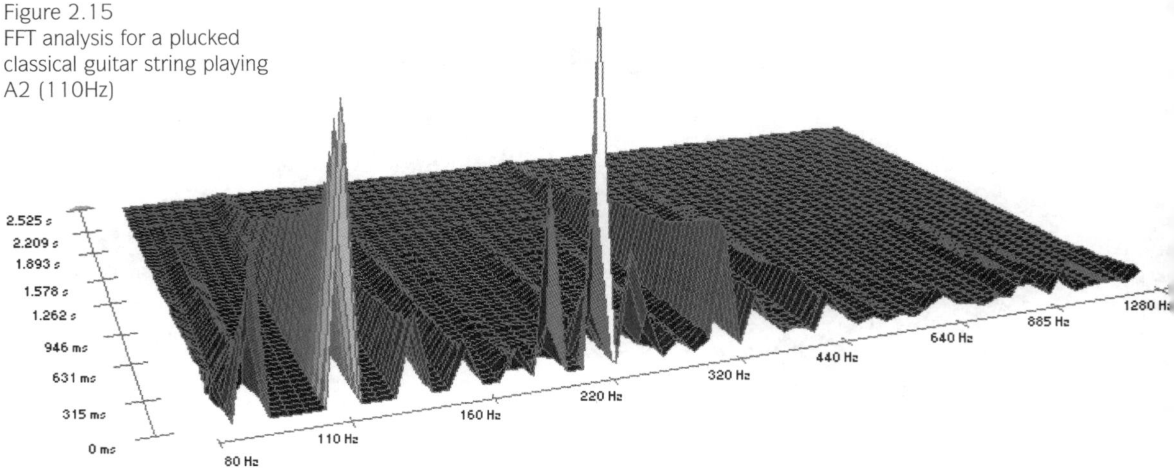

Figure 2.15
FFT analysis for a plucked classical guitar string playing A2 (110Hz)

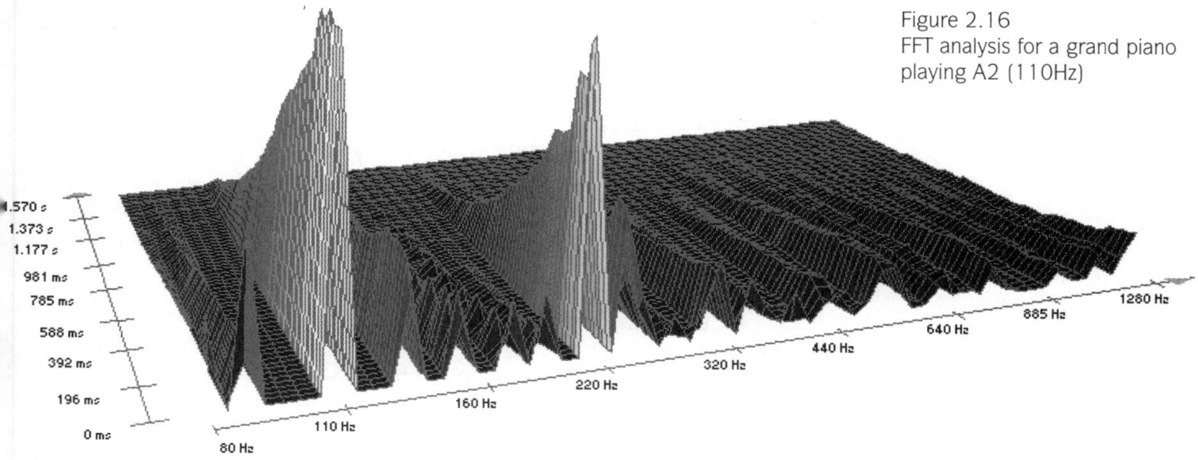

Figure 2.16
FFT analysis for a grand piano playing A2 (110Hz)

components prevail throughout the rest of the sound's evolution. These are accompanied by a wide range of lower level harmonic and inharmonic spectra distributed throughout the rest of the spectrum.

Figure 2.17 shows the FFT analysis of the cymbal crash displayed in Figure 2.10. The complete duration of the event (approximately 6.5s) is shown. The evolution of the event is considerably more complex than those of the other instruments shown above since we are looking at an inharmonic sound. There are a multitude of peaks at largely non-harmonically related frequencies throughout the evolution of the sound. The attack is particularly prominent, as would be expected in a crash of this kind, with a marked intensity between around 900Hz and 4kHz. The sound features a steady decay with the higher frequencies dying out sooner than the lower frequencies.

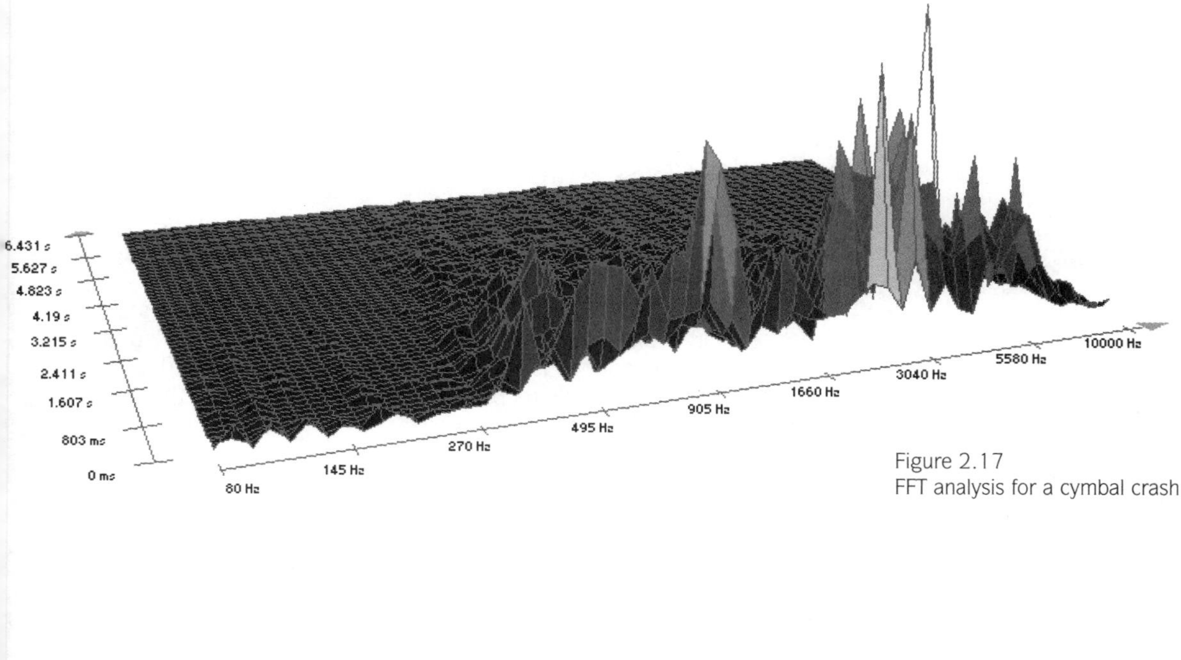

Figure 2.17
FFT analysis for a cymbal crash

The importance of the attack phase

All the instrument tones displayed in the above FFT analyses are in their maximum state of change during the attack phase. This is a common feature of most acoustic musical instrument sounds and is due, in particular, to the manner in which the harmonic components tend to behave. The guitar and piano tones (above) show a marked difference between the amplitudes of the spectral components in the attack phase and those in the decay phase. Similar attributes are normally also present in other timbres like brass, wind and bowed instruments. The attack is the primary cue for our recognition of the sound's timbre and an appropriate attack phase is fundamental to the production of a pleasing instrument tone. A dynamic attack phase endows the tone with liveliness and interest. This is valuable information for anyone attempting to synthesize authentic instrument or lively synth tones.

Vibrato and tremolo

Other important elements in the production of authentic and musically interesting instrument tones include vibrato and tremolo effects. Vibrato is a periodic variation in the pitch and tremolo is a periodic variation in the amplitude of a tone. Both are present to some extent in many acoustic instrument and particularly human sung vocal sounds and provide important auditory cues for the perception of a pleasing and authentic result. They are most often applied during the steady-state phase of the tone. In practical sound synthesis, when using a keyboard-based sound synthesizer, vibrato and/or tremolo are often applied in real-time using the modulation wheel on the front panel of the instrument. This provides an authentic performance-based approach which is appropriate to the application of these effects.

Info

Vibrato is a periodic variation in the pitch and tremolo is a periodic variation in the amplitude of a tone.

Summary

So why all this detailed theory about sound? The answer is that sound is the medium we use for sound synthesis. If we understand the parameters which govern its behaviour then we can really start to get inside the medium and experiment. Knowing about sound in theory helps us develop skills and a certain intuition which will be useful in practice. The idea of getting 'inside' a sound is a helpful analogy, even though there are limits to how far we can actually achieve this. Once inside we can start to transform and shape the medium and eventually synthesize our own sounds.

After having read this chapter, readers will hopefully find themselves at least partially immersed in the medium of sound. In order to go on to synthesize your own sounds it also helps to become familiar with at least some of the sound synthesis techniques involved. This forms the subject matter of the next chapter.

3 Sound synthesis techniques

This chapter describes some of the main sound synthesis techniques, many of which are used within real-world synthesizers and VST Instruments. These include subtractive, additive, FM, physical modelling and granular synthesis, and sampling. This provides background knowledge which helps in the creation of your own sounds and serves as a useful reference for those who are already familiar with sound synthesis. Understanding sound synthesis is not always an easy task and this chapter may therefore occasionally require considerable effort.

Analogue and digital traditions in sound synthesis

The development of sound synthesis techniques has tended to be a double-edged sword involving, on the one hand, academic research and, on the other hand, the development of experimental and commercial sound synthesis instruments. Historically, analogue sound synthesis precedes digital sound synthesis. Digital synthesis is a relatively recent phenomenon.

The development of analogue sound synthesis began, in theory, in 1807 when Jean Baptiste Fourier (1768–1830) published his theorem describing how any periodic waveform could be broken down into a number of sine waves. This formed the basis for additive synthesis. Synthesizing sound electronically began in 1897 when Thaddeus Cahill (1867 – 1934) patented his 'Telharmonium', the first significant electronic musical instrument. The working model was presented to the public in 1907, weighing in at an astonishing 200 tons. After this, the Theremin (1919), the Ondes Martinot (1928), the Hammond tonewheel organ (1935) and a number of other devices made significant contributions to the creation of sound electronically. However, it was not until the development of the RCA synthesizer in 1956 that it was possible to produce a wide range of sounds using a single instrument. The RCA synth featured a programmable sound controller in the form of a punched paper roll and the manner in which it synthesized its sounds was an early example of subtractive synthesis.

The basis for modern sound synthesis as we know it today came into existence in 1964 when Robert Moog developed the idea of voltage-controlled synthesis using voltage-controlled oscillators, amplifiers and filters and in 1965 built the first Moog synthesizer. The first commercially available embodiment of Moog's ideas was the Moog modular synthesizer, released in 1968. This was quickly followed by the development of the Mini Moog in 1969, the world's first truly portable sound synthesizer. Up to the mid 1970s sound synthesis implementations remained largely analogue in nature but in 1973, in the academic world, John Chowning was already laying the foundations for the digital revolution in sound synthesis with his paper on FM sound synthesis entitled 'The Synthesis of Complex Audio Spectra by Means of Frequency Modulation'. The Yamaha Corporation were to develop his ideas for use in commercial sound synthesis products ten years later, the most popular of which became the all-digital Yamaha DX7 FM synthesizer, released in 1983. Digital synthesis and the use of computers for musical purposes had actually already began in 1975 with the release of the New England Digital 'Synclavier' (an all-digital sampler and synthesizer), and in 1979 with the release of the Fairlight CMI (computer musical instrument).

Throughout the late 20th century and into the 21st century digital techniques have grown to dominate the world of sound synthesis both in terms of research and the release of commercially available sound synthesis instruments. However, the 'analogue' sound is still very much sought after and many synthesis techniques which are now implemented digitally actually find their roots in the analogue tradition. Some of the newer forms of sound synthesis are exclusively digital in nature and could only ever have been achieved using digital techniques. The types of synthesis which find their roots in the analogue tradition include additive, subtractive, amplitude modulation and ring modulation. Digital methods include FM, physical modelling, waveshaping, granular synthesis and digital sampling. Hybrid sound synthesis methods include wavetable and sample and synthesis (S&S) techniques. However, you should bear in mind that the main sound synthesis techniques are not mutually exclusive. For example, it is perfectly feasible to create FM tones in a system designed for subtractive synthesis or to use additive synthesis techniques in a system designed for FM synthesis.

The terms 'analogue synthesis' and 'digital synthesis' are commonly associated with specific kinds of timbres. Analogue sounds are often described as being 'fat', 'big', 'warm' and 'resonant', while digital sounds are often described as being 'clean', 'bright', 'sparkling' and 'accurate'. There is indeed a particular quality to many classic analogue synthesizer tones born of the fact that the voltage-controlled circuitry which produces the sounds is imperfect. This imperfection is often pleasing to the human ear. Digital synthesis instruments can sometimes justifiably be criticised for producing lifeless or cold sounds since, by their very nature, they are totally accurate and predictable. However, software engineers are now programming imperfections and variations into digital synthesis instruments so that they can replicate imperfect analogue behaviour.

Confusion between analogue and digital

There is some confusion in the world of sound synthesis with regard to the terms analogue and digital. Strictly speaking, analogue synthesis uses 'voltages and currents' to directly create audio and control signals, whereas digital synthesis uses 'numerical data' to represent these same audio and control signals. For example, in analogue synthesis the waveform of a sound is represented by an electronic signal which (theoretically) has a value at every point in time. There are no steps between each point and the changes in the electronic signal are directly analogous to the vibrations of a sound signal in air. In digital synthesis the waveform of a sound is represented by a series of numbers which measure the characteristics of the signal in discrete steps. The numbers are *not* directly analogous to the vibrations of a sound signal in air. Before we can hear a digital representation of a sound signal it must be converted into analogue form (digital to analogue conversion).

Most synthesizers commercially available at the time of writing are essentially digital synthesizers and, strictly speaking, this includes absolutely all software synthesizers and VST instruments. However, many synthesis instruments are digital models of analogue systems. This is particularly apparent in the large number of VST instruments which are described as 'virtual' analogue synthesizers. It is important to separate analogue and digital systems for academic and theoretical reasons but, for the most part, throughout the course of this book the main concern is with the user interface and the practical implications of each synthesis technique. For example, we should acknowledge that the synthesis engine which drives Native Instruments' Pro 52 (see Chapter 5) is essentially digital in nature but our contact with the instrument revolves around the user interface and this is modelled upon an entirely analogue system. In order to create your own sounds with this synthesizer you need to be familiar with classic analogue subtractive synthesis rather than the precise details of what goes on at the deeper level of the instrument.

Using the term 'analogue synthesis' to describe what is actually 'subtractive synthesis' may also lead to some confusion. It is important to bear in mind that, strictly speaking, subtractive synthesis is only one type of analogue synthesis and that it is only in popular usage that the two terms have tended to become synonymous. Analogue synthesis, as implemented in most synthesizers, is more precisely a form of subtractive synthesis. Subtractive synthesis has proved to be a particularly popular form of sound synthesis due to its comparative ease of use, its intuitive nature and its elegant implementation. It is common to many of the VST instruments described in Chapter 5.

Finding your place

Finding your place in the world of sound synthesis is not necessarily an easy task. Many readers may be wondering where they actually belong on the sound synthesis evolutionary ladder and what they really need to know.

When presented with the front panel controls (or graphical user interface) of a synthesizer many of us immediately start adjusting the parameters without necessarily knowing too much about the precise function of each. This starts a learning process which involves judging what we are achieving by listening to the audible results of each parameter movement. This might be described as real-time audio feedback and in the synthesis world is often referred to as 'tweaking' the parameters. Experimenting with synthesizer parameters like this plays an important role in the practical synthesizing of new sounds and it helps us become familiar with the sound possibilities of a synthesizer. There is nothing wrong with remaining at this point, and you might find yourself there right now, but one of the aims of this book is to help you delve into sound synthesis a little more deeply. This involves gaining a real appreciation of how the parameters interact and how each synthesis technique is endowed with its own particular strengths and weaknesses.

Of course, your interests in sound synthesis may also depend very much on what kind of synthesis instrument you possess or intend to acquire. Hopefully, Chapter 5 will be of assistance in this area. You may already be an experienced sound synthesist searching to enrich your knowledge of VST Instruments, in which case you need to assess which parts of this text are particularly relevant to your needs.

Source and modifier theory

Conventional musical instruments and a number of sound synthesis techniques follow a 'source and modifier' pattern of behaviour. The source is the part of the instrument which produces the initial energy input for the system while the modifier is responsible for shaping the source in terms of its pitch, amplitude and timbre (see Figure 3.1). The two elements in these configurations are inseparable if you wish to retain the characteristic sound of the instrument concerned.

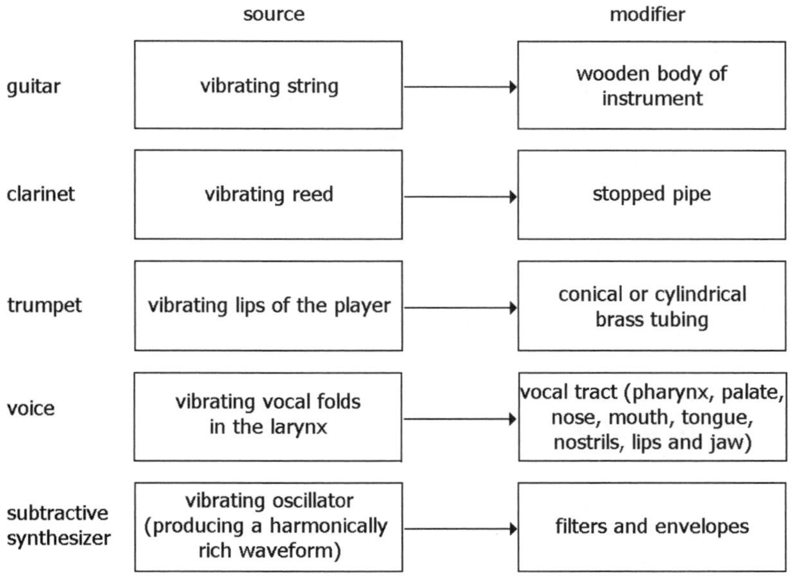

Figure 3.1
Musical instruments as models of the source and modifier theory

Exploring real-world acoustic musical instruments in 'source and modifier' terms helps us to understand some of the fundamentals of sound synthesis. Take an acoustic guitar, for example. The source is the guitar string which is stretched from the bridge, across the main body of the instrument, up to the machine heads on the neck. The modifier is the body of the instrument and the manner in which all the physical components have been assembled. Sound occurs when energy is added to the system by plucking the stretched string, which vibrates accordingly. Owing to the manner in which it is attached to the body of the instrument, the vibrations of the string produce a characteristic 'guitar' sound. The original source sound of the plucked guitar string is significantly modified according to the resonant properties of the wood and other materials used in the construction of the instrument and how they interact. If you were to separate the stretched string from the main body of the instrument then it would lose most of its harmonic identity (i.e. its 'guitar-like' sound) and it would also suffer a drastic reduction in amplitude level. To maintain its tonal properties the source and modifier parts of a guitar need to be linked in a mutually balanced and inter-dependent fashion so that the elements which contribute to the sound interact in a specific manner.

An analysis of the design of a trumpet (or other brass instrument) reveals a similar configuration. The source sound (the vibrating lips of the player in the mouthpiece) is significantly modified according to the resonant properties of the brass tubing. As with the guitar, the source and modifier are coupled in a mutually balanced and inter-dependent fashion.

The source and modifier theory can also be used to describe the functional principles of subtractive synthesis (explained in more detail below). In subtractive synthesis, the source is an oscillator providing a tone which is normally rich in harmonics (such as a sawtooth, square, pulse or triangle wave). The modifier part of the system includes filters and envelopes. A filter modifies the harmonic structure of the source while an envelope generator changes the way its amplitude evolves over time. The filter itself can also be modified according to an envelope generator providing a method by which the harmonic content of the sound can also evolve over time. The design principle of subtractive synthesis can be likened, therefore, to that found in real-world acoustic musical instruments. If you were to separate the source (the oscillator) from the modifier (filters and envelopes) then you would be left with a rather bland and musically uninteresting tone.

This section has described a global theory which can be applied to a number of different acoustic musical instruments and sound synthesis techniques. The following section describes a number of elements which can be applied specifically to sound synthesis.

Basic building blocks

Chapter 1 described how sound synthesis involves the creation and processing of sound using a number of building blocks. Synthesis implies the creation of a composite whole from a number of separate elements. These include a control interface, such as the parameters found on the front panel (GUI) of most synthesizers, and a synthesis engine, such as a network of electronic or digital circuits designed to interpret the parameter settings and produce the sound. There are a number of key parameters which are common to many types of sound synthesis and these are worth exploring before proceeding to specific synthesis techniques. There is often a direct relationship between the control parameter and the component which is being addressed (particularly in subtractive synthesis). This results in a user interface which is fairly close to the synthesis engine itself. The following descriptions are good for both the analogue or digital versions of the same element. These elements also happen to be those encountered in classic subtractive synthesis.

Oscillators

An oscillator is an electronic or digital device designed to produce a regular alternating signal between two values. Oscillators are often referred to as VCOs (voltage controlled oscillators) or DCOs (digitally controlled oscillators). The signal produced by an oscillator can be easily converted into a regular sound wave (i.e. vibrations in air). Oscillators are good at generating periodic waveforms which can be used as sound sources in a synthesizer. Popular periodic waveforms include sine, square, sawtooth, triangle and pulse waves (see Chapter 2 for a detailed explanation).

As well as its waveform type, an oscillator can be changed in terms of its frequency (or pitch) and its amplitude. Frequency is the number of times it 'oscillates' per second (measured in hertz). In musical terms this would be known as pitch (measured in semitones and cents). Amplitude is a measure of the level at which the signal 'oscillates' (or 'how much' the oscillator 'oscillates') and in subtractive synthesis, for example, the overall amplitude is a function of the values of the parameters in the amplifier section (see 'Amplifiers and Envelope Generators' below).

Low frequency oscillators (LFOs)

Oscillators can be used as sound sources (as above) or as modifiers. If you take the frequency of an oscillator down to a very low rate it becomes what is known as a low frequency oscillator (LFO). An LFO is used as a modifier rather than an audible sound source. A typical function of an LFO would be to apply vibrato to a sound source. Vibrato is a continuous periodic variation in the pitch of a tone (producing a 'warbling' effect). LFOs are typically adjustable between frequencies of around 0.03Hz and 20Hz.

Filters

In sound synthesis a filter performs a similar function to devices of the same name in other walks of life. A coffee filter 'filters' the larger particles of coffee from the source coffee mixture. An air filter 'filters' the larger particles of air-born dust from the air which passes through it. Similarly, a sound filter 'filters' various sound particles (harmonics) from the raw source sound which passes through it. However, a coffee filter is normally of one type only which is designed to filter the raw coffee mixture in one specific fashion to produce the perfect cup of coffee. The original coffee mixture can be changed but the 'parameters' of the coffee filter itself remain the same. This is in contrast to sound filters which are designed to filter the sound in a multitude of different ways using various user-changeable parameters. In addition, a number of different filter types are available. These have names such as low-pass, high-pass, band-pass and band-reject. The essential idea of a filter in sound synthesis is that of a device which modifies the harmonic structure of the sound which passes through it (see 'Filters in detail' below).

Amplifiers and envelope generators

Many sound synthesis configurations include an amplifier section. The function of the amplifier is to make the source sound louder. The amplifier section is also usually comprised of an envelope generator. An envelope generator is a device which controls the evolution of the amplitude of a signal over time. Envelope generators vary in design but among the most popular is the ADSR type. ADSR is short for 'attack, decay, sustain, release', referring to four elements which control how the amplitude of the sound evolves over time. Envelope generators of this type also feature the idea of a 'gate' time. This is the length of time between the point when the note is activated at the beginning of the attack stage and the point when the note is released just before the release stage. This is usually viewed in terms of a key on a keyboard instrument being held down to produce a note and then released to terminate it (see Chapter 2, Figure 2.12). As well as being applied to the amplitude of a sound, envelope generators can also be applied to the action of a filter.

Info

In analogue synthesis, an oscillator is often referred to as a VCO (voltage controlled oscillator), a filter is often referred to as a VCF (voltage controlled filter) and the amplifier section is often referred to as a VCA (voltage controlled amplifier). The abbreviations also tend to be used to describe any oscillator, filter or amplifier section, whether it be in an analogue or a digital system.

Designing a simple synthesizer

Synthesis is the creation of a composite whole from a number of separate elements. It implies the mixing together of two or more things to create something new. So let's take a number of the elements described above and start building a simple modular synthesizer (see Figure 3.2).

Building a simple synthesizer helps take the sound synthesist beyond the level of tweaking control parameters by promoting a more intimate knowledge of how the parameters actually interact to produce the resulting timbre. It also helps you to become familiar with where the building blocks can be placed within the chain of parameters.

Figure 3.2 shows an extremely simple synthesis model which helps us get started in assembling the basic building blocks into something meaningful. Here, an oscillator produces a simple sine tone which is modified by an envelope generator. As we already know, a sine wave features a single harmonic and produces a rather bland, uninteresting tone. Applying an amplitude envelope improves matters slightly since the tone has the possibility of possessing a more natural start and end or some kind of evolution over time. However, using this very simple set-up leaves us a long way from producing a tone which resembles that made by a real-world acoustic instrument or, at least, something which is musically or acoustically interesting.

Figure 3.2
Design plan for a simple sound synthesizer

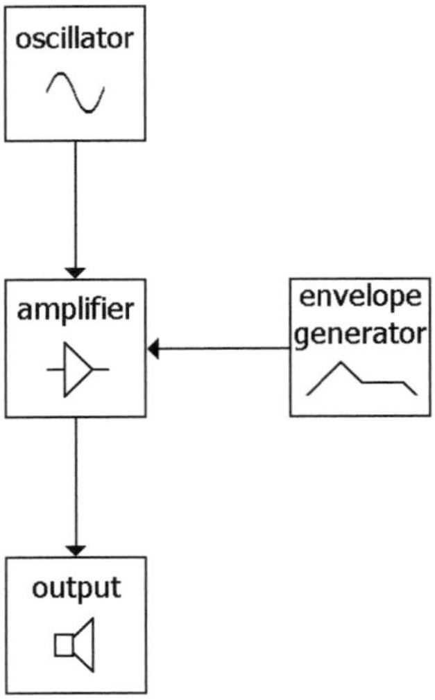

Figure 3.3 takes us closer to realising a model for the synthesizing of more authentic timbres. It shows a basic configuration for subtractive synthesis. The essential difference between this configuration and that shown in Figure 3.2 is the addition of a filter. Subtractive synthesis takes the form of a 'source and modifier' configuration, as outlined above. In Figure 3.3, an oscillator generating a sawtooth wave provides the source sound and a filter, amplifier and two envelope generators modify it.

You may ask why this particular configuration should be of use and how it was discovered in the first place. Early experiments in sound synthesis revealed that applying various types of filter to a sound source which is rich in harmonics was particularly fruitful for producing a wide range of timbres. In addition, it could achieve this with relatively few basic parameters and there was an intuitive and predictable relationship between the adjustment of the parameters and the sonic result.

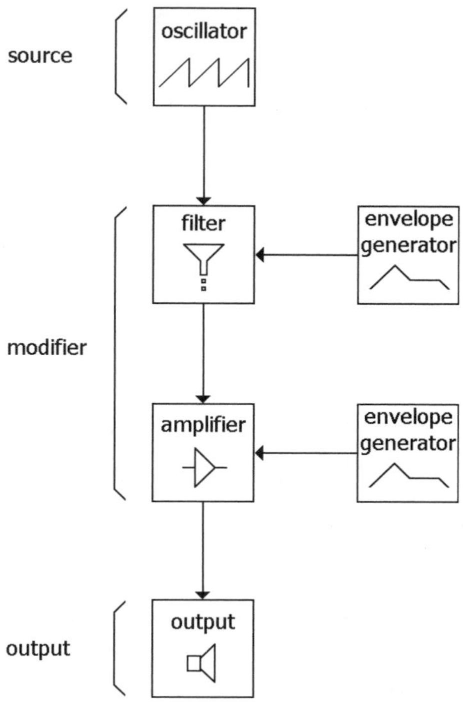

Figure 3.3
Basic model for subtractive synthesis

Since subtractive synthesis is so popular and has been instrumental in establishing many of the core principles of modern sound synthesis, it is appropriate to explore this first in the next section.

Subtractive synthesis

In subtractive synthesis a sound is generated by one or more oscillators (or noise sources) and it is then modified by subtracting a chosen part of the frequency spectrum using a filter. The filter can be one of various different types. For example, a low-pass filter allows those frequencies below a set point in the frequency spectrum to pass through with little change while those above are significantly reduced. The set point at which the filter begins to have an effect is known as the cut-off frequency (or cut-off point). The characteristics of the filter's response around the cut-off frequency are modified by means of a resonance control. The action of the filter is also regulated by a control device known as an envelope generator (filter envelope). This provides a manner of controlling how the frequency spectrum of the sound evolves over time. The manner in which the overall amplitude of the sound evolves over time is regulated according to a second envelope generator (amplifier envelope, sometimes referred to as the loudness contour).

Some of the essentials of subtractive synthesis have already been outlined in 'Basic building blocks' and 'Designing a simple synthesizer', above. Figure 3.3 also showed a basic model for subtractive synthesis. However, to really appreciate the essence of subtractive synthesis requires the exploration of a more elaborate model (see Figure 3.4) and, in particular, the exploration of envelopes and filtering (see below).

Subtractive synthesis in detail

Figure 3.4 shows the configuration for classic subtractive synthesis. Variations on this model are used in the vast majority of subtractive synthesizer designs. This involves two oscillators (VCO1 and VCO2), each

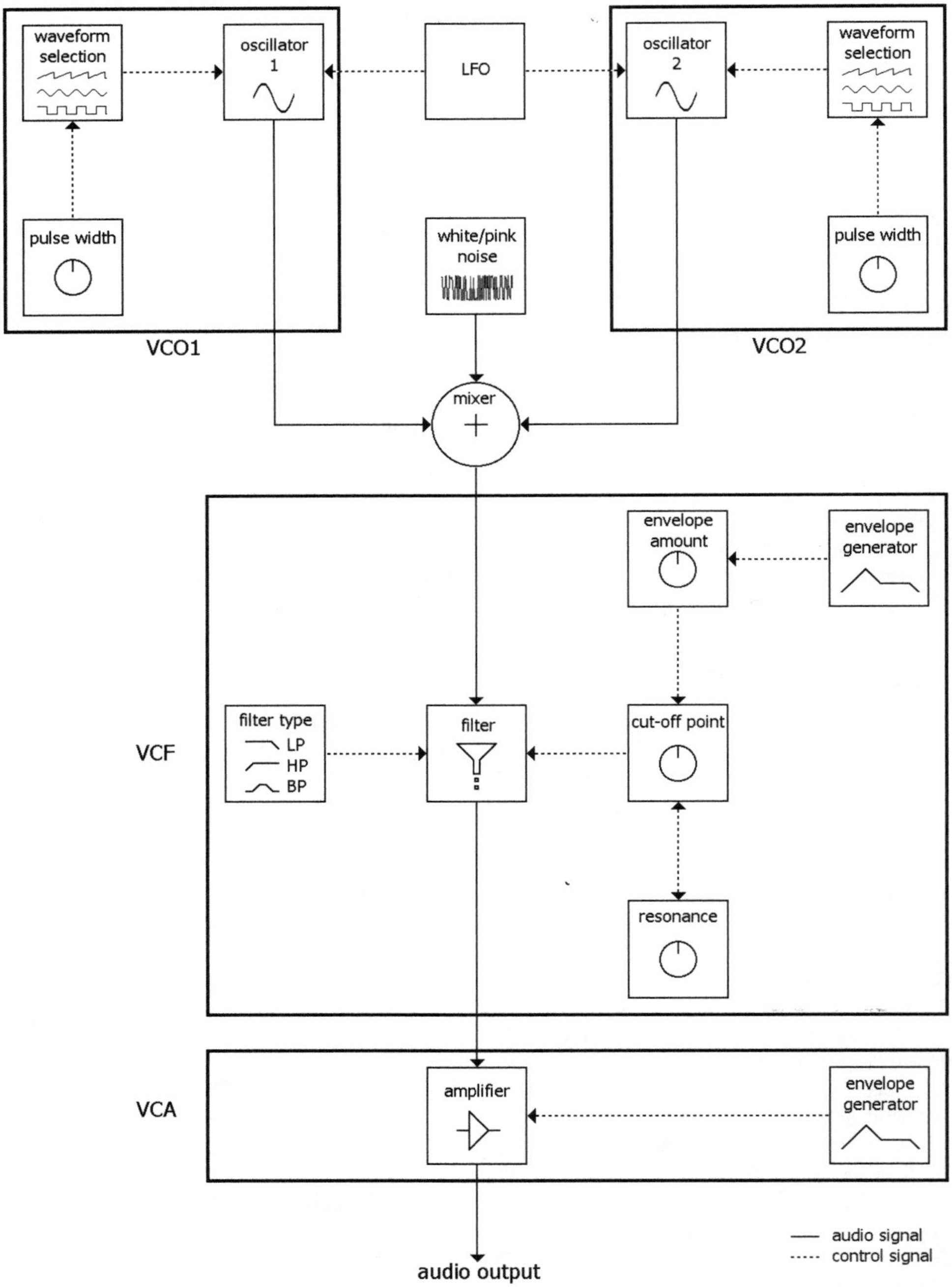

Figure 3.4 Classic subtractive synthesis

with variable frequency and waveform selection, and a white (or pink) noise generator. When a pulse wave is selected the width of the pulse is chosen using a pulse width control. Varying proportions of the source waveforms can be mixed together as desired. The composite mix is passed through a filter where its frequency spectrum is modified according to the chosen filter type and its cut-off and resonance settings. The action of both the filter (VCF) and amplifier (VCA) are modified according to envelope generators. Vibrato effects are achieved by using a low frequency oscillator (LFO) which is applied to the source oscillators. The following describes the parameters in more detail:

Oscillator

Each oscillator generates a periodic waveform (usually heard as a musical tone of a prescribed pitch). This forms the raw material which is subsequently modified and shaped with the other controls of the synthesizer. Classic subtractive synthesis usually involves two or more oscillators since this allows:

(a) the combining of different waveforms to create richer sounds
(b) the detuning of the oscillators for chorusing and chord effects and
(c) the modulation of one oscillator by another.

Waveform selection

The waveform of the oscillator may be changed to various different shapes. These usually include sine, sawtooth, triangle and pulse waves. The waveform varies the frequency spectrum of the sound. (If you need to make the link between the basic waveform shapes and the audio result and you are also an owner of a recent version of Reaktor, check out the presets of the 'Soundforum' synthesizer, Library/New in Reaktor 3/Soundforum Synth R3.ens).

Pulse width

When a pulse wave is chosen as the waveform for an oscillator, its characteristics are governed by the pulse width control. Pulse width determines the length of time for which the signal is in the compression (or positive) part of its cycle, expressed as a percentage of one complete cycle. For example, a pulse width of 50% produces a regular square wave, with its characteristic 'hollow' tone, whereas a pulse width of 10% (for example) produces a narrow pulse waveform with a more aggressive 'buzzy' timbre.

White/pink noise generator

Since noise is fundamentally different to regular, periodic waveforms, it is produced more conveniently using a separate generator. White noise produces a signal with (theoretically) the same amount of acoustical energy at all frequencies, resembling a 'hissing' sound. Pink noise is similar but with a roll-off in the higher frequencies at a rate of 3dB per octave. Noise can be used on its own or mixed with the other waveforms and is useful for producing drum and percussion sounds and tones which need a 'breathy' or 'hard-edged' character.

LFO

Whereas the oscillators described above are used as sources, a low frequency oscillator (LFO) is a sub-audio signal which is used as a modifier (i.e. you hear its effect but you do not hear the oscillator itself since it is below the audible frequency range). An LFO's most common use is to modify (modulate) the frequency of a source oscillator to achieve vibrato effects. LFOs typically operate between 0.03Hz and 20Hz.

Filter type
The filter type determines what kind of filtering action takes place on the source signal. Each filter type has specific characteristics which are fundamental to the manner in which the filtering action takes place. The main filter types include low-pass, high-pass, band-pass and band-reject.

Filter cut-of frequency
The cut-off frequency determines the frequency at which the filter begins to have an effect. In the case of a low-pass filter those frequencies below the cut-off point are allowed to pass through unchanged while those above are significantly reduced. The cut-off point of a low-pass filter therefore regulates the overall 'brightness' of the tone.

Filter resonance
Filter resonance is also referred to as Q or emphasis. This emphasises the frequencies around the cut-off point thereby regulating the 'sharpness' or resonant character of the tone.

Filter envelope generator
The filter envelope generator imposes a time-based envelope shape (contour) upon the filter cut-off frequency. This determines how the frequency spectrum of the sound evolves over time. The envelope shape is usually viewed on a graph of amplitude against time. One of the most common types is the ADSR envelope (attack, decay, sustain, release – see below for more details).

Filter envelope amount
The filter envelope amount determines the depth of the effect of the filter envelope generator upon the cut-off frequency.

Amplifier envelope generator
The amplifier envelope generator imposes a time-based envelope shape (contour) upon the amplifier. This determines how the overall amplitude of the sound evolves over time. The envelope shape is usually viewed on a graph of amplitude against time. One of the most common types is the ADSR envelope (attack, decay, sustain, release - see below for more details).

Other possibilities (modulation)

The above list of functions covers the most popular parameters in their principal applications when linked together as in Figure 3.4. Various of the parameters can also be arranged in more unusual ways, providing still more sound-sculpting possibilities. Most of these involve ways of modulating a source signal with a control signal. This might be two signals of the same type such as one oscillator modulated by a second oscillator, or something slightly more difficult to grasp, like the modulation of an oscillator by an envelope generator. Keep in mind that modulation involves the use of one signal to affect another. Modulation sources include oscillators, LFOs, envelope generators and key position. One example of modulation which has already been outlined is the modulation of the frequency of an oscillator by a low frequency oscillator (LFO) producing the popular effect known as vibrato. It is also possible to modulate the frequency of an oscillator according to an envelope generator to produce pitch sweep effects. Other possibilities include the following:

Frequency modulation (FM)
If the frequency of an oscillator is modulated by a signal higher than the usual LFO (i.e. when the modulator is another oscillator operating within the normal hearing range), multiple frequencies (sidebands) are added to the output signal producing FM effects (FM synthesis is described in detail below). Check out the frequency modulation features of the Bitheadz Retro AS1 or the rgcAudio Pentagon I.

Amplitude modulation (AM)
Low frequency (LFO) modulation of the amplitude of an oscillator produces tremolo effects. At higher frequencies, (i.e. when the modulator is another oscillator operating within the normal hearing range), amplitude modulation effects are produced, where additional frequencies are added to the output signal. The original frequency (the carrier) remains present in the output.

Ring modulation
Ring modulation is a variation of amplitude modulation where two oscillator signals are combined in a way that produces the sum and difference of their frequencies in the output. In the case of ring modulation (and unlike both FM and AM) the original frequency of the carrier is *not* present in the output. Ring modulation is typically used to produce alien speech effects and metallic, abstract sounds.

Pulse width modulation (PWM)
Pulse width modulation most often involves the automatic variation of the pulse width of a pulse waveform in a repeated cycle according to an LFO. This results in the continuous shifting of the harmonic spectrum of the source waveform. Modern synthesis techniques allow the changing of the width balance of waveforms other than pulse shapes, and the modulation source might also be an envelope generator or key position. Check out the PWM features of the NI Pro-52 and Muon Tau Pro.

Cross-modulation (CM)
Cross-modulation is the technique of connecting the outputs of two oscillators to each other's frequency inputs resulting in a complex frequency-modulated signal.

LFO modulation
You can also modulate one LFO by another LFO to produce vibrato and tremolo effects which do not have a fixed rate. In this context, it is also worth bearing in mind that LFOs can operate with waveforms other than

Info

Modulation effects (especially vibrato) are often programmed to be controlled by the position of the modulation wheel found on the front panel of most synthesizers.

sine waves. Popular waveforms for LFOs include sine, triangle, square, sawtooth and pulse and it is common to be able to mix two or more waveforms simultaneously to produce hybrid waveforms for special effects.

Envelope generators in detail

Basic envelope theory was explored in the 'Envelopes' section of Chapter 2. This showed how most sounds 'sit inside' an amplitude envelope (loudness contour). This envelope determines the evolution of the amplitude of the sound over time. In sound synthesis the envelope for the sound is provided by a device known as an envelope generator. There are a number of different types of envelope generator as shown in the examples below. However, let's go back one step and consider what takes place when an envelope is imposed upon the amplitude of a sound source within a synthesizer.

Opening the gate

There has to be a mechanism for deciding at what point in time an envelope generator should start 'generating' its contour and when it should stop. This mechanism usually involves a trigger, a short pulse which tells the synthesizer to start an event like a note or the onset of an envelope and a device called a 'gate', which determines the length of time between the trigger point of the event and the point when it is terminated. The on and off points for this gate mechanism are often viewed in terms of the pressing and releasing of a key on a musical keyboard. When the key is pressed (key on) the gate is opened and the envelope generator begins to generate its loudness contour. When the key is released (key off) the gate is closed and the envelope generator ceases the generation of its loudness contour (the amplitude is reduced to zero). Note that the trigger and the start of the gate occur simultaneously. Some synthesizers do not implement a separate trigger and use only a gate to control the onset and termination of note events. However, a separate trigger is advantageous since it ensures that the event is re-triggered accurately regardless of the state of the gate, which may not be able to open and close quickly enough for some synthesizer playing styles.

In subtractive synthesis, once you have decided what waveforms to generate in the source oscillators and how they are to be mixed, tuned and routed, this source signal is being generated on a continuous basis. It is only when you decide to trigger this continuously generated source that you will actually hear anything. The envelope generator, therefore, governs what happens once the gate is opened and the sound is allowed through.

Envelope generator types

Gate

The simplest possible envelope which can be implemented is that which closely follows the action of the gate mechanism itself. The gate envelope simply switches the sound on or off instantaneously according to the key on and key off points. There is no amplitude evolution since the tone is either on at its maximum level or off at zero.

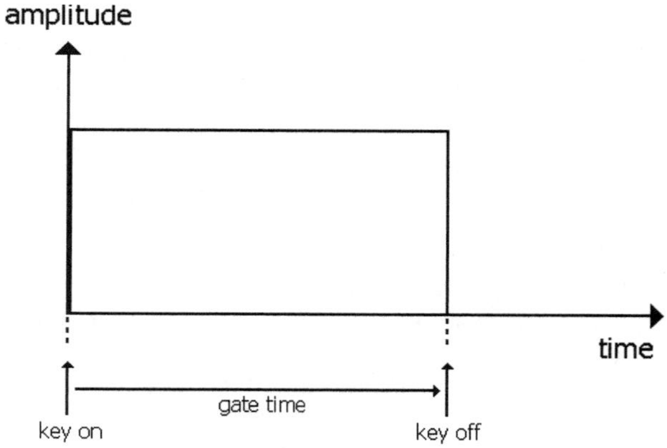

Figure 3.5
Simple gate envelope

AD

An AD (attack, decay) envelope features just two parameters which function as follows:

- attack – determines the length of time for the amplitude to rise from zero to its peak level.
- decay – determines the length of time for the amplitude to fall from its peak level to zero.

The key on marks the point at which the envelope generator begins to generate its loudness contour. This is also the point at which we begin to hear the sound event. The attack stage begins as soon as the gate is opened. If the gate is held open for long enough, the amplitude rises to its peak level and then immediately begins to decay to zero. The AD envelope does not feature a sustain element.

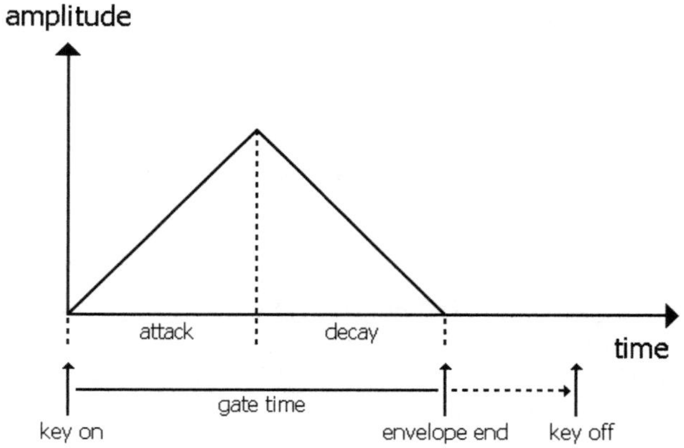

Figure 3.6
AD (attack, decay) envelope

Key off points which occur after the sound has decayed to zero have no effect on the sound since it has already been terminated. However, when the key off occurs before the full evolution of the attack and decay segments, the sound is terminated at that point in time. AD envelopes are useful for drum and percussive sounds.

ADSR

The ADSR (attack, decay, sustain, release) is the most common of all the envelope types. The four parameters function as follows:

- attack – determines the length of time for the amplitude to rise from zero to its peak level.
- decay – determines the length of time for the amplitude to fall from its peak level to its sustain level.
- sustain – determines the level of the sound which continues for as long as the note is being held. (On a keyboard instrument like an organ, for example, the sound remains at this stage for as long as the key continues to be held down).
- release – determines the time for the amplitude to fall from its sustain level to zero when the sound is terminated (when the key is released on a keyboard instrument, for example).

Figure 3.7
ADSR (attack, decay, sustain, release) envelope

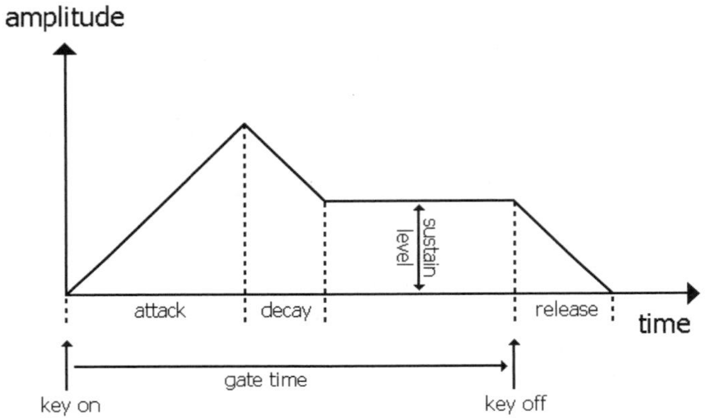

Similar to the AD envelope (above) the attack stage of the ADSR envelope begins as soon as the gate is opened by the key on event. If the gate is held open for long enough, the envelope rises to its peak level and then decays to its sustain level. The sustain level continues for as long as the gate is held open. The release stage begins as soon as the gate is closed by the key off event. When the key off occurs the amplitude of the sound event is reduced to zero according to the rate set in the release stage. Note that the sustain segment is level-based and not time-based.

ADSR envelopes are suitable for an extremely wide range of contours but due to the fixed level sustain segment cannot produce an envelope which gradually fades out during the steady-state segment of the sound (such as is found in piano tones, for example).

AHDSR

AHDSR envelopes are similar to the standard ADSR envelope except that they insert an extra 'hold' segment between the attack and decay. The five parameters function as follows:

- attack – determines the length of time for the amplitude to rise from zero to its peak level.
- hold – determines the length of time for which the amplitude is held at its peak level.

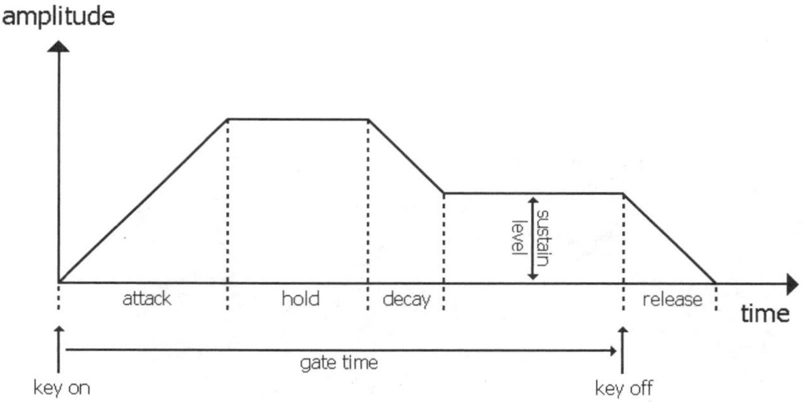

Figure 3.8 AHDSR (attack, hold, decay, sustain, release) envelope

- decay - determines the length of time for the amplitude to fall from its peak level to its sustain level.
- sustain - determines the level of the sound which continues for as long as the note is being held.
- release - determines the time for the amplitude to fall from its sustain level to zero when the sound is terminated.

The implementation of a hold segment allows the peak level to be sustained for a period of time before the onset of the decay segment. This is helpful if you need to give detailed attention to the attack and decay parts of the sound event when you may not require the level to begin its decay phase quite so soon after it has reached its peak.

Other envelope types
There are many more envelope types than those that have been described above. One popular technique to augment the possibilities is the use of break-points. Break-points divide an envelope into multiple segments which allow the implementation of two or more decay segments or multiple attack, decay and release segments or even multiple segments which loop continuously for as long as the gate is open.

For a practical insight into the possibilities take a look at the envelope section of the Native Instruments FM7 VST instrument. The FM7 features all of the envelope types described above, and many others, preprogrammed in the presets menu (Figure 3.9).

The FM7 allows the insertion of multiple break-points for extremely complex envelope contours and envelope looping effects. Listen to the first patch,

Figure 3.9
FM7 envelope presets menu

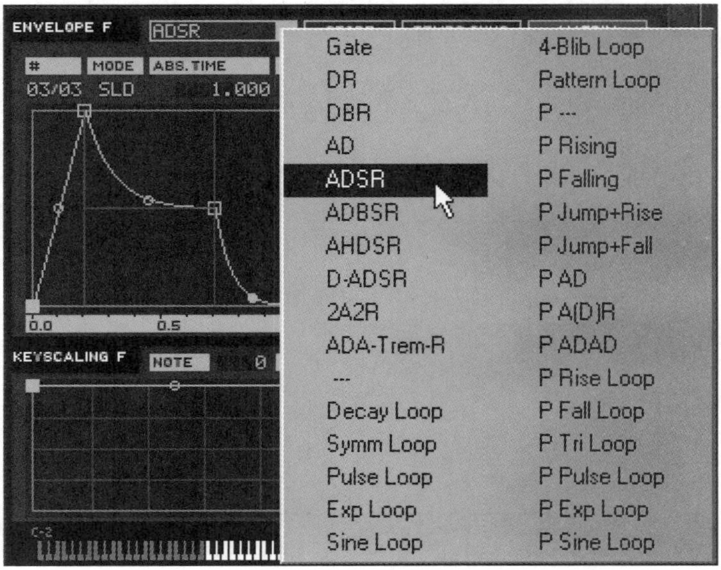

named 'Exciting', in the default patch library. The amplitude contour of this sound loops around the complex multiple break-point envelope shown in Figure 3.10 for as long as you hold a sustained note (in this case, the loop is synchronised to the tempo of the host software).

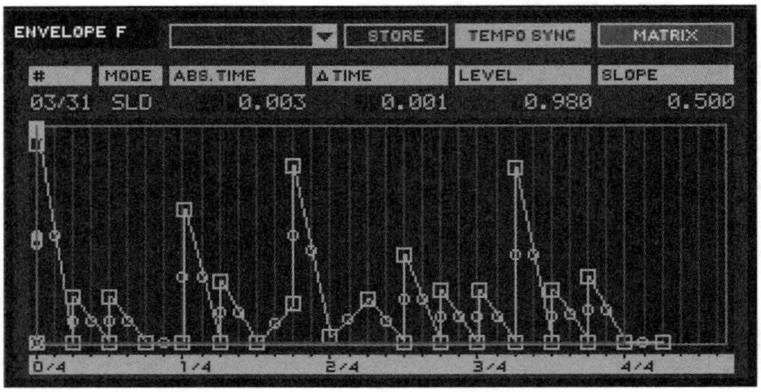

Figure 3.10
Multiple break-point envelope used in the Native Instruments FM7 'Exciting' sound, designed by Peter Krischker

Filters in detail

Filter types

The four basic types of filter are low-pass, high-pass, band -pass and band-reject. Variations and combinations of these are known by different names in popular EQ processing, such as notch filtering and parametric EQ. However, understanding the action of the four basic types is the first step in becoming familiar with the details.

Filter types are generally recognised by their amplitude response. This is shown on a graph of amplitude against frequency (see Figures 3.11 to 3.14, below). Each filter type is characterised by one part of the frequency spectrum which is allowed to pass through, known as the pass band, and another part of the spectrum which is significantly reduced, known as the stop band. The point at which the filtering action begins, (when the amplitude response passes from the pass band to the stop band), is known as the cut-off frequency (or cut-off point). There is always a transitional area between the pass band and the stop band. The rule for defining the exact point for the cut-off frequency is generally accepted as that point where the signal has fallen 3dB below the level of the pass band. It is, therefore, true to say that a significant number of frequencies below (or above) the cut-off point will have already been attenuated (cut) before the cut-off point itself is reached.

Low-pass

A low-pass filter allows those frequencies below the cut-off point to pass through with little change while those above are significantly reduced.

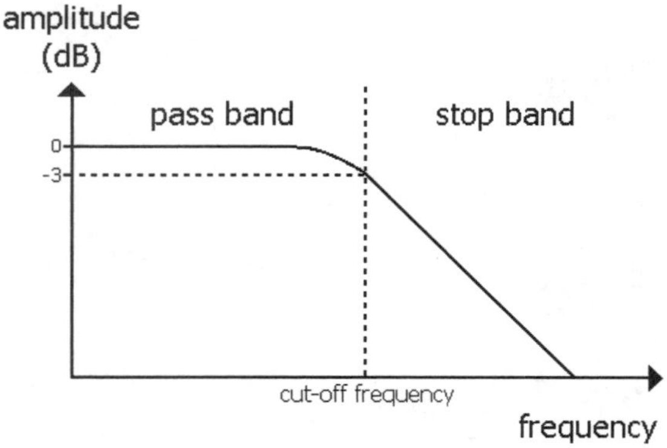

Figure 3.11
Amplitude response of a low-pass filter

High-pass
A high-pass filter significantly reduces those frequencies below the cut-off point while those above are allowed to pass through with little change (the opposite of the low-pass filter).

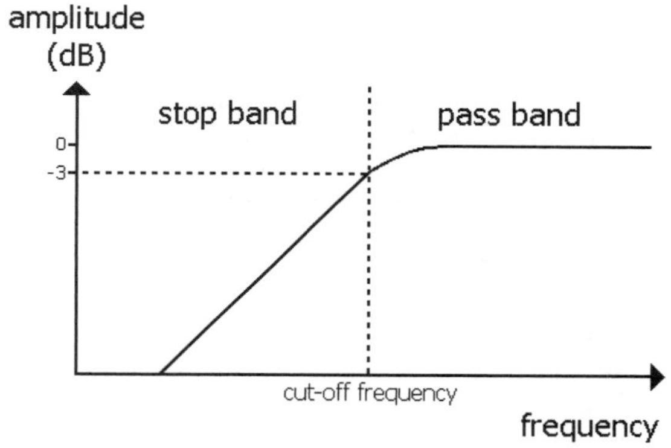

Figure 3.12
Amplitude response of a high-pass filter

Band-pass
A band-pass filter allows a band of frequencies to pass through between two cut-off points while significantly reducing frequencies both above and below the pass band. The mid-point of the amplitude response curve is referred to as the centre frequency and the frequency range between the lower and upper cut-off points is known as the bandwidth.

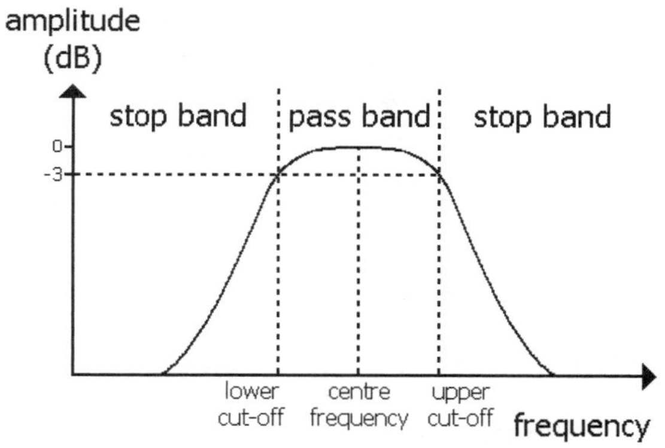

Figure 3.13
Amplitude response of a band-pass filter

Band-reject
A band-reject filter attenuates (rejects) a band of frequencies between two cut-off points while allowing the rest of the signal to pass through with little change (the opposite of the band-pass filter). The mid-point of the amplitude response curve is referred to as the centre frequency and the frequency range between the lower and upper cut-off points is known as the bandwidth.

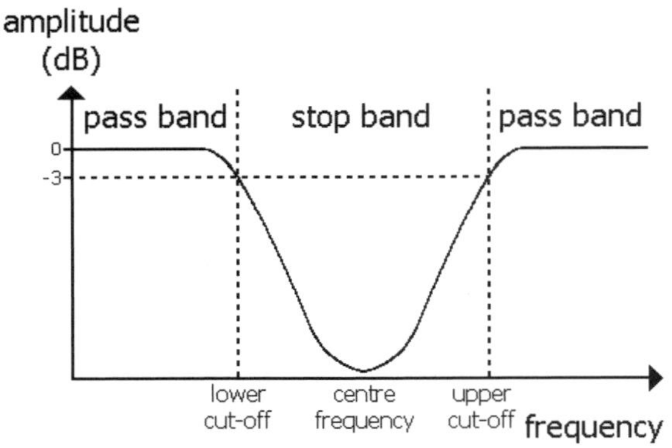

Figure 3.14
Amplitude response of a band-reject filter

Filter slopes

In its most basic form, a low-pass filter (for example) is regulated using a single parameter, the cut-off frequency. This governs the point at which the upper frequencies in the sound begin to be reduced, (attenuated), thereby controlling how the spectrum is modified. However, this attenuation takes place according to a slope as the filter passes between the pass band and the stop band. This slope describes the rate at which the upper frequencies are attenuated and is generally measured in terms of dBs per octave. The slope varies according to the manner in which the filter has been designed. In voltage-controlled circuitry, for example, the rate is governed, among other things, by the number of resistors and capacitors used in the circuit. A simple passive filter with one resistor and one capacitor in the circuit is known as an RC filter and this has an attenuation slope of 6dB per octave. Other common rates include 12dB per octave, 18dB per octave and 24dB per octave. These slopes can be plotted graphically in terms of relative attenuation against frequency.

Another manner in which to describe filters is in terms of the number of 'poles', such as two-pole or four-pole filters. A two-pole filter is equivalent to a filter with a 12dB per octave attenuation slope and a four-pole filter is equivalent to a filter with a 24dB per octave attenuation slope. Each pole is equivalent to one resistor/capacitor pair as in the simple RC filter described above. Each pole results in an additional 6dB per octave of attenuation in the filtered signal.

Filter phase response

As well as changing the amplitude of the signal which passes through it, a filter also changes the phase. As explained in Chapter 2, a complex signal can be broken down into a number of sine waves which represent the different frequency components of a sound. Phase refers to the relationships between these components in terms of the position of the compression and rarefaction parts of their waveforms (see 'Phase considerations' in Chapter 2). This is expressed in degrees. Another way of expressing the phase effects of combining waveforms is to suggest that it is, instead, a filtering effect. It is, therefore, correct to suggest that just as changing the phase of the components produces a filtering effect so filtering a signal changes the phase of its components.

The phase response of a simple filter invariably resembles that shown in Figure 3.15.

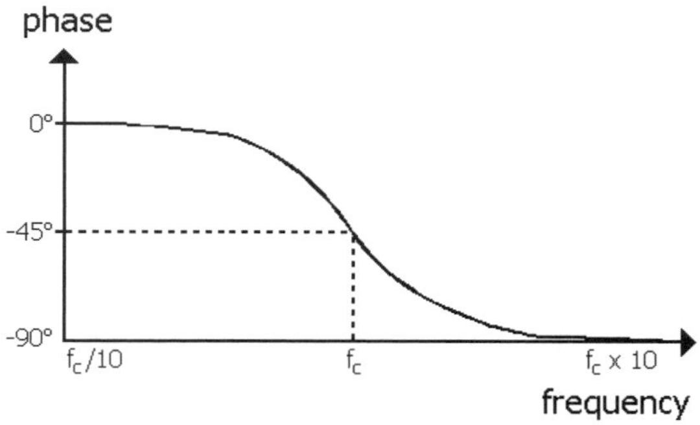

Figure 3.15
Phase response of a simple filter

Figure 3.15 reveals that the low frequency components pass through the filter unchanged in terms of their phase whereas the higher frequency components are progressively moved more negatively out-of-phase. The phase change at the cut-off frequency is invariably -45 degrees. There is 0 degrees phase change at around 1/10th the cut-off frequency and -90 degrees phase change at around 10 times the cut-off frequency. Passing a complex signal through a filter therefore results in noticeable changes in the timbre due to the phase response (in addition to those which are due to the amplitude response).

Filter resonance (emphasis)

Resonance can be defined as the frequency or frequencies at which an object vibrates in sympathy with itself or with external vibrational phenomena. Filters, too, can be endowed with this kind of behaviour. Passive RC filters have no resonant frequencies and simply filter the source according to their amplitude and phase response. However, active filters can be designed to produce a boost in the response around the cut-off frequency.

All synthesizers which feature resonant filters include a parameter which is used to regulate the amount of resonance. The parameter is commonly referred to as resonance, emphasis or Q. Figure 3.16 shows what happens to a low-pass filter's amplitude response for low, high and maximum resonance values.

When the resonance control parameter is set to low or medium positions the bandwidth of the emphasised frequencies is quite wide and they are only boosted by a small amount (Figure 3.16a). For higher resonance values the bandwidth of the emphasised frequencies is quite narrow and they are boosted by a large amount (Figure 3.16b). As the resonance is increased the lower frequencies are progressively attenuated. At maximum resonance the lower and upper frequencies virtually disappear from the filtered signal leaving a single harmonic which oscillates at the cut-off frequency (Figure 3.16c). With real world filters, an amount of the source signal still passes through.

The effect of resonance can be summarised as follows: resonance results in the emphasising of a narrow band of frequencies (harmonics) in the source signal located around the cut-off point. This narrow band can be moved around within the frequency spectrum by changing the frequency of the cut-off point. This results in effects which are particularly pleasing to the ear. At extreme resonance values, when the filter

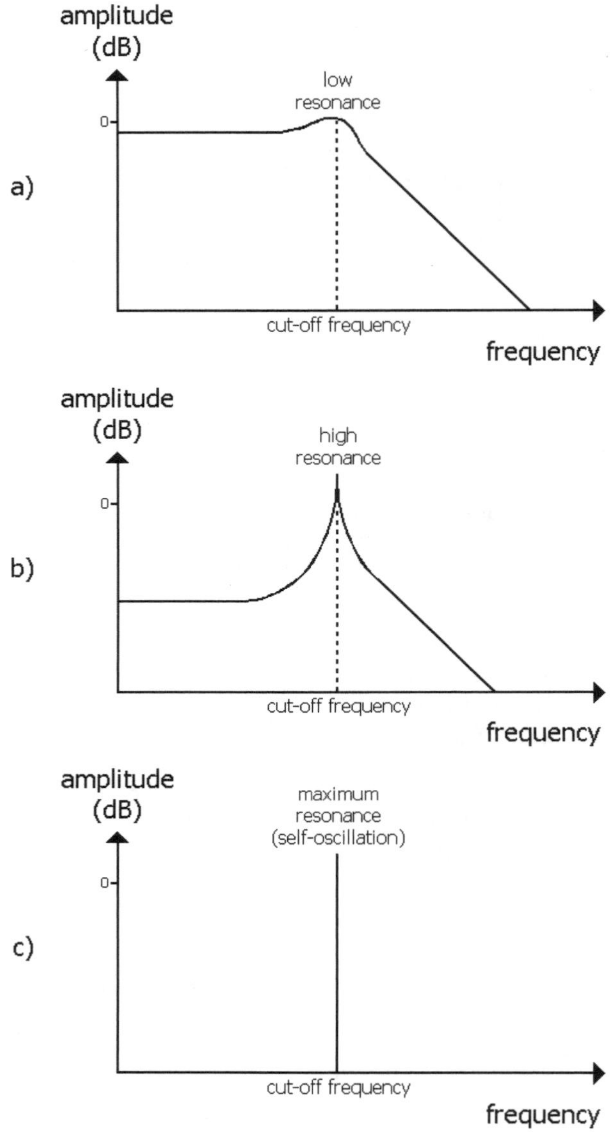

Figure 3.16
The effect of resonance on a low-pass filter's amplitude response

enters a state of self-oscillation (as in Figure 3.16c), special effects and pitched tones can be produced.

The resonant low-pass filter has, more than any other filter type, been responsible for some classic subtractive synthesis effects. Setting up a medium to high resonance level and then sweeping the cut-off frequency up and down has been used in innumerable synth patches. The addition of resonance to a filter increases the sound-sculpting possibilities some way above the basic non-resonant filter type and gives the sound synthesist a powerful means by which to really add character and expression to the source signal. As well as its implementation in low-pass filters, resonance is also commonly implemented in high-pass filters.

Filters in reality

As in many aspects of sound synthesis there are idealised versions of a component and then there is what actually happens in reality. The filter types described above have been idealised to help with the learning curve. However, it is important to appreciate that filters rarely attenuate the chosen frequencies in a strictly linear and entirely predictable fashion. The amplitude attenuation characteristics are invariably imperfect and show marked irregularities (particularly with analogue filters). For example, a filter designed to attenuate the frequencies in the stop band at a rate of 24dB per octave may, in reality, attenuate lower frequencies in the spectrum at a rate of 6dB per octave, mid frequencies at a rate of 12dB per octave, and only achieve its full 24dB per octave rating for the higher frequencies in the spectrum.

As we have also seen, the filtering action actually starts some way before the chosen cut-off frequency and a sound passed through any filter (analogue or digital), is invariably also changed in terms of its phase. Filters are also subject to different resonant characteristics and whereas simple RC filters are passive circuits involving resistors and capacitors, the filters in most analogue synthesizers are more complicated active devices involving the addition of op-amps in the circuit. The components within a real-world analogue filter can be fine-tuned for an optimum response but setting up one part of the circuit also simultaneously effects the other elements. This means that setting up an optimum amplitude response may result in an undesirable phase response or vice versa. In reality, filter design involves a compromise between desirable and not-so-desirable attributes. This is also the case for the digital filters used within software synthesizers and VST instruments.

All this is actually good news for the sound synthesist since it means that each filter design imparts a different tone colour into the resulting sound. Filter design plays a large part in the classic synthesizer tones produced by Moog, Arp, Oberheim and others, and it is equally important for determining the character of synthesizers in the digital world (including software synthesizers and VST instruments).

What happens to the source sound when it is filtered?

So what is actually happening when a sound rich in harmonics is filtered? Of course, firstly, it depends on what kind of filter is being used. Let's assume that it is the popular low-pass filter type.

A low-pass filter allows the lower frequencies in the source sound to pass through while attenuating (cutting) the upper frequencies. Figure 3.17 shows what this action means in terms of harmonics. In this example, the frequency axis is displayed logarithmically which means that, for each successive harmonic shown, the frequency is always doubled. In musical terms this means that the distance between each harmonic on this scale is one octave. The first, second, fourth, eighth, 16th, 32nd, 64th, 128th and 256th harmonics are shown for a sawtooth wave with a fundamental frequency of 55Hz. This is passed through a low-pass filter with its cut-off frequency (f_c) at 220Hz and with a response curve of 12dB per octave. This means that in the resulting spectrum shown in the figure, the eighth harmonic (440Hz) is attenuated by 12dB, the 16th harmonic (880Hz) is attenuated by 24dB, the 32nd (1760Hz) by 36dB and so on. The resulting waveform would therefore sound significantly more 'dull' than the original.

Figure 3.17
The resulting spectrum for a sawtooth wave passing through an idealised low-pass filter

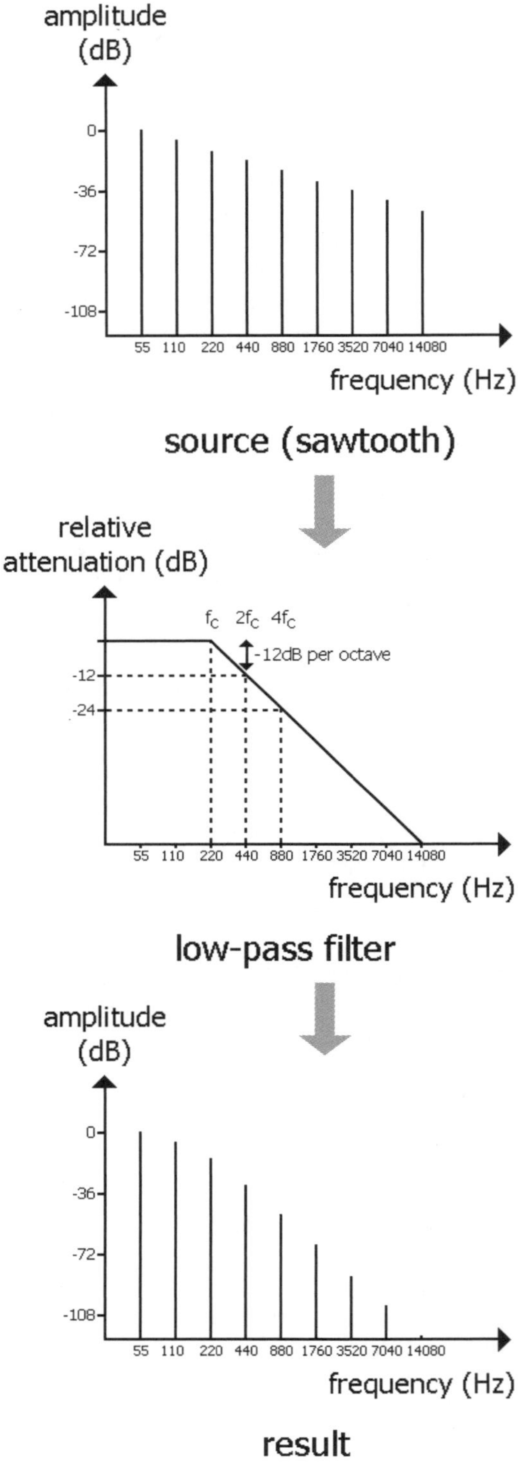

Adjusting the upper harmonics of a sound can radically alter how it is perceived. Imagine also making the change in upper harmonics a function of time using an envelope generator. You could set the attack segment to a short duration containing a large amount of high frequency energy followed by a steady-state segment which contains mainly the lower harmonics. A rapid attack phase containing more upper harmonics than the rest of the sound matches the behaviour of many real-world acoustic musical instruments and synthesizing a tone which approximates this behaviour using a sawtooth wave is likely to resemble a brass-like instrument.

Figure 3.17 shows an idealised filter in order to clarify the filtering process but passing a sound through a real filter (particularly an analogue filter), never changes the amplitudes of the harmonics in a strictly linear fashion.

Hearing the results

Since envelope generators and filtering, in particular, are so important in subtractive synthesis, it is worth linking some of what you have learnt so far in this chapter to a practical listening exercise. This requires the use of Native Instruments Reaktor (or Dynamo) and the 'ManyMood' synthesizer. 'ManyMood' is found in the NI Premium Library in the Subtractive Synths folder (Library/Premium/Synths – Subtractive/ManyMood.ens). This synthesizer is a Moog emulation featuring a 24dB-per-octave resonant low-pass filter. It is particularly useful for linking the graphical material of this chapter to the audible result since it includes dynamic graphic displays which react according to the parameter settings and the triggering of notes (see Figure 3.18).

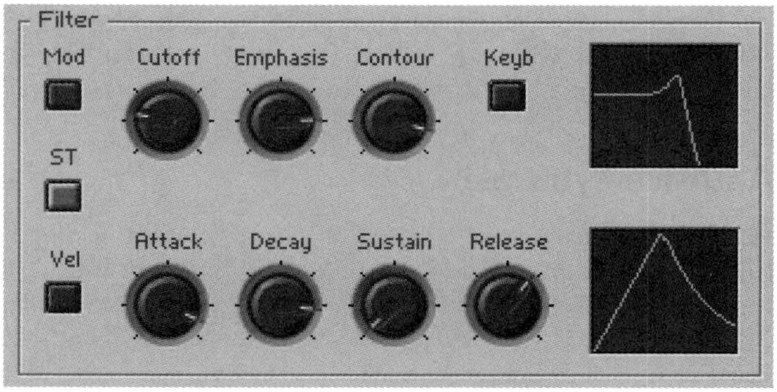

Figure 3.18
Filter section from Reaktor's 'ManyMood' synthesizer

Load the synth into Reaktor (or Dynamo) and select preset number 4, 'Dirty boy' (in order to be able to see the presets, ensure that 'Many Mood' is selected in the left-most menu of the instrument toolbar). Observe the low-pass filter section as shown in Figure 3.18, above. Play and hold any note on your triggering keyboard. The filter response curve moves slowly to the right indicating that the filter cut-off frequency is being shifted upwards. More of the harmonics of the source sound are allowed through as the filter opens up. This occurs according to the attack of the ADSR filter envelope, which is set quite slow. If you hold the note down for long enough the cut-off frequency eventually returns to its initial position, according to the exact contour of the whole ADSR filter envelope (as shown in the lower graphic display). Try changing the filter envelope amount (contour dial). A lower envelope amount results in a smaller change in the sweeping effect (of the cut-off frequency) and this is reflected in the smaller movement of the cut-off position in the filter response display on the screen.

What kinds of sounds can be produced with subtractive synthesis?

Using the subtractive filtering technique with different source waveforms results in a surprisingly wide range of timbres. The following is a basic guideline to what kinds of timbres can be produced with each of the commonly available waveforms and with various waveform combinations:

- sawtooth wave – brass, strings and guitar
- square wave – clarinet and woodwind
- triangle wave – flute
- pulse wave – oboe, bassoon and reed instruments
- pulse and triangle wave combinations – piano, strings
- sawtooth and pulse wave combinations – bass guitar, organ
- white noise – drums and percussion

Subtractive synthesis can therefore produce reasonable approximations of the majority of real-world acoustic musical instruments, hence its popularity. If you were to add ring modulation to your basic synthesis configuration you could also produce bell-like and gong tones.

VST instruments which use subtractive synthesis

There are a wide range of VST instruments which use subtractive synthesis. Notable among these are the NI Pro 52, NI Absynth, Bitheadz Retro AS-1, Steinberg Model E, Muon Tau Pro, rgcAudio Pentagon I, and the subtractive synths found within NI Reaktor and Dynamo.

Additive synthesis

Additive synthesis was touched upon in Chapter 2 since its principles run in parallel with classic harmonic theory and the understanding of sound and timbre. Additive synthesis involves the adding together of sine waves of different frequencies to produce a composite, complex waveform. This is based upon the research of Jean Baptiste Fourier (1768 – 1830) who showed that any complex periodic waveform could be broken down into a number of separate sine waves, each oscillating at different frequencies and possessing differing amplitudes (see Chapter 2 for more details). Additive synthesis is the process of adding them back together again to make up the various harmonics which constitute a complex sound.

An ideal additive synthesizer might use 64 harmonics or more but most practical implementations would use far less. The harmonics might be arranged according to the natural harmonic series i.e. each of the components is an integer multiple of the fundamental frequency. For example, sawtooth, square, triangle and pulse waves are made up of varying proportions of the harmonics in the natural harmonic series (see Chapter 2 for more details about harmonics). Timbres which more closely resemble real-world sounds, such as those from acoustic musical instruments, would normally need to include a number of inharmonic components for an authentic recreation of the sound. Inharmonic components are those which do not bear any whole integer multiple relationship to the fundamental.

Although the concept is relatively straightforward, additive synthesis has proved difficult to implement in commercially available synthesizers since a large number of parameters are required. Each harmonic component would normally be comprised of frequency, level, phase and a number of envelope parameters. If you take a sound comprised of just 24 harmonics, for example, a total of over 150 parameters would be required. This is a large processing overhead which also presents problems when attempting to design a readily accessible user-interface. In addition, additive synthesis is not particularly intuitive. You are not likely to be able to predict the sonic result of changing one or a small number of the parameters. Working with additive synthesis is more likely to be an experimental process or based upon the detailed analysis of real-world sounds in order to be able to create a synthetic version. One notable exception is found in organ technology. The classic drawbar organ is essentially a specialised type of additive synthesizer.

Practical realisations of additive synthesis instruments

Although additive synthesis has its roots in analogue synthesis, practical implementations tend to be digital in nature. Digital systems lend themselves more efficiently to the simultaneous production of a wide range of frequencies using digitally controlled oscillators (DCOs) and the processing of large numbers of control parameters. Figure 3.19 shows a basic model for digitally controlled additive synthesis.

Figure 3.19
Additive synthesis with eight oscillators

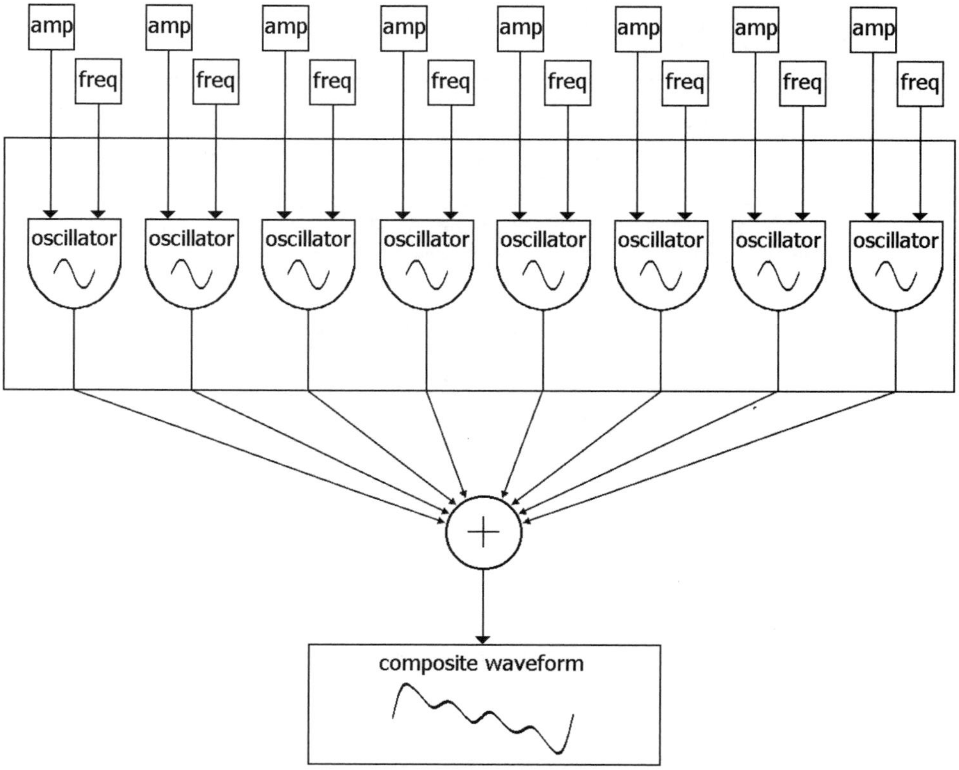

Eight digitally controlled oscillators are shown, each with amplitude and frequency parameters. These are added together to produce a composite waveform. The amplitude and frequency parameters can be substituted with actual values. The chosen values govern the shape and spectral content of the resulting waveform.

Figure 3.20 substitutes values for the control parameters of each oscillator. The odd-numbered harmonics in the natural harmonic series have been chosen at the amplitude ratios shown in the diagram. This results in a waveform which resembles a square wave (see Chapter 2 for more details about square waves). To arrive at a perfect square wave a theoretically infinite number of harmonics would be required. In additive synthesis it has been shown that an authentic sounding timbre is achieved using a relatively small number of harmonics. Thus the perceived timbre of the square wave produced in Figure 3.20 (which contains eight components up to the 15th harmonic) would possess the characteristic 'hollow' tone of a typical square wave even though the resulting waveform is not perfectly square.

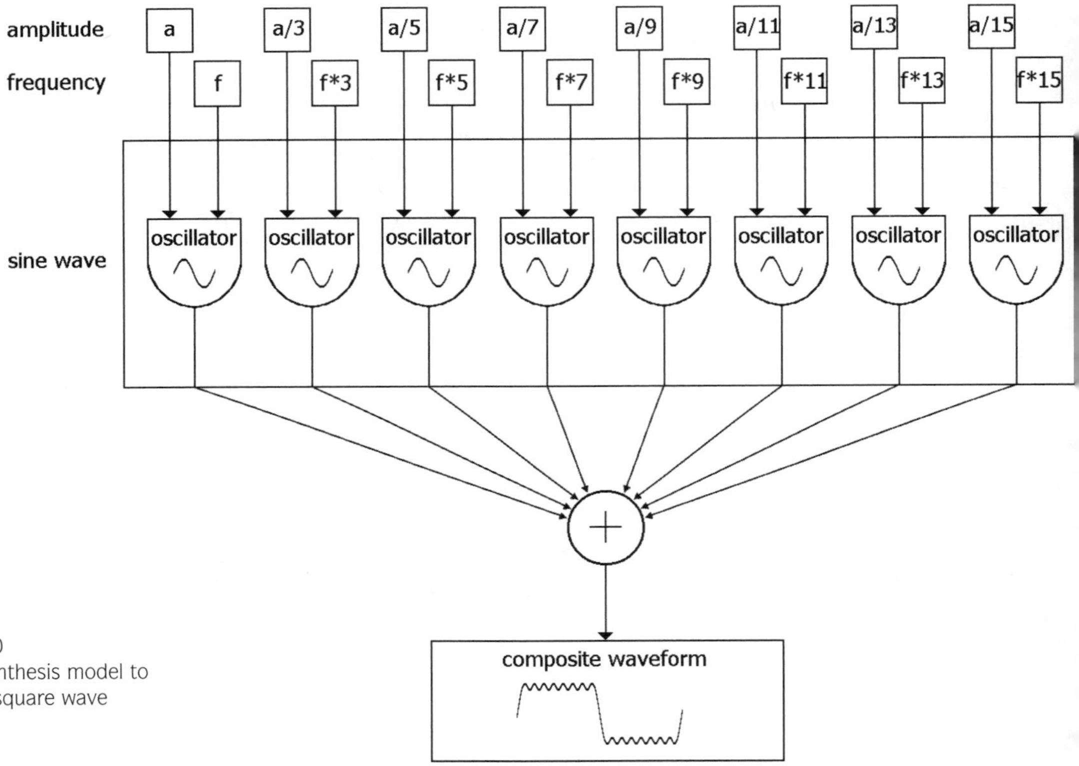

Figure 3.20
Additive synthesis model to produce a square wave

To produce authentic timbres matching real-world sounds a far more elaborate additive synthesis model might be required. To find the components necessary for synthesizing a real-world sound it is common practice to analyse a sampled real-world sound to find how its spectrum is arranged (usually achieved using FFT analysis, see Chapter 2 for more details). The additive synthesis instrument used to replicate the sound would need to control the amplitude of each oscillator using envelope generators in an attempt to match how each component evolves over time. Real-world instrumental sounds invariably include inharmonic components and this complicates the process still further.

Additive techniques have been successfully used to synthesize a wide range of tones (notably bell-like tones as described in Jean-Claude Risset's 'Introductory Catalogue of Computer Synthesized Sounds'). It is also well-disposed towards the creation of organ tones since all drawbar organs are essentially examples of additive synthesizers. Figure 3.21 shows an additive synthesizer model with the values required to produce an organ tone.

Figure 3.21
Additive synthesis model to produce an organ tone

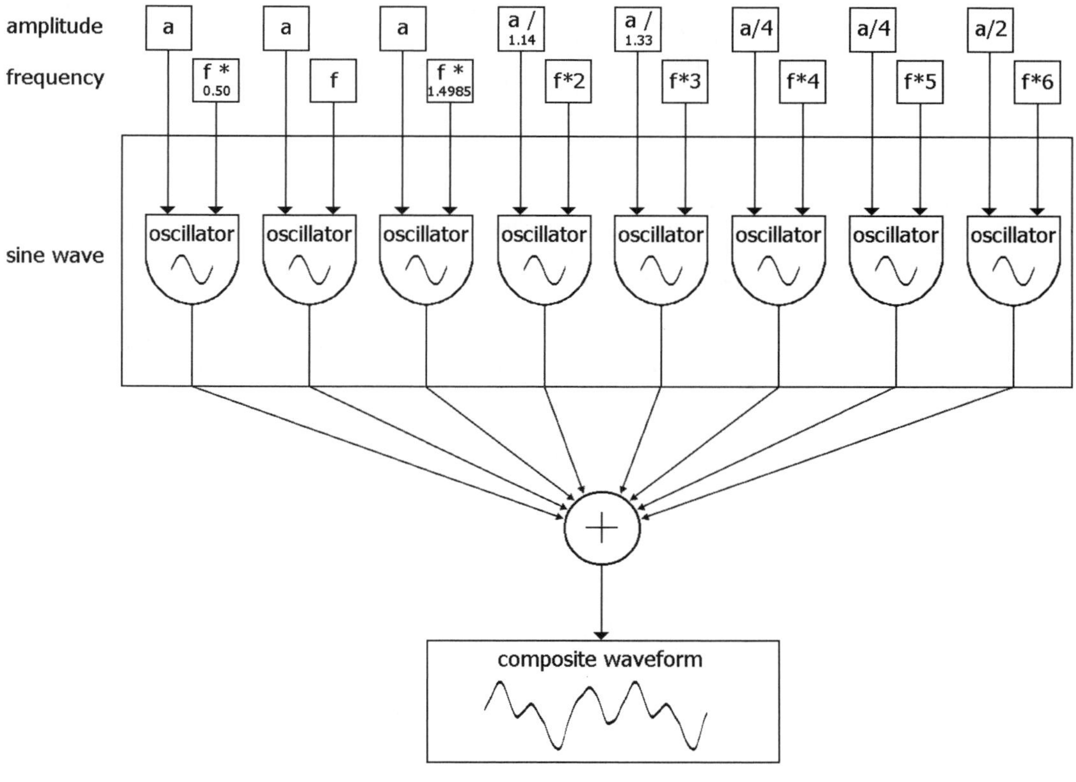

VST instruments which use additive synthesis

The NI B4, like real-world tonewheel organs, uses additive synthesis to create its sound. The NI FM7 can be used for simple six oscillator additive synthesis by using the six operators as parallel carriers connected directly to the output with no modulation. NI Reaktor and Dynamo may also be used for additive synthesis.

FM synthesis

FM synthesis is a digital form of sound synthesis which can produce complex, time-varying audio spectra using relatively few initial building blocks. It was first developed by John Chowning at the Centre for Computer Research in Music and Acoustics (CCRMA) at Stanford University. Chowning's research resulted in the publication of a paper entitled 'The Synthesis of Complex Audio Spectra by Means of Frequency Modulation' in 1973 (*Journal of the Audio Engineering Society*, Volume 21, Number 7). This was to prove highly influential and the technique was later to be adopted by Yamaha in their DX range of synthesizers, the most popular of which became the Yamaha DX7.

Chowning discovered that sounds with surprisingly realistic and complex spectral evolutions could be produced with relative ease using just two oscillators. Thus, the computational overhead for FM synthesis techniques was very small while the sound synthesis possibilities remained very large. Despite being a rich source for the synthesis of interesting timbres, FM synthesis lacks the intuitive nature of subtractive and other forms of synthesis. Its basis resides in mathematics and the resulting timbre for any given set of parameters has a reputation for being difficult to predict.

Regardless of the difficulties it is worth persevering with the theory of FM synthesis since this can result in overcoming many of the obstacles involved in the practical programming of FM sounds.

FM basics

FM stands for 'frequency modulation' and simple FM synthesis produces its tones by modulating one oscillating frequency with another. The theory of FM already had a history in the world of radio transmission before it was used for sound synthesis. FM radio involves the transmission of sound via radio waves, using what is known as a 'carrier' frequency to 'carry' another frequency known as the 'modulator'. The modulator forms the intended audible part of the signal whereas the carrier is a very high frequency signal used for transmission purposes only. The carrier is not intended to be included in the final audio which we hear in the radio transmission and, in order to hear the desired audio, the composite signal must first be decoded (i.e. the modulator must be separated from the carrier).

FM synthesis, on the other hand, involves reducing the frequency of the carrier so that both the carrier and the modulator are in the audible frequency range. When this is the case a vast range of audio spectra can be produced.

One form of musically related modulation with which most readers will be familiar is vibrato. Vibrato can also help us understand FM synthesis and it was indeed experimentation with vibrato which initially led to an understanding of the potential of FM in sound synthesis. Vibrato is the periodic variation of the pitch of a tone and in sound synthesis is often implemented by the use of an LFO (low frequency oscillator). The rate of vibrato applied to a tone in the musical world rarely exceeds around 10Hz. FM synthesis involves increasing the vibrato to a rate which is closer to the frequency which is being modulated. At higher frequencies the modulating effect is no longer referred to as vibrato. Instead, it is referred to as a 'modulation frequency' and its effect is somewhat different.

At a normal vibrato rate (between 1 and 10Hz) a periodic fluctuation in pitch is clearly perceptible but when the rate is increased beyond 10Hz the periodic fluctuation in pitch gradually disappears. Surprisingly, as the vibrato is increased, additional spectral components are introduced into the signal and the harmonic structure of the tone becomes progressively more complex and enriched with high frequency components. If we were to set the rate of the vibrato (modulating frequency) to a fixed amount and then experiment with the vibrato depth we would find that the number of frequency components increases as the depth increases. In FM synthesis, vibrato depth is known as 'frequency deviation'.

A preliminary model for FM synthesis

If you refer back to the beginning of this chapter you will remember how subtractive and other forms of synthesis can be understood in terms of a number of building blocks that can be arranged to create a model for sound synthesis. These same building blocks can be applied to FM synthesis except that they are arranged in a different manner. Basic FM synthesis can be organised into two sections as in Figure 3.22.

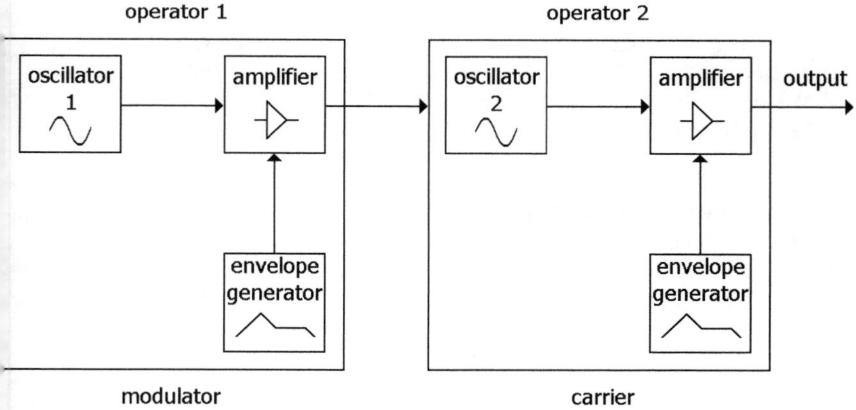

Figure 3.22
Simple FM synthesis

Oscillator 2 provides the centre frequency (pitch) for the final audio output. In FM synthesis, the centre frequency is known as the 'carrier'. The frequency of the carrier is modulated by a second signal, oscillator 1 (i.e. it has a form of 'vibrato' applied to it). In FM terminology, this modulating signal is known as the 'modulator'. The modulator has a frequency and an amplitude which, in FM terminology, are referred to as the 'modulating frequency' and the 'frequency deviation'. Thus, in simple FM synthesis there are only three preliminary parameters: the carrier frequency, the modulating frequency and the frequency deviation. These are commonly represented by the following three symbols respectively: f_c f_m and DELTA f. Early implementations of FM synthesis used oscillators which generated only sine waves, but modern FM systems allow the use of a number of different waveforms.

Figure 3.22 also includes an envelope generator for each of the oscillators. In the case of the carrier, the envelope generator governs the overall amplitude characteristics of the final sound. The carrier is also simultaneously modulated according to the modulating frequency and the frequency deviation (width) of the modulator. The level of the modulator, like the carrier, is controlled by its own envelope generator. This provides a manner in which complex, time-evolving spectra can be created according to the envelope shape of the modulator.

In classic FM synthesis of the type implemented by Yamaha in their DX range of synthesizers, each oscillator/amplifier/envelope generator unit is known as an 'operator'. This structure has been adopted in the Native Instruments FM7 VST instrument which emulates the classic Yamaha DX7 and additionally takes FM synthesis into another dimension (see Chapter 5 for more details). Each of the two units shown in Figure 3.22 can, therefore, also be referred to as an operator. An operator can be designated as a carrier or a modulator.

In this configuration, the frequency of the modulator determines the harmonic structure of the resulting sound while the level of the modulator determines the number of harmonics present. It is worth noting here that the interaction of the carrier and modulator produces additional frequencies below, as well as above, the carrier frequency. This means that the carrier is not always perceived as the fundamental pitch for the resulting FM tone. Increasing/decreasing the level of the modulator can be likened to raising/lowering the cut-off point of a low-pass filter in subtractive synthesis.

The basics outlined above form the fundamental ideas which can lead to an understanding of FM synthesis but in order to be able to predict what kinds of timbres can be produced in detail we need to know something about how the different elements interact. This is outlined in the next section.

FM parameter interaction

The effect of modulation (vibrato) can be somewhat confusing. A modulation effect like vibrato can be expressed as a waveform plotted on a graph of frequency deviation against time. At lower modulation rates, (those producing vibrato), it is the change in frequency deviation which directly produces the perceived fluctuation in pitch in the target waveform. Figure 3.23a shows a slow modulation signal of this type at a frequency of around 10Hz which produces a regular vibrato effect. In order to understand FM synthesis in more detail we need to be aware of exactly how the frequency of the modulator effects the carrier waveform in terms of sound pressure against time. Figure 3.23b shows a sound pressure against time graph for a target signal (carrier) of 110Hz when it is modulated by the 10Hz signal shown in Figure 3.23a. The modulation effect modifies the waveform of the carrier on the horizontal axis (time). The centre frequency of the carrier is continually speeded up and slowed down by the modulator, and this can be perceived graphically as compressed and not-so-compressed parts of the waveform. Finally, Figure 3.23c shows what happens when the modulating frequency is increased to the same rate as the frequency of the carrier (both at 110Hz). The result is a complex waveform typical of FM synthesis.

Of course, in FM synthesis, the modulating effect takes place extremely quickly. In addition, the effect is accentuated or not-so-accentuated according to the frequency deviation. At higher levels of frequency deviation the effect of the modulation on the carrier frequency is greater. Another way of looking at frequency deviation (or vibrato

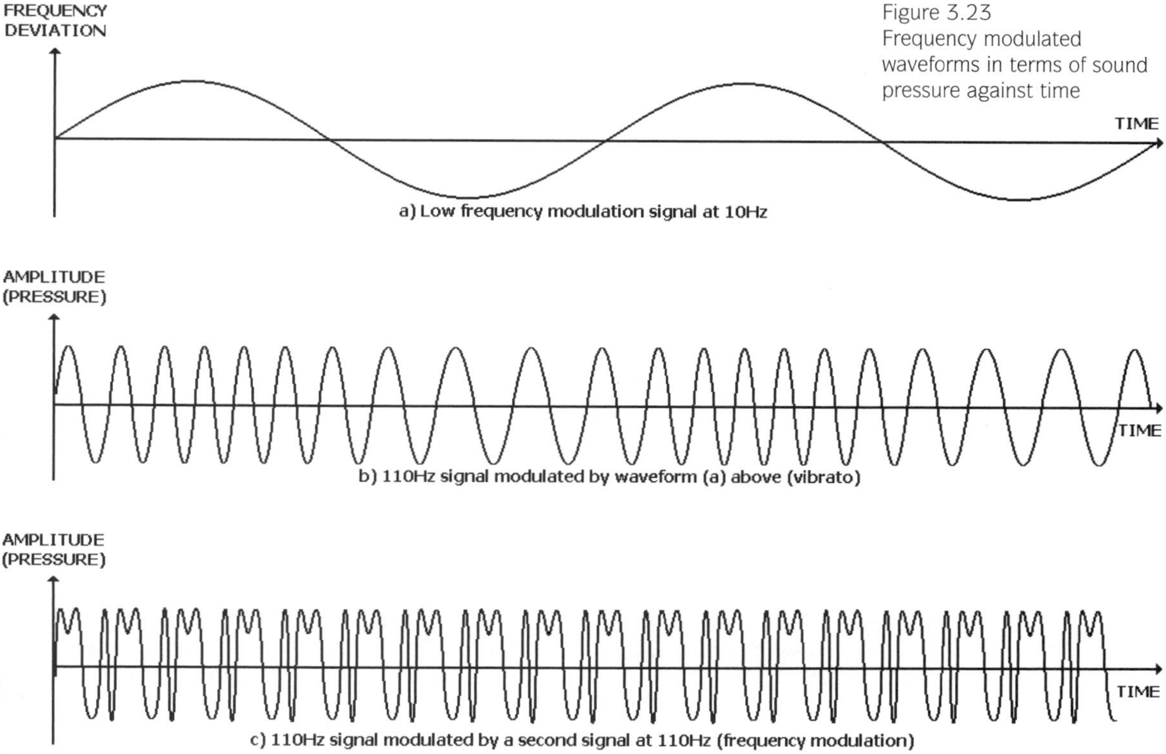
FREQUENCY
DEVIATION
TIME
a) Low frequency modulation signal at 10Hz
AMPLITUDE
(PRESSURE)
TIME
b) 110Hz signal modulated by waveform (a) above (vibrato)
AMPLITUDE
(PRESSURE)
TIME
c) 110Hz signal modulated by a second signal at 110Hz (frequency modulation)

Figure 3.23
Frequency modulated waveforms in terms of sound pressure against time

depth) is in terms of width. Frequency deviation can be expressed in hertz as the maximum width above and below the carrier frequency by which the signal is modulated. This deviation in the frequency of the carrier occurs at the rate of the frequency of the modulator. Thus, for a frequency deviation value of 220Hz with a modulating frequency of 110Hz, a centre frequency of 880Hz (for example) is modulated between 660 and 1100Hz at a rate of 220Hz (220 times per second). The resulting waveform for these values is shown in Figure 3.24.

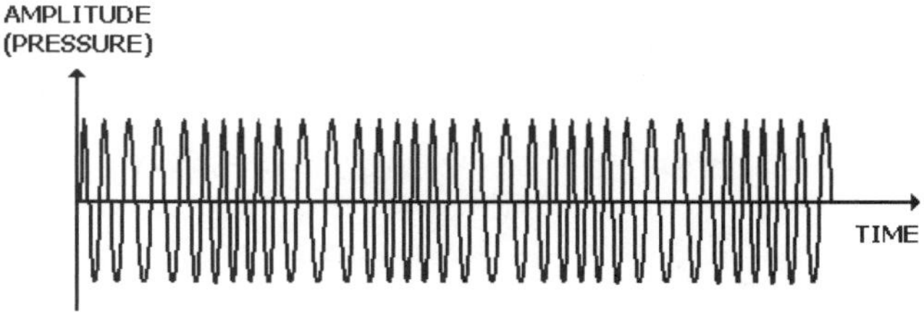
AMPLITUDE
(PRESSURE)
TIME

Figure 3.24
Resulting waveform for a frequency deviation of 220Hz with a 880Hz carrier and 110Hz modulator

Although time-domain graphs are useful in helping us to imagine the effect of frequency modulation, it is actually more valuable to view the spectral components in the frequency domain (Figure 3.25). This shows the details of the frequency components and gives an indication of what the resulting timbre might actually sound like.

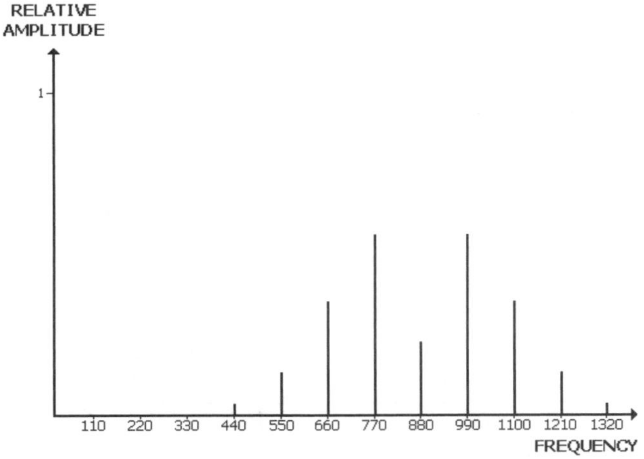

Figure 3.25
Frequency domain plot for the waveform shown in Figure 3.24

Predicting the results

FM synthesis is not the most intuitive type of sound synthesis and it is often difficult to predict the results for any given set of parameter values. However, there are a number of ground rules which can help us turn FM synthesis into something which is at least manageable. The secret is to be able to predict what relationships between the basic parameters produce what kinds of timbres. For this purpose, and also for the purpose of further clarification of the theory, FM synthesis has adopted an additional parameter which expresses the ratio between the modulating frequency and the frequency deviation. This is known as the 'modulation index' which is normally designated the symbol 'I'. The modulation index is found by dividing the frequency deviation by the modulating frequency. For example, for an FM signal with the carrier at 110Hz, the modulator at 440Hz and the frequency deviation at 880Hz, the modulation index is equal to 880Hz divided by 440Hz (frequency deviation divided by the modulating frequency). The result is a modulation index of 2. (If the modulation index is already known, or has been chosen, the frequency deviation can be calculated by multiplying the modulation index by the modulating frequency.)

It can be shown that there is a special relationship between the carrier and the modulating frequency. In order to maintain the same spectral identity when the pitch of the note is changed, both the carrier and the modulating frequency must be multiplied by the same factor. For example, to transpose the FM timbre outlined above by one semitone multiply both the carrier frequency (110Hz) and the modulating frequency (440Hz) by a factor of 1.059, or to transpose the same tone up by one octave multiply both values by a factor of 2. In order to maintain exactly the same spectral components as the pitch is transposed, the frequency deviation must also change by the same factor. However, the modulation index is used to achieve this automatically since it is inextricably linked to the modulating frequency. The modulation index can, therefore, be fixed at the same value for all transpositions of an FM synthesized tone. If you ever need to know the frequency deviation for any set of FM values you can simply multiply the modulation index by the modulating frequency. In addition, the carrier and modulator can be expressed in terms of a ratio, rather than fixed frequencies, and this ratio remains constant throughout all transpositions of the tone. This is clarified in the following table where the FM tone with the carrier at 110Hz, the modulator at 440Hz and a modulation index of 2 (as described above) is transposed up by one semitone, by one octave and by two octaves respectively.

Table 3.1
FM carrier-modulator relationships expressed as ratios

	carrier (Hz)	modulator (Hz)	modulation index	ratio (c:m)
FM tone at 110Hz	110	440	2	1:4
up one semitone (x 1.059)	116.49	465.96	2	1:4
up one octave (x 2)	220	880	2	1:4
up two octaves (x 4)	440	1760	2	1:4

c = carrier
m = modulator

The parameters are now slightly more under control with respect to their relationship with one another. The carrier and modulator relationship can be managed entirely in terms of ratio rather than discrete frequencies and, when the FM tone is transposed, the ratio values are simply multiplied by a common factor. The modulation index remains fixed at the same value for all transpositions. This constitutes a system which can be used for predicting the results of FM synthesis manipulations which is slightly easier to understand.

For example, we can safely predict that carrier:modulator ratios made up of whole integers produce periodic tones whose spectra are harmonically related and whose pitch can be clearly perceived. These ratios are best for producing real-world instrument emulations and FM tones which have a clear sense of pitch. Non-integer carrier:modulator ratios produce complex aperiodic tones whose spectra are inharmonic and whose pitch is not always clearly perceptible. These ratios produce bell-like, percussive or abstract FM tones.

The ratio of the modulator to the carrier determines the basic structure and distribution of the spectral components. Increasing the modulator ratio spreads the frequency components further apart across a wider frequency range while increasing the modulation index increases the number and bandwidth of the frequency components contained within the sound. Bear in mind that components are generated both above and below the frequency of the carrier. In certain circumstances, a small change in index can produce a large change in timbre. The modulation index should not, therefore, be considered as a parameter which operates in a strictly linear or predictable fashion.

It is useful to note that carrier:modulator ratios of 1:2, 1:4, 3:2, 3:4, 5:2 and 5:4 (where the modulator is an even number) all produce timbres with only odd-numbered harmonics present and therefore resembling the classic 'hollow' tone associated with square waves. Ratios of 1:1, 2:1, 3:1 etc. (where the modulator = 1) contain both odd and even-numbered harmonics and produce spectra resembling a sawtooth wave. Ratios of 1:3, 2:3, and 4:3 contain spectra resembling a pulse wave where every third harmonic is missing. Non-integer carrier:modulator ratios like 1:1.4 and 1:2.66 produce FM bell-like tones.

Info

Carrier: modulator ratios made up of whole integers produce periodic tones whose spectra are harmonically related and whose pitch can be clearly perceived. These ratios are best for producing real-world instrument emulations and FM tones which have a clear sense of pitch. Non-integer carrier:modulator ratios produce complex aperiodic tones whose spectra are inharmonic and whose pitch is not always clearly perceptible. These ratios produce bell-like, percussive or abstract FM tones.

In order to make more precise predictions about the kind of timbre which is produced by a given set of parameter values we need to delve a little deeper into the theory.

Deeper into the theory

It has already been established that there are three essential elements which interact to create a sound using FM synthesis. These parameters are the carrier, the modulator and the modulation index. The carrier and modulator are more usefully viewed in terms of ratio rather than fixed frequencies. The ratios can then be multiplied by a given factor to transpose the pitch of the timbre, while the modulation index remains at a constant value. This arrangement ensures that the timbre remains the same at different frequencies. However, many readers familiar with FM synthesis as implemented in the Yamaha DX range of synthesizers, will be wondering why there is no mention of modulation index within the DX synthesizer parameters. As mentioned above, the DX range and the Native Instruments FM7 VSTi use building blocks known as operators (units containing an oscillator, VCA and envelope generator). An operator can be designated as a carrier or a modulator. The reason that the modulation index is not apparent is that each time an operator is designated as a modulator its output level is arranged so that it also automatically governs the modulation index.

It would be possible at this stage to suggest that since the DX range of synthesizers managed to hide the modulation index then we could do the same and simply forget about its existence. Although it is true that for most practical FM synthesis it could largely be ignored, it forms a fundamental stepping stone in the understanding of the theory and is always worth bearing in mind during the practical programming of FM sounds.

To explore FM synthesis in further detail now requires the use of some basic mathematics. The frequencies of the spectral components for any given carrier:modulator ratio can be calculated using the following table :

Table 3.2
Equations table for calculating the spectral components for any given carrier: modulator ratio

frequency component	*calculation*
carrier frequency	c ± (0 x m)
upper 1st order side band	c + (1 x m)
lower 1st order side band	c - (1 x m)
upper 2nd order side band	c + (2 x m)
lower 2nd order side band	c - (2 x m)
upper 3rd order side band	c + (3 x m)
lower 3rd order side band	c - (3 x m)
upper 4th order side band	c + (4 x m)
lower 4th order side band	c - (4 x m)
and so on	c + (n x m)

c = carrier
m = modulator

The spectral components are arranged in pairs above and below the carrier frequency and these pairs are known as 'side bands'. To calculate the frequency of each component the modulator is multiplied by its corresponding side band number and then added to and subtracted from the carrier to derive the upper and lower side bands. The carrier is calculated only once.

To derive the approximate number of side bands which should be calculated simply add 2 to the value of the modulation index for any given set of parameters.

For example, consider the case of an FM signal with the carrier at 440Hz, the modulator at 110Hz and the modulation index at 1. Firstly, you derive the number of side bands by adding 2 to the modulation index. The result here is 3. Thus, you need to add and subtract the frequencies (as in the table above) three times to produce three pairs of side bands. This process is shown in the following table :

frequency component	*calculation*	*resulting frequency*
carrier frequency	440 ± (0 x 110)	= 440Hz
upper 1st order side band	440 + (1 x 110)	= 550Hz
lower 1st order side band	440 – (1 x 110)	= 330Hz
upper 2nd order side band	440 + (2 x 110)	= 660Hz
lower 2nd order side band	440 – (2 x 110)	= 220Hz
upper 3rd order side band	440 + (3 x 110)	= 770Hz
lower 3rd order side band	440 – (3 x 110)	= 110Hz

Table 3.3
Calculating the spectral components for an FM signal with the carrier at 440Hz, the modulator at 110Hz and the modulation index at 1 (using Table 3.2 above)

These calculations produce the frequency spectrum shown in Figure 3.26.

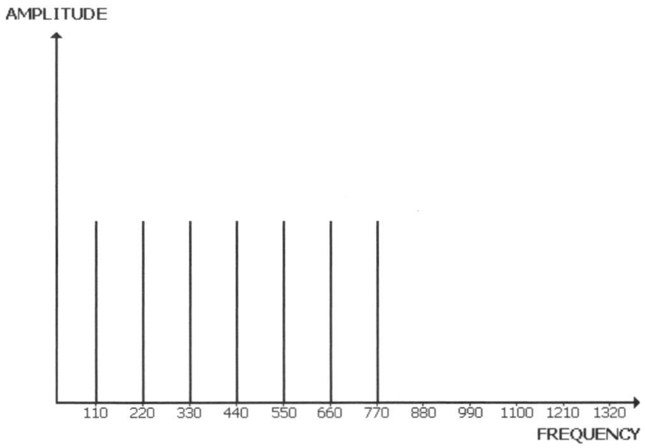

Figure 3.26
The number and locations of the spectral components for an FM signal with the carrier at 440Hz, the modulator at 110Hz and with a modulation index of 1

This is fine but, up to now, there is no indication of how the amplitude for each component is calculated. For this we need to use something called a Bessel function. Bessel functions provide a specific curve (set of values) for the carrier and each pair of side bands which determines the amplitude for each component in relation to the modulation index. This can be read from a graph (of amplitude against modulation index) or from a mathematical table (see Table 3.4).

Table 3.4
The carrier and first to fourth order side band Bessel function values for modulation index values between 0 and 10 (whole integers only)

		side bands			
modulation index	*carrier*	*1st order*	*2nd order*	*3rd order*	*4th order*
0	1.000	0.000	0.000	0.000	0.000
1	0.765	0.440	0.115	0.019	0.002
2	0.224	0.577	0.353	0.129	0.034
3	-0.260	0.339	0.486	0.309	0.132
4	-0.397	-0.066	0.364	0.430	0.281
5	-0.177	-0.327	0.046	0.365	0.391
6	0.151	-0.277	-0.243	0.115	0.358
7	0.300	-0.004	-0.301	-0.167	0.158
8	0.171	0.234	-0.113	-0.291	-0.105
9	-0.090	0.245	0.145	-0.181	-0.265
10	-0.246	0.043	0.255	0.058	-0.219

To find the amplitudes for the components within an FM signal you need to read off the amplitude level according to the modulation index and the relevant band numbers. For example, for a modulation index of 1, the carrier has an amplitude of approximately 0.76 and the three pairs of side bands which would need to be taken into account occur at amplitudes of approximately 0.44, 0.11 and 0.02 (on a relative amplitude scale of -1 to +1). For the values indicated in Figure 3.26, the final normalised spectrum for the FM signal is shown in Figure 3.27.

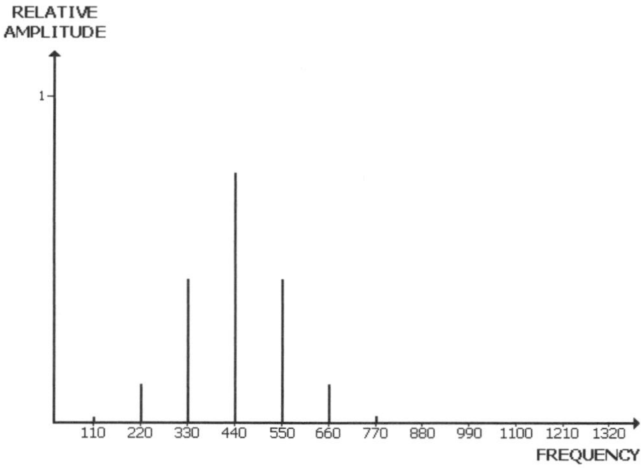

Figure 3.27
Final normalised spectrum for an FM signal with the carrier at 440Hz, the modulator at 110Hz and with a modulation index of 1

Further complications

Note that all the examples outlined above have been idealised to help ease the learning curve. In reality, calculating the spectral components of an FM signal often includes negative and out-of-phase frequency components. In order to arrive at the standard frequency domain representation of the signal (similar to that shown in Figure 3.27), any negative frequency components must be reflected around the 0Hz point and then, according to their phase characteristics, must be added to, or subtracted from, the positive frequency components. There are various mathematical rules which govern how this is managed. The full details of these rules and the many other intricacies of FM synthesis are beyond the scope of this text. For further information, readers are advised to consult alternative texts on the subject. These provide such things as Bessel function tables and other mathematical data, (one of the best sources on the subject is *FM Theory and Applications* by John Chowning and David Bristow, 1986, Yamaha Music Foundation).

It is worth bearing in mind that the modulation index, like the carrier:modulator ratio, is on a continuous scale and can, therefore, be non-integer. Additionally, the waveforms used for the carrier and modulator can be other than a sine wave and the Bessel function values used to define the amplitudes for each spectral component can have negative values, as well as positive values. In addition, the Bessel function amplitude values for all odd-numbered lower side band frequencies must be multiplied by -1. All this means that the mathematics used to calculate the resulting timbres can be prohibitively complicated. Luckily, an understanding of the finer details of the mathematics is not essential knowledge for gaining an appreciation of FM synthesis.

Algorithms

The Yamaha implementation of FM synthesis involves arranging operators into interacting carrier:modulator networks known as algorithms. The DX7 synthesizer features 32 such algorithms, each containing six operators connected in various different configurations.

The six operator principle has also been adopted by Native Instruments in their FM7 VST Instrument but, rather than fixed presets (as in the DX7), the algorithms of the FM7 can be configured by the user. This is achieved in a special matrix where virtually any operator can be connected to any other. In addition to the standard operators, the FM7 also features two special operators, one for distortion or noise-generating applications and the other for filtering (see Chapter 5 for a full description of the FM7 and see also the FM synthesis tutorial in Chapter 6).

Figure 3.28 shows various ways in which operators can be joined together to form algorithms.

Figure 3.28 Algorithms for 6 operator FM synthesis

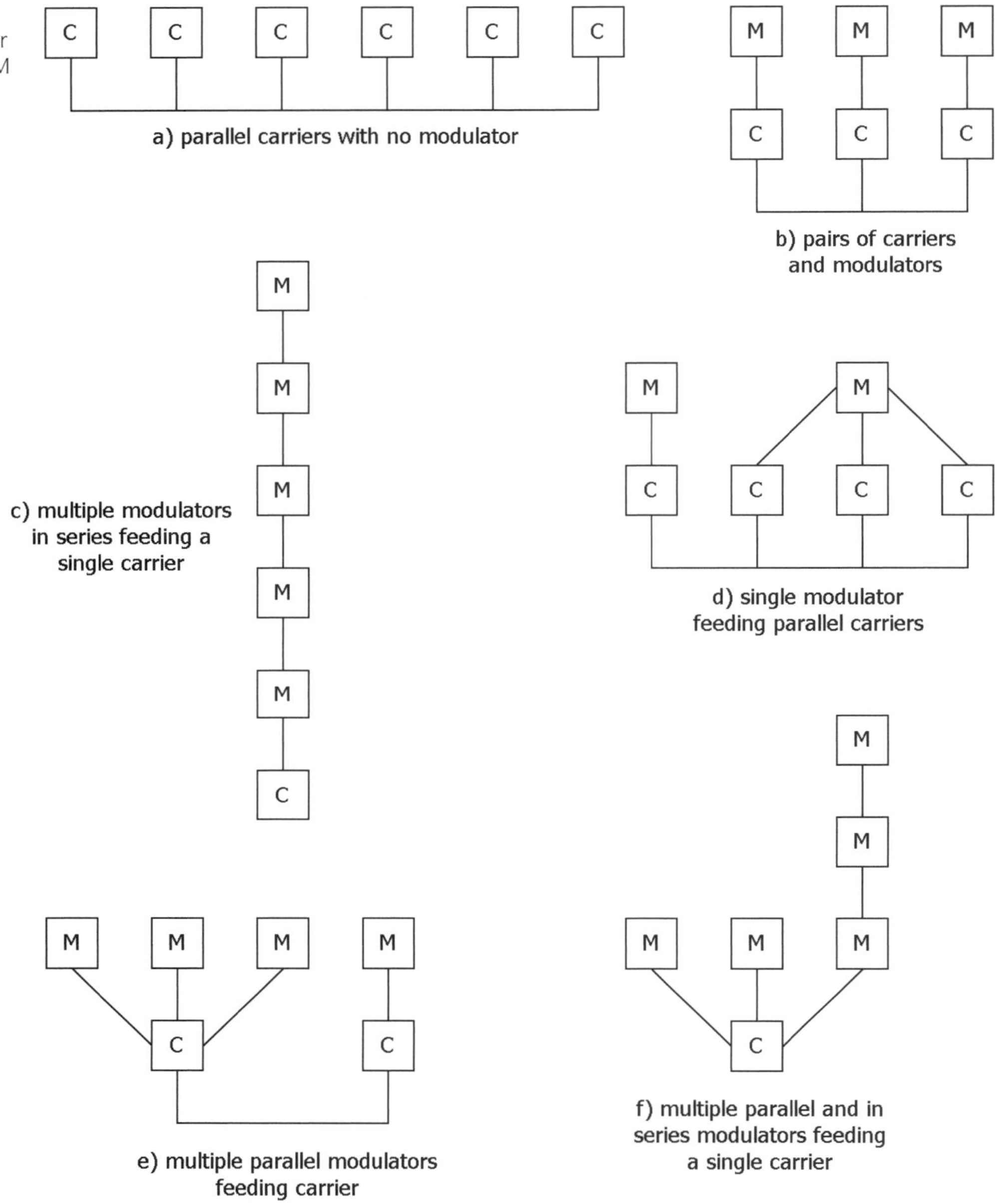

Algorithm (a) is comprised of six carriers with no modulator which means that it cannot produce an FM tone in the normal way. However, any of the carriers could provide its own modulator by using feedback (see below). This algorithm was included in the original DX7 where it could be used for simple tones and basic additive synthesis. Algorithm (b) arranges the operators into carrier:modulator pairs, a standard FM configuration useful for synthesizing a wide range of tones. Algorithm (c) shows how modulators can be linked in series so that the carrier at the end of the chain is eventually modulated by a highly complex signal rather than the usual sine wave of a standard, single operator. This configuration produces sounds which are particularly rich in harmonics.

Algorithm (d) shows how a single modulator can simultaneously modulate a number of carriers (in this case, three). This produces three instances of the same FM tone and, by detuning (or otherwise modifying) each of the carriers, rich composite FM sounds can be produced. The algorithm also includes a standard carrier and modulator pair which might be used for synthesizing another element within the sound. Algorithm (e) shows the opposite of the previous algorithm. One carrier is simultaneously modulated by three different modulators. In this case, each modulator might be adjusted to synthesize a different part of the required spectrum. Once again, this algorithm also includes a standard carrier and modulator pair which might be used for synthesizing another element within the sound. Algorithm (f) shows how a mixture of both in-series and parallel modulators can be arranged to modulate a single carrier. This algorithm features the advantages of both algorithms (c) and (e).

In most implementations of FM synthesis, the output of an operator can be fed back to its own input (feedback). The use of feedback provides another manner in which you can add additional frequency components to an FM tone (see Figure 3.29). For example, using feedback on the modulator operator in a carrier:modulator pair with a ratio of 1:1 produces noise, or applying an amount of feedback to a single carrier produces a sawtooth wave.

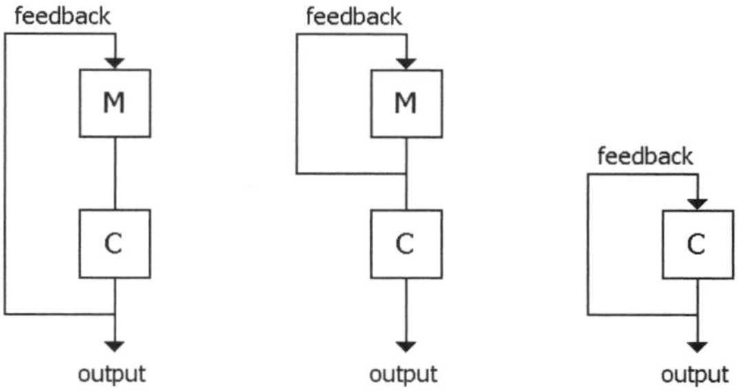

Figure 3.29
Common FM operator feedback configurations

Brief summary of FM

The aim of the above text has been to provide an introduction to the theory of FM which helps you appreciate the details of the process during the practical synthesis of your own FM tones. To help clarify matters, let's consider some of the main principles of FM synthesis again:

1 FM synthesis produces complex spectra with only a small number of basic parameters. However, it is not a particularly intuitive synthesis technique and so requires an effort to understand the theory in order to program new sounds effectively.
2 Simple FM synthesis involves the interaction of three basic elements: a carrier, a modulator and a modulation index (operator output).

3 FM synthesis, as implemented by the Yamaha Corporation, involves the use of 'operators'. An operator is an oscillator/amplifier/envelope generator unit which can be designated either as a carrier or a modulator.
4 The ratio of the modulator to the carrier determines the basic structure and distribution of the spectral components (side bands). Increasing the modulator ratio spreads the frequency components further apart. Increasing the modulation index (or the output level of an operator designated as a modulator), increases the number and bandwidth of frequency components contained within the sound.
5 Manipulations of the modulation index (operator output level) using an envelope generator can produce complex time-evolving spectra which match the behaviour of real-world acoustic musical instruments.
6 The amplitudes of the carrier frequency and side bands are governed by Bessel functions. Bessel functions are fixed amplitude curves which determine the level of each frequency component relative to the modulation index (operator output level).
7 The Bessel function curves are highly variable so, when time-evolving spectra are created using the modulation index (operator output level), the amplitude of each of the spectral components contained within the sound evolves in a fashion which is not immediately predictable.
8 During frequency modulation, spectral components (side bands) are produced both above *and below* the carrier frequency. This means that the carrier is not always perceived as the fundamental pitch for the resulting FM tone.
9 Whole number integer carrier:modulator ratios produce harmonic spectra whereas non-integer ratios produce inharmonic spectra.
10 Operators (oscillator/amplifier/envelope generator units) can be arranged into interacting carrier:modulator networks known as algorithms. As well as being connected to other operators, the output of any unit can be connected back to its own input (feedback). Algorithms can be designed to help produce tones of a specific timbre.

FM in practice

The theory above is easier to understand if you attempt to put it into practice. For this purpose, it is proposed that you go to the tutorial entitled 'FM synthesis: linking the theory to the practice' in Chapter 6. This makes use of the Native Instruments FM7 VST Instrument to provide the link between the theory outlined in this chapter and the audible result.

VST Instruments which use FM synthesis

VST Instruments which use FM synthesis include Native Instruments FM7, Reaktor and Dynamo, and LoftSoft's FM Heaven. The FM7 is a dedicated FM synthesis instrument which emulates the classic Yamaha DX7. The FM7 takes FM synthesis into the 21st century and yet presents the technique in a comparatively easy-to-use format. Reaktor employs a modular approach to sound synthesis in general and features a number of FM synthesizer modules in its library as well as allowing users to build their own FM instruments. FM Heaven is a general-purpose FM synthesizer which is available as shareware.

Sampling

The word 'sampling' is derived from digital audio recording and has assumed two slightly different meanings. In the pure digital recording sense, sampling involves the conversion of an audio signal into a stream of binary numbers before it is stored on a hard disk or other digital medium. This involves taking a snapshot of the audio at successive moments in time. Each of these snapshots is known as a 'sample' and the act of recording sound using this technique is known as 'sampling'. However, in the context of computer musical instruments known as 'samplers', the word 'sampling' has taken on a subtly different meaning. It describes the act of recording whole segments of digital audio and not necessarily the details of the recording process itself. The word 'sampler' is used to describe those computer musical instruments which record, edit, modify and play back segments of digitally recorded sounds. Rather confusingly, each recorded segment of digital audio is also referred to as a 'sample' and collections of such samples are known as 'sample libraries' (often found on CDs).

Working with a sampler normally involves the recording of relatively short segments of audio. Once recorded, the data is stored temporarily or permanently and can later be played back, usually at various pitches. A piano-style musical keyboard is often used to trigger the sounds (samples) which are normally assigned to individual keys or key ranges. The act of simply recording (sampling) a signal and then replaying it is not a pure sound synthesis technique in the usual sense of the term since the basis for the sound is a simple recorded source. However, most sampling instruments now feature sophisticated envelope, filtering and editing functions whereby sampled sounds can be timbrally transformed, looped, spliced, reversed, pitch changed and otherwise modified. This takes sampling out of the realms of a simple audio replay technique and into the world of sound synthesis.

Early samplers

The basis for creative tape-based 'sampling' techniques had often been to modify or change the context of the recorded sound. This dates back to experiments with tape recorders in the 1950s (notably by Pierre Schaeffer at his 'Studio de Musique Concrete' in Paris). This involved the creative splicing and re-arranging of segments of recorded magnetic tape. In this context, the tape recorder might be viewed as an early example of a sampler. Just like a modern-day sampler, sounds could be recorded (sampled), stored and replayed. And just like a modern-day sampler the act of manipulating and transforming the stored data before it was replayed was a form of sound synthesis. Serious recorded sound manipulation became practical only with the introduction of plastic tape covered with a thin layer of magnetic particles. Plastic tape is easy to cut and splice and the mechanics of passing the tape over record/playback heads is fairly straightforward. Tape recorders involve two spools, one which is initially loaded with the tape and the other which is used to receive the tape after it has passed over the record/playback heads. The heads are situated between the two spools and the tape is pressed against them using a pinch wheel and capstan (a revolving rod) which, together with the spool motors, pull the tape across the heads at a constant rate and tension. One obvious sound manipulation which can be achieved using a tape recorder is to change the rate at which the tape passes over the heads (during recording or playback). The change in speed results in a change in pitch when played back.

The use of tape-based systems in a sampling sense was also apparent in tape-based echo units. These used magnetic tape loops which were passed over record/playback heads to produce echo effects. However, one of the main forerunners for modern-day samplers was a tape-based sample replay keyboard instrument known as the 'Mellotron'. This was, in fact, the most well-known of a number of instruments of the same type conceived in the 1950s with names like the 'Chamberlin' and the 'Birotron'. The Mellotron's flute sounds can be heard on the classic Beatles song *Strawberry Fields Forever*.

The essential idea with the Mellotron was the use of a discrete tape recording (sample) for each key on the keyboard. As each key was pressed, a pre-recorded tape was pulled across a playback head, thus producing the sound. There was no looping mechanism so each sound had a finite length. Each tape contained several tracks so the sound could be changed without necessarily changing all the tapes. Since each key required a different recording, the preparation of tapes for such a system was prohibitively time-consuming and consequently instruments like the Mellotron tended to be viewed as replay only machines. However, this should not be allowed to obscure the fact that the Mellotron was highly significant as one of the first instruments to employ 'multi-sampled' sounds across the entire range of a musical keyboard.

Info

The Mellotron was one of the first instruments to employ 'multi-sampled' sounds across the entire range of a musical keyboard.

VST technology provides us with an emulation of the Mellotron in the guise of G Force's M-Tron VST instrument. Although it may not have quite the same charisma, the M-Tron produces all the classic tones associated with the original, allows the easy changing of sample 'tapes' and encourages the re-exploration of the instrument (see Chapter 5 for more details).

Digital sampling in detail

In order to understand sampling in terms of the techniques involved with real-world samplers and software samplers it is helpful to understand the theory of the digital sampling process itself. As already mentioned, the term 'sampling', in its more detailed sense, describes the process of recording sound digitally and any kind of digital audio recording, whether it be onto digital audio tape, onto a CD or into a 'sampler', involves the process of sampling. The details of how analogue sound can be digitally sampled warrants further exploration since it is an important concept in digital audio, sound synthesis and sampling technology.

Digital sampling is a two-way process involving, firstly, the conversion of an analogue sound signal into digital form (for recording purposes) and, secondly, once stored, the conversion of the digital signal back into analogue form (for playback purposes). The first stage includes taking a snapshot of the analogue signal at regular intervals in time and then converting these snapshots into digital form using an analogue-to-digital converter (ADC). The digital information is then stored (either temporarily or permanently) and, when it needs to be replayed, it is converted back into analogue form using a digital-to-analogue converter (DAC). The rate at which the snapshots are taken at the recording stage is known as the sampling rate.

Sampling rate

The higher the sampling rate the more accurate the digital representation of the analogue signal (although accuracy also depends upon the sample resolution, see below). The effect of higher sampling rates upon accuracy can be demonstrated by viewing a graphic representation of a sampled waveform as shown in Figure 3.30

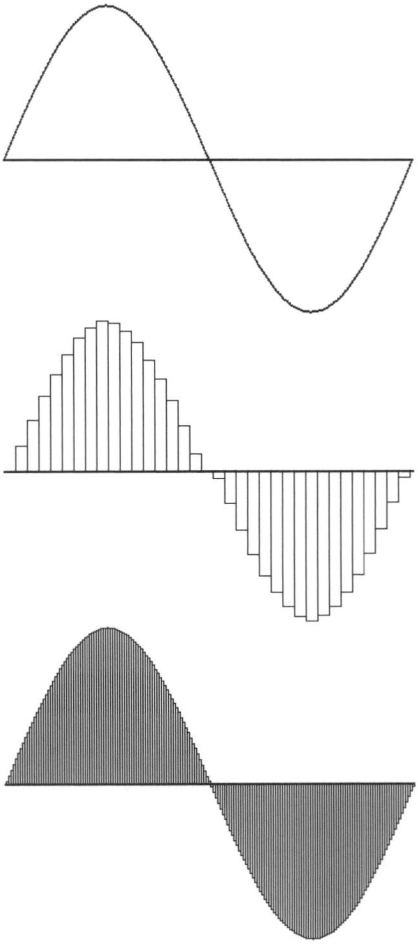

a) original analogue waveform

b) waveform (a) sampled at low sampling rate

c) waveform (a) sampled at high sampling rate

Figure 3.30
The effect of sampling rate upon a sampled waveform

The original analogue waveform (Figure 3.30a) has a smooth contour with (theoretically) a value at every point in time. When the signal is sampled at a low sampling rate (Figure 3.30b) the measurement of the signal features discrete points in time, the rate of which produces only a coarse representation of the original waveform. As the sampling rate is increased (Figure 3.30c) the measurement of the signal produces discrete points which are much closer together and thus provides a more accurate representation of the signal.

Info

Sampling rate is measured in hertz (Hz). For example, a sampling rate of 10kHz measures the signal 10,000 times per second. CD-quality digital audio uses a 44.1kHz sampling rate, i.e. the signal is measured 44,100 times per second.

Sample resolution

Like all digital systems, sampling systems have a finite number of values which can be used to measure analogue audio signals. This is known as the sample resolution, sometimes referred to as the 'bit depth'. Whereas the sampling rate (described above) is time-based, the sample resolution is value-based. In other words, the resolution is the number of values available within a given range which can be used for the measurement of the signal (see Figure 3.31). Sample resolution is usually expressed in 'bits'. You may ask why this should be and what the word 'bit' actually means. The short answer is that bits are the fundamental data unit used by digital systems and to understand what a digital system is doing we need to speak the same language.

Figure 3.31
The effect of bit resolution when sampling a waveform

a) 2-bit system
(very low resolution)

b) 4-bit system
(slightly higher resolution)

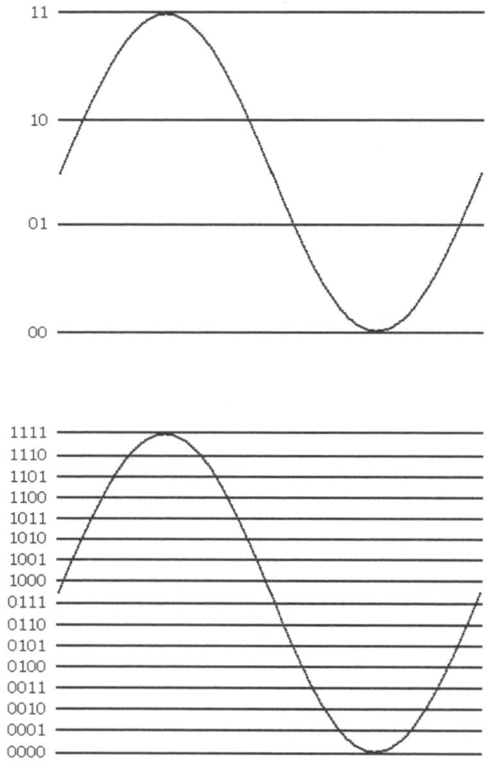

And now for the slightly longer answer to the above question. Digital systems use binary numbers. Binary numbers are represented by 0s and 1s which are known as binary digits or more commonly 'bits'. Binary numbers are often expressed in groups of four, eight, sixteen, twenty-four, thirty-two etc. Hence the terms 4-bit, 8-bit, 16-bit etc. and their corresponding binary number formats:

0101
0100 0111
0001 0011 1010 0100
etc.

Each bit in a binary number can either be on or off (1 or 0); each bit, therefore, has only two possible states. When a bit is on (i.e. when it has a value of 1) it assumes a different decimal value according to its bit position in the binary number. The first bit (the right-most digit) assumes the decimal value 1 (2^0) when it is on (binary 0001, decimal 1). The second bit assumes the decimal value 2 (2^1) when it is on (binary 0010, decimal 2). The third bit assumes the decimal value 4 (2^2) when it is on (binary 0100, decimal 4) and so on.

Thus the 2-bit resolution shown in Figure 3.31a expresses only four different values (binary 00–11, decimal 0–3). The crossing points of the waveform with the horizontal lines are the *only* points where the measurement is 100% accurate. Whenever a snapshot coincides with any other levels within the waveform the reading must be rounded up or down (resolved) to the nearest available measurement point. In other words this system is unable to read the parts of the waveform which appear between the lines. A digital sampling system measuring sound at this resolution would only be able to provide a very crude version of the original waveform when it came to be replayed since it does not possess the fine resolution required to capture the detail of the original waveform. This could be likened to attempting to measure your height with a ruler which has only metres marked on its scale and no centimetres or millimetres. You would never be able to take a precise measurement.

To improve matters with digital audio it is necessary to increase the sample resolution. Figure 3.31b shows what happens if we measure the same waveform on a 4-bit scale. 4-bit resolution is a slight improvement but it still does not provide the detail we require for high quality audio.

The dynamic range for a digital audio system is generally measured as a ratio of the number of decibels (dB) between the loudest part of the signal and the noise floor. The dynamic range for a sampling system can be roughly calculated from the number of bits using the following equation:

dynamic range (in dB) = 6 x n (where n equals the number of bits).

A 4-bit system, therefore, only gives around 24dB of dynamic range whereas the idealised dynamic range for CD-quality digital audio is 96dB. To achieve CD quality we would require 16-bit resolution (6 x 16). 16-bit resolution provides 65,535 discrete values, a vast improvement on the 2-bit and 4-bit resolutions shown in Figure 3.31. Anything lower than 16-bit (i.e. 8-bit, 12-bit) produces what is commonly described as 'grainy' sound reproduction resulting from the loss of fine detail and the subsequent noise which is introduced when the signal is reconstructed.

Pulse code modulation (PCM)

Pulse code modulation is the method by which analogue signals are converted into digital form during the sampling process. As already described above, sampling involves taking a snapshot of an analogue signal at each instant in time. This instant in time is represented by a binary number which, in turn, is coded into a group of electrical pulses. (A bit like Morse code for binary numbers). This coding scheme is known as pulse code modulation and is fundamental to the technique of sampling.

The sampling theorem

The mathematician Harry Nyquist laid down one of the cornerstones of sampling theory known as the 'sampling theorem', when he calculated that a sound signal must be measured at a sampling rate which is greater or equal to twice the highest frequency component within that signal. Failing to do so, results in a particular type of distortion known as 'aliasing', which becomes apparent when the signal is reconstructed. Aliasing manifests itself as additional frequency components which do not form part of the original signal. It occurs when the sampling rate is not high enough to capture the details of the upper frequency components. For example, Figure 3.32 shows how an anomaly occurs when a high frequency component is sampled at too low a rate.

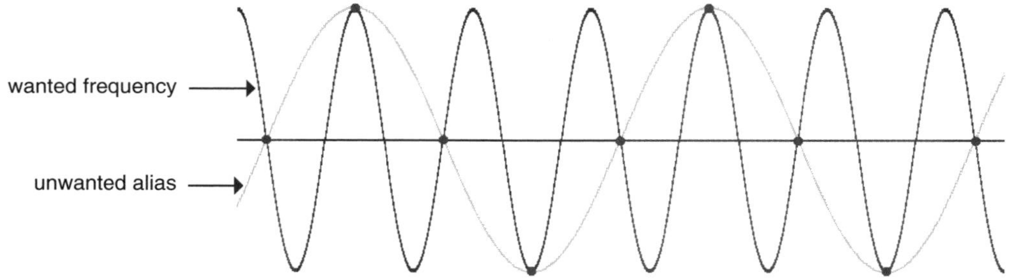

Figure 3.32
The aliasing effect

When the sampling system attempts to reconstruct the signal it has no way of knowing that the sample points do not represent the original higher frequency so it creates an alias at a lower frequency. A more scientific description of aliasing is provided in the statement that frequencies greater than half the sampling rate are reflected back below the half sampling rate point by the amount with which they overshoot it. For example, with a sampling rate of 48kHz, the half sampling rate is 24kHz. If a frequency of 34kHz (overshooting the half sampling rate by 10kHz) was introduced into this system it would be reflected back down below the half sampling rate threshold and would be heard as an unwanted alias at 14kHz.

The structure of a sampling system

In practice, the sampling rate is not the only factor which is used to avoid the creation of alias frequencies and ensure a clean reproduction of the original signal. Sampling systems also incorporate high-quality filters before the sampling stage and before the sound is reconstructed to ensure that only the desired signal is reproduced. This involves a bandlimiting filter (a low-pass filter with a very sharp cut-off slope) just before sampling occurs to limit the maximum frequency which will be recorded, and a reconstruction filter (a second low-pass filter with a very sharp cut-off slope) to prevent aliasing distortion after digital-to-analogue conversion (see Figure 3.33).

Figure 3.33
Structure of a sampling system

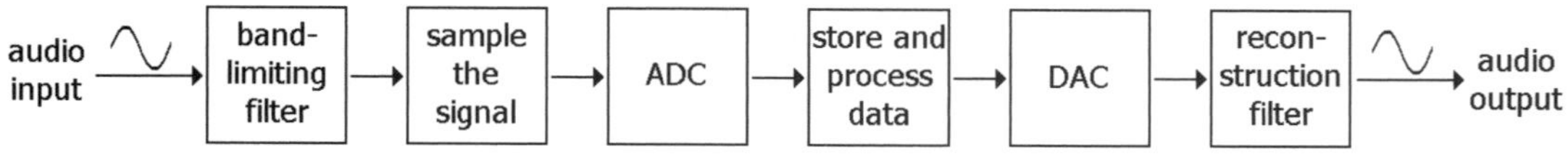

Applying the sampling theorem

Following Nyquist's sampling theorem to establish what sampling rate might be needed for CD-quality audio, we can assume the following:

1 Since the ear is sensitive in the frequency range 20Hz–20kHz, the maximum frequency we need to sample is 20kHz.
2 Following Nyquist's rule that the sampling rate should be equal to or greater than twice the highest frequency component in the target audio signal we, therefore, need at least twice 20kHz, resulting in a sampling rate of 40kHz.
3 A sampling rate of slightly more than twice the highest frequency component is preferable to make up for the deficiencies of the filters and other system components (which in the real-world may be less than ideal). Let's add another 4kHz to our sampling rate to make up for this. The final figure is 44kHz.

This final figure will be familiar to many readers since 44.1kHz is the standard sampling rate for CD-quality digital audio. Of course, when 44.1kHz was originally chosen it was not an arbitrary decision, it was based upon the above criteria and various other technical considerations.

What is a sampler?

The digital recordings made by sampling techniques are commonly known as 'samples' and the device responsible for recording these samples is commonly known as a 'sampler' (see Figure 3.34).

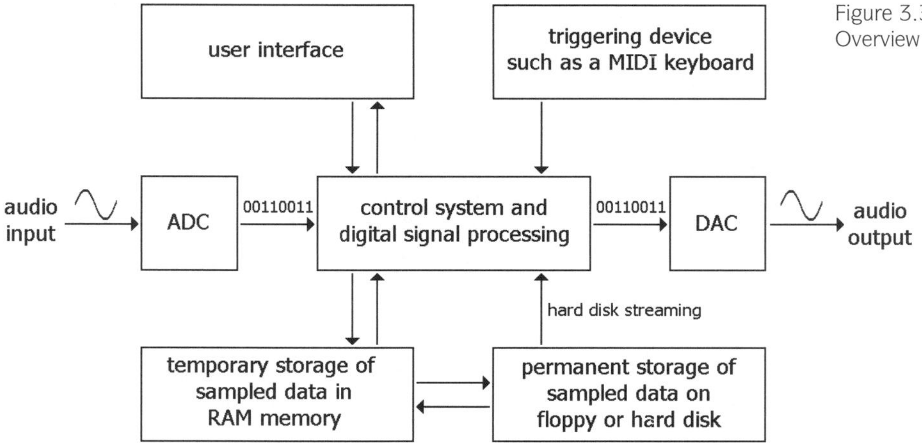

Figure 3.34
Overview of a digital sampler

A sampler differs from a standard digital audio recording device, like a DAT machine, in the sense that the recordings are initially stored temporarily in RAM memory whereas with a standard recording device the recording is stored directly onto a permanent recording medium such as digital audio tape. The other difference is that samplers are designed to record and play back relatively short multiple segments of sound whereas the design principle of standard digital audio recording devices is the recording and playback of relatively long segments of audio. (It is worth bearing in mind that these differences are fast becoming less of an issue since software samplers are now using data streaming techniques which allow the playback of extremely long segments of audio directly from hard disk and negate the need for large amounts of RAM memory.) A sampler is also designed to allow the samples to be triggered (usually via MIDI using a musical keyboard). The other important area in which samplers differ from standard digital audio recording devices is that, once the sample has been recorded and stored in temporary RAM memory, it can be immediately trimmed, looped and modified in fine detail. Once a successful sample has been 'captured', it can be stored onto permanent media such as floppy or hard disk. When you need to play back the samples which are stored on permanent media they must first be recalled into RAM memory before playback can commence. Samplers also allow the significant modification of samples during playback using filters, envelopes and LFOs.

Primary functions of a sampler

The following are the primary functions involved when recording, editing and playing back sounds with a digital sampler:

1. The recording of the source signal into the sampler. (The analogue sound is converted into a stream of numbers using an analogue-to-digital converter and is stored in RAM memory. The recorded data is referred to as a sample.)
2. The playback (triggering) of the recorded sample. (The digital representation of the signal stored in RAM memory is converted into analogue form using a digital-to-analogue converter and is sent to the audio output of the sampler.)
3. The editing of the samples in RAM memory. (Digital signal processing allows the easy trimming, looping, re-sampling, reversing, splicing, crossfading etc. of the samples in memory.)
4. The copying of the samples onto permanent storage media such as diskette, hard disk, DAT tape, CD etc. (Samples stored in this way must first be recalled into RAM memory before they can be played back. This is not necessarily the case for software samplers since they often use disk streaming which reads the samples directly from hard disk. Overall, the permanent storage process allows the building up of large and useful libraries of samples which can be mixed and matched as required.)
5. The arranging of the samples into meaningful groups, key zones and velocity layers. (Samples are normally assigned to various key zones across the range of the musical keyboard. It is common practice to use a number of samples recorded at different pitches when producing an authentic representation of a single musical instrument, and each sample is then assigned to a single key or to a specified zone of the keyboard range, normally according to its original pitch. This technique is referred to as multi-sampling. Similarly, multiple samples can be assigned to the same key, to be triggered according to the velocity with which the key is struck. This helps match the dynamic performance of acoustic musical instruments, drums and percussion where the timbre changes significantly according to the energy input.)
6. The real-time processing of samples to change their timbral and envelope characteristics. (Filtering, envelope and LFO parameters

allow the real-time modification of samples as they are played back. This endows samplers with envelope and spectral modification features which match those found in conventional sound synthesizers.)

Sampler design and RAM memory

The fact that samples must be recalled into RAM memory before they can be played back results in a design imperative for as much RAM as possible. At the onset of sampling technology this was prohibitively expensive, and early commercially available digital samplers were provided with very limited memory capacity. In order to maximise what was available, a less-than-ideal sample resolution was provided (8-bit or 12-bit) resulting in the characteristic 'grainy' sound of early machines. For similar reasons the sampling rate was also limited.

For example, the first Fairlight CMIs (one of the first sampling instruments, released in 1979) featured 8-bit resolution with a 10kHz sampling rate. The Ensoniq Mirage (1985) provided 8-bit resolution with a variable 8 – 33kHz sampling rate. The RAM memory of the Mirage was 144kbytes, allowing only around 1 second of sample time at its maximum sampling rate. The Akai S900 (1986) improved matters by providing 12-bit resolution with a variable 7.5 – 40kHz sampling rate. Its standard RAM memory of 750kbytes provided 11.75 seconds of sampling time at its maximum sampling rate of 40kHz. All these early machines featured 8-note polyphony.

It was not until the Akai S1000 (1988) that a truly affordable 'CD quality' digital sampler became available. The S1000 provided 16-bit stereo sampling with 22.05kHz or 44.1kHz sampling rates and 2Mb of RAM memory as standard, giving 23.76 seconds of sampling time at 44.1kHz. The RAM memory was expandable up to a total of 32Mb. The S1000 quickly became an industry standard and the sample libraries created for it are still in popular use today. It has since been followed by other S series samplers including the advanced S5000 and 6000.

RAM memory is still an issue in contemporary digital samplers and, from the outset, sampling technology established techniques to make the most of the available RAM. These include looping, re-sampling and the use of key zones (with multi-sampled instruments). Although these began as practical memory-saving techniques, they are now also used for purely creative purposes.

RAM memory is less of an issue with contemporary software samplers since they tend to make use of hard disk streaming techniques. Hard disk streaming allows the reading of data and the playback of audio directly from the hard disk without needing to firstly load it into RAM. However, the common sample manipulation techniques remain in the design features of almost all samplers, whether they be software or hardware models.

Common sample manipulation techniques

Looping

Looping is one of the main techniques for cutting down on the amount of RAM required for sample playback. It is also a creative technique in its own right. The essential idea with looping is to define a segment within the recorded sample which resembles (or could be used as) the steady-state portion of the sound. This is applicable, therefore, to those tones which would normally feature a sustained segment, such as string, bass, woodwind or organ sounds. Looping can also be used for special effects and for creating drum and rhythmic loops.

Finding a successful loop point is not always an easy task. The following procedure outlines the steps involved to create a loop for a sustained note:

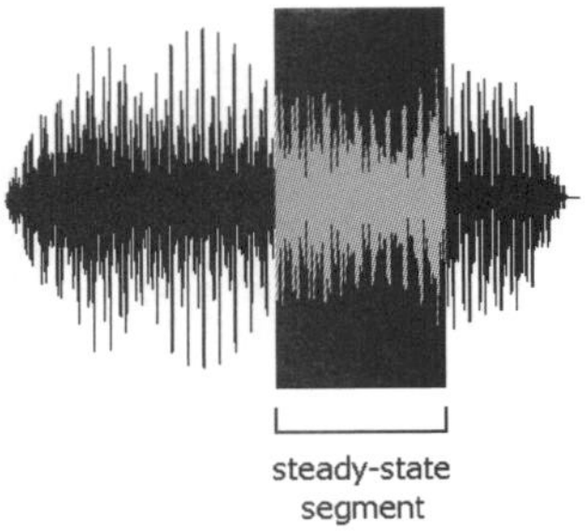

Figure 3.35
Find the steady-state segment of the sample

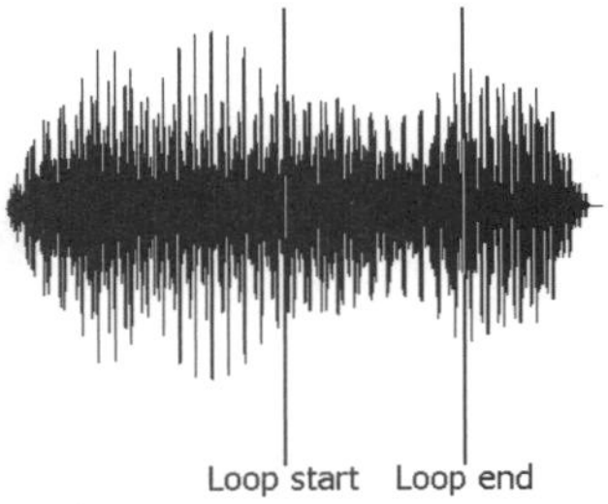

Figure 3.36
Define the start and end loop points

1 Decide which part of the sample corresponds to the steady-state segment of the note. This can often be achieved visually by looking at the overall waveform and aurally by judging where the sound has reached a stable level and timbre (Figure 3.35).
2 Define the start and end loop points somewhere within the chosen segment (Figure 3.36).
3 Fine tune the loop points so that there are no clicks or glitches in the sound by (a) ensuring that the start and end loop points are at zero-crossing points in the waveform, (b) carefully matching the level and pitch at the loop points and (c) carefully matching the waveform's slope, shape and period at the loop end point to those at the loop start point (Figure 3.37).

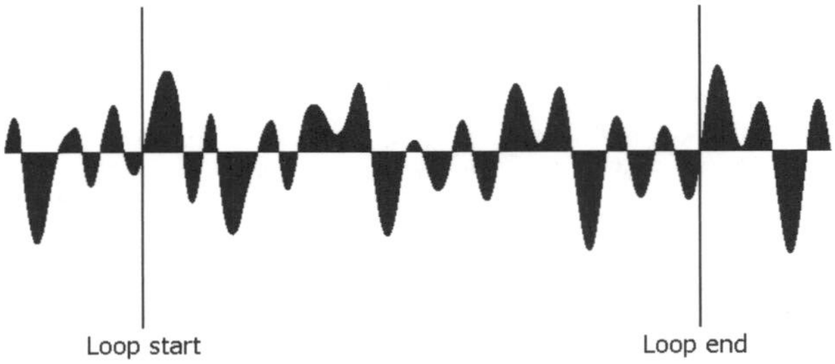

Figure 3.37
Fine tune the loop points for matching waveform characteristics

4 The loop start and end points may alternatively be viewed in the same way as the splice point on a section of magnetic tape (Figure 3.38). This gives a better idea of the join.

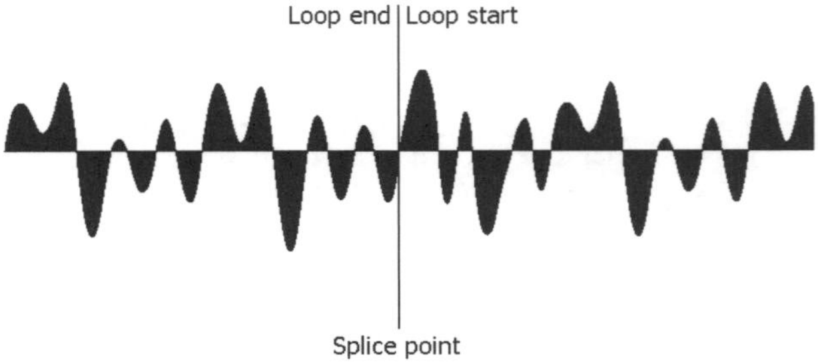

Figure 3.38
Viewing the loop points as a splice point on a section of magnetic tape

Finding a successful loop point for a drum or rhythmic loop is slightly easier since it involves specifying the point at which the rhythm has reached a prescribed number of beats, at which time the sample loops back upon itself. However, it is still a skilled operation to create a rhythm that loops for the exact number of beats required, and without a click or glitch at the loop point. Indeed, one of the greatest difficulties for any kind of looping operation is finding a click-free splice point.

Some samplers feature automated loop point functions which can sometimes help. Samplers also often feature 'crossfade looping' functions which create a crossfade between the start and end points of the loop. This can help disguise a glitch at the loop point. Matching the timbre at the loop point can be just as problematic as clicks and glitches. This is particularly true for samples taken from real-world acoustic instruments since, as mentioned in Chapter 2, acoustic instrument tones tend to feature continuously changing spectra. Reversing the audio alternately each time the audio is looped is another common feature of samplers and, in certain cases, this may provide a more convincing loop. However, the art of loop creation remains a skilful task relying, for the most part, on intuitive and trial-and-error techniques.

Once a successful loop has been created, the newly looped sample normally comprises its normal attack and decay phases, followed by the loop, which remains for as long as the note is held, and finally the sound may enter its own natural release phase, or may be comprised of an amplitude envelope which releases the held note while it is still looping. Some samplers incorporate multiple looping functions so that different sections of a sample can be looped a specified number of times one after the other.

The Akai S1000, for example, features no-less-than eight definable looped sections for each sample. The HALion VST sampler features an easy-to-configure sustain loop which is looped for as long as you hold down a key and includes crossfade smoothing at each end for seamless loop points. It has a second loop known as the release loop which plays after the key is released. Native Instruments Kontakt software sampler/VST instrument features eight loops for each sample with independent pitch and number of repeats for each looped section. It also includes loop crossfading, automatic find for loop start and end points and changeable loop start points via MIDI controllers. Features like these are effective in producing more natural sound evolutions and are also useful for special effects.

Re-sampling

The primary function of re-sampling is to 're-record' a sample at a lower sampling rate in order to reduce the number of memory bytes used to store the signal. This tends to be employed as a final resort when more RAM memory is required. Sounds treated in this way suffer a loss in high frequency detail and, in extreme cases when the sampling rate is greatly reduced, aliasing distortion. For these reasons, it is bass sounds and those samples with less high frequency content which can have their bandwidth reduced without obvious audible side-effects. Re-sampling can also be used creatively to re-sample samples or parts of samples along with any modifications which may have been applied to them in the filtering, envelope and editing sections of the sampler.

Info

The primary function of re-sampling is to 're-record' a sample at a lower sampling rate in order to reduce the number of memory bytes used to store the signal.

Multi-sampling and key zones

The ideal sampling of a musical instrument implies recording a separate sample for each semitone step in the musical scale (commonly known as multi-sampling). It might also imply the recording of extremely lengthy samples allowing each note to decay naturally rather than using any loops. With conventional hardware sampling technology this would be prohibitively expensive in terms of system resources. The traditional solution is to multi-sample the instrument once every four or five semitones and to use loops to cut down on the RAM memory requirements. Each sample is assigned to a key zone with a range of a few semitones and the key zones are then arranged to cover the full range of the musical keyboard. The sampler transposes the source samples so that they play back at the correct pitch for each note in the key zone. Although the transpositions involve slight changes in the timbre of the sampled tones, these go unnoticed as long as the range of the key zone for one sample is not too wide.

Other techniques

Other popular techniques within hardware and software samplers include time-stretching, pitch shifting, the use of velocity layers, reversing, sample joining, enveloping and filtering.

Time stretching and pitch shifting

One of the advantages of digital signal processing is that time and pitch are not inextricably linked. In the world of analogue magnetic tape, raise the speed of the tape machine and the pitch goes up while the length becomes shorter and vice versa. With sampling technology, time-stretching changes the length of the sample without changing the pitch and pitch shifting changes the pitch of the sample without changing the length. Pitch shifting is useful for re-tuning samples which are out of tune and time stretching is excellent for establishing new tempos for rhythmic material. Both techniques can be used for creating sound effects.

Velocity layers

Most samplers allow the assigning of several samples to the same key on the musical keyboard. Each sample can then be set to be triggered according to the velocity with which the key is struck. In other words, each sample is set to its own velocity range and is only triggered when the key is struck somewhere within that range. This helps match the dynamic performance of acoustic musical instruments where the timbre changes significantly according to the energy input.

Reversing

Digital signal processing allows the easy and instantaneous reversal of samples so that they can be played backwards. This is good for special effects and crescendo-like effects, especially with samples of cymbals and drum hits (preferably those with a reverb tail).

Sample joining

The splicing of different samples together is a common technique for the creation of new instrument tones and effects. For example, sampling technology allows the easy splicing of the attack segment of one sample onto the sustain (or decay) segment of another. Using this technique, the attack of a piano sound might be spliced onto the sustain of a string sound or the attack of a cymbal crash might be spliced onto the decay of the sound of breaking glass.

Enveloping and filtering

The majority of samplers provide enveloping and filtering functions which match those found on conventional sound synthesizers. Enveloping and filtering are used to fine tune or radically alter the final timbral characteristics of the sample before it arrives at the audio output (for more information about envelopes and filters see the Subtractive Synthesis section, above).

VST instruments which use sampling technology

VST instruments which use sampling technology include:

- Steinberg HALion
- Steinberg/Wizoo The Grand,
- Steinberg LM4, LM7 and LM9 VSTi drum modules
- G Force M-Tron
- Native Instruments Kontakt, Reaktor, Dynamo and Battery
- Spectrasonics Stylus, Atmosphere and Trilogy
- Speedsoft Virtual Sampler
- Creamware Volkszampler
- Bitheadz Unity DS1.

HALion and the Grand stream the samples directly off hard disk and use a small amount of RAM to play back the first part of each sample. The LM series stores the samples used in each drum kit entirely in RAM memory. (See Chapter 5 for more details of VSTi samplers and drum modules.)

Physical modelling

The manner in which the parameters of conventional sound synthesis techniques interact is *not* often directly analogous to the manner in which real acoustic musical instruments actually function. For example, creating 'brass-like' tones using subtractive or FM synthesis does not take into account the physical engineering of how a brass instrument is put together. You are merely building the sound directly using parameters which happen to create the desired result when arranged in one particular configuration. This configuration is often arbitrary to how a real brass instrument produces its sounds. Physical modelling, however, re-constructs all the interacting parts of a real (or imaginary) musical instrument and when the sound is triggered the elements in the model interact just like the real thing. Models like this are created using mathematical equations and computer algorithms. Sound is produced according to the laws of physics which govern the behaviour of the constituent parts. This is directly analogous to the manner in which real acoustic instruments function. A physical model possesses a sense of already being alive and feels and reacts very much like the real thing. Physical modelling, therefore, does not generally use any of the traditional sound synthesis building blocks such as oscillators, envelopes, preset waveforms or samples and the user interface might also be radically different.

Physical modelling in more detail

The use of mathematical and computer generated models to simulate the behaviour of phenomena found in the real world already has a long history in the worlds of science and technology. Mathematical equations and computer algorithms can be used to simulate the behaviour of just about any kind of real-world phenomena including such things as weather systems, earthquakes and seismic activity, flight simulation and even the re-creation of how dinosaurs might have moved around. It is not surprising, therefore, that this approach can also be applied to the vibrations, resonances and acoustic phenomena found in real-world musical instruments.

Non-mathematicians might be wondering how on earth something like the behaviour of a musical instrument can be reduced to a series of equations and computer algorithms, but if you can visualise the movement of a vibrating string then you may be able to get one stage closer to grasping what physical modelling involves. You may well begin by thinking about a vibrating string in one of its most obvious dimensions : the amount of displacement from its rest position as it vibrates and the rate at which this displacement occurs (Figure 3.39). This information is analogous to the amplitude and frequency of the vibrating string and might be simulated mathematically with relative ease. The movement of the centre point of the idealised string shown in Figure 3.39 could be approximated using the mathematical sine function which would result in a simple sine wave.

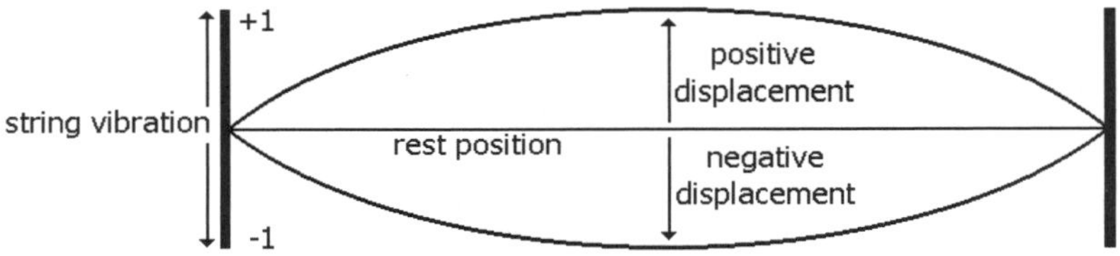

Figure 3.39
An idealised musical instrument string plucked at its centre point

However, in reality, a plucked string never produces a pure sine wave. In addition, the amount and rate of displacement do not tell us the whole story about the physics of a vibrating string and, in particular, do not indicate its timbral qualities. A real-world plucked string actually has the potential to generate a wide range of simultaneous frequencies and these vary according to where it is plucked along its length. The potential frequencies are known as modes. Modes describe those frequencies where there are sympathetic resonances in the string. They are based upon whole number multiples of the string's length and produce the harmonic content of the resulting sound when the string undergoes excitation. Figure 3.40 shows the first five potential modes of vibration for a string stretched between two points. The points where the string is fixed and those points in the modes of vibration where there is zero displacement are known as displacement 'nodes'. Nodes are points of zero potential energy. Those points where there is maximum displacement are known as 'antinodes'. Antinodes are points of maximum potential energy. Whenever a node coincides with the plucking point along the length of the string, its corresponding modal frequency is *not* included as part of the resulting waveform. For example, plucking the string shown in Figure 3.40 at its centre point coincides with the nodes of the second and fourth modes (and all other even-numbered modes thereafter). Plucking the string at the centre point therefore results in a waveform containing frequency components corresponding to only the odd-numbered modes (although the pure case of only odd-numbered mode excitation depends upon a pluck position which is at an exact integer multiple of the string length). Typically, this results in a triangle waveform at the onset of the sound. Plucking the string at other points along its length results in a different combination of harmonic components based upon which modes are emphasised and which modes are de-emphasised. All this is vital knowledge if you intend to use mathematics to model the string's behaviour since it becomes obvious that the point at which the string is plucked along its length plays a primary role in determining the resulting timbre.

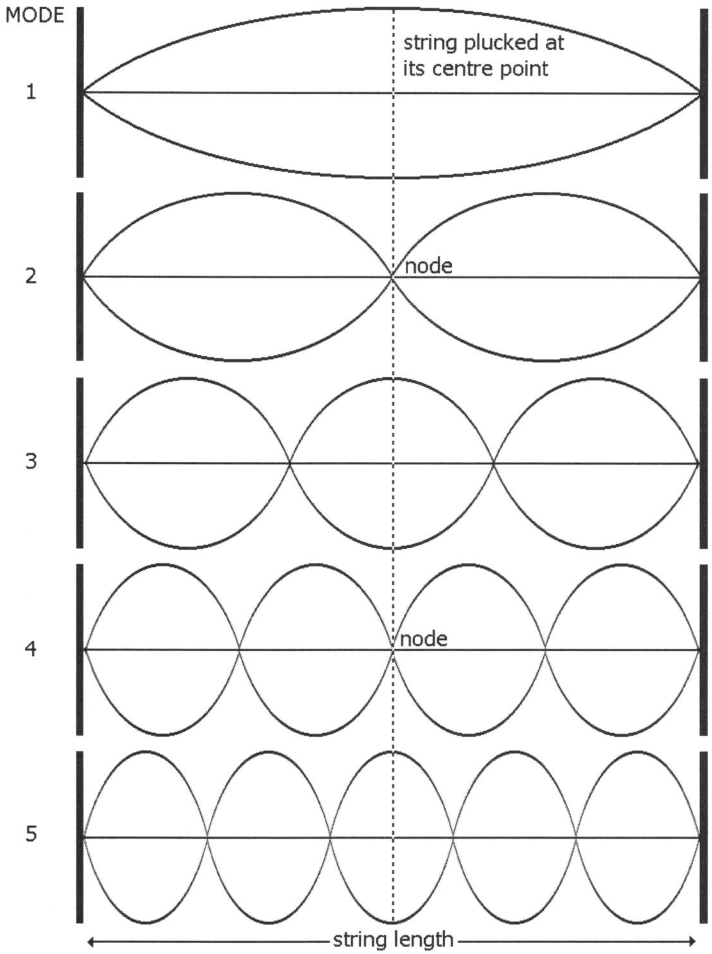

Figure 3.40
The first five modes of potential vibration for a string stretched between two points

The physical modelling of a real-world plucked string would also need to take into account a wide range of other parameters. These include the shape and stiffness of the plectrum or finger which plucked the string, the length, tension stiffness and density of the string, the resonant properties of the body of the instrument to which the string is attached, how far it is pulled from its rest position as it is plucked, the direction in which it is plucked, how the string is attached at the bridge and the nut of the instrument, the rate of energy loss due to friction at these end points, the rate of energy loss due to friction with the surrounding air, the rate of energy loss due to the elastical properties of the string itself and so on.

As you can see, physical modelling quickly takes us into the worlds of physics and engineering. Just as the physics aspects of a vibrating string are enormously complex so are the mathematical equations needed to express them. These complexities are such that a detailed explanation is beyond the scope of this text.

Types of physical modelling

There are a wide range of different approaches to physical modelling. The following categories are among the most common:

- driver-resonator modelling
- vibrating mass-spring networks
- modal synthesis
- waveguide synthesis

Driver-resonator modelling

Driver-resonator modelling involves dividing an acoustical system into two parts, in a very similar fashion to the source and modifier theory (explained in the 'Source and Modifier' section, above).

The driver is the part of the system where the energy is added. For example, the driver for a guitar is a plectrum or a finger pulling or plucking the string, in a brass instrument it would be the vibrating lips of the player in the mouthpiece, in a violin it would be the bow scraping across the string and so on. If we were to examine the behaviour of a stretched acoustic guitar string in more detail we would find that energy is added by pulling the string from its rest position and then letting go. This initial energy input is then dissipated over a short period of time as the string moves back and forth, producing vibrations. The input of energy in this case is quite sudden and in physical modelling terms would be referred to as an impulse. Impulsive models include plucked and struck instruments. Other drivers provide a continuous energy input such as with bowed and blown instruments like violins and clarinets. These are referred to as continuous models.

The resonator is the part of the system which amplifies and modifies the impulse or the continuous vibrations and couples the energy to the surrounding air. For example, the resonator for a guitar or violin is the bridge and body of the instrument and for a brass or wind instrument it would be the pipe or tubing.

The interaction between the driver and resonator produces the resulting sound of the instrument. From a physical modelling point of view the engineer modelling the system needs to know an enormous number of details about how such a configuration is put together in physics terms. As mentioned above, in the case of a stretched string a wide range of data would be required including the length, tension, density and stiffness of the string, where along its length it is plucked, how far it is pulled from its rest position as it is plucked, and so on. As far as the resonator (the guitar body) is concerned, its dimensions, the size of the sound hole, the density of the materials used, the overall construction and specific resonant properties would all be required. Of equal importance is the precise manner in which the driver and resonator are coupled together.

Once all the required data has been assembled, each part of the system must be modelled using mathematical equations and computer algorithms. Producing a successful result with driver-resonator physical modelling depends as much on the accuracy of the original analysis of the physics of the acoustical system as on the accuracy of the mathematics used to express it.

Vibrating mass-spring networks

Vibrating mass-spring networks attempt to model acoustical systems by using idealised mechanical units known as masses, dampers and springs. These elements are represented mathematically and are arranged in networks to approximate the behaviour of various vibrating media. The 'mass' and 'spring' elements were derived as a manner in which to express two of the fundamental properties of vibrating media, density and elasticity. The mathematical equations which govern these elements take into consideration such things as the force driving each mass, the forces driving each spring and various friction coefficients. A succession of masses might be connected together, for example, with a spring and damper in parallel at each connection point to model the behaviour of a vibrating string or a column of air in a tube.

Modal synthesis

Modal synthesis is based upon the fact that any object which produces sound can be represented as a number of vibrating sub-structures. Each sub-structure vibrates according to its modal properties i.e. its specific resonant characteristics. A mode is a particular excitation within the sub-structure which causes every point to vibrate at the same frequency. Different sub-structures can be assembled to create a model for a musical instrument. Typical sub-structures include such things as bodies, bridges, tubes, plates, membranes and bells. The modal synthesis method has been developed mainly at IRCAM in Paris, France under the name 'Modalys'.

Waveguide synthesis

Waveguide synthesis involves the use of delay lines to model the behaviour of waves travelling along a vibrating string or travelling up and down the column of air within a tube. An early version of this kind of synthesis was that developed by Karplus and Strong in 1983. This is known as the Karplus Strong plucked string algorithm and simulates what happens when a string is plucked or a bar is struck.

The Karplus Strong algorithm involves the use of a delay line to represent the length of a string (or bar). The output of the delay line is fed back to the input of the system via a low pass filter which approximates the energy loss of a real string due to friction at the end points and the reflections of the wave in the string (or bar). When an impulse noise is fed into the system resonant behaviour occurs which is very similar to that found in a plucked string or a struck bar.

If you are the experimental type and happen to be an owner of the Steinberg Karlette plug-in delay unit, a similar effect can be created by feeding a short burst of white noise (around 30 – 40ms) into its input. Use the Karlette as a send effect, switch the 'sync' button to the off position and set its output mix to fully wet. Activate only one delay line with its volume on full, the damp control set to '200', pan to centre and feedback set to around '995' (almost full). Dial in a delay between 5ms and 10ms and play the short burst of white noise through the Karlette. This results in something resembling a plucked string. Experiment with other settings and try mixing in another delay line. (When experimenting you are advised to test at low levels to avoid damaging your speakers !)

To physical model or not to physical model

Some would argue that any synthesizer which exists in the virtual world is an example of physical modelling and there is undoubtedly much truth in this argument. However, physical modelling begins with the premise that an object from the physical world is modelled by analysing its particular behaviour. Not all virtual synthesizers are designed in this way. It could be argued that 'pure' physical modelling involves an element of modelling something from the tangible 'real' world, otherwise everything that exists in software form instantly becomes physical modelling. Certainly, the original idea was the modelling of the physical parts of a real-world acoustic musical instrument.

In any case, whether or not a virtual synthesizer is created using physical modelling is not the direct concern of this text. In a practical sound synthesis sense, the user is more concerned with how to 'interact' with the system and this involves the user interface. Naturally, the next question is 'Is there a common user interface for physical modelling instruments ?' The answer is 'not really'. Physical modelling suffers from a number of dilemmas with regard to how we might interact with it since its design structure is so adaptable. In effect, each instrument produced by physical modelling techniques might require a different user interface and there may be relatively few common parameters. It could be argued that Steinberg's VB1 (virtual bass) VST instrument has a physical modelling type of interface. With the VB1 we change the sound by moving various representations of the physical parts of the system on the graphical user interface. This includes pick position, pickup position, damping, volume and tone controls etc. It is doubtful, however, that the internal architecture of the instrument is based upon a real-world bass guitar.

In order to get further ideas of how we might interact with a physical modelling instrument the next section proposes a brief exploration of one of the first commercially available real-world physical modelling instruments, the Yamaha VL1 virtual acoustic synthesizer.

A brief exploration of the Yamaha VL1

The Yamaha VL1 is a virtual acoustic synthesizer which models the acoustical behaviour of several real-world acoustic musical instruments. It has a maximum polyphony of two notes and is thus principally designed as a solo 'performance' synthesizer. Due to its extreme internal complexity, the core parts of the physical models available inside the VL1 are not accessible to the user. Instead pre-programmed models are provided (including woodwind, brass and string configurations) which can be modified in various ways.

Each of the VL1's physical models is made up of three elements: controllers, instrument and modifiers (Figure 3.41).

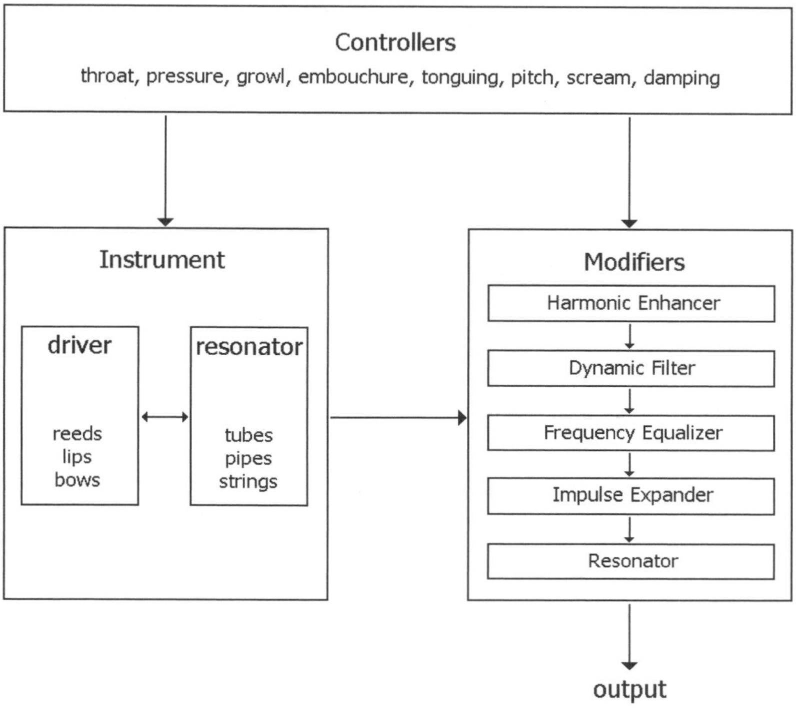

Figure 3.41
Yamaha VL1 design overview

Instrument

The Instrument section governs the essential timbre for the physical model, and although its finer details are not accessible it can be significantly modified by the settings of the Controllers section (see below) which provides detailed control of the expressive capabilities of the chosen instrument. The Instrument section is arranged in a classic driver-resonator setup providing such things as reeds, lips and bows as drivers and tubes, pipes and strings as resonators. Almost any driver can be coupled with any resonator, allowing the creation of hybrid virtual acoustic instruments which are not found in the real world.

Controllers

The Controllers section governs how the instrument responds in terms of performance or playing style. This includes such things as lip and breath control, arm movements when using a bow, and how the sound is modified by the keys, tone holes or frets. Yamaha established a special set of parameters to handle the VL1's extended expressive range. These parameters function as follows:

- Throat – controls the 'throat' characteristics of the player in a wind instrument or the bowing arm characteristics in a string instrument.
- Pressure – governs the amount of breath pressure applied to the mouthpiece or bow velocity.

- Embouchure – governs the tightness of the lips on the mouthpiece or the force with which the bow is pulled across the string.
- Pitch – changes the length of the air column or string.
- Growl – governs a special kind of pressure modulation or bow velocity modulation.
- Tonguing – mimics a 'half-tonguing' technique as used with reed instruments.
- Scream – applies a special chaotic oscillation effect particular to the VL1.
- Damping and absorption – simulates string or pipe-based air friction and high frequency damping due to friction at the ends of the pipe or string.

These parameters represent a particularly wide range of real-time performance controls and to accommodate this the VL1 has been equipped with hardware controller features over and above the average synthesizer. These include a velocity and aftertouch sensitive keyboard, two modulation wheels and one pitch-bend wheel, a breath controller input (with sophisticated breath controller parameters), two footswitch inputs and two foot controller inputs. Any of the controller parameters can be assigned to any of these hardware controllers.

Modifiers

The Modifiers section allows significant changes to be made to the timbre of the sound by the application of various sound processing modules. These modules are intimately related to the sound making model within the instrument so they are more than just ordinary sound effects. They allow radical harmonic structure variations via the Harmonic Enhancer, sophisticated high-pass, band-pass, band-stop and low pass filtering via the Dynamic Filter, five band parametric equalisation via the Frequency Equalizer, instrument resonant cavity simulation via the Impulse Expander (this is particularly suited to the simulation of the metallic resonances found within brass instruments), and more 'wooden' sounding resonance simulation via the Resonator.

Physical modelling and the VL1 interface

Exploring the VL1 can teach us a lot about how the interface for a physical modelling instrument based upon the simulation of real-world acoustic instruments might be designed. It also exposes some of the difficulties found in the sound synthesis world and, in particular, in the physical modelling world, with performance-based manipulation of a sound synthesis instrument. If you are playing a wind instrument via a controller like a standard musical keyboard then it is inherently difficult to inject the same kind of performance nuances as you would with the real thing. A keyboard simply does not react in the same way as a bowed string or a blown reed. This problem is compounded in physical models of real-world acoustic instruments since these kinds of instruments behave so much more like the real thing. In many ways, the player of a physical modelling instrument like this might be expected to 'learn' how to play the chosen model and it would only be through consistent practice that the best results would be obtained.

VST Instruments and physical modelling

Readers may be wondering why this text has outlined physical modelling at such length. The reasons for this coverage are two-fold. Firstly, physical modelling techniques present an alternative manner in which to think about acoustic musical instruments which helps us appreciate how they propagate their sound in physics terms. This helps when we synthesize our own sounds. Secondly, all VST instruments might be classed as physical modelling instruments, if you accept the fact that any synthesizer which exists in the virtual world (in software) is automatically an example of physical modelling.

It is often unclear precisely how each VST instrument has been programmed at the deeper level, and there are relatively few VST instruments which are overtly described as physical modelling instruments. Exceptions are Sonic Syndicate's Plucked String VST instrument and Applied Acoustics Systems' Tassman acoustic modelling synth. Steinberg's VB1 also resembles a physical modelling kind of approach. Most other virtual instruments tend to be emulations of other kinds of synthesis techniques or emulations of specific synthesizers. Future VST instruments which are overtly based upon physical modelling are likely to be modular 'acoustic modelling' synths in the tradition of Applied Acoustics Systems' Tassman. (See Chapters 5 and 6 for in-depth coverage of Tassman.)

Granular synthesis

Granular synthesis is a comparatively unusual form of sound synthesis involving the creation of sound events by joining together a large number of very short sonic particles or 'grains'. Each grain typically lasts around 10 to 50 milliseconds and on its own is simply a very short burst of energy but, when joined together with thousands of other similar grains, forms a single large-scale audio event. This concept follows the ideas of Dennis Gabor (1947), a physicist who suggested that sound can be broken down into a succession of discrete, microscopic energy bursts.

It is known that the ear perceives individual sound events as a rhythm when they are between a few beats per minute and around 20 beats per second. 20 beats per second equates to a duration of 50ms between each event. 50ms is known to be the approximate threshold of the timing resolution of the human ear. Events occurring closer than this start to become fused together into a single sound event which is perceived as a pitch rather than a rhythm. This is the basis of granular synthesis.

Granular parameters

Granular synthesis, as developed by Curtis Roads (1991, 1995), features a number of parameters which modify the contents of each grain and the manner in which they are sequenced together to form what Roads described as grain 'clouds'. These include the following:

- Waveform – each grain can theoretically take its sound contents from any available sound source such as noise, simple waveform or sampled sources. The contents may also mutate from one waveform to another throughout the course of the resulting grain cloud. (See Figure 3.42.)

Figure 3.42

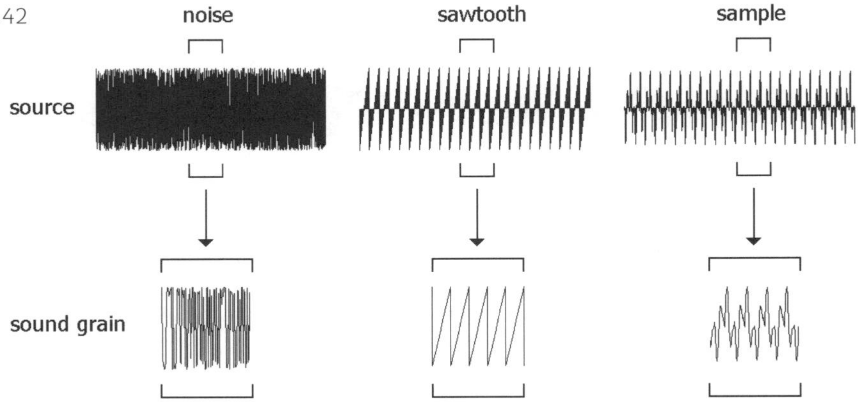

- Duration – the duration of each grain can be varied between 1 and 100 milliseconds. Most artists using granular synthesis have found that grain durations between 10 and 50 milliseconds are the most effective.

Figure 3.43

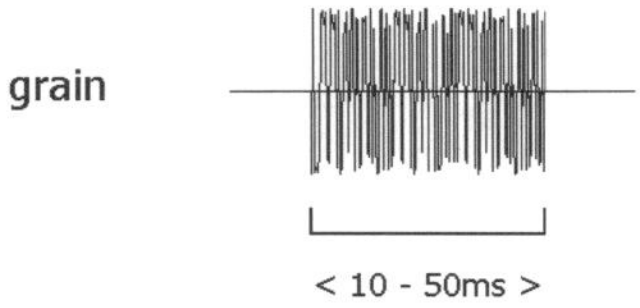

- Envelope shape – once inside a grain, the waveform is invariably modified using an envelope generator. The envelope is typically bell-shaped and invariably starts and finishes at zero amplitude in order to ensure a smooth transition from one grain to the next and to avoid clicks.

Figure 3.44

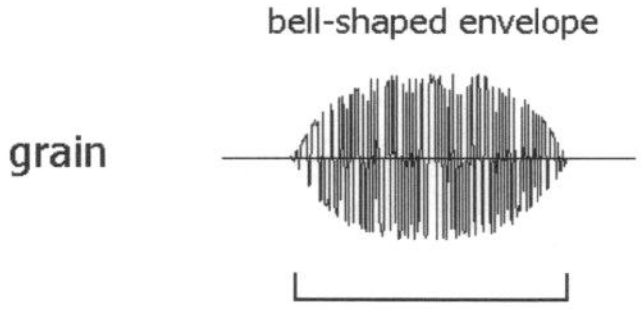

- Frequency – the frequency or 'repeat time' determines the rate at which the grains are repeated within a given time frame.

Figure 3.45

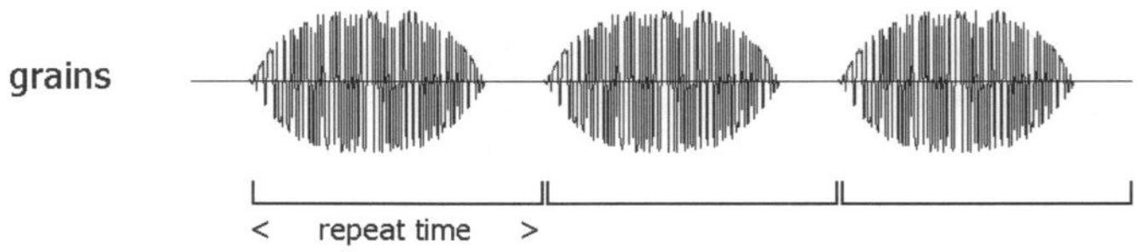

- Delay time – the delay time determines the duration of a short delay between each grain (typically 0-5ms).

Figure 3.46

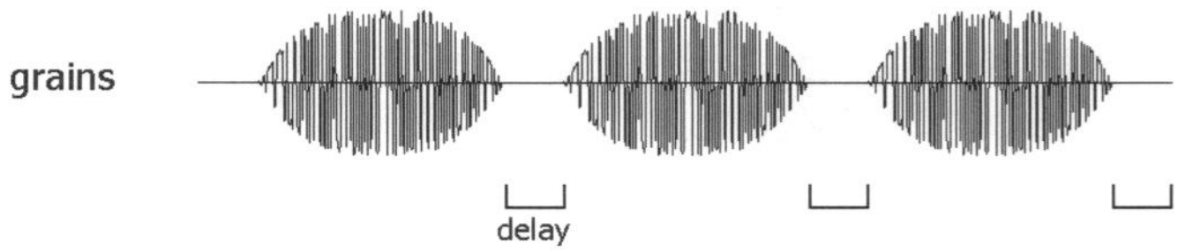

- Spatial location – each grain can be endowed with spatial characteristics which determine where it is located in a stereo (or multi-speaker) sound environment. This allows, for example, the creation of sound effects which sweep across the stereo soundfield.

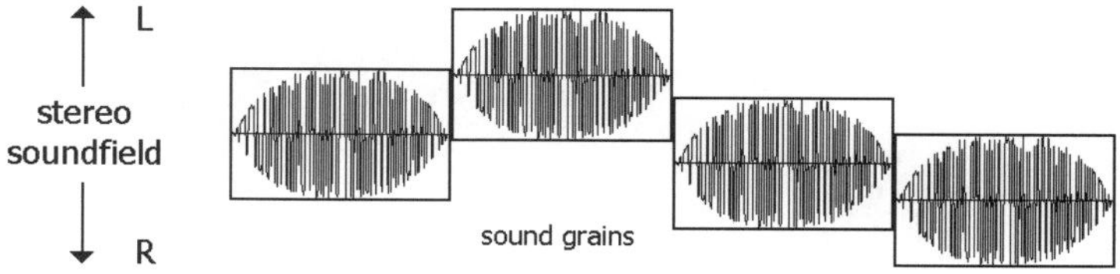

Figure 3.47

A number of global parameters controlling the resulting larger scale audio event (cloud) may also be implemented, such as the density of the grains and the duration, bandwidth and overall amplitude of the 'cloud'.

Granular synthesis in practice

Complex granular synthesis where discrete parameters are set for each grain is largely impracticable with current computer technology. There may be literally thousands of events to process in every minute and this produces a very large computational overhead. Popular granular synthesis implementations involve the generation of a stream of identical grains, the parameters of which are modified as a function of time. For example, it has been shown that simply changing the shape of the envelope can produce dramatic changes in the perceived timbre, as can changing the duration and delay parameters. There is however no obvious or intuitive correlation between the parameter which is being changed and the resulting timbre.

The granular synthesis technique described above is more precisely known as 'asynchronous granular synthesis' (AGS). This is good at producing what Curtis Roads described as sound 'clouds' and large scale audio events. The results are not easily produced by conventional musical instruments or other synthesis techniques but, equally, simulating existing sounds with granular synthesis is extremely difficult. The main strength of granular synthesis, as it is normally implemented, is for the creation of new and inspiring sound events.

VST Instruments featuring granular synthesis

Native Instruments Reaktor and Dynamo feature granular synthesis modules in a number of their NI Premium Library ensembles. These include Formanter, Plasma, rAmpler, Grain States and Travellizer.

4 Meet your hosts

This chapter describes the installation and basic use of VST Instruments within two of the main MIDI + audio sequencers, Steinberg's Cubase VST and Emagic's Logic Audio, both of which support VST 2.0 technology.

System requirements and performance issues

VST Instruments require a VST 2.0-compatible host application like Steinberg Cubase VST, Cubase SX, Nuendo or Emagic Logic Audio and most run on both the PC and Mac computer platforms. Your chosen host software should already be running successfully on the computer before you install a VST Instrument. Once installed, the VST Instrument is loaded and activated inside the host application similar to a regular plug-in effect. The sounds are triggered via MIDI, either in real-time using an external MIDI keyboard (or other controller), or from a recorded MIDI Track. There are a number of computer hardware factors which affect the performance and playability of a VST Instrument. Paramount among these are CPU speed, the amount of RAM memory and audio hardware latency.

- CPU speed and RAM – software synthesis, software sampling and software effects processing are CPU-intensive activities. The number of voices available for any software instrument is, therefore, directly related to the amount of CPU power available. The drain on CPU power varies according to the number of notes being played simultaneously and according to the complexity of the tone being produced by the instrument. Many software samplers and sample-based drum modules require substantial amounts of RAM in order to run smoothly. This is particularly true for those which use disk-streaming techniques where greater use of RAM memory results in less strain on the hard disk.
- Latency – latency is the delay between the user input and the time it takes for a digital audio system to respond and process the data through its hardware and software, expressed in milliseconds. This affects real-time performance with VST instruments since it imposes a slight delay between the moment you press a note on your MIDI keyboard and the moment you hear the sound from the instrument. If the delay is too long then it becomes impossible to play in real-time. (Real-world electronic musical instruments also suffer from a similar delay.) For real-time performance the audio hardware should be capable of latency times of less than 20ms. Achieving this requires a

high-quality audio card/hardware with a special ASIO driver. Dedicated ASIO drivers producing low latency times are also beneficial for the general operation of the host software. (See relevant internet sites and software/hardware developer documentation for precise details of ASIO drivers and hardware system recommendations.)

Info

Most performance based problems with VST Instruments are likely to be directly related to your computer's CPU power, RAM memory or audio hardware driver (and *not* the host application or VST Instrument itself). To ensure the best performance, high speed CPUs, large amounts of RAM and audio cards/hardware with dedicated ASIO drivers are highly recommended.

Installing and using VST Instruments within Cubase VST

For use with Cubase VST, VST Instruments are installed on your computer in a similar fashion to regular plug-ins. Follow the installation instructions supplied with the chosen VST Instrument and, when complete, you normally find the relevant file(s) located in the Cubase 'vstplugins' folder alongside the regular plug-in files. In some cases, you may need to manually drag the installed plug-in file into the vstplugins folder. When you next launch Cubase VST, the newly installed VST Instrument is added to the list of available instruments within the software.

Before you can play or open the graphical user interface for a VST Instrument it must first be activated in one of the slots of the VST Instruments rack (similar to a regular plug-ins rack). This is opened by selecting 'VST Instruments' in the Panels menu (Figure 4.1).

Figure 4.1
VST Instruments rack

To load a VST Instrument into one of the rack's slots, click on the name display in the centre of the front panel (which reads 'No VST Instrument' if no VST Instrument is currently loaded). This opens a pop-up menu containing the VST Instruments which are available on your system. Selecting a VST Instrument from the menu loads it into the rack and its name appears on the front panel. Activate the VST Instrument by clicking on the power button. Once activated, two or more VST Instrument channels are automatically created in the VST Channel mixer. These are used to regulate the volume, pan position, EQ and routing of the audio output signal from the instrument, just like a regular audio channel. The appropriate number of channels is also automatically created for those VST Instruments featuring multiple output channels (e.g. Kontakt, HALion, Model E, Battery, DR-008). To open the graphical user interface for the VST Instrument click on the Edit button of the VST Instrument rack front panel (Figure 4.2).

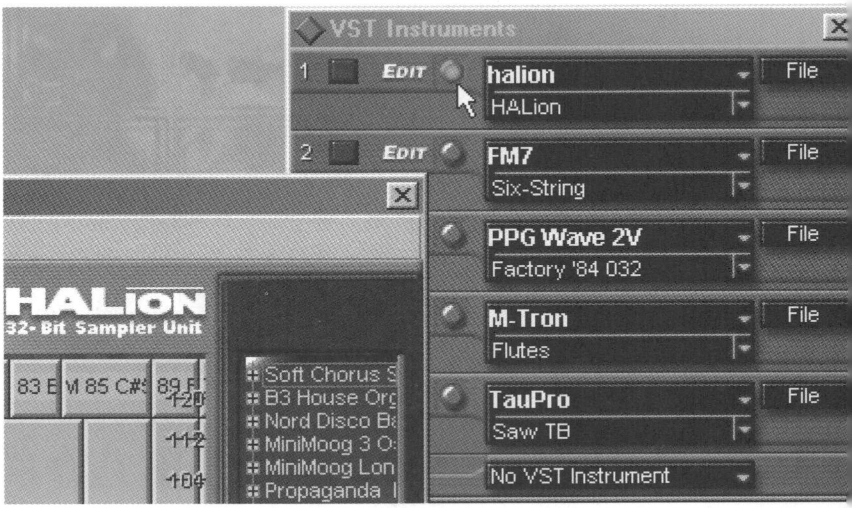

Figure 4.2
Click on the Edit button to open the interface for the VSTi

In order to trigger the VST Instrument via MIDI you must first allocate a spare MIDI Track to the instrument in the Arrange window Output column. Click in the Output column of the chosen Track. This opens the output menu where the name of any currently active VST Instruments are found alongside the other output ports (Figure 4.3). Select the desired VST Instrument and choose an appropriate MIDI channel (not necessary with all VST Instruments since many are permanently set to Omni mode). With the Track selected you can now play the VST Instrument from an external MIDI keyboard. If desired, you can make a recording onto this Track. You can also trigger the VST Instrument using an existing pre-recorded MIDI Track if you set the Track's output port to the VST Instrument.

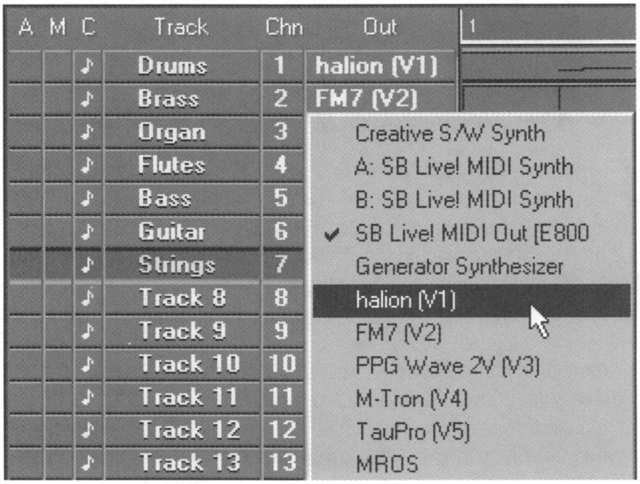

Figure 4.3
Allocate a MIDI Track to a VST Instrument in the Output column

VST Instrument automation within Cubase VST

Automation is understood here to mean the recording of manipulations of the control parameters of a VST Instrument. In Cubase VST, this is achieved by recording MIDI System Exclusive or Controller data onto a regular MIDI Track.

Most VST Instruments support the System Exclusive method. Before you can record SysEx automation data you must first make sure that System Exclusive is *not* filtered in the MIDI Filtering dialogue (Options/MIDI Setup/Filtering). Next, select an empty MIDI Track, activate record in the normal way and then tweak (move) the controls of the chosen VST Instrument. When you play back the Track, the controls you manipulated now move automatically according to the recorded data.

Some VST instruments, notably Native Instruments Reaktor, Pro-52 and B4, feature controls which send and receive MIDI Controller data and use this, instead of SysEx, for automation purposes in Cubase VST. In many ways this is more convenient. It allows tweaking of the parameters from a remote control surface and the manipulations can be recorded simultaneously into Cubase VST. Alternatively, moving the parameters using the mouse on the computer screen equally produces MIDI controller data which can be recorded into Cubase VST. The other advantage of using controller data is that it can be viewed and edited in Cubase VST's Controller editor (Edit/Controller). Figure 4.4 shows the editing of Pro-52 filter cut-off and resonance automation. Cut-off is assigned to MIDI controller 70 and resonance to 71.

Tip

VSTi automation is excellent for producing filter sweeps and special effects and can add an extra dimension to synthesizer parts. Almost all VST Instruments are capable of automation within Cubase VST.

Figure 4.4
Editing Pro-52 filter cut-off and resonance data in Cubase VST's Controller editor

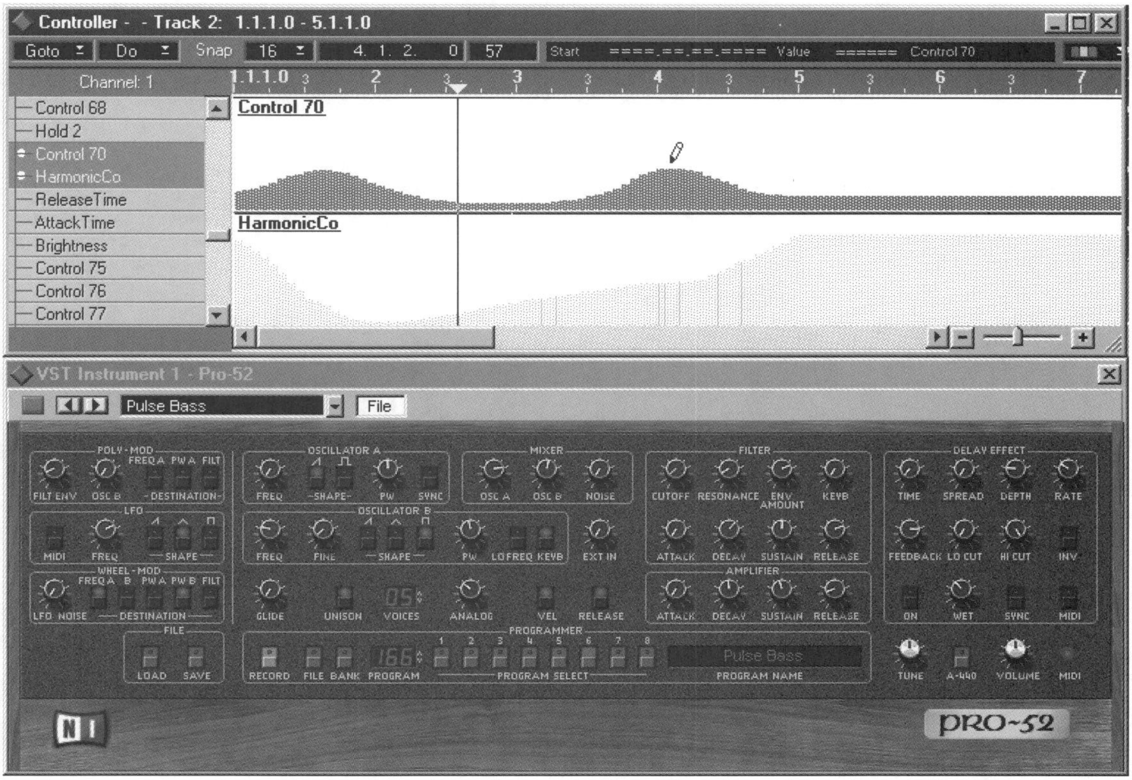

Converting VSTi Tracks into regular audio Tracks in Cubase VST

VST Instrument Tracks can be converted into audio files for use on regular audio Tracks using Cubase VST's Export audio function (File/Export/Audio Tracks, see Figure 4.5). Export audio exports non-muted audio data and VSTi Tracks between the left and right locators to an audio file. This is helpful when your computer is running out of system resources since regular audio Tracks use less CPU and less RAM than VSTi Tracks.

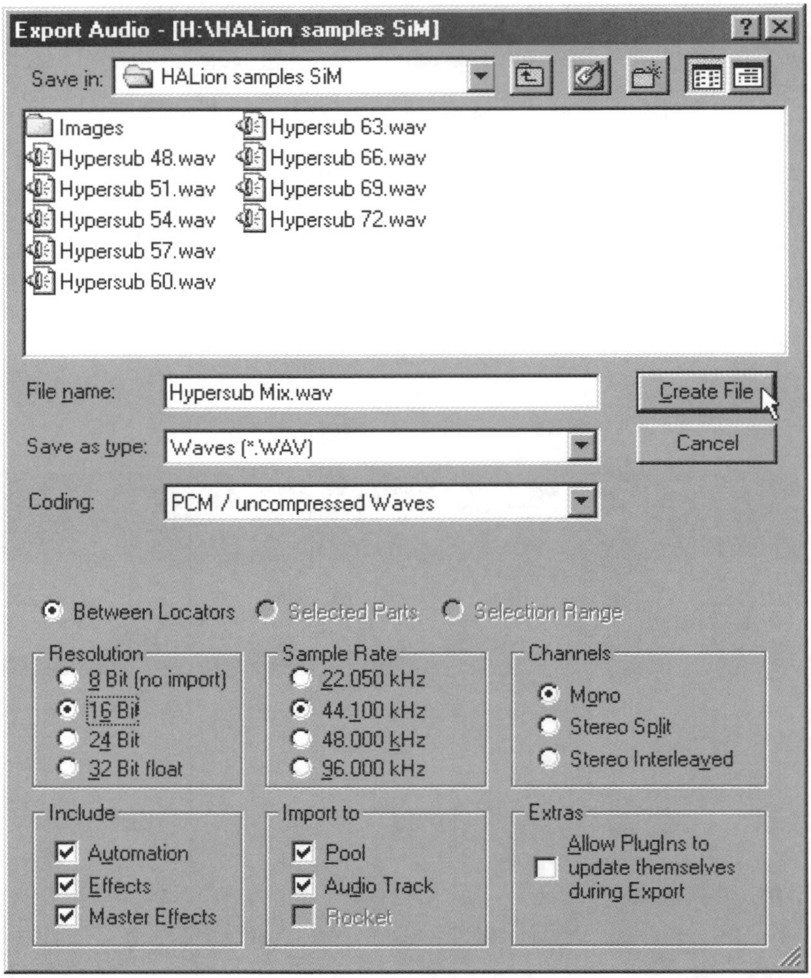

Figure 4.5
Use Cubase VST's Export Audio function to convert VSTi tracks into audio files

Installing and using VST Instruments within Logic Audio

For use with Logic Audio, VST Instruments are installed on your computer in a similar fashion to regular plug-ins. Follow the installation instructions supplied with the chosen VST Instrument and, when complete, you normally find the relevant file(s) located in the Logic 'VstPlugIns' folder.

In some cases, you may need to manually drag the installed plug-in file into the VstPlugIns folder. When you next launch Logic, the newly installed VST Instrument is added to the list of available instruments within the software.

Before you can play or open the graphical user interface for a VST Instrument, it must first be activated on an Audio Instrument channel. To achieve this, select an existing Audio Instrument Track in the Arrange window or create a new Track using Ctrl+Enter on the computer keyboard. Convert the new Track to an Audio Instrument Track by clicking and holding on the Track name and selecting Audio/Audio Instrument/AudioInst1 from the pop-up menu (Figure 4.6).

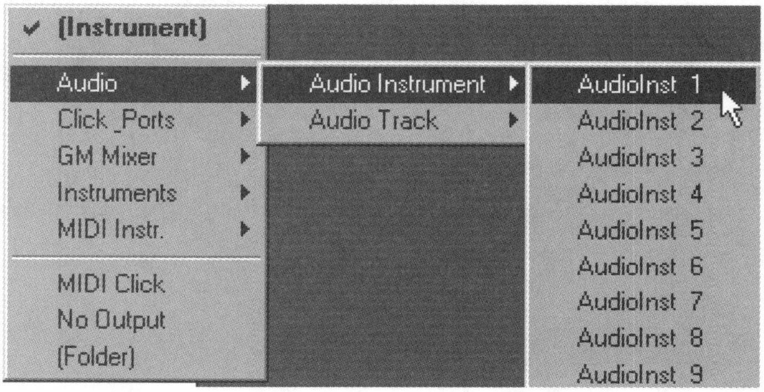

Figure 4.6
Select an Audio Instrument channel in Logic's Arrange window

Double-click on the Audio Instrument Track to open the Environment window. Logic automatically scrolls to the fader strip for your selected Audio Instrument Track. VST Instruments are inserted into the top insert slot of the Audio Instrument channel. Click and hold on the insert slot and select the desired VST Instrument from the Stereo/VST menu which contains the instruments which are available on your system (Figure 4.7).

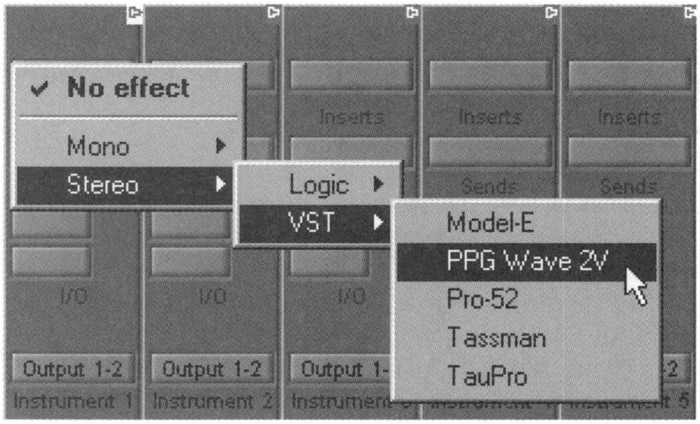

Figure 4.7
Click on the top insert slot of the Audio Instrument channel to insert a VST Instrument

The name of the VST Instrument appears on the insert slot and the GUI for the instrument is automatically launched (Figure 4.8). The instrument is now ready to be played using an external MIDI keyboard or other controller. Opening the user interface for an already-active VST Instrument is achieved by double-clicking on the insert button.

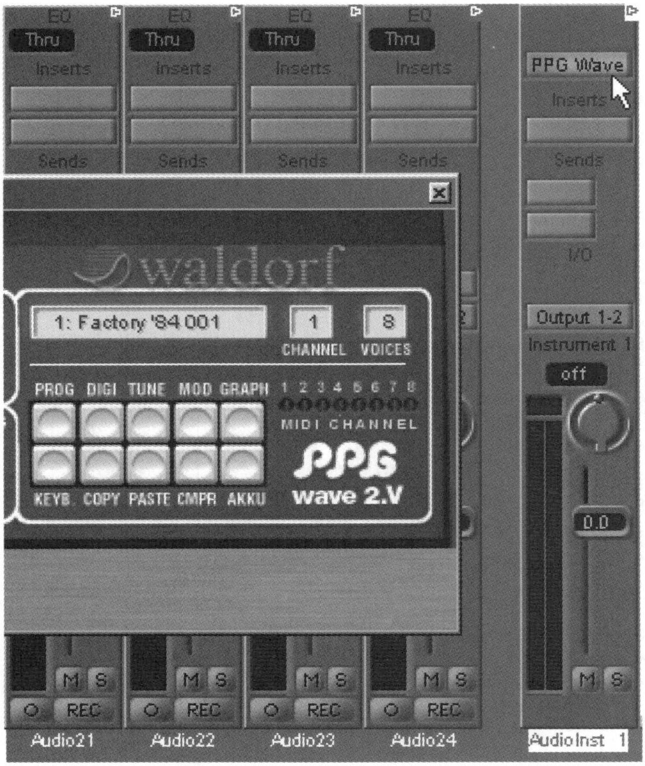

Figure 4.8
The graphical user interface for the VSTi is automatically launched when the instrument is first activated

Recordings can be made with the VST Instrument in the same way as with a regular MIDI Track, and any MIDI Tracks with pre-recorded MIDI data can be changed to play back via the VST Instrument (click and hold on the Track name and select an Audio Instrument from the pop-up menu). Logic does not support multiple outputs for VST Instruments (at the time of writing).

VST Instrument automation within Logic Audio

Automation is understood here to mean the recording of manipulations of the control parameters of a VST Instrument. In Logic (version 5 and later), this is achieved using the Track Automation system. Logic Track Automation data is recorded independently of all MIDI data and has 32-bit resolution for the recording of very precise and smooth automation. Most VST Instruments function well with Track Automation.

To prepare for Track Automation, double-click on the VST Instrument Track in the Arrange window, select 'Touch' in the automation mode field of the Audio Instrument channel and double-click on the insert button on the VST Instrument channel strip to open the user interface (Figure 4.9).

'Touch' is the standard automation mode. It replaces existing data per parameter for as long the control is manipulated. This allows you to go on improving your tweaks in real-time until you are completely happy with the effect (by continuously cycling on the relevant segment of the song, for example). To record the automation, put Logic into play

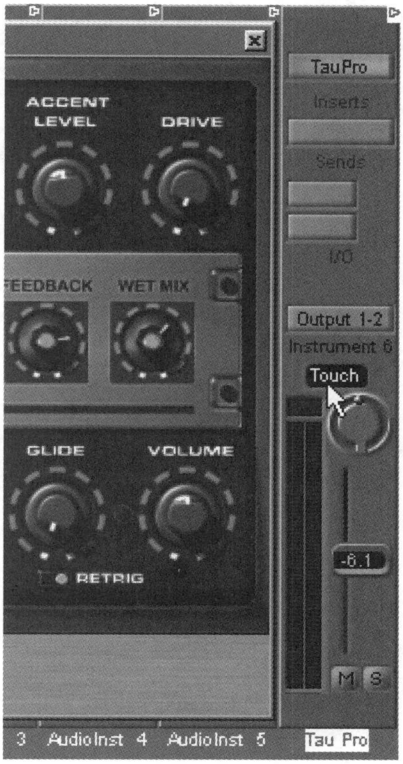

Figure 4.9
To record Track Automation select 'Touch' mode in the automation mode field

(record mode is not necessary) and tweak the VST Instrument's controls as desired. All parameter movements are recorded for as long as you are in Touch mode. When you have finished manipulating the parameters you can change the Automation mode to Read mode. This implements read-only status for the channel.

To edit the data, open the Arrange window, select the Audio Instrument Track containing the automation and activate Track Automation in the View menu. The vertical zoom level is automatically set appropriately. The automation data for one of the parameters should be visible in the sequence of the chosen Track. If not, click in the centre field of the expanded Track and choose a parameter from the lower section of the pop-up menu. Several parameters can be shown simultaneously by clicking on the small right-facing arrowhead at the lower left position of the Track. This shows additional parameters in sub-Tracks. Figure 4.10 shows cut-off, Q and envelope modulation automation for the Muon Tau Pro VSTi. Note that Logic's Track Automation allows the drawing of automation 'curves' for the creation of very smooth parameter movements (see Logic's documentation for more details about Track Automation).

In Logic version 5.0 (and later), to record automation with VST Instruments which use preset MIDI controller numbers for each of their control parameters (such as NI Pro-52 and B4), select 'Software Instruments use MIDI Controller as standard MIDI controls' in the MIDI options dialogue (Options/Settings/MIDI options). This allows the normal

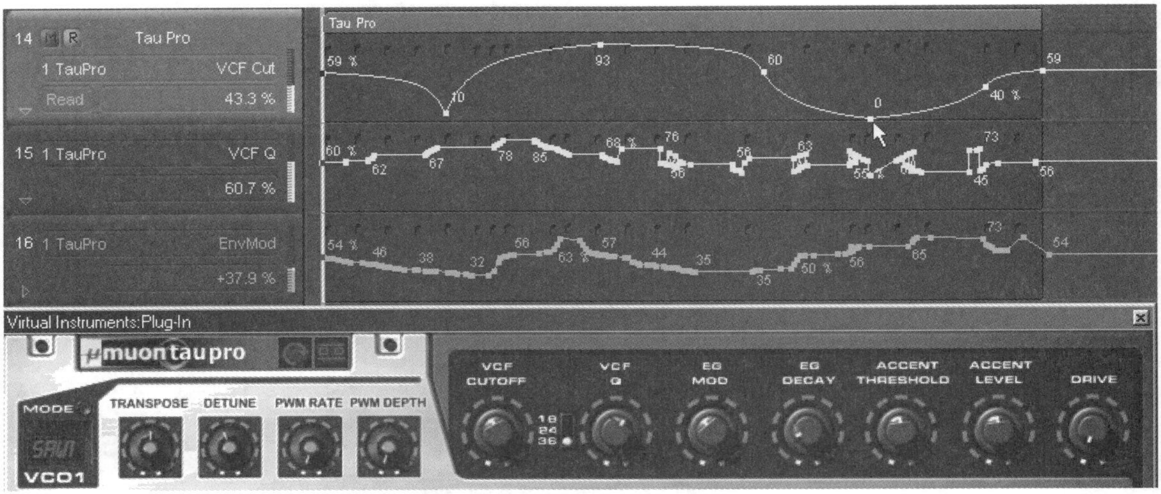

Figure 4.10
Editing Tau Pro automation data using Logic's Track Automation system

recording of automation using external controllers like the modulation wheel of a synthesizer or the faders and dials of a remote control surface. Controller data can be edited in the Arrange window using Hyper Draw (View/Hyper Draw/Other). For convenience, it may need to be merged first (Functions/Merge/Objects).

VSTi automation is excellent for producing filter sweeps and special effects and can add an extra dimension to synthesizer parts. Almost all VST Instruments respond to Logic's Track Automation system.

Converting VSTi Tracks into regular audio Tracks in Logic

VST Instrument Tracks can be converted into audio files for use on regular audio Tracks using Logic's Bounce function found on the Master audio object in the Environment window (Figure 4.11). Bounce transfers non-muted audio data and VSTi Tracks in the selected region in the Arrange window to an audio file. This is helpful when your computer is running out of system resources since regular audio Tracks use less CPU and less RAM than VSTi Tracks.

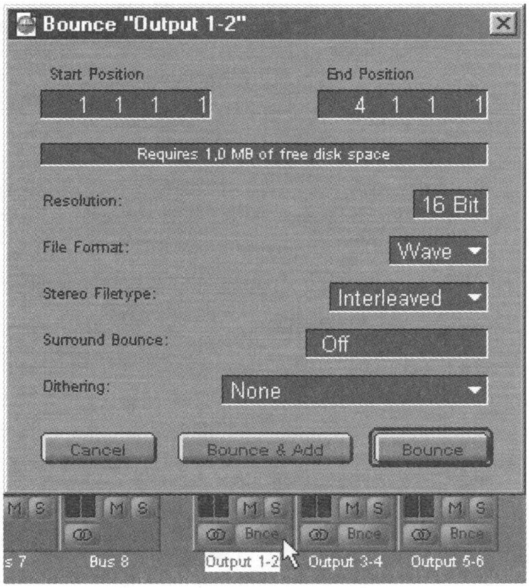

Figure 4.11
Use Logic's Bounce function to convert VSTi tracks into audio files

5 VST Instruments directory

This chapter provides detailed descriptions of a selection of VST Instruments. This helps readers appreciate how the synthesis techniques outlined in Chapter 3 have been implemented and provides 'fast-track' user guidance to those who already own one or more of the products. It also helps those who are searching for a new VST Instrument/software synthesizer/software sampler.

General concepts

Software synthesis, software sampling and software effects processing are CPU and RAM-intensive activities. All the software instruments described below vary in performance according to the resources available in the host computer. The number of voices available for any instrument is directly related to the amount of CPU power available. The drain on CPU power varies according to the number of notes which are being played simultaneously and according to the complexity of the tone being produced by the instrument. Many software samplers and sample-based drum modules also require substantial amounts of RAM in order to run smoothly.

The other main issue to consider is the latency. Latency is the delay between the user input and the time it takes for the computer to respond and process the data through its hardware and software, expressed in milliseconds. This affects real-time performance with VST instruments since it imposes a slight delay between the moment you press a note on your MIDI keyboard and the moment you hear the sound from the instrument. If the delay is too long then it becomes impossible to play in real-time. For real-time performance with VST Instruments the computer system should be capable of latency times of less than 20ms. To achieve this usually requires a high-quality audio card with a special ASIO driver. (See relevant internet sites and software developer documentation for precise details of hardware system recommendations.)

General options for instruments vary slightly between different platforms, different host applications and when you run in stand-alone mode. There are also a number of different interface standards relating to the use of software instruments with different applications and these are outlined below.

Interface standards

At the time of writing, the following were the main interfacing standards for software synthesis and sampling instruments:

- VST 2.0 – the most popular virtual instrument interfacing standard developed by Steinberg which is responsible for the birth of VST instruments (Virtual Studio instruments) and has helped fuel the creation of software instruments in general. VST 2.0 allows the instrument to run as a plug-in within the convenient environment of the host software. Supported in Cubase VST, Cubase SX, Nuendo, Logic and other VST compatible host software.
- DXi – interfacing standard for the running of instruments using Microsoft's Direct X technology. This is supported in Cakewalk Sonar.
- MAS – audio streaming interface for use with MOTU Digital Performer when using the instrument in stand-alone mode.
- DirectConnect audio streaming protocol allowing software synthesizers and samplers to be integrated into the Pro Tools TDM mixing environment when they are used in stand-alone mode (not compatible with all Pro Tools systems).

The VSTi Directory

The following descriptions are compatible with the use of instruments as plug-ins within VST 2.0 compatible host software (they are also largely accurate for the use of instruments in other kinds of software and as stand-alone applications). The Directory is divided into two main sections 'VSTi close-ups' and 'VSTi quick views'. Both sections present the VST Instruments in simple alphabetical order (according to the VSTi name) and no attempt is made to provide rankings or preferences. In the included screenshots, the windows within which the VST Instruments appear may vary according to the host application.

VSTi Close-ups

This section describes a selection of VST instruments in detail and provides the reader with an in-depth appreciation of the range and features of the available products.

Muon Atom Pro

Instrument type:	virtual analogue synthesizer
Polyphony:	12
Number of outputs:	1
Number of program slots:	16
Supported interfaces:	VST 2.0
Platform:	PC, Mac

Description

The Atom Pro is Muon's entry level software synthesizer. It is a two oscillator device featuring a 24dB/octave low pass filter and a high performance 64-bit audio engine (Figure 5.1).

Figure 5.1
Muon Atom Pro virtual analogue synth

Control interface

The front panel controls are arranged into groups according to their function and include the following:

Oscillator section

- MIX – blends the outputs from oscillators 1 and 2. Oscillator 1 is a fixed sawtooth wave and oscillator 2 is a variable pulse wave. Oscillator 1 (sawtooth) is fully left and oscillator 2 (pulse) is fully right while any position in between blends the corresponding percentage of the two waveforms.
- PW – manually governs the pulse width for oscillator 2. The centre position produces a square wave, fully left produces a narrow, in-phase pulse wave and fully right produces a narrow, opposite phase pulse wave.
- PWM (5-way 'ladder' control) – modulates the pulse width according to four preset LFO rates and depths. When set to OFF the PWM control has no effect and the pulse width is determined only by the PW control (above). When set to I, II, III or IV the PW control is disabled.

Filter section

- CUTOFF – determines the cut-off frequency of the low pass filter between 30Hz (fully left) and 12kHz (fully right).
- Q – determines the emphasis/resonance of the filter. More than 30-40% will cause the filter to go into self-oscillation for special effects.
- ENVMOD – determines the depth of the filter envelope modulation between negative modulation (fully left) and positive modulation (fully right). The centre position produces no modulation.
- Filter envelope with standard ADSR parameters.

Amplifier section

The amplifier section features a similar standard ADSR envelope generator to that of the filter section.

User Guide

Like many analogue synthesizers, preliminary experimentation with the Atom Pro might revolve around the cut-off and Q controls in conjunction with the filter's ADSR envelope. The Atom Pro's cut-off and Q controls are more expressive than most and a rich set of synth tone colours can be extracted just by tweaking these along with the envelope modulation control. Try setting Q and ENVMOD to their 2 o'clock positions and then listen to the effect of the cut-off control by slowly sweeping it from its lowest to highest position.

The four active positions of the PWM 'ladder' control (I, II, III and IV) are useful for enlivening and thickening those sounds which contain the pulse waveform. The four positions add progressively greater amounts of pulse width modulation. Positions I and II produce subtle slow modulation effects while positions III and IV produce deeper and faster, 'chorus-like' effects which are good for strings and pads.

Summary and applications

The Atom Pro's main strength is its intelligent simplicity. The front panel controls are very responsive and easy to use. The 64-bit audio engine produces a crystal-clear sound quality which cuts through in the mix and the 24dB-per-octave filter can produce classic 'squelchy' synth effects. Despite the absence of a user adjustable LFO and oscillator frequency tuning, the instrument manages to produce inspiring results. The Atom Pro is good for bass, pad and synth tones.

Waldorf Attack

Instrument type:	virtual analogue drum and percussion synthesizer
Polyphony:	up to 64
Number of outputs:	8 (2 stereo, 4 mono)
Number of program slots:	each Attack bank contains up to 16 kits
Supported interfaces:	VST 2.0
Platform:	PC, Mac

Description

Attack is an innovative software drum module for the synthesizing of analogue-style drum and percussion sounds. It is also good for creating bass, lead and pad synth sounds (Figure 5.2).

Control interface

The Attack control interface features a solo button, edit menu, preset menu, polyphony parameter, twenty-four sound select buttons and oscillator, mixer, filter, amplifier, envelope and delay sections. Drum kits (programs) and banks of kits (up to 16) are saved and loaded using standard VST 2.0 program and bank files (.fxp and .fxb file extensions).

Solo button, menus and polyphony

When activated, the solo button mutes all other sounds apart from the currently selected sound. The edit menu provides copy, paste, compare and recall functions for sounds and kits. The preset menu provides ini-

Figure 5.2
Waldorf Attack

tialisation and randomisation functions for sounds and kits, and a number of preset sounds and kits ready to load. The number of voices for Attack is adjusted by clicking on the polyphony setting and dragging the mouse vertically.

Sound select buttons

To see the settings of each sound in an Attack kit click on any one of the sound select buttons found in the left part of the window. Once displayed the sound may be edited as desired.

The lower twelve sound select buttons are intended primarily for drum and percussion sounds and are assigned to MIDI notes C1 to B1/36 to 47 (one sound per note). The upper twelve sound select buttons can equally be used for drum and percussion sounds, this time assigned to MIDI notes C2 to B2/48 to 59 (one sound per note). The upper twelve buttons can also be used to trigger pitched synth sounds polyphonically between C3/60 and the upper limit of the keyboard. C3/60 might be viewed as a keyboard split point. The pitched sounds are triggered according to MIDI channel, where upper buttons 1-12 correspond with MIDI channels 1-12 respectively. Another way of understanding this configuration is that all the sounds between C1 and B2, mapped with one sound per note, and one sound between C3 and G9 are available for each of MIDI channels 1-12.

To re-name any of the twenty-four sounds hold down ‘alt’ while clicking on its sound select button.

Oscillator section

Attack has two similar oscillators. The following describes the features of oscillator 1 which is applicable to both oscillators (oscillator 2 differs only in that it does not feature the FM section of oscillator 1):

- Semitone – determines the pitch of the oscillator in semitone steps (-50 to +50 semitones)
- Detune – fine tunes the pitch in cents (-50 to +50 cents)
- Pitch – determines the pitch in terms of Hertz (0.007984 to 20000Hz)
- Shape – determines the shape of the waveform generated by the oscillator. Triangle, sine, pulse, sawtooth, sample and hold, noise and sampled closed hi-hat, open hi-hat and crash cymbal are available.
- Env (pitch envelope) – allows an amount of pitch modulation to be applied to the oscillator using either envelope 1 or 2 as the modulator (-100% to +100%).
- Vel (pitch velocity) – determines the amount of pitch envelope modulation according to the velocity of incoming MIDI notes. This is combined with the pitch envelope amount to give an overall amount of pitch modulation (-100% to +100%).
- FM (frequency modulation) – determines the amount of frequency modulation applied to oscillator 1 by oscillator 2.
- FM env (FM envelope) – regulates the amount of time-based influence over the frequency modulation using envelope 1 or 2 as the modulator (-100% to +100%).
- FM vel (FM velocity) – determines the amount of FM envelope effect according to the velocity of incoming MIDI notes. This is combined with the FM envelope amount to give an overall amount of frequency modulation.

Mixer section

The mixer section features the following controls:

- Osc 1 – regulates the level of oscillator 1 (0-100%).
- Osc 2 – regulates the level of oscillator 2 (0-100%).
- Env (envelope) – regulates the amount of influence of either envelope 1 or envelope 2 upon the level of oscillator 2 (-100% to +100%).
- Vel (velocity) – determines the amount of envelope control over level change according to the velocity of incoming MIDI notes. This is combined with the envelope amount to give an overall level for oscillator 2 (-100% to +100%).
- Rmod (ring modulation) – determines the level of the ring modulation of oscillators 1 and 2. Ring modulation involves the multiplication of the signals of oscillators 1 and 2 (0-100%).
- Crack – adds the sound of the 'crack' modulator to the mix. This is a special amplitude modulation signal designed for the synthesis of handclap sounds. When activated it affects all other mix signals (0-100%).
- Crack speed – sets the frequency of the crack modulator (1-5000Hz).
- Crack length – sets the number of modulations of the crack modulator (0-infinity).

Filter section

After being mixed the composite signal is routed to the filter section. This consists of a 12dB per octave resonant filter with the following controls:

- Type – selects the amplitude response for the filter to either low-pass, high-pass, band-pass, notch, lo-hi shelf EQ or bell-type EQ.
- Cut-off – determines the cut-off or centre frequency for the different filter types (11.56-18794Hz).
- Resonance – emphasises the frequencies around the cut-off point for low-pass, high-pass, band-pass and notch filter types (0-100%).
- Env (filter envelope amount) – regulates the amount of influence of either envelope 1 or 2 upon the cut-off frequency of the filter (-100% to +100%).
- Vel (filter velocity) – determines the amount of envelope control over filter cut-off according to the velocity of incoming MIDI notes. This is combined with the filter envelope amount to give an overall envelope influence over the cut-off frequency (-100% to +100%).
- Drive – adds harmonics and distortion to the signal (0-54dB).
- Sync – synchronises Attack's LFO to key-on or to a tempo-based modulation of the filter cut-off frequency. Select key to cause the LFO's triangle waveform to always start at maximum amplitude. Select a note value to synchronise the LFO to the desired division of the bar at the current tempo of your host application.
- Mod speed – determines the frequency (speed) of the LFO (S&H random-1000Hz).
- Mod depth – determines the amplitude of the LFO and therefore the depth of the modulation effect (-100% to +100%).

Amplifier section

The amplifier section includes the following controls:

- Output – determines the stereo or mono audio output for the currently selected sound.
- Volume – determines the volume for the currently selected sound (-infinity to 0dB).
- Vel (velocity) – determines how the volume is affected by the velocity of the incoming MIDI notes (-100% to +100%).
- Pan – determines the stereo position of the currently selected sound whose output has been set to one of the stereo audio outputs (100%R to 100%L).
- Mix – determines the dry/wet mix of the untreated and the delay signal (100% dry – 100% wet).
- XOR group – assigns the currently selected sound to a monophonic XOR group for the creation of monophonic synth sounds and for the monophonic triggering of open and closed hi-hats.

Envelope section

Attack provides two envelopes for the creation of time-based control signals. Envelope 2 is pre-set for control of the amplifier level. Both envelopes can be directed to other relevant sound parameters. The envelope parameters include attack, decay and release segments with a 'shape' control. Shape allows the shaping of the decay and release segments of the envelope according to various exponential, linear and

Info

Attack's amplifier section is always controlled by envelope 2.

inverse-exponential envelope curves. For sustained sounds, set decay to maximum and release to any setting other than zero.

The envelopes are adjusted using the rotary controls or by clicking on the relevant handle in the envelope display and dragging it to a new position.

Delay sections

Attack features two delay effects sections. Delay 1 is selected automatically when a sound is routed to stereo audio outputs 1 and 2. Delay 2 is selected automatically when a sound is routed to stereo audio outputs 3 and 4. The control parameters are as follows:

- Spread – spreads the delay across the stereo image for the creation of ping-pong delay effects.
- Speed – produces modulation of the delay time according to an LFO (0.01-10Hz).
- Depth – determines the depth of the LFO delay modulation effect (0-100%).
- Lo-cut – controls low frequency dampening for each successive loop of the delay.
- Hi-cut – controls high frequency dampening for each successive loop of the delay.

User guide

Attack's parameters have been organised in a way which is favourable for the creation of analogue drum and percussion sounds. One of the best ways of learning about its potential is to load in one of the preset sounds (808 kick, 909 kick etc. in the presets menu) and attempt to understand the 'how and why' of its parameter settings.

The original 808 bass drum sound was made by triggering a special kind of oscillator with a short accented impulse. The oscillator featured a feedback path which controlled the decay rate of the sound. The signal was then routed to a low-pass filter to remove an amount of the upper frequencies.

One way of approximating the sound of an 808 bass drum in Attack is to assign a sine wave shape to oscillator 1 with its pitch set at G#1. Apply a small amount of positive pitch modulation using envelope 1 set to a short impulse envelope shape. This provides the bass drum click at the beginning of the sound. Adjust envelope 2 for the fastest attack with a short exponential decay. The decay parameter controls the length of the bass drum. This is the manner in which the preset '808 kick' is configured in Attack.

Another more generalised technique (which is applicable to analogue synthesizers in general) is to trigger the sound of a self-oscillating filter (created with a high resonance setting) with a short impulse from one of the oscillators. In these circumstances the cut-off frequency controls the pitch (tone) of the bass drum and the amount of resonance controls its length. An envelope modulating the filter cut-off to produce a fast sweep down in the pitch produces a click for the attack of the bass drum. The sound is also affected by the pitch of the oscillator impulse if it is within the normal audible bandwidth. (A more detailed explanation of this patch is provided in Chapter 6 'Programming a synthesized bass drum').

The use of Attack's random functions sometimes produces interesting sounds and are worth trying just to get a feel for the more wildly abstract side of Attack's sound palette. Synth bass, lead and pad sounds can easily be programmed in Attack using traditional subtractive synthesis techniques. For sustained sounds set the decay to maximum and the release to any setting other than zero for envelope 2.

Summary and applications

Attack allows you to create your own analogue style drums and percussion as well as producing authentic re-creations of the sounds from classic analogue drum machines. This moves away from traditional practice where many of the old analogue sounds are triggered in sample form. Attack is advantageous since you can trigger the virtual analogue sounds directly from within your favourite sequencing application without the headache of the operation of some of the classic real-world instruments.

Attack is supplied with two excellent sound banks containing a total of 32 kits (in VST 2.0 bank format, .fxb extension). Where possible the kits are arranged across the keyboard according to standard GM mapping. They include kits designed for specific musical styles like House kit, Techno kit, Jungle kit, Latin kit, 808 kit, and 909 kit, and kits containing analogue style sound effects such as the Electro FX kits, Chaos kit, Arcade Fever kit and 23rd century kit. Overall, Attack is an adventure into the world of analogue-style drums, percussion and inspiring electronic sound effects. It is particularly suited to dance floor styles. Its potential for the synthesizing of pitched lead and bass sounds and analogue pads means that for certain kinds of music it can produce entire arrangements all on its own.

Native Instruments B4

Instrument type:	virtual tonewheel organ
Polyphony:	tonewheel-based polyphony limit with a maximum of 91 tones
Number of outputs:	1 stereo
Number of program slots:	120
Supported interfaces:	VST 2.0, DXi, MAS, DirectConnect
Platform:	PC, Mac

Description

The B4 is a software emulation of Hammond's B3 tonewheel organ (Figure 5.3).

The first Hammond Tonewheel organs were introduced by Laurens Hammond in 1935 and the Hammond B3 was in production between 1955 And 1974. The B3 is considered by many to be the definitive Hammond organ. It features a split level control interface with 61-key upper and lower keyboards, (known as 'manuals' in organ terminology), and 25-note foot pedals. Its particular sonic identity is due to the tonewheel technology which produces the sound. Tonewheels are specially shaped wheels (with bumps or notches) which rotate on an axle,

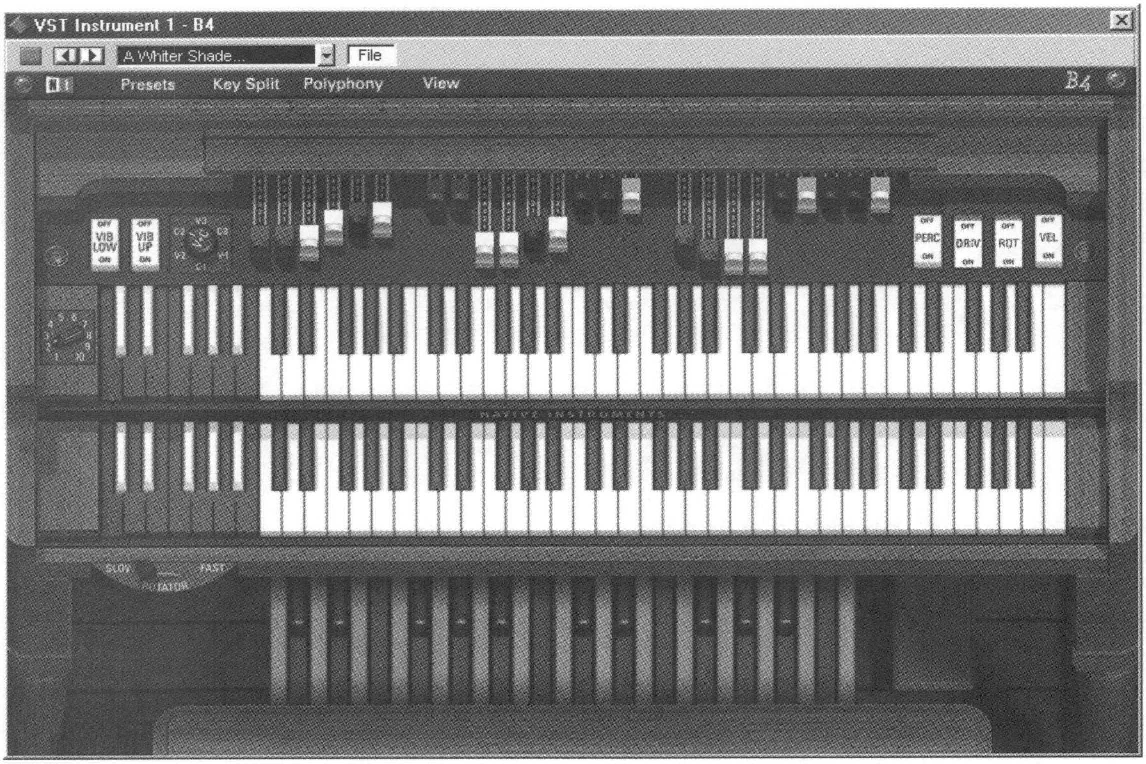

Figure 5.3
Native Instruments B4

each adjacent to its own pickup (magnet and coil assembly). The irregularities and rotation speed of each wheel produces an electrical current in the pickup which when converted into an audible signal produces a tone of a prescribed pitch. The B3 features 91 such tonewheels, a number of which are used to produce the sound each time you press a key (depending on how many harmonics are being used to produce the organ sound – see below).

The B3 uses additive synthesis to produce its different timbres. This involves adding harmonics from the natural harmonic series, the only difference with organ technology being that the harmonic controls are configured in terms of pipe lengths rather than harmonic numbers. The control devices which govern the level of each harmonic are known as 'drawbars', named after the drawbar technology dating from earlier pipe organs. Each drawbar represents a different length of pipe and each is responsible for producing a different harmonic in the composite sound. Combining the drawbars in differing proportions allows the creation of a wide range of organ tones. The final output signal is invariably delivered via a rotating speaker system. This configuration resulted in the classic organ tones used in some of the great R&B, jazz and rock music of recent times.

The Native Instruments B4 recreates the classic sound of the original in software form. This includes the accurate modelling of the behaviour of the original tonewheel and rotating speaker systems.

Control interface

The B4 features two interface windows, the 'keyboard view' and the 'control view'.

Keyboard view

The keyboard view (Figure 5.3 above) displays all the main operational parameters of the B4. It also gives access to the Presets, Key split, Polyphony and View menus. The control parameters displayed in the keyboard view include the following:

- upper and lower manuals and foot pedals – 61-note virtual keyboards and 25-note foot pedals which can be used to audition sounds by clicking with the mouse on the keys. The keys also register the presence of any incoming MIDI data.
- the swell pedal – corresponds with MIDI controller 11 (expression) for the dynamic control of volume.
- the rotary speaker control – for changing the speed of the rotary speaker simulation effect between slow and fast.
- the upper and lower manual vibrato switches and vibrato setting switch – when activated, produce a vibrato/chorus effect for the upper or lower manuals. The foot pedals use the setting of the lower manual vibrato switch.
- the drawbars – three sets of drawbars regulate the tone of the foot pedals, lower manual and upper manual. There are six drawbars for the foot pedals and nine for each of the lower and upper manuals.
- the percussion switch – when activated produces a lightweight, percussive signature to the front of each note. The percussion effect does not occur on notes which are played legato.
- the overdrive switch – when activated adds distortion to the organ tone according to the setting of the tube amplifier drive control in the control view.
- the rotator speed control switch – switches the rotating speaker simulator between slow and fast settings. The slow and fast settings are regulated using the treble and bass rotor controls in the control view.
- the velocity switch – when activated, incoming MIDI velocity affects the volume of the B4.
- bank select switch – selects a bank for the recall or storing of B4 presets.
- upper and lower preset selector keys – inversely coloured keys for the recall or storing of B4 presets. The upper preset selector keys save all the drawbar and effect settings whereas the lower preset selector keys store only the lower manual and foot pedal settings.

The menus include the following:

- Presets menu – for the storing of the current settings in one of B4's 120 onboard presets using 'store' or 'store as'. 'Store' saves to the current preset location. 'Store as' saves to the preset you select using the rotary bank selector switch followed by an upper or lower preset selector key. Choosing an upper manual preset selector key saves all the drawbar and effect settings whereas choosing a lower manual preset selector key stores only the lower manual and foot pedal settings. The presets menu also allows the importing and exporting of single B4 sounds or all the B4 sounds in B4 format, and the dumping of the current settings as MIDI controller data. If you have alternative tonewheel sets these can be chosen from the presets menu (Native Instruments supply the B4 'Vintage Collection' which includes tonewheel sets for Vox Continental, Farfisa and Indian Harmonium).

- Key split menu – for the selection of keyboard split positions so that you can play the upper and lower keyboards and foot pedals from a single MIDI keyboard. The key split menu also allows the transposition of any of the upper, lower or foot pedal keyboards up or down by one octave.
- Polyphony menu – for the adjustment of the polyphony of the B4 to suit the processing power of the host computer (50 tones is suitable for most applications).
- View menu – switches between keyboard view and control view.

The control view

The control view page (Figure 5.4) is where you can adjust all the control parameters of the B4 in fine detail.

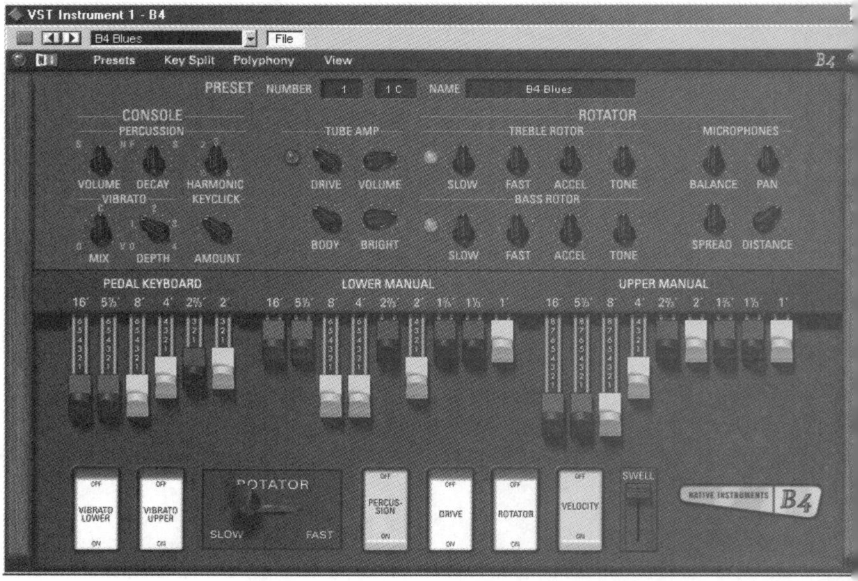

Figure 5.4
The B4 'control view' window

The parameters include the switches, slow-fast speaker rotation selector, swell pedal and drawbars as displayed in the keyboard view page. These are shown in the lower half of the control view and have exactly the same function as in the keyboard view. Changes made here are reflected in the keyboard view (and vice versa). The upper half of the control view includes the following:

- percussion section – configures the percussion effect which is introduced into the sound when the percussion switch is activated. The volume control regulates the amount of percussion effect, the decay control regulates its decay phase and harmonic determines which drawbar is used to create the percussive timbre.

- vibrato section – regulates the vibrato/chorus effect applied to the sound when either of the vibrato switches are activated. Mix determines the type of effect between virtually no effect at lower settings, chorus effects at mid-range settings and vibrato effects at high settings. Depth controls the depth of the effect.
- keyclick – adds a slight click to the start of the sound (typical of many organ tones and useful for helping the sound to cut through in the mix).
- tube amp section – adds tube amplifier warmth and distortion to the output signal of the B4. The drive control regulates the amount of distortion introduced into the sound and is active only when the overdrive switch is activated. The volume control determines the overall volume level of the tube amplifier. The body parameter provides tone control in the mid frequency range. The bright parameter provides tone control in the high frequency range.
- treble rotor section – the speaker rotation system of the B4 includes a treble rotor and a bass rotor. The two rotors can rotate independently at different speeds. The slow control regulates the speed of the rotor when the rotator speed control switch is set to slow (between 0 and 85rpm). The fast control regulates the speed of the rotor when the rotator speed control switch is set to fast (between 85 and 700rpm). The accel control determines the time it takes for the rotator speed to change when switching between slow and fast settings. The tone control alters the perceived size and shape of the rotor.
- bass rotor section – identical in operation to the treble rotor above.
- microphone section – the B4 features two virtual microphones which are responsible for capturing the output signal from the rotary speakers. These can be placed in various positions around the rotors giving a wide range of variations in the kind of sound which is produced. The balance control determines the amount of bass or treble rotor sound in the mix with more bass rotor when turned to the left, more treble rotor when turned to the right and both bass and treble in equal amounts when in the centre position. The pan control splits the treble and bass rotors between the two channels of the B4's output. The default centre position sends equal amounts of the treble and bass rotors to both speakers. The spread control distributes the left and right microphone positions progressively wider apart around the rotors. The distance control determines the distance of the microphones from the rotors and affects the amount of amplitude modulation in the signal.

Tip

To quickly change the presets of the B4 right-click on the preset number field in the control view and drag the mouse vertically (PC only).

User guide

Most programming of the B4 revolves around the drawbar settings and the percussion, vibrato and rotator switch settings. Once a basic sound has been established, refinements can be added using the tube amp, microphone settings, chorus and percussion controls in the control view.

The drawbar settings are the key to setting up the basic organ tone and it is important to have an idea of how they function in order to use them to their best effect. Drawbars find their roots in earlier pipe organ technology where each drawbar controlled an organ pipe of a different length. Each pipe produced a different note according to its length which constituted a different harmonic in the natural harmonic series. These harmonics could be added together to produce a composite timbre. This was an early example of additive synthesis (see Chapters 2 and 3 for more details about harmonics and additive synthesis). The B4 follows in the same tradition and each of its drawbars is labelled according to a pipe length rather than a note or frequency in the harmonic series. Each drawbar also has a level indicator marked from 1 to 8. The following are the pipe length labels (which are marked in feet) with their corresponding note names, frequencies and harmonic numbers for a note played at middle C (equal-tempered scale, middle C = C4 / 261.63Hz):

16'	C3	130.81Hz	Subharmonic fundamental
5 1/3'	G4	392.00Hz	Subharmonic third harmonic
8'	C4	261.63Hz	Fundamental
4'	C5	523.25Hz	Second harmonic
2 2/3'	G5	783.99Hz	Third harmonic
2'	C6	1046.50Hz	Fourth harmonic
1 3/5'	E6	1318.51Hz	Fifth harmonic
1 1/3'	G6	1567.98Hz	Sixth harmonic
1'	C7	2093.00Hz	Eighth harmonic

Notice that the drawbars do not start at the fundamental (the frequency which usually gives the composite sound its pitch) and the seventh harmonic is missing. The notes actually start an octave below the fundamental at C3 (16' pipe), along with its third harmonic G3 (5 1/3' pipe). These are used to boost the bass end of the sound. These subharmonic drawbars are colour-coded in brown. The white drawbars mark the positions of the fundamental and one, two and three octaves above. The black drawbars are where the remaining harmonics are found.

When you start to create an organ tone you might start with an amount of the fundamental and then build the tone using varying proportions of the other drawbars. Using the white drawbars alone produces 'cheesy organ' sounds. As you add the black drawbars you can produce more jazz-style organ tones and pulling out all the drawbars almost, or completely, to their maximum level you can produce tones suitable for rock music.

In Hammond organ terminology each set of drawbar values is known as a registration. This is a sequence of nine numbers which represent the setting of each of the nine drawbars of either the upper or lower manuals. Two spaces are normally added to help read the numbers (e.g. 84 7767 666). Registrations for the pedals are expressed in a similar sequence but, this time, of six numbers (e.g. 85 8000). The drawbar setting might be viewed as the 'cake' of the sound and the other controls of the organ are the 'icing' which you add later. There are a large number of drawbar registrations available in organ documentation and on the Internet. These can help you get started with Hammond-style organ programming (also see the section 'Programming organ tones on Native Instruments B4' in Chapter 6).

To get started try the following: 32 7645 222, 00 7373 430 and 88 8888 888. Once you have established a basic sound, changing the status of the percussion, vibrato and rotator switches can radically alter the timbre. The B4 provides still more possibilities than the original instrument since it allows the changing of the mix of the chorus/vibrato effect and its depth, the detailed adjustment of the percussion effect, and the changing of the speed and tonal characteristics individually for each of the treble and bass rotors. Try setting the chorus/vibrato settings to C for the mix dial and 2 for depth for a generic chorus/vibrato effect suitable for the majority of organ tones or percussion volume to S, decay to F and harmonic to 2 or 3 to produce a jazz style percussion effect. Try the rotator system with the rotator switch set to slow, the treble rotor slow dial set to 3 o'clock and the tone dial set to 11 o'clock, the bass rotor slow dial set to 12 o'clock and the tone dial set to minimum to achieve a mellow tone with dynamic movement. Sending the sound through the tube amplifier section adds warmth and character to the sound. Try adding drive to a sound with all the drawbars at maximum for a distorted rock organ sound. For sub-bass pedal sounds try turning the body and bright dials fully to the left. Finally, the B4 allows you to place virtual microphones in different positions around the rotating speakers for added realism in the final output signal.

Info

The B4 is installed with an additional effects module (B4fx) providing a way to process other signals with the tube amplifier and rotating speaker system.

For sound synthesists, it is surprising to learn that there are no envelope controls in the B4 interface. The sound starts and stops quite suddenly. In addition, all the programming revolves around the timbre of only one type of sound, the organ tone. Some might think that this would result in a restrictive and uninteresting instrument but, on the contrary, with the B4 (like the real-world Hammond organs), 'less is more'. By concentrating on a comparatively small number of parameters, organ instruments like the B4, deliver a highly distinctive and inspiring set of tone colours.

Summary and applications

Similar to The Grand VSTi piano, Native Instruments' B4 is dedicated to the production of a single type of sound. If you want exceptionally authentic organ tones in a convenient, well-designed virtual instrument then the B4 delivers. It also provides the perfect learning tool for anyone interested in organ technology.

The B4 is supplied with a bank of 120 presets. These include many of the standard settings used in church, classical, jazz, rock and house music. The names of some of the presets contain references to the personalities, hits and groups of the 60's and 70's which made the Hammond legendary in the popular music field, such as Jimmy McG, Jimmy (Smith), A Whiter Shade..., Emersons Basic, Purple, Samba Pa Ti, Small Faces, Gimme Some Lovin' and so on.

The B4 is suitable for all organ styles from jazz to classical and from rock to house. It can produce anything from screaming overdrive organ solos to massive sub-bass organ tones. Its sound processing engine can also be used as an insert effect for any other audio signals in your VST2.0 compatible sequencer. Great for applying rotating speaker and tube amp effects to other audio signals (see 'Programming organ tones in Native Instruments B4' in Chapter 6).

Native Instruments FM7

Instrument type:	FM synthesizer
Polyphony:	up to 64
Number of outputs:	1 stereo
Number of program slots:	128
Supported interfaces:	VST 2.0, DXi, MAS, DirectConnect
Platform:	PC, Mac

Description

The FM7 is an innovative FM synthesizer with extended design features including eight operators, user-configurable algorithm structures and an easy-edit page (Figure 5.5).

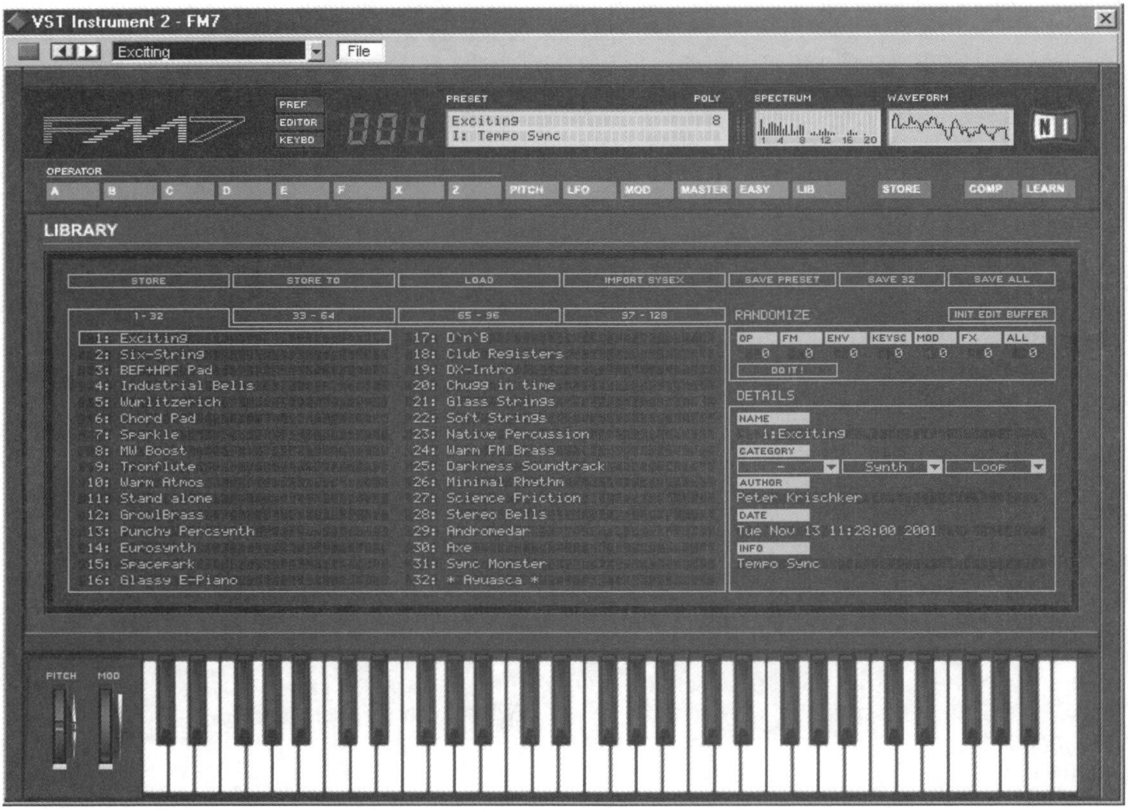

Figure 5.5
Native Instruments FM7

The FM7 is modelled upon the original DX7 FM synthesizer, released in 1983. The DX7 was an all-digital instrument and among the first FM synthesizers to be produced. It became one of the best-selling keyboard instruments of all time. FM (frequency modulation) is a digital synthesis technique classed as a distortion (or non-linear) type of synthesis. Simple FM synthesis manages to produce a wide range of timbres using a comparatively small number of parameters (see the FM synthesis section in Chapter 3).

The FM7, like the DX7, is based upon FM algorithms, sets of modulators and carriers (known as operators) linked in various configurations. In the DX7 the algorithms were pre-set but the FM7 features user-configurable algorithms arranged in a unique matrix page. There are six conventional operators and two specialised operators for distortion and filtering of the signal. Other features of the FM7 include an easy-edit page, a choice of 32 different waveforms for each operator, 64-voice polyphony, 128 preset memory slots and a dedicated delay effects section.

Control interface

When the graphical user interface for the FM7 is first activated it appears with the Common parameters strip at the top of the screen and the first 32 (of 128) presets visible in the main page display (as in Figure 5.5). This is the Library page, one of the 14 main edit pages of the FM7. Each page is accessed by clicking on the respective green selector buttons just above the page display (A-F, X, Z, PITCH, LFO etc.). The default display also features the usual virtual keyboard and pitch-bend and modulation wheels which are convenient for the auditioning of sounds using the mouse. The functions of each aspect of the FM7 and each of the main pages is now described.

Common parameters strip

The Common parameters strip is always visible at the top of the FM7 control interface. It features three small buttons just to the right of the FM7 logo. The Pref button opens the Preferences dialogue where you can set options for memory protect, velocity characteristics, controller handling and randomize behaviour. You can also enter your name in the author field so that it appears in the information section for any patches you create. The Editor button opens/closes the editing part of the interface. The Keyboard button shows/hides the virtual keyboard.

The Preset name display shows the currently selected FM7 sound preset. Click on the number and move the mouse vertically to change the preset. The green Preset info display shows the name of the preset and the current polyphony of the FM7 on the first line. You can click directly on the preset name to enter a new name and the polyphony can be adjusted by clicking in the polyphony field and dragging vertically. Clicking on the second line in the display reveals, in turn, the number of voices in use with the current CPU load, the category (C), author (A), date (D), info (I) and the currently selected editing parameter (P). (Category, author, date and info are entered in the details section of the Library page, see below). The Common parameters strip also includes an output meter, spectrum display and waveform display.

Library page

The main feature of the Library page is the Preset list which appears in four banks of 32 sounds. Clicking on any of the names selects the corresponding preset. There is a Master control strip above the Preset list which allows the storing of the current sound to the current preset slot (STORE) or to another slot (STORE TO), the loading of soundbanks (LOAD), the importing of DX7/DX7II/DX200 System Exclusive banks (IMPORT SYSEX), and the saving of single presets, banks of 32 or all 128 presets (SAVE PRESET, SAVE 32 and SAVE ALL). The right segment of the Library page features a Randomize section where you can selectively randomise different parts of the current patch (for creating new sounds based upon serendipity) and an Init edit buffer button for initialising the current patch to default values as the starting point for the creation of a new sound. The Details section allows you to enter preset name, category, author, date and info details (these details also appear in the Preset info display in the Common parameters strip, as mentioned above).

Algorithms and the algorithm matrix

The heart of FM synthesis with the FM7 is the programming of an algorithm and the operators which form the building blocks of this algorithm. An algorithm is a network of operators arranged together in an interactive configuration. Each operator has a waveform, a frequency and an amplitude level and is designated as a carrier or a modulator according to the way it is linked in the algorithm matrix (see the FM synthesis section in Chapter 3 for more information about carrier and modulator operators).

The algorithm matrix is accessed by clicking on any of the green operator buttons (A–F, X or Z) and selecting 'matrix' in the upper right corner of the envelope display. The same green operator buttons are used to select the parameters page for each operator.

Figure 5.6a shows a very simple algorithm where operator E modulates operator F (i.e. operator E is the modulator and operator F is the carrier). This is compared to the highly complex algorithm (Figure 5.6b) used in FM7 default preset number 32, Eric Young's 'Ayuasca', which features all eight operators linked in an interactive feedback and cross-modulating network. This results in a highly imaginative patch which forms an abstract piece of music in its own right. When you hold down a note you hear a sound which develops continuously over more than a whole minute.

Operators are connected to create interacting networks by clicking in the matrix at the point where the vertical axis of one operator meets the horizontal axis of another and then dragging the mouse vertically to enter an output level. Dragging this level back down to zero disconnects

Figure 5.6
From highly simple to highly complex algorithms in FM7's algorithm matrix

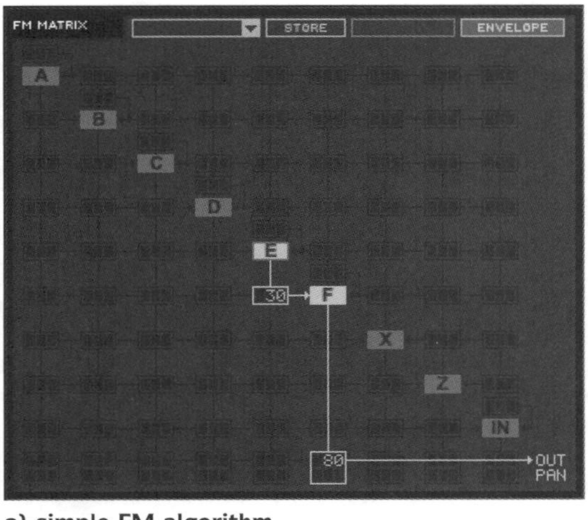

a) simple FM algorithm

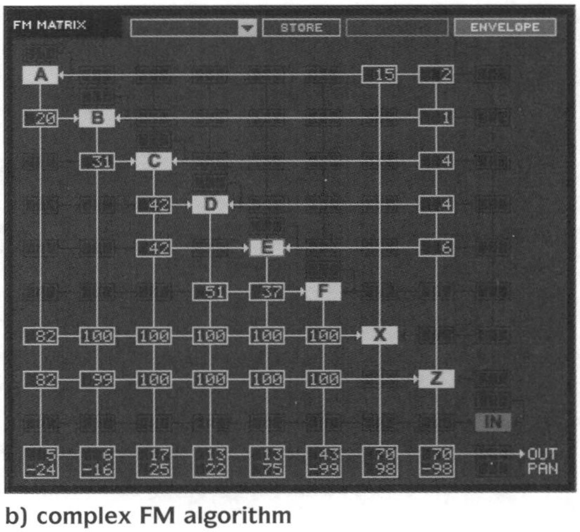

b) complex FM algorithm

the two operators. For example, to connect operator E to operator F, click in the slightly darkened rectangular area just below operator E (and to the left of operator F) and drag the mouse vertically upwards. In this case, operator E is designated as a modulator since it is modulating operator F. If operator F is connected to the main output in the lower part of the matrix then it has been designated as a carrier (see Figure 5.6a). Clicking and dragging the mouse vertically in the slightly darkened rectangular area just above any operator allows the adding of an amount of feedback. Any one operator can be modulated simultaneously by a number of other operators (see Figure 5.6b). Completed algorithms are stored and recalled using the algorithm preset menu above the algorithm matrix display (or are loaded and saved as part of the preset).

Tip

Try using the algorithm preset menu above the algorithm matrix display to recall existing algorithm presets and produce instant radical timbral changes in the currently selected patch.

Operator pages A-F

The parameters for each of the six regular operators (A-F) are identical and accessible separately by clicking on the corresponding green selection button (see Figure 5.7).

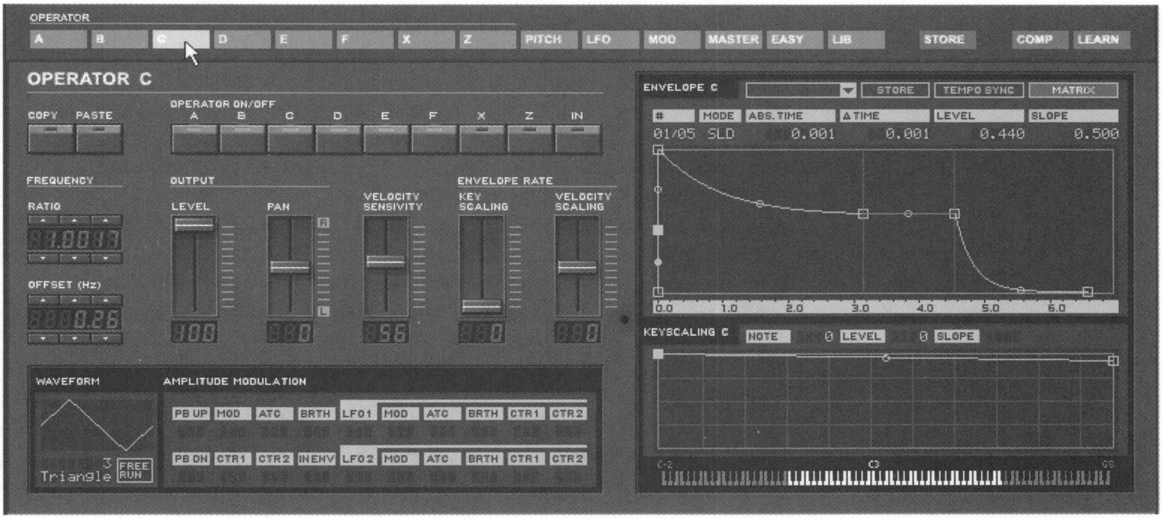

Figure 5.7
FM7 operator page

Each operator features the following parameters:

- operator on/off buttons (OPERATOR ON/OFF) – allows you to choose which operators are active to help focus on the part of the sound you are currently programming. Active operator buttons have an illuminated red LED.
- copy/paste buttons (COPY, PASTE) – for copying/pasting the settings from one operator to/from another.
- frequency ratio (RATIO) – provides a ratio by which the frequency of the currently played note is multiplied to determine the frequency of the operator. For example, for a frequency ratio of 1.0000, a note played at A4 (440Hz) gives a result of 440Hz (i.e. 1 x 440, the same pitch at the fundamental frequency). For a frequency ratio of 2.0000 a note played at A4 (440Hz) produces a result of 880Hz (i.e. 2 x 440, one octave higher or the second harmonic). A frequency ratio of 3.0000 produces the third harmonic and so on.

Frequency ratios are especially useful for establishing the ratio between operators designated as carriers and those designated as modulators (see the FM synthesis section in chapter 3 for more details about operators, carriers and modulators).

- frequency offset (OFFSET) – offsets the frequency of the operator by a set amount (-999Hz to 9999Hz).
- waveform selection (WAVEFORM) – determines the waveform for the operator from a total of 32 different waveshapes. Key sync mode resets the phase of the oscillator each time a note is activated. In Free run mode there is no phase reset.
- operator output level (LEVEL) – sets the master output level for all connection points of the operator on the algorithm matrix where the slider shows the highest value if there are more than one. Useful for raising or lowering multiple outputs of an operator when the relative levels need to be maintained.
- operator pan (PAN) – determines the pan position of the operator when it is designated as a carrier. Mirrored in the pan position field in the algorithm matrix. Likewise, changes to the pan position in the algorithm matrix are reflected on the operator pan slider.
- Velocity sensitivity (VELOCITY SENSITIVITY) – determines how much the amplitude envelope is affected by the velocity of incoming MIDI notes. This results in more amplitude level the harder you hit the keys, if the operator is a carrier, and a brighter timbre, if the operator is a modulator.
- key scaling (KEY SCALING) – determines how much the keyboard pitch affects envelope times where higher keyscaling settings mean that the higher you play on the keyboard the shorter the envelope times become.
- velocity scaling (VELOCITY SCALING) – determines how much the velocity of incoming MIDI notes affect envelope times where positive values mean that high velocities shorten the envelope times and negative values mean that high velocities lengthen the envelope times.
- amplitude modulation matrix (AMPLITUDE MODULATION) – determines the amount by which various modulation sources, (such as modulation wheel, aftertouch, breath control and LFOs 1 and 2), affect the amplitude of the operator's output signal. The amplitude modulation matrix is a replication of that found in the main modulation matrix page (see Modulation page below).
- operator amplitude envelope (ENVELOPE) – governs how the amplitude level of the operator changes over time according to a time-based multiple breakpoint envelope. The envelope time ruler below the envelope display shows time in seconds and milliseconds. Breakpoints are displayed as square handles along the contour line of the envelope. The level of each breakpoint is measured between zero (minimum level) and 1 (maximum level). A small circle between each pair of breakpoints allows the shape of the envelope contour to be modified between concave and convex slopes. Two vertical red lines mark the position of the sustain segment of the envelope. If there are any breakpoints specified between the red lines then the sustain segment is treated as a loop and cycles continuously until the note is released. Right-click (PC)/ ctrl-click (Mac) to insert/delete breakpoints at the desired positions along the envelope contour.

Tip

Drag left or right in the operator envelope time ruler to reveal different parts of the envelope. Drag left or right (PC: right mouse button/Mac: ctrl + mouse button) in the operator envelope time ruler to zoom in or out of the envelope display. Double-click on the operator envelope time ruler to show the whole of the envelope in a single envelope display.

- Envelope parameter strip (#, MODE, ABS TIME, TIME, LEVEL, SLOPE) – the envelope section features a useful parameter strip above the display. The #(number) field shows the currently selected breakpoint number out of the total number of breakpoints. The Mode field can be changed to 'SLiDe' mode or 'FIX' mode where Slide mode keeps the absolute time values of adjacent breakpoints when you edit the time between one pair of breakpoints (changing the overall envelope time) and Fix mode compresses and expands the breakpoints relative to the changes you make between one pair of breakpoints (keeping the overall envelope time the same). 'Abs' (absolute) time displays the time between the onset of the envelope and the selected breakpoint. 'Delta' time displays the time gap between the selected breakpoint and the breakpoint to its left. 'Level' displays the level of the currently selected breakpoint on a scale between 0 and 1. 'Slope' displays the value of the currently selected contour marker which determines the shape of the envelope contour between each pair of breakpoints.
- Envelope function strip ([PRESET], STORE, TEMPO SYNC, MATRIX) – the envelope function strip at the top of the operator envelope pane allows you to recall envelope presets, store your own envelopes as presets, regulate the timing of your envelopes according to tempo by activating tempo sync (the ruler displays note values rather than seconds and milliseconds), and select the FM7 algorithm matrix to display the overall operator configuration for the current patch.
- Keyscaling graph (KEYSCALING) – governs how the operator amplitude changes over the range of the keyboard. The top of the graph represents full amplitude and whenever the curve descends below this point the amplitude is reduced by the chosen amount at the corresponding range of the keyboard. The range of a standard 5-octave keyboard is indicated by the white area in the keyboard display below the graph. The keyscaling curve is created similarly to a standard operator envelope curve using breakpoints and the small circular curve-shaping handles.

Operator X

Operator X is similar to the conventional operators except that it generates noise instead of a periodic waveform. It can also process input signals from other operators. The noise output passes through a low-pass filter and is mixed with the input signal (if present). The mixed signal then passes through a saturation (distortion) stage. Operation X features the following parameters:

- Page 2 and bypass switches (PAGE 2, BYPASS) – page 2 opens the second page of parameters and bypass switches off the operator X effects (for quickly comparing the signal with and without the effects).
- Saturation curve display (SATURATION CURVE) – shows the waveform produced by adjusting the saturation controls (for display purposes only)
- amplitude modulation matrix (AMPLITUDE MODULATION) – similar function to the regular operator amplitude modulation matrix where various sources can be set to affect the amplitude of the operator X output signal (see above).

Page 1 parameters

- noise amplitude slider (AMP) – determines the level of the noise signal.
- noise cut-off slider (CUTOFF) – determines the cut-off frequency of the noise generator's low-pass filter.
- noise resonance slider (RESO) – determines the amount of resonance at the chosen cut-off frequency of the noise generator's low-pass filter.
- saturator gain (GAIN) – determines the level of the signal which is routed to the saturator.
- saturator asymmetry (ASYM) – determines how much the saturation is offset towards the negative amplitudes in the signal.
- saturator limit (LIMIT) – clips the upper and lower limits of the waveform's amplitude where a value of 100 produces no clipping and lower values introduce more clipping.

Page 2 parameters

- Page 2 features a duplication of the noise amplitude slider of page 1 (as described above) and output, velocity sensitivity and envelope rate sliders which are identical to those of the regular operator page described in the 'Operator pages A-F' section, above.

Envelope and keyscaling parameters

- These are identical to the similar functions of the regular operator page as described in the sections 'Operator amplitude envelope' and 'Keyscaling graph', above.

Operator Z

Operator Z is a special signal processing operator which includes two multimode 2-pole 24dB per octave filters. Operator Z features the following parameters:

- Page 2 and bypass switches (PAGE 2, BYPASS) – operate in an identical manner to the equivalent switches of operator X (see above).
- filter curve display (FILTER CURVE) – shows the waveform produced by adjusting the filter controls (for display purposes only).
- Cut-off modulation matrix (CUTOFF MODULATION) – functions in a similar manner to the amplitude modulation matrix of a regular operator except that the modulation for operator Z affects cut-off frequency rather than amplitude.

Page 1 parameters

- cut-off (CUTOFF) – determines the base cut-off frequency for both filters.
- resonance (2 x RESO sliders) – determines the amount of resonance at the chosen cut-off frequency for the corresponding filter.
- envelope amount (ENV AMOUNT) – determines the amount of envelope modulation of the cut-off frequency where positive values increase the effect and negative values decrease the effect.
- mode (2 x MODE sliders) – changes the response of the corresponding filter continuously between low-pass, band-pass and high-pass filter types.

- Cut-off spread (CUTOFF SPREAD) – offsets filter 2's cut-off frequency relative to that of filter 1.
- Serial/parallel (SERIAL PARAL) – changes the routing configuration of the filters continuously between serial (filter 1 followed by filter 2) and parallel (outputs of filters 1 and 2 mixed after processing the same input signal).
- Filter mix (FILTER MIX) – determines the amount of signal from each filter which is heard in the final output signal.

Page 2 parameters

- Page 2 features a duplication of the cut-off slider of page 1 (as described above) and output, velocity sensitivity and envelope rate sliders which are identical to those of the regular operator page described in the 'Operator pages A-F' section, above.

Envelope and keyscaling sections

- These are identical to the similar functions of the regular operator page as described in the sections 'operator amplitude envelope' and 'keyscaling graph' above, except that frequency cut-off is affected rather than amplitude. The keyscaling graph features an additional 1:1 button which, when activated, implements linear tracking of the cut-off frequency across the range of the keyboard.

Pitch page

The pitch page governs all those parameters which are related to pitch. The following parameters are available:

- portamento on/off switch (ON/OFF) – switches portamento on or off. Portamento is the smooth sliding of pitch from one note to another (otherwise known as glissando).
- portamento auto (AUTO) – when activated, portamento only occurs when there is no gap between successive notes (i.e. only when you play legato).
- portamento time (TIME) – determines how long it takes to slide from one note to another.
- analog slider (ANALOG) – emulates the behaviour of analogue circuitry by introducing slight pitch changes in the output signal.
- pitch envelope amount (AMOUNT) – determines the amount by which the envelope affects the pitch.
- pitch envelope velocity sensitivity (VELOCITY SENSITIVITY) – determines how much the pitch envelope is affected by the velocity of incoming MIDI notes. Higher values result in a greater pitch envelope effect the harder you hit the keys.
- pitch envelope key scaling (KEY SCALING) – determines how much the keyboard pitch affects envelope times where higher keyscaling values mean that the higher you play on the keyboard the shorter the envelope times become.
- pitch envelope velocity scaling (VELOCITY SCALING) – determines how much the velocity of incoming MIDI notes affect envelope times where positive values means that high velocities shorten the envelope times and negative values means that high velocities lengthen the envelope times.

- mode (PITCHBEND MODE) – adjusts the pitch bend response between four modes. Normal provides conventional pitch bend response, highest bends only the highest of several simultaneous notes, lowest bends only the lowest of several simultaneous notes and keyon bends notes only for as long as they are held down.
- pitch bend tune (TUNE) – detunes the pitch bend by a fixed amount.
- pitch bend transpose (TRANSP) – transposes the pitch bend by a fixed amount (-24 to +24 semitones).
- pitch modulation matrix – functions in a similar manner to the amplitude modulation matrix of a regular operator except that the modulation affects pitch rather than amplitude.
- microtuning matrix – provides a tuning matrix where you can set up your own tuning scheme or load in presets from the microtuning presets menu. The presets provide many choices including equal-tempered (the standard Western music tuning system), bagpipe, just intonation, Pythagorean, stretch tuning and so on.
- pitch envelope section – This is similar to the envelope section of the regular operator page as described in 'operator amplitude envelope' and 'envelope parameter strip' above, except that pitch is affected rather than amplitude. The pitch envelope has no keyscaling graph.

LFO page

The LFO page features parameters for LFOs 1 and 2. The controls are identical for both LFOs and include the following:

- waveform (WAVEFORM) – determines the waveform for the operator from a total of 32 different waveshapes and allows the setting of a positive or negative sign for the waveform (this inverts the wave). Key sync mode resets the phase of the oscillator each time a note is activated. In Free run mode there is no phase reset.
- on/off (ON/OFF) – switches the LFO on or off.
- tempo sync (TEMPO SYNC) – when activated, regulates the frequency of the LFO according to the current tempo of the host software.
- rate (RATE) – determines the frequency of the LFO.
- delay (DELAY) – specifies a delay time before the LFO reaches its full amplitude (for the gradual onset of a vibrato effect, for example).
- key scaling (KEY SCALING) – determines how much the keyboard pitch affects the LFO rate where higher keyscaling values mean that the higher you play on the keyboard the faster becomes the LFO rate.
- velocity scaling (VELOCITY SCALING) – determines how much the velocity of incoming MIDI notes affect the LFO rate, where higher values means that high velocities speed up the LFO rate.
- LFO modulation matrix – functions in a similar manner to the amplitude modulation matrix of a regular operator except that the modulation affects the amount of LFO rather than amplitude.

Modulation page

The modulation page features a matrix of modulation sources on the horizontal axis and targets for the modulation effect on the vertical axis. The sources are connected to the targets in a similar manner to the connection of operators in the algorithm matrix (see 'Algorithms and algorithm matrix' above). Direct modulation sources include pitch bend wheel, modulation wheel, aftertouch, breath controller, two other controllers (as chosen in the Master page), LFO1, LFO2 and the amplitude envelope of an input signal. The amount of modulation effect of LFOs 1 and 2 can also be regulated according to modulation, aftertouch, breath controller and chosen controllers 1 and 2. The pitch bend value fields can include positive or negative values. A lower strip below the matrix displays the current level of all modulation sources, allows manipulation of the levels with the mouse and provides a reset button which returns all levels to zero.

Tip

Double-click on any numerical value in the modulation matrix, pan positions in the algorithm matrix or slider values in the easy edit page to reset the corresponding parameter to zero (disconnect the target from the modulation source).

Master page

The Master page contains a number of global parameters for the FM7 in the Master section and the parameters for the onboard Effect section. Note that those parameters featuring green digits are not saved as part of a preset.

Master section

The Master section parameters include the following:

- output volume and level meters – the output volume slider regulates the overall level of the FM7. The level of the output signal is shown in the output level meters.
- input volume and level meters – the input volume slider regulates the overall level of any signal routed to the FM7 (when using it as an effects processor). The level of the input signal is shown in the input level meter.
- polyphony (VOICES) – determines the available polyphony for the FM7 up to 64-voice polyphony.
- mono switch (MONO) – when activated implements unison mode where the FM7 performs as a monophonic synthesizer (one note at a time)
- unison voices (UNISON VOICES) – determines the number of voices used per note when in unison mode.
- unison detune (UNISON DETUNE) – detunes the voices used in unison mode for producing rich, chorus-like effects for synth sounds.
- analog (ANALOG) – models the behaviour of analogue circuitry. Higher values result in more 'imperfect' analogue behaviour.
- digital (DIGITAL) – modifies the bit-resolution of the output signal. Higher values result in less bit-resolution and a slightly noisier signal.
- master tune (MASTER TUNE) – provides overall tuning adjustment for the FM7.
- transpose (TRANSPOSE) – transposes the pitch up or down in semitones (+/- two octaves).
- Controller define (CONTROLLER DEFINE) – allows the assignment of controllers to two generic controller parameters (controller 1 and controller 2) which are used for modulation purposes in the modulation matrix.

Tip

Using a combination of the Master page analog and digital sliders helps add 'dirt' and analogue-style 'warmth' to FM sounds, especially in unison mode.

Effect section

The Effect section produces high quality delay, echo, chorus, flange and reverb-like effects for the sounds of the FM7. The parameters are as follows:

- on/off button (EFFECT ON/OFF) – switches the effect section on or off.
- tempo sync button (TEMPO SYNC) – when activated, synchronises the delay time to the current tempo of the host software.
- dry/wet (DRY WET) – regulates the mix between the wet and dry signal where higher values give more of the effect sound.
- delay time (TIME) – determines the initial time delay between each repeat of the delay processor.
- delay feedback (FEEDBACK) – determines how much of the output signal is fed back to the delay input where higher feedback levels result in more repeats.
- delay diffusion (DIFFUSION) – at the zero position a standard single delay effect is produced. As the diffusion slider is set higher a 4-tap stereo delay effect is produced where each delay tap varies slightly in time and is spread across the stereo image.
- delay invert button (INVERT) – inverts the phase of the delay repeats.
- sync delays button (SYNC DELAYS) – synchronises the LFO modulation rate with the delay time.
- filter low-cut (LOW CUT) – reduces the low frequency content of the delay signal where a slider setting of zero produces no effect and higher settings produce progressively more low frequency attenuation.
- filter hi-cut (HI CUT) – dampens the high frequency content of the delay signal where a slider setting of 100 produces no dampening and lower settings produce progressively more high frequency dampening.
- modulation rate (RATE) – determines the rate at which the effect section LFO modulates (changes the length of) the delay times where higher values equal faster modulation rates.
- modulation depth (DEPTH) – determines the depth of the modulation of the delay times or how much the delay times are changed within each cycle of the LFO where a zero setting gives no modulation and higher values result in greater modulation.

Easy edit page

The Easy edit page is an easy-to-use editing environment which reduces the extremely wide range of FM7 parameters to more manageable proportions. This is particularly useful for experimentation and provides a quick way of discovering new sounds. The page includes an effect select section and five groups of sliders which address different aspects of the sound. The parameters are as follows:

- apply (APPLY) – when you have edited the sound clicking on the apply button makes the changes a permanent part of the patch (at which time all the sliders return to zero).
- reset (RESET) – resets all sliders back to zero, returning the sound to its pre-edit state.
- effect selection (EFFECT) – allows the selection of a preset effect for the sound (changing the Master page Effect section accordingly). 'Original' gives the original effect of the sound before any edits were made and 'Off' switches the effect off. The intensity of the effect can be increased or reduced using the 'FX strength' field.
- timbre brightness (BRIGHTNESS) – positive values increase and

negative values decrease the high frequency content of the sound (by raising the output level of operators designated as modulators).

- timbre harmonic (HARMONIC) – changes the harmonic content of the sound. Positive values tend towards more abstract timbres while negative values tend towards simpler sounds (by changing the ratios of the operators).
- timbre detune (DETUNE) – changes the pitch of the carrier operators in multiple-operator algorithms in order to 'thicken' the timbre and create chorus effects.
- timbre envelope amount (ENVELOPE AMOUNT) – determines the amount by which the timbre envelope affects the sound.
- timbre velocity sensitivity (VELOCITY SENSITIVITY) – determines the amount by which the timbre is affected by the velocity of incoming MIDI notes (i.e. how hard you hit the keys).
- timbre envelope (ATTACK, DECAY, SUSTAIN, RELEASE) – provides a global ADSR envelope for how the timbre evolves over time which causes multiple envelope changes within the sound patch. Positive slider values increase the time of the corresponding envelope attack, decay and release segments or increase the level of the sustain segment while negative values decrease the settings.
- LFO rate (RATE) – changes the rate of multiple LFO settings within the patch where positive values increase and negative values decrease the rate.
- LFO vibrato (VIBRATO) – changes the amount by which the LFO settings modulate pitch where positive values increase and negative values decrease pitch modulation.
- LFO timbre (TIMBRE) – changes the amount by which the LFO modulates the timbre of the sound where positive values increase and negative values decrease the effect.
- LFO tremolo (TREMOLO) – changes the amount by which the LFO modulates the amplitude of the sound where positive values increase and negative values decrease the amplitude modulation.
- output volume (VOLUME) – changes the output level of the preset (the overall output level of the FM7 is still controlled by the main output level parameter in the Master page).
- output stereo width (STEREO WIDTH) – at positive settings pans the outputs from multiple operators across a wider stereo field and at negative settings pans all operators further towards the centre of the stereo image.
- output velocity sensitivity (VELOCITY SENSITIVITY) – determines the amount by which the velocity of incoming MIDI notes affects the overall amplitude. Positive values give increased velocity response and negative values give reduced velocity response.
- amplitude envelope (ATTACK, DECAY, SUSTAIN, RELEASE) – provides a global ADSR envelope for how the amplitude evolves over time which causes multiple envelope changes within the sound patch. Positive slider values increase the time of the corresponding envelope attack, decay and release segments or increase the level of the sustain segment while negative values decrease the settings.

User guide

The FM7 features a vast range of sound synthesis parameters but remains comparatively easy to program (at least, by FM synthesis standards). Like any synthesizer, the first steps in getting to know the instrument revolve around listening to the presets and experimenting with the controls. As mentioned above, the heart of FM synthesis with the FM7 is the programming of an algorithm and the programming of the operators which form the building blocks of this algorithm. Rather than directly program the intricate details of the operators themselves it is better to start with some basic slider adjustments in the Easy edit page. Manipulations in the Easy edit page still affect the operators and other parameters but the changes occur 'behind the scenes'. The following three steps quickly transform an FM7 preset into a new sound and demonstrate how simple strategies can produce fruitful results:

1 Select factory default preset 105 ('Electric Harp' by Peter Krischker). Click on any one of the regular operators A to F and select the algorithm matrix using the 'MATRIX' button above the envelope display. Change the algorithm by selecting '4C 4M #2' (meaning 4 carriers and 4 modulators) from the algorithm preset menu. The harp changes into an electric piano (almost!). Click on the 'COMP' button to compare the two sounds. This shows how simply changing the algorithm can radically alter the sound.
2 Following on from (1) above, you might like to change the electric piano-like sound further. Operator D produces a sustaining harmonic which is unsuitable for the piano-like sound. Switch it off by clicking on operator D's on/off switch. Open the Easy edit page and change the current echo effect to a chorus effect by selecting 'Chorus' in the preset effects menu. You are now a little closer to an acceptable patch. Click on the Apply button to write the changes into the edit buffer. Click on the 'COMP' button to compare the current sound with the original harp sound.
3 Although the sound is now different from the original it still retains some of the quality of the original harp. Let's try changing it into something very different; a vibes-like percussion instrument. While still in the Easy edit page, set all the timbre envelope sliders to -99. Set the amplitude envelope decay slider to -9 and the sustain slider to -99. You may now like to add some more spice to the sound. Try setting the timbre harmonic slider to +4, the LFO rate slider to +50, the LFO vibrato slider to +35 and perhaps the amplitude envelope attack to a gentler +20. This creates a brighter and more harmonically interesting tuned percussion instrument. Click on the Apply button to write the changes into the edit buffer. Click on the 'COMP' button to compare the current sound with the original harp sound. You can now hear just how far we have travelled away from the original patch with relatively few manipulations of the parameters.

Let's now consider what actually happened to the operator parameters in the main editing pages when we made the various changes in Easy edit in step 3, above. Setting all the timbre envelope sliders to -99 radically reduced the envelope times of all those operators designated as modulators (which resulted in a percussive attack for the sound). The adjustments to the amplitude envelope sliders altered the amplitude envelope characteristics of all those operators designated as carriers (changing the final decay and sustain characteristics of the sound). Setting the timbre harmonic slider to +4 altered the frequency ratios of two of the modulator operators and one carrier (adding more upper harmonics to the signal). The LFO adjustments affected the main LFO modulation of the pitch (producing a vibrato effect).

Note that the most radical changes involved the envelopes and frequency ratios. This gives you a clue as to how you might approach direct programming in the operator pages themselves.

If you are searching for other ideas, the Randomize function in the Library page might be worth a try. Set OP to 0, FM to 30, ENV to 20, KEYSC to 0, MOD to 10, FX to 5 and ALL to 0. Set the Randomize behaviour to 'Cautious' in the Preferences window. Select any preset and click on the Randomize 'Do it' button. The above settings maintain some of the character of the original throughout several clicks of the 'Do it' button. More extreme settings tend to obliterate the original patch and produce highly abstract sounds.

For more FM7 programming tips and FM synthesis theory see the FM synthesis sections in Chapter 3 and Chapter 6.

Summary and applications

The FM7 is an extremely well-designed and powerful synthesis instrument. It eases the burden of synthesizing FM sounds by providing a wide range of editing pages, a user-configurable algorithm matrix and, in particular, an Easy edit page. It can produce typical FM tones reminiscent of the original DX7 but, due to its extended design, its main strength lies in its ability to produce its own unique timbres. It is particularly stable and has an extremely full MIDI specification. It is supplied with two banks of 128 FM7 presets, one bank of 32 DX200 presets and one bank of 128 original DX7 presets. There are also a wide range of sounds available for download from various sources on the Internet and the instrument can import SysEx soundbanks in DX7, DX7II and DX200 format.

The FM7 is particularly suited to the creation of bass, brass, electric piano, harp, bells, vibes and bright pad and string sounds. It is also capable of very good guitar and flute sounds (check out default preset number 2, Six String and number 9, Tronflute) and produces good lead synths and inspiring tempo sync effects. For the more adventurous, it can process an external audio signal when used as an FX processor within your host software (check out default preset numbers 126 and 127).

Steinberg HALion

Instrument type:	VST sampler
Polyphony:	up to 256
Number of outputs:	12 (4 stereo / 4 mono)
Number of program slots:	128 (16 part multi-timbrality)
Supported interfaces:	VST 2.0
Platform:	PC, Mac

Description

HALion is a VST software sampler supporting 8 to 32-bit samples and featuring extensive, editing, modulation and filtering features (Figure 5.8).

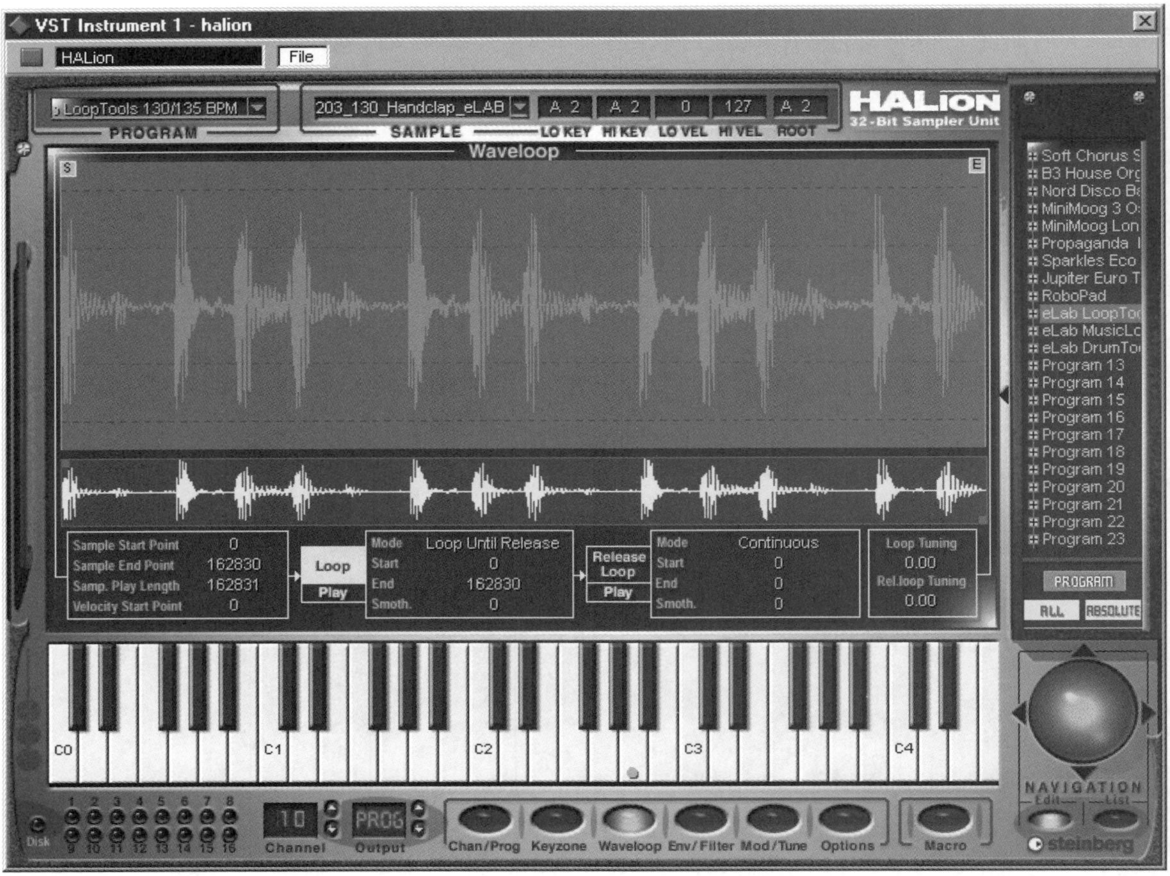

Figure 5.8
Steinberg HALion VST sampler

HALion is comprised of a Macro page and six other pages which are dedicated to different parts of the HALion system. You can navigate to any of these pages by clicking on the corresponding oval blue button (located below the virtual keyboard). HALion is arranged in a classic sampler configuration where groups of samples are assigned to different key and velocity zones. These groups of samples are arranged within programs which can be stored and recalled as required.

Control interface

Macro page

The Macro page is selected by clicking on the Macro button. It shows a number of global parameters which affect all the samples in the currently displayed program. A program is selected using the top left program menu. Try selecting one of the programs which are loaded by default when you first launch HALion, such as 'MiniMoog Osc 3 Bass'. You can then check out the available controls while playing the sound.

Global editing can be made to affect the sound in an absolute sense or relative to any settings which have already been made for individual samples within the program by selecting either 'Edit absolute' or 'Edit relative' in the Macro page options menu. The available parameters on

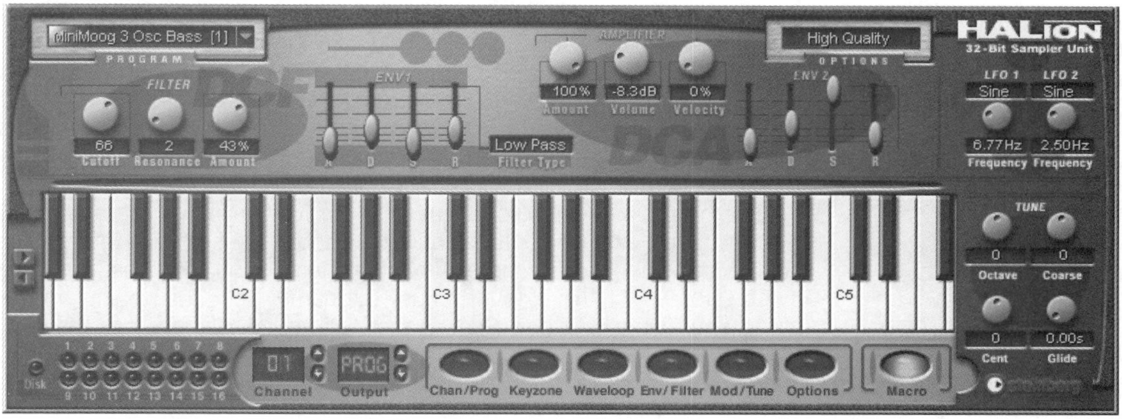

Figure 5.9
HALion Macro page

the Macro page include filter cut-off, resonance, envelope amount, filter ADSR envelope, filter type, amplifier volume, amplifier envelope amount, velocity sensitivity, amplifier ADSR envelope, LFO and tuning settings. If the filter controls produce no effect it is likely that the filter has been bypassed in the Envelope/Filter page. You can also change the output for the program and the MIDI channel. When you change the MIDI channel the current settings in the display change according to any programs which are already loaded into the respective channels. You can monitor incoming MIDI data in the 16 MIDI monitoring LEDs in the lower left corner.

The generic page frame and program list

You can learn a lot about HALion just by experimenting in the Macro page but the heart of the system is found within the other six pages. The other six pages open within a generic frame which contains a virtual musical keyboard, program selection menu, a sample selection menu, key and velocity range menus, the root note for the selected sample, MIDI input activity LEDs, MIDI channel select, audio output channel for the selected MIDI channel and the six blue oval selection buttons (see Figure 5.8). Please note that the screenshots of each page below show only the page itself and do not show the generic frame which is exactly the same for each page.

A trackball-style navigation tool is found to the right of the virtual keyboard. The trackball is used for scrolling and zooming on any editable element within the edit pages or for scrolling in the program list (click on the item you wish to edit). It also allows scrolling the keyboard range in all page views except the macro and waveloop pages.

A program list is found above the navigation tool which is used to display a list of the currently loaded programs and their samples. Programs can be selected here and the samples contained within each program can be viewed and selected by opening the program folder (by clicking on the plus sign to the left of the program name). A range of samples can be selected by holding shift while clicking. You can also decide whether editing affects all samples or only the selected samples by clicking on the ALL button which toggles between 'all' and 'select' mode. This is a very important button since it determines the behaviour of HALion for all editing operations. Editing operations can also be designated as absolute, where the settings follow the exact chosen values, or relative, where editing is relative to any previous settings, by using the ABSOLUTE button which toggles between 'absolute' and 'relative' mode. This is only relevant when you have selected all or a multiple number of samples. The PROGRAM button displays whether you have selected 'all' or 'select' mode and if you are in select mode, it displays whether one or multiple samples have been selected.

The program list is also where you can load in new programs from your hard disk or from other sources. Choose an empty program slot and then select the instrument loading function of your host software (with Cubase VST this is found under the name 'Load Instrument' in the File menu above HALion). Choose the desired file, and the data is loaded into the selected program slot. Alternatively, use 'Import audio files' in the Options page (see below).

The Channel/Program page

The Channel/program page is used to set which program is assigned to each of the 16 MIDI channels and the choice of virtual output for each. Clicking on any of the program slot downward-pointing arrows opens a menu of the currently loaded programs (up to 128).

Figure 5.10
Channel/Program page

The Keyzone page

The Keyzone page shows the velocity and key ranges of each sample on a two dimensional display where the horizontal axis represents the key range and the vertical axis represents the velocity range. The velocity scale is shown on the right of the page and the key range is in relation to the position of the keys on the virtual keyboard. Each sample is displayed as a strip whose size can be dragged to the required proportions within the display using graphic handles. The settings are reflected in the key and velocity range fields above the display which can be used as a guide and to make fine adjustments.

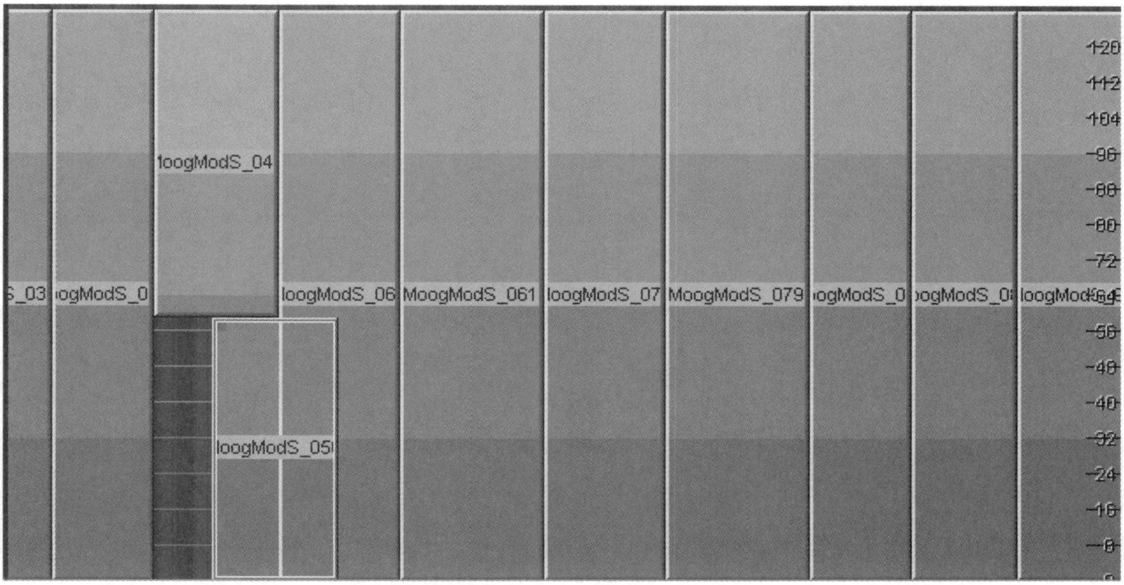

Figure 5.11
Keyzone page

Clicking on a sample selects it. You can also make multiple selections by dragging a selection rectangle around the required samples. This provides an alternative to selecting samples in the program list. A yellow border around the sample (in the page display) indicates that the sample is 'view selected' but not selected for editing. 'View selected' means that this sample's parameters are shown when viewing any information within HALion which refers to the settings of a single sample. A red/yellow border around the sample indicates that the sample is selected for editing and view selected. A red border around the sample indicates that the sample is selected for editing but not view selected. The currently view selected sample is shown in the sample select field above the page display.

The easiest way of editing in the Keyzone page is to drag the sample boxes using the handles. You can move samples to new positions by clicking in the middle of a sample box and dragging. After having moved a sample you may need to change the root key in the root field so that the sample plays back at the correct pitch. Note that all editing also depends upon the status of the ALL/SELECT button located below the program list (see explanation above).

The Waveloop page

The Waveloop page displays the waveform and loop points (if set) for the currently selected sample. To quickly view the samples assigned to each key select 'key activates sample' in the Options page. Now when you press a key on the keyboard the sample assigned to that key is shown in the page view.

The Waveloop page allows you to set a sustain loop, which sustains for as long as you hold down a key, and a release loop which is activated when the key is released. To create a loop, activate the required loop button (Loop or Release Loop) and drag the mouse in the waveform display. You can add crossfades to the sustain loop for click-free looping

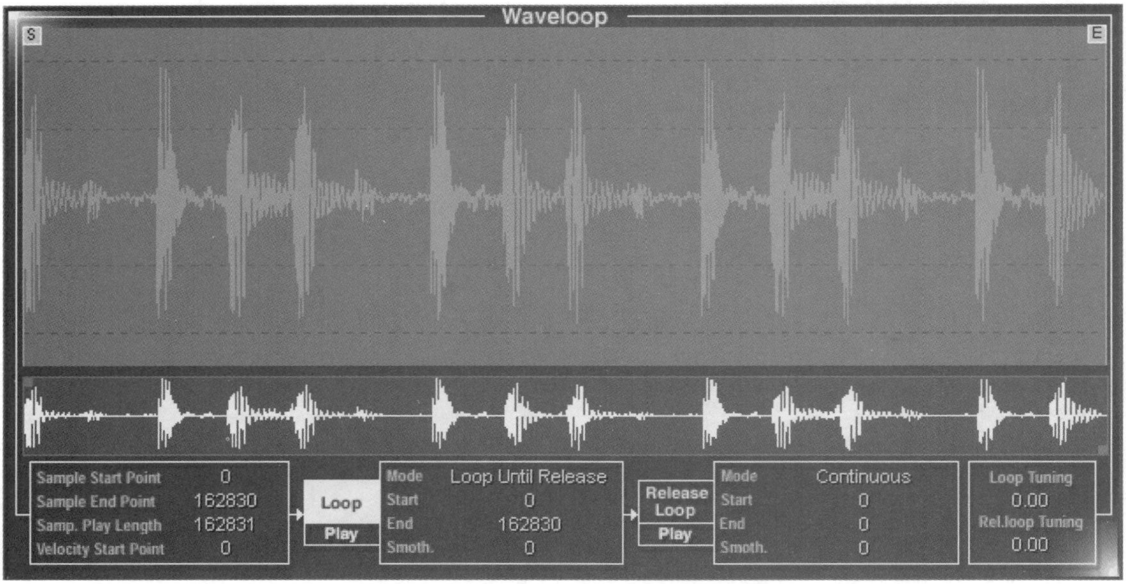

Figure 5.12
Waveloop page

by holding alt and dragging the mouse pointer outside of the loop range. Loops can be set to play back in several modes in the Mode fields and include Loop until release, Loop once, Play until end and Play reverse modes for the sustain loop and Continuous release loop or Single release loop for the release loop.

The Waveloop page also features a thumbnail view of the waveform. You can drag the handles found therein to zoom in to specific segments of the waveform or to show the entire waveform. The start and end points of the sample are shown in the main waveform display with 'S' and 'E' handles. These handles can be dragged to new positions, if required. The looped parts of the waveform are shown in light blue. All parameters in the Waveloop page can also be changed by clicking directly in any of the value fields.

The Envelope/Filter page

The Envelope/Filter page allows the setting of filter and envelope settings for all or a number of selected samples. The parameters are largely the same as those found on the Macro page but arranged on the screen in a different manner. The main difference is that the amplifier and filter ADSR envelopes can be edited graphically. The page also contains a fatness control which adds tube distortion to the signal.

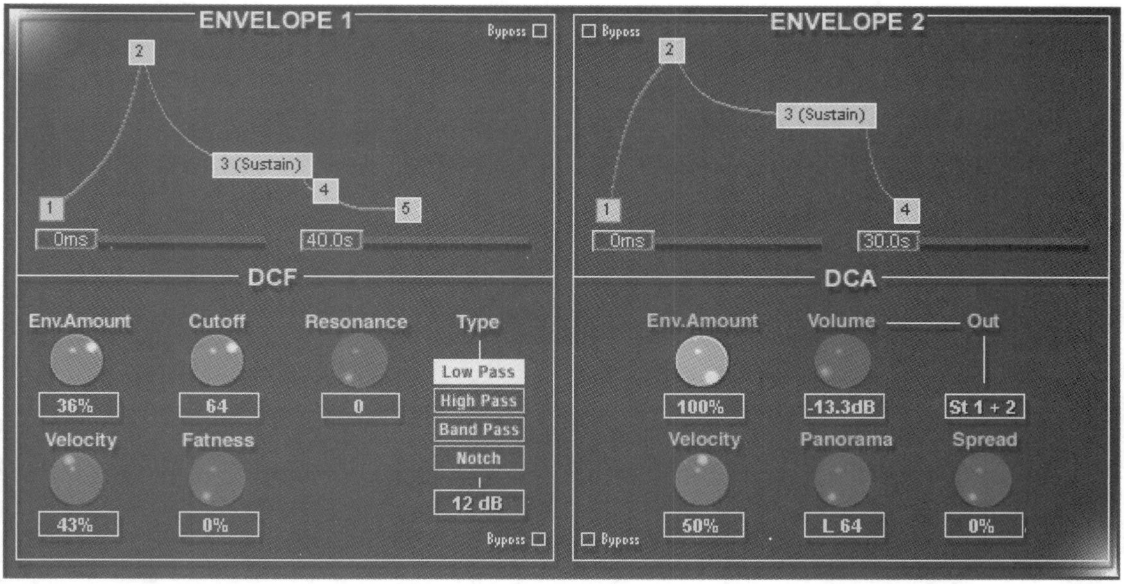

The Modulation/Tune page

The Modulation/Tune page features a modulation matrix and LFO, tuning and grouping sections. The modulation section features source, amount and destination fields where the source is the chosen signal which does the modulating, amount is how much the source modulates the destination (expressed as a simple amount or as some kind of controller) and destination determines which parameter is modulated. The menus for both the source and amount fields are identical. A typical example might be the creation of vibrato effects by using the modula-

Figure 5.13
Envelope/Filter page

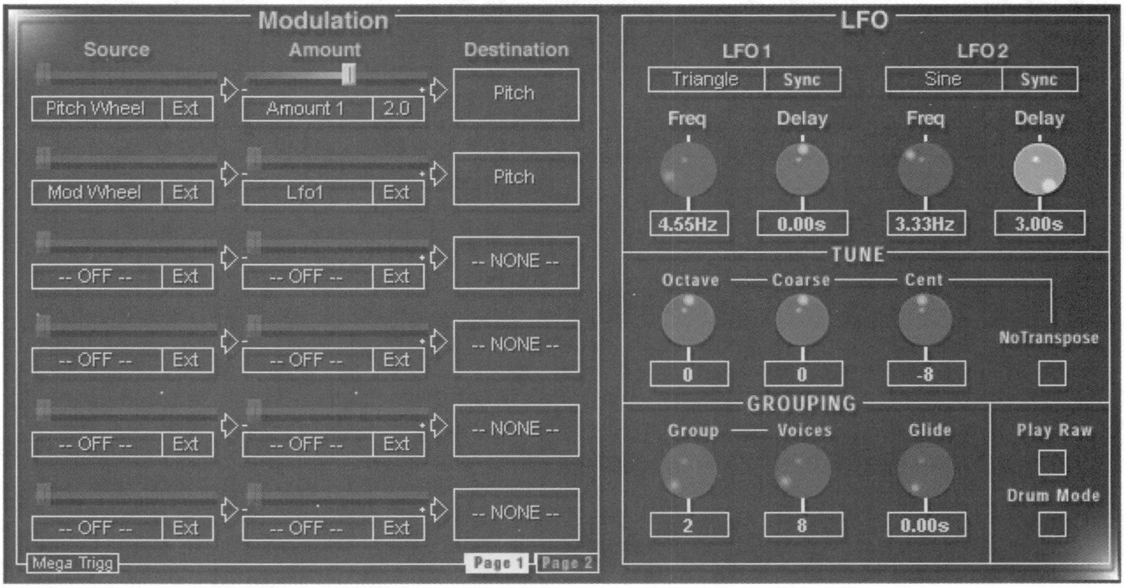

Figure 5.14
Modulation/Tune page

tion wheel. In this case, set the source to modulating wheel, the amount to LFO and the destination to pitch.

The LFO section contains two LFOs with sine, triangle and pulse waveforms and variable frequencies between 0 and 30Hz. The LFOs are selected in the 'source' and 'amount' modulation menus (see above). Tuning controls provide octave, semitone and cent tuning for all or selected samples. Activating the 'No Transpose' field means that samples play back with the same pitch across the entire keyboard. Glide initiates a glissando effect between successive notes (0-3secs). Grouping allows the assignment of samples to 'polyphony groups' (1-16). The number of voices available to each group is regulated using the 'voices' parameter.

The Options page

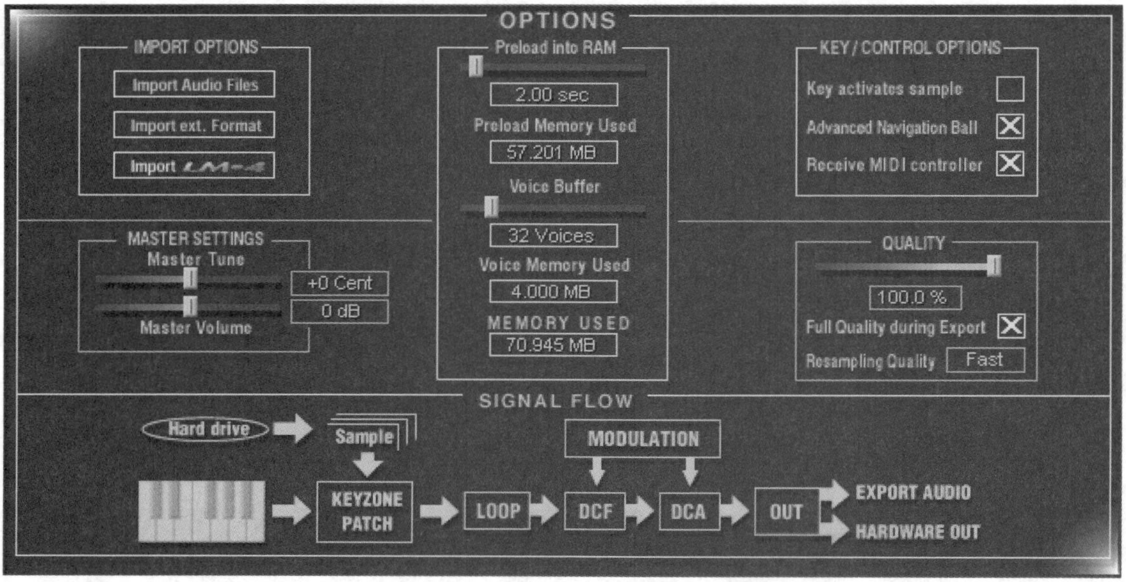

Figure 5.15
Options page

The Options page includes import, master tune and master volume, preload into RAM and voice buffer settings, key and control options and quality setting.

Supported import formats include:

- audio files, HALion bank or instrument files (.fxp or .fxb file extensions) and LM4 MkII bank or instrument files via the 'Import audio files' option.
- soundfonts 2.x, Akai S1000, S2000, S3000, EMU 3, 3X, ESI, 4, 4K, E64, E64000, Esynth, Ultra, REX, REX2 and GIGA via the 'Import ext. Format' option.
- LM4/LM9 script files via the 'Import LM4' option.

The pre-load into RAM and voice buffer settings allow the management of HALion in relation to your computer's resources. The first part of each sample is played from RAM memory rather than directly from the hard disk to ensure instantaneous playback. If you have a large amount of RAM (Steinberg recommend 512MB or more) then you can try allocating more of each sample to RAM to avoid clicks and pops during playback. Allocating more of the sample to RAM takes the strain off the hard drive and helps the smooth operation of HALion. With around 512MB of RAM (or more) you can usually safely raise the pre-load into RAM to around 4 seconds. Playback performance is also dependent upon the number of voices you have allocated in the voice buffer field. A large number of voices demands more from your computer's resources. Between and 16 and 32 voices might be sensible preliminary settings. If you suffer from playback problems then you may need to reduce the pre-load into RAM and voice buffer settings. You can also reduce the playback quality using the quality slider which will provide smoother playback but at a lower resolution. This does not prevent you from exporting your work at full quality by activating the 'full quality during export' option.

Another useful parameter on the Options page is the 'Key activates sample' option. When this is activated, playing a sample activates it in the generic frame above the page display, in the program list and in the Keyzone, Waveloop, Env/Filt and Mod/Tune pages. This provides a quick way of viewing the settings for any sample within a program when editing. It's best to set this to off during normal playback.

User guide

Most users of HALion start by exploring the samples supplied with the program before creating their own sample programs. These are included on four contents CDs (which are best copied to a hard disk in the host system). Once you have chosen which MIDI channel upon which you intend to audition the sounds in the host sequencer software, you need to choose a method of loading in HALion bank or instrument files. Users of Cubase VST can load these using the File load menu just above the HALion display. The alternative is to use 'Import Audio Files' in the Options page. Try using the instrument file type which loads a single program. When using 'Import Audio Files' this can be merged with the current program (if one is in memory) or it can replace the current data. Merging data can be useful for building up a drum/percussion program or for layering sounds together. By selecting new empty program slots in the program list for loading different programs you can build up a number of presets (up to 128). You can later choose from these using the program select field (which opens a menu containing all the programs currently in memory). Loading a bank replaces all the programs currently in memory. Loading samples alone places them in the currently selected program (raw samples loaded in this manner need to be mapped appropriately across the keyboard before you can play them).

For multi-timbral operation use the Channel/Program page to select which program plays back on which MIDI channel. This is also where you decide which virtual audio output is used for each sound.

The first step in any basic editing is to set the All/Select button below the program list. This directs editing to all samples in the currently displayed program, to a single selected sample or to a multiple selection of samples.

HALion works extremely well as a playback device for preset programs and many users may be happy to use it entirely for this purpose. However, many others will be keen to create programs from their own original samples using HALion's Keyzone, Waveloop and other pages.

Please see the section entitled 'Creating your own sample program in Steinberg's HALion' in Chapter 6, which outlines this process in detail.

Summary and applications

HALion is a powerful, fully-featured sampler which equals the performance of hardware units. It is supplied with a generous sample library on four contents CDs (around 2Gb) which includes drum kits, drum loops, vocal samples, music loops and sound effects supplied by eLAB, and acoustic piano, nylon string guitar, 6-string bass, drums, percussion, electric piano, clavinet, organ, electronic drums, synth basses and much more supplied by Wizoo. Setting up your own samples in HALion is particularly quick and easy due to the intelligent, intuitive user interface. It performs particularly well when run within Cubase. It fulfils a wide range of musical tasks and with the right sample library and sufficient CPU power/RAM memory manages entire arrangements with ease.

Steinberg LM-4 MARK II

Instrument type:	virtual drum module (using sample playback)
Polyphony:	64 (18 polyphonically playable drum pads with up to 20 velocity zones per pad)
Number of outputs:	12 (3 stereo / 6 mono)
Number of program slots:	each LM-4 MK II bank can contain up to 20 drum sets
Supported interfaces:	VST 2.0
Platform:	PC, Mac

Description

The LM-4 MK II is a virtual drum module which uses samples loaded into RAM memory to produce its sounds (Figure 5.16). It features super accurate timing resolution difficult to match on external MIDI controlled devices.

Control interface

The LM4 MK II interface features a default view, as in Figure 5.16 above, and layer and edit modes which are displayed by clicking on the layer and edit buttons (see Figure 5.17, below).

The default view

The LM-4 MK II's default appearance features 18 virtual drum pads each with a name, volume and tuning faders for each pad and master volume and tuning dials in the right panel. The details of the controls are as follows:

- Drum pads – the drum pads are located in the lower half of the LM-4 MK II window. Each drum pad triggers a separate sample or series of velocity layered samples previously loaded into the unit. Each pad has a name which varies according to which drum set has been selected. As well as being loaded from a bank or program, samples can be assigned by directly dragging WAVE or AIFF onto the pads from the computer's desktop. Samples can also be loaded using a file

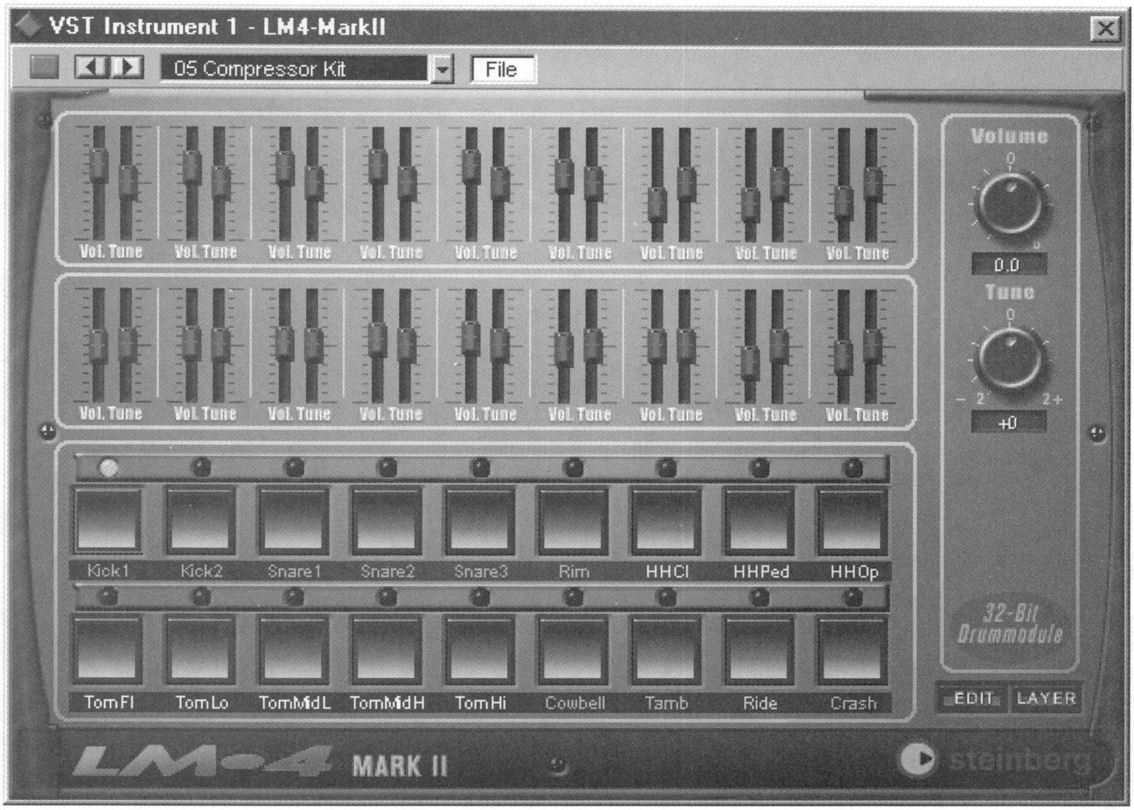

Figure 5.16
Steinberg LM-4 MK II drum module default interface

dialogue, copied or pasted between pads, or deleted, by right-clicking (PC)/ctrl-clicking (Mac) on the pad and selecting the appropriate function from the pop-up menu.

- Volume and tuning faders – the volume and tuning faders are arranged in pairs in the upper half of the LM-4 MK II window. Each pair controls the volume and pitch of the pad in the corresponding position in the lower half of the window. To centre the tuning or volume click on the fader while holding 'Ctrl' on the computer keyboard.
- Volume and tuning dials – the master volume and tuning dials provide overall volume and tuning control for the unit.

Layer and edit mode

Clicking on the layer and/or edit buttons above the Steinberg logo reveals the other aspects of the control interface. The edit display replaces the volume and tuning faders and the layer display replaces the master volume and tune parameters in the right-hand display. The 18 pads remain visible at all times.

The edit interface displays the information for the currently selected pad (illuminated in yellow) and features the following:

- Replica volume and tuning sliders and additional velocity slider – the volume and tuning sliders mirror the sliders of the default interface.

Figure 5.17
LM4 MK II drum module with layer and edit modes displayed

The velocity slider regulates the amount of velocity response for the currently selected pad when the LM-4 MK II is triggered via MIDI.

- Graphic amplitude envelope – when the envelope bypass switch is not activated an envelope can be set up in the graphic envelope display to control the amplitude envelope of the currently selected sound. Use the graphic handles or manipulate the dials. A zoom switch allows you to zoom in on the attack segment of the envelope.
- Bitcrusher and reverse functions – allow the creation of effects by changing the bit-resolution of the sample or reversing it.
- Group and voicing – allow the distribution of the LM4's potential 64 voices among 10 groups so that you can program open and closed hi-hat chokes, for example. The names under the 18 pads are colour-coded according which groups are assigned. The Global option in the Group menu allows the setting of the number of voices available to the LM4 as a whole.
- Output and panorama – allows the selection of an output for the currently selected pad. Each pad can be allocated to any of the three stereo outputs or six mono outputs.
- Panorama – determines the pan position of the currently selected pad in the stereo mix, assuming that a stereo output has been chosen.

The layer display shows the sample(s) assigned to the currently selected pad (illuminated in yellow) and features the following:

- Velocity stacking window – when more than one sample has been assigned to a pad they are stacked in the layer display. The velocity setting for each sample is changed by dragging the small handle at the top of each sample block. The order of the samples is changed by alt-clicking and dragging the sample block. A local menu for other sample-related functions is opened by right-clicking (PC)/ctrl-clicking (Mac) in the layer display.
- Key range fields – the upper and lower key range for each sample is adjusted using the key range fields below the layer display.

User guide

Banks are loaded into the LM-4 MK II using standard VST 2.0 .fxb files and these may contain up to 20 drum sets. Once the bank is loaded, each drum set is accessed by selecting a different program number. It is also possible to save and load single drum sets using standard VST 2.0 effects files (.fxp extension).

For recording purposes, the LM-4 MK II can be triggered via MIDI or from the on-screen pads, (to enable the pads click on the LM-4 MK II logo). Sample files can be dragged directly onto the pads or directly into the layer display and samples can be copied and pasted between pads (see Drum pads, above). Up to twenty layers can be assigned to a single pad and pads respond polyphonically. The key ranges of pads can overlap.

When programming you own settings make sure you have selected the correct pad before making the adjustments. Any changes are memorised and may be saved as part of a program or bank and are also retained if you save the song in the host application.

> **Tip**
>
> To define a default bank which is automatically loaded each time you launch the LM4 MK II, assemble the bank of kits as desired (making sure that all samples have been found) and then store the bank in the same folder as the LM4 MK II, naming it as 'lm4MKIIdef.fxb'.

Summary and applications

The LM-4 MK II is supplied with an additional CD containing 35 excellent kits. These include velocity mapped kits, kits with vinyl-style special effects, big reverberant kits and processed studio kits. Those needing to expand their library can build their own kits very quickly since samples can be dragged directly onto the pads and the user interface is generally highly intuitive.

The LM-4 MK II is a fully functional and highly accurate drum module which fulfils any role which might normally be assigned to such a device. Once the MIDI part is recorded, the samples are triggered with pinpoint accuracy which is difficult to match in a real-world unit. The load on the CPU is minimal since the LM-4 MK II triggers samples which are loaded into RAM memory.

Steinberg Model E

Instrument type:	virtual analogue synthesizer
Polyphony:	up to 64 note simultaneous multi-timbral playback on 16 MIDI channels
Number of outputs:	4 stereo
Number of program slots:	128
Supported interfaces:	VST 2.0
Platform:	PC, Mac

Description

The Steinberg Model E is a multi-timbral virtual analogue polyphonic synthesizer based upon the design of the original Minimoog Model D (Figure 5.18).

Figure 5.18
Steinberg Model E virtual analogue synth

Control interface

The controls of the user interface are located in a number of separate groups on the front panel, the first of which features the following parameters:

- Oscillator Modulation switch – activates/de-activates modulation of the oscillators for vibrato and other effects via the modulation wheel of an external MIDI keyboard or an existing track containing modulation data.
- Tune – regulates the global tuning for the current user interface panel.
- Glide – introduces a glissando or 'slide' effect between successive notes. When set at its minimum position Glide has no effect and the pitch steps between notes as normal.
- Modulation Mix – determines the ratio of the modulation signal between oscillator 3 and a noise generator. This becomes the modulation source for the pitch of the oscillators or for the frequency of the cut-off (according to the status of the oscillator modulation and filter modulation switches).
- Mono switch – switches the current Model E channel into monophonic mode where only one note at a time may be triggered.
- Oscillator 3 switch – activates/de-activates MIDI triggering of oscillator 3. When activated oscillator 3 responds to incoming MIDI notes in the same way as oscillators 1 and 2 and can be used as part of the signal you hear to create 'thicker' tones. When de-activated it becomes a pure signal generator which does not respond to incoming

MIDI notes and which is normally used as an LFO source. In this mode, the volume level for oscillator 3 would normally be set to zero.

The VCO section

The VCO (Voltage Controlled Oscillator) section is where you choose the octave and the waveform for each of the three oscillators using the Range and Waveform rotary switches. The tuning of oscillators 2 and 3 can be further adjusted using the Frequency dials and oscillator 3 can be used as an LFO (Low Frequency Oscillator). The details of the VCO controls are as follows:

- Range control – selects the octave for the oscillator between six octave bands. When using oscillator 3 as an LFO, its range control would usually be switched to LO.
- Frequency dial – governs the tuning of oscillators 2 and 3 relative to oscillator 1 over +/- 7 semitones.
- Waveform control – selects the wave shape for the oscillator between triangle, triangle/sawtooth combination, sawtooth, wide square, medium square and narrow square.

The Mix section

The Mix section regulates the levels of the three oscillators and allows the possibility of adding white or pink noise to the signal. The details of the Mix section controls are as follows:

- Oscillator faders – regulate the respective levels for each of the oscillators.
- Noise fader – regulates the level of noise which may be added to the signal.
- White/pink noise switches – toggles the type of noise generated.

Filter section

The filter elements for the Model E include the following parameters:

- 2 pole/4 pole switch – toggles the filter type between 2 or 4 pole operation. The poles refer to the number of elements in the circuit which are used to produce the filtering effect, where each element represents 6dB of attenuation. The 2 pole setting therefore reduces frequencies above the cut-off point at a rate of 12dB/octave and the 4 pole setting reduces frequencies at a rate of 24dB/octave. (The 4 pole setting uses more processing power).
- Filter Modulation switch – when activated, allows the modulation of the filter using the LFO.
- Keyboard control switches – govern whether the MIDI keyboard controls the cut-off frequency of the filter ('key tracking').
- Cut-off – determines the frequency cut-off point .
- Emphasis – emphasises the frequencies around the cut-off point .
- Amount – determines the amount of filter envelope control over the cut-off frequency. When set to its highest position the envelope exerts its maximum effect.
- Attack, decay and sustain – modulates the cut-off frequency to create changes in the spectral evolution of the sound over time (similar to a standard ADSR envelope).

VCA (Voltage Controlled Amplifier)

Identical attack, decay and sustain controls are provided below the filter envelope controls of the same name. These behave in the same manner as the filter envelope controls except that they determine how the amplitude of the sound changes over time. The VCA also includes a Release On switch which, when activated, adds a release segment to the sound (a portion of the sound which dies away after you release the key on the MIDI keyboard). The duration of the release phase is determined by the value of the decay dial.

Lower panel parameters

The Model E features a lower panel which contains a number of miscellaneous displays and parameters. These include the following:

- MIDI activity LEDs – monitor the presence of incoming MIDI data on the Model E's 16 MIDI channels.
- Channel selector – allows the selection of the MIDI channel and corresponding interface panel for each of the 16 channels.
- Output selector – allows the selection of one of four audio outputs for the currently active interface panel.
- Program selector – allows the selection of one of the 128 programs in the currently loaded bank. Clicking and holding directly in the number display opens a menu containing all the program names of the current bank.
- Program display – displays the name of the currently selected program.
- Copy, paste, and compare buttons – allow the copying and pasting of programs to different program locations and the comparison of a currently edited program with the previously edited status.
- VCF velo control – determines the sensitivity of the filter to the velocity of incoming MIDI notes.
- VCA velo control – determines the sensitivity of the amplifier to the velocity of incoming MIDI notes.
- Spread – determines the amount of random auto-panning which is applied to each note.
- Volume – governs the output volume of the current channel.
- Panorama – governs the pan position of the output in conjunction with the Spread control.
- Voices selector – determines the number of voices which are available for each channel. The Model E allows a total polyphony of 64 voices.

User guide

The four outputs of the Model E can be routed to four separate stereo audio channels in host applications which support multiple outputs. The sound output of any of the 16 channels can be directed to any of these four outputs and by using the panorama dial to pan the sound to the extreme left or right two different sounds can be routed through the same output to arrive in the host application's audio mixer on separate monophonic channels. The latter is useful for increasing the number of sounds which can be individually output from the Model E. Of course, several sounds can also be routed through the same output.

In order to avoid confusion when using several channels simultaneously make sure that the MIDI channel of the Track you are currently using in the Arrange window corresponds to the channel number of the currently displayed Model E front panel.

Preliminary experimentation with the Model E might revolve around the cut-off, emphasis and amount controls in conjunction with the filter's envelope generator. In 4 pole mode the cut-off and emphasis are more responsive and the results tend to be warmer. The choice of six waveforms per oscillator means that a wide range of tone colour can be achieved just by changing the waveform combination. Try selecting the triangle wave for all three oscillators as a good starting point for bell and flute-like tones. Try combinations of wide, medium and narrow square waves as starting points for piano and clarinet-like tones and combinations of sawtooth and mixed triangle/sawtooth waveforms for brass-like tones. To 'thicken' or add 'chorus' to the sound use the tuning dials of oscillators 2 and 3.

Careful attention should be given to the VCF velo and VCA velo dials to make sure that the Model E is performing as desired relative to the velocity of incoming MIDI notes. The spread dial is convenient for adding a sense of dynamic movement to a musical arrangement but care should be taken not to over-use the effect.

Summary and applications

The Model E is supplied with five banks of sounds each containing around 70 patches created by various sound designers. These give a good idea of the range of tone colour available and make good starting points for creating your own patches. This instrument can produce classic rich synth sounds and is excellent for bass, pad, brass and pure bell-like tones. It can also be used effectively to create automatic chords and special tunings using all three oscillators. Its multi-timbral capability is its main strength and some very big sounds and complex arrangements can be achieved by using two or more modules simultaneously.

GForce M-Tron

Instrument type:	sample playback instrument
Polyphony:	35
Number of outputs:	1
Number of program slots:	up to 54 (according to currently available sound library)
Supported interfaces:	VST 2.0
Platform:	PC, Mac

Description

The GForce M-Tron is a virtual emulation of the classic Mellotron keyboard instrument (Figure 5.19).

The concept of the Mellotron was originally developed in the USA by Harry Chamberlin in the 1950's. Following reliability problems with early designs the idea was later developed in the UK by the Bradley brothers and was in production between 1963 and 1986. The instrument featured a 35-note keyboard where each key triggered the playback of a different sound stored on 3-track 3/8 inch tapes. Each key triggered its

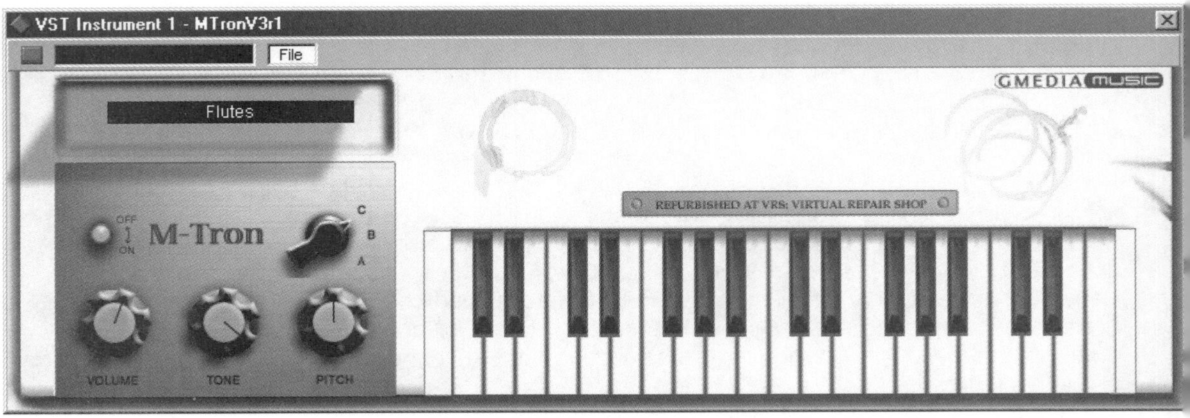

Figure 5.19
GForce M-Tron

own tape and there were no loops involved. The standard maximum playback time was around 8 seconds.

GForce have kept most of the features of the original instrument in their M-Tron emulation and have paid particular attention to the authenticity of the sound samples. The sound library is at the heart of the sonic identity of the M-Tron.

Control interface

M-Tron features a single interface window with a virtual keyboard which can be played using the mouse button. The control parameters have deliberately been kept at a simple level so as not to differ too much from the characteristics of the real-world instrument. They include the following:

- volume – changes the output level of the M-Tron.
- tone – produces no filtering at its maximum position and filters progressively more high frequencies as it is turned to the left.
- pitch – changes the pitch up or down by 15%. Produces the original pitch when at its centre position.
- 3-position function dial – when set at position A you hear the default sound of the M-Tron and the panel lid is closed. Position B opens the panel lid where you can adjust the attack and release characteristics for the currently loaded sound. Position C allows you to select other 'tape banks' from a pop-up menu.

Tip

The vintage sounds of M-Tron can benefit from effects processing using the available plug-ins of your host software. Try echo, delay, chorus, flanging or phasing effects, especially on the choir, string and brass sounds. You can also layer sounds by loading more than one instance of M-Tron.

User guide

The M-Tron is installed onto the hard drive of your choice which allows you to decide where the samples are to be stored. This is useful since the samples take up a considerable amount of hard disk space (around 600MB). The m-tron.dll file can later be dragged into your vst plugins folder. You are given the choice as to which samples you want copied to your hard drive during the installation procedure.

The operation of M-Tron is very easy due to its deliberately simple interface. Its MIDI response is also deliberately simple in an effort to ensure that the instrument plays like the original. The attack and release controls provide simple envelope shaping which is appropriate for the vintage approach of M-Tron.

Summary and applications

The design principle of the M-Tron is to reproduce as faithfully as possible the original sound and performance characteristics of the real-world Mellotron. To this end GForce have endowed their emulation with carefully recorded samples from the original tapes including the hiss, wow and flutter. There are no loops and the instrument is not velocity sensitive, just like the original. They even went as far as including coffee stains on the front panel! The only slight downside is that the samples take a short while to load each time you select a new sound.

M-Tron is suitable for musical applications which require the warmth and character of classic, vintage sounds. It provides a refreshing alternative to the clean, often clinical, sounds of modern sampling technology. The original installation CD is supplied with a range of 28 sounds including brass, choirs, flutes, accordions, rhythms, strings, vibes and saxophones. GForce supply a further bank of 26 sounds called 'Tape Banks Vol.1' which features other similar vintage instruments like the Chamberlin, Birotron and the Roland VP330 (as well as the Mellotron) and includes clarinet, double bass, cello, woodwind, choirs, strings, organs, guitar and wine glasses. To store all of the sounds of either one of these banks requires around 600MB of free hard disk space.

Native Instruments Pro-52

Instrument type:	virtual analogue synthesizer
Polyphony:	up to 32 voices
Number of outputs:	1
Number of program slots:	512
Supported interfaces:	VST 2.0, DXi, MAS, DirectConnect
Platform:	PC, Mac

Description

The Pro-52 is a virtual emulation of the Prophet 5 analogue synthesizer featuring a user interface which matches the control surface of the original instrument (Figure 5.20).

The Prophet 5, developed by Sequential Circuits Incorporated, was released in 1977. It featured five note polyphony and was the first truly polyphonic synthesizer offering memories that stored every parameter. Due to its distinctive warm sound and programmability the Prophet 5 soon became a legend and is now a collectable vintage instrument. The Pro-52 is a digital replica and its characteristics are based upon an analysis of the analogue circuitry of the original instrument. It is an impressive feat of software engineering and Native Instruments have excelled in producing a realistic emulation of the real thing.

Control interface

The front panel controls are arranged in groups according to their function and are comprised of the following:

Oscillator A

Oscillator A generates a periodic waveform which is normally used as

Figure 5.20
Native Instruments Pro-52 virtual synthesizer

the predominant tuned pitch element of the sound. It has the following parameters:

- FREQ (frequency) – determines the base pitch of the tone (4 octaves in semitone steps).
- SHAPE (waveshape) – selects the shape of the waveform (sawtooth, pulse or both).
- PW (pulse width) – when the pulse wave is selected, PW varies the percentage duration (or width) of the positive component of the waveform (1% to 99%)
- SYNC – forces Oscillator A to restart its waveform in synchronisation with the waveform of Oscillator B. In sync mode, the frequency of Oscillator A affects the timbre and the pitch is governed by Oscillator B.

Oscillator B

Oscillator B is used for the production of a second tone or as a modulation source for Oscillator A. It can be disconnected from the incoming MIDI data to allow independent operation.

- FREQ (frequency) – determines the base pitch of the tone (4 octaves in semitone steps). When in Lo Freq mode it determines the low frequency modulation between 0.3 and 30 Hz.
- FINE – fine tunes the base pitch of the tone over a range of one semitone.
- SHAPE (waveshape) – selects the shape of the waveform (sawtooth, triangle or pulse).
- PW (pulse width) – functions the same as the pulse width control for oscillator A.
- LOFREQ (low frequency switch) – when activated, oscillator B becomes a low frequency oscillator (LFO) with a frequency range of

0.3 to 30Hz.
- KEYB (keyboard switch) – when activated, the pitch of oscillator B is governed by incoming MIDI notes.

Mixer

The mixer combines the outputs from oscillators A and B and, if desired, allows white noise to be included before sending the resulting signal to the Filter. The mixer features three controls as follows:

- OSCA (oscillator A) – determines the level of the signal from oscillator A.
- OSCB (oscillator B) – determines the level of the signal from oscillator B.
- NOISE – determines the level of white noise.

Filter section

The Pro-52 filter is a 24dB-per-octave low pass resonant filter with a dedicated ADSR envelope generator. It features the following parameters:

- CUTOFF – determines the frequency cut-off point .
- RESONANCE – emphasises a band of frequencies around the cut-off .
- ENV AMOUNT (envelope amount) – determines the amount of filter envelope control over the cut-off frequency.
- KEYB (keyboard switch) – when activated, the cut-off frequency varies according to any incoming MIDI notes.
- Standard ADSR filter envelope .

Amplifier section

The amplifier section features a similar ADSR envelope generator to that of the filter section .

POLY – MOD section

The poly-mod section allows the modulation of any combination of the frequency of oscillator A, the pulse width of oscillator A and the filter cut-off. The choice of modulator for this purpose is either the filter envelope or oscillator B, or a mix of both.

LFO section (low frequency oscillator)

The LFO section generates a low frequency modulation signal for the wheel-mod section. The frequency control adjusts the frequency range between 0.04Hz and 20Hz. When the MIDI switch is activated the LFO locks to any incoming MIDI clock data, the resolution of which is then governed by the frequency control. The shape of the modulation signal is determined by selecting any combination of sawtooth, triangle or square waveforms.

WHEEL-MOD section

Once the LFO section is generating the modulation signal, the wheel-mod section determines where this signal is routed. The LFO/NOISE control determines the mix between the LFO section's signal and an additional pink noise signal. When set at its minimum position the LFO signal alone is employed. The final modulation signal can be routed to any combination of the frequencies of oscillators A and B, the pulse width of oscillators A and B or the filter cut-off.

Other controls

The Pro-52 has a number of other controls distributed over the front panel which include the following:

- GLIDE – introduces a portamento or 'slide' effect between successive notes.
- UNISON – switches the Pro-52 into monophonic response where all voices are allocated to the currently playing note.
- VOICES – displays/adjusts the number of voices currently available to the Pro-52 synthesis engine.
- ANALOG dial – regulates the behaviour of the Pro-52 between digital mode (the minimum dial setting), when the synthesis engine behaves with mathematical precision analogue mode, when the synthesis engine emulates the actual behaviour of real analogue circuitry (the higher the setting the more analogue-style imperfections are introduced into the signal).
- VEL (velocity sensitivity) – when enabled, varies the amplifier envelope by 90% and the filter envelope by 70% according to the velocities of incoming MIDI notes.
- RELEASE – when enabled, allows normal release response as set by the filter and amplifier envelopes. When disabled, all release times are set to their minimum values.
- TUNE (rotary control) – provides global master tuning over a range of three semitones.
- A440 – provides a continuous A-440Hz signal when activated.
- VOLUME – provides global output level control.
- MIDI – is for MIDI monitoring purposes and flashes whenever MIDI data is received.

Effects section

The Pro-52 also features an effects section where the output signal can be processed with chorus, flanging and delay effects. This features the following:

- TIME – sets the basic delay time of 4 parallel delay lines between 1msec and 1sec.
- SPREAD – spreads the delays of the 4 delay lines to different times for diffusing the delay effect.
- DEPTH – applies LFO modulating signals to each of the delay times for chorus and flanging effects.
- RATE – determines the rate of the LFO modulation between 0.25 and 25Hz.
- FEEDBACK – feeds back the output of the effect to the input for longer lasting echo and other effects.
- LPF and HPF – low and high pass filtering for the effect signal.
- WET – determines the mix of the wet (effected) and dry signal.
- INV – inverts the phase of the effects signal.
- SYNC – synchronises the LFO modulation of the 4 delay lines and ensures that the delay times are rhythmically related.
- MIDI – synchronises the delay times to MIDI tempo (according to the resolution set by the Time dial).

Load, Save and Programmer functions

The load and save buttons allow the import and export of sound programs (patches) to disk. Sounds can be loaded or saved in several formats which can be identified by the file extension. The options are as follows:

- .p5a is for all 512 programs.
- .p5f is for a file (64 programs loaded into or saved from the currently selected file).
- .p5b is for a bank (8 programs loaded into or saved from the currently selected bank).
- .p5p is for a single program.

The currently selected file, bank and program numbers are shown in the Programmer section display and new programs can be selected by clicking the desired combination of file, bank and program number buttons. The name of the current selection is shown in the standard name display at the top of the window.

To store an edited program within the Pro-52, enable the record button and then select a program location. At this point the red light of the record button goes out indicating that the edited program has been stored at the chosen location.

User guide

The rotary controls of the Pro-52 are adjusted by clicking on the chosen control and then moving the mouse up or down vertically. For fine adjustments hold down the shift key at the same time. (An alternative rotary action for adjustments can be selected by clicking on the NI logo while holding down the shift key). A retractable keyboard is included with the interface which can be opened/closed by clicking on the Pro-52 label. The keyboard includes virtual pitch and modulation wheels. The modulation wheel position is saved along with the rest of the program.

Patches can be dialled up very quickly by clicking directly in the program number display in the programmer section and moving the mouse up or down vertically. Alternatively use the numbered buttons in the 'program select' section in combination with the file and/or bank buttons. (See also 'Exploring the presets of the NI Pro-52' in Chapter 6.)

Tip

If your controller keyboard features a modulation wheel (or sliders) which can be assigned to MIDI controller numbers try manipulating the Pro-52's cut-off, resonance or envelope amount parameters in real-time performance by assigning wheels or sliders to MIDI controller numbers 70, 71 or 72.

Summary and applications

The Pro-52 is a sophisticated instrument capable of a wide range of expressive tones and it sounds and feels like a real-world synthesizer. It has the luxury of an enormous patch memory capacity of 512 which comes filled with an excellent collection of factory presets. Just like the original Prophet 5 it is particularly suited to the creation of warm strings and pads, powerful lead synths and rich bass sounds.

Native Instruments Reaktor

Instrument type:	state-of-the-art multiple synthesizer/sampler/sequencer/effects processor and modular synthesizer/sampler creation environment
Polyphony:	up to 64
Number of outputs:	1 stereo
Number of program slots:	128 per instrument
Supported interfaces:	VST 2.0, DirectX, DXi
Platform:	PC, Mac

Description

Reaktor is a modular sound synthesis and musical processing environment for the creation of your own unique synthesizers, samplers, drum modules and effects processors or for the exploration of the preset instruments (ensembles) found in Reaktor's extensive libraries (Figure 5.21).

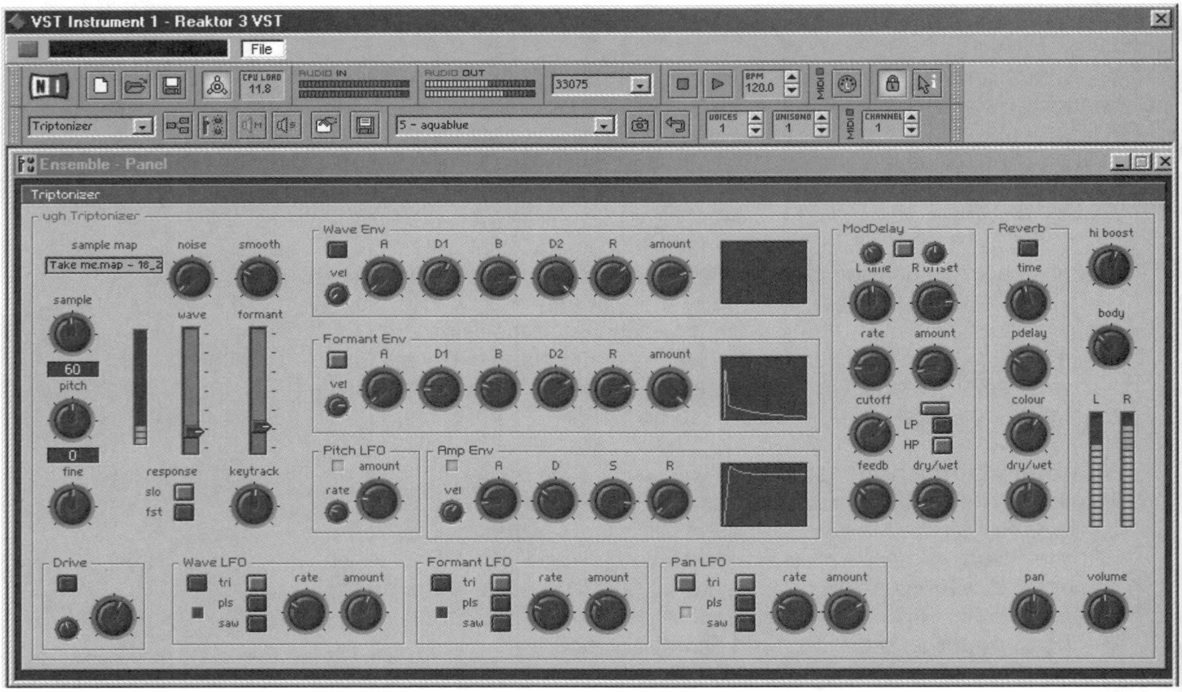

Figure 5.21
Reaktor modular software for synthesis, sampling and effects processing. Here, a control panel for a sample manipulation instrument called Triptonizer is loaded in the ensemble panel window.

Reaktor already has a history as a stand-alone software application dating back to 1996 so it benefits from several years of development and refinement. It is a sophisticated modular software environment into which you can load pre-constructed virtual musical instruments or in which you can design and build your own creations, using modular building blocks. The supplied instruments include subtractive synthesizers, samplers, FM synthesizers, wavetable (waveset) synthesizers, granular synthesizers, virtual drum machines and modules, sequencers, sound processors and all kinds of weird and wonderful hybrid instruments. These virtual musical instruments are known as ensembles in Reaktor and are found on the CD, or in the installed Native Instruments directory, in the 'Premium' and 'Essentials' folders. The sheer number and quality of the supplied ensembles is enough to satisfy many of its users but the heart of Reaktor is its provision of a streamlined modular environment where you can build your own original musical instruments. Reaktor can therefore become many different things according to which kind of supplied instrument is loaded or which kind of instrument you have created yourself. Its availability as a VST Instrument means that you can bring Reaktor's power into the convenient environment of your host VST 2.0 application.

Control interface

The basics

When used as a VST Instrument, Reaktor launches in a window similar to that shown in Figure 5.22. This is an empty ensemble window.

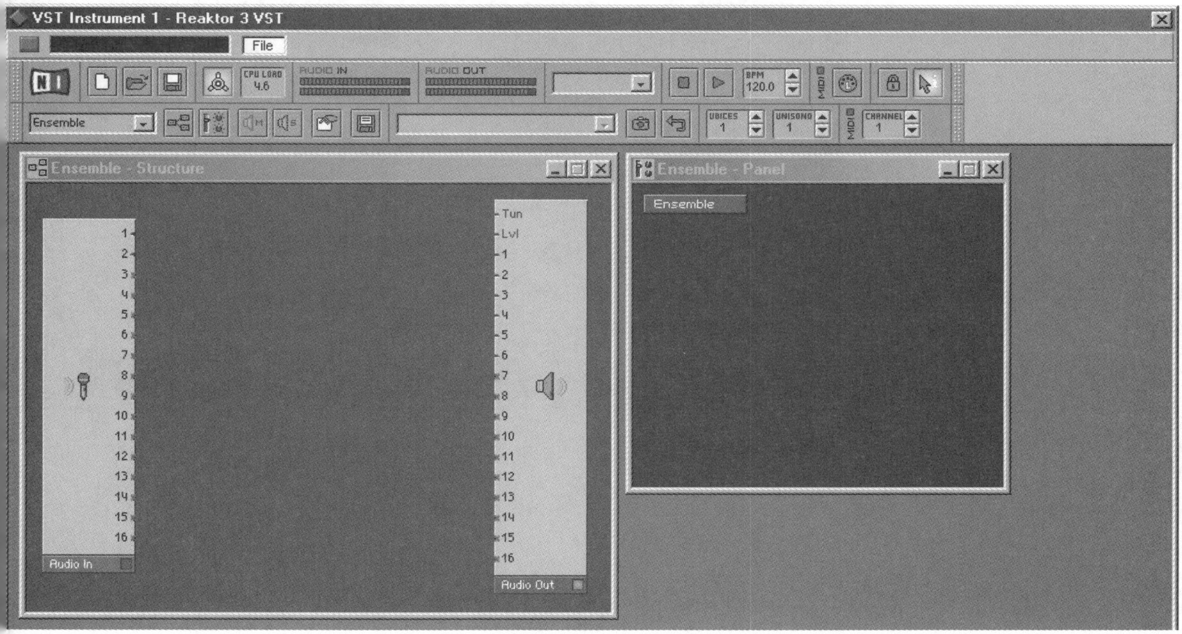

Figure 5.22
Reaktor empty ensemble structure and ensemble panel windows

The empty ensemble is Reaktor's blank sheet which is waiting for you to begin construction of your own instrument. Alternatively, you can load a preset ensemble (which overwrites Reaktor's current contents). Construction projects are managed in the structure window (left) and the control panel for a structure is created in the panel window (right). Either window can be hidden or re-sized. Preset ensembles usually load as control panels similar to that shown in Figure 5.21 and, in this case, the internal structure of the instrument is usually hidden.

The internal structure of a Reaktor musical instrument (known as an Ensemble) is made up of interconnected modular building blocks. These are known as Modules. Modules arranged into small functional groups can be stored within units known as Macros. Macros (and Modules), in turn, can be arranged into functional groups and stored within units known as Instruments. Modules, Macros and Instruments 'live' inside the Ensemble. To see the structure inside a preset Ensemble control panel, click on the structure button in the Instrument toolbar (see below). To take a look at the Modules and the supplied Macros and Instruments, right-click (PC)/ctrl-click (Mac) in empty space in the Ensemble structure window (see Figure 5.23).

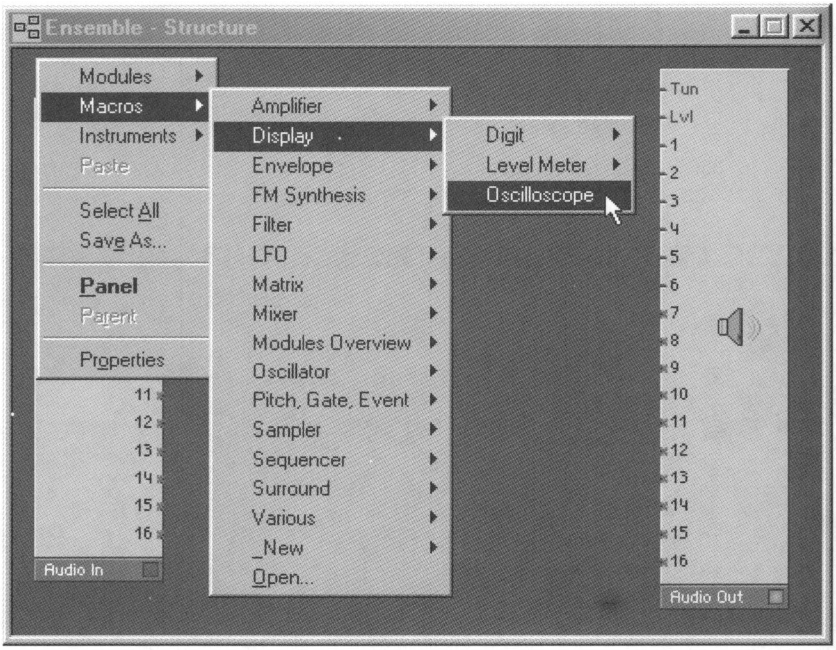

Figure 5.23
Right-click (PC)/ctrl-click (Mac) in the Ensemble structure window to open the Module, Macro and Instrument menus

Modules can have inputs and/or outputs and each appears on screen as a unique object. Modules, Macros and Instruments are connected by clicking on an input or output and dragging the resulting virtual cable (known as a wire) to another unit. There are two classes of signal which are transmitted/received between modules; audio signals and event signals. Audio signals are comparable to the sound signals and control voltages of the analogue world and the terminals for this kind of signal are shown in black on the module. Event signals are for transmitting control messages and changing values between Modules and the terminals for this kind of signal are shown in dark red. Wires can only be connected between out-ports and in-ports and a single out-port can be connected to up to 16 in-ports. Event in-ports cannot directly process audio signals. An event in-port can be fed by up to 16 event out-ports but an audio in-port can only be fed by a single out-port.

When a structure has been built using the various building blocks, right-click (PC)/ctrl-click (Mac) in empty space in the Ensemble structure window and click on Panel in the pop-up menu to create a control panel.

The controls for the instrument can be dragged around the screen when the Lock button (see below) is de-activated. This allows the creation of an ergonomic and logical control interface for the instrument. When you want to tweak the parameters of the completed control panel the Lock button must be activated (see below).

The toolbars

The main screen includes the Ensemble and Instrument toolbars above the display window which are important for the basic operation of Reaktor.

Ensemble toolbar

Figure 5.24

The ensemble toolbar is concerned with the global status of Reaktor and features the following buttons and controls (from left to right):

- New button – creates a new ensemble.
- Load button – opens a file dialogue for loading an ensemble from disk.
- Save button – saves the current ensemble.
- Main Reaktor switch – switches all Reaktor audio processing on or off. Using this switch causes a re-initialisation of all audio processes.
- CPU load display – shows the current load on the CPU.
- Audio input meters – display the level of any audio signal arriving at Reaktor's audio input.
- Audio output meters – display the level of Reaktor's audio output signal.
- Sample rate menu – selects the sample rate of Reaktor's internal processing where higher sample rates give better sound quality but use more CPU power.
- MIDI file player stop button – stops the master clock and any MIDI file which has been imported into Reaktor's MIDI file player. Not applicable when using Reaktor as a VST Instrument within a host sequencing application.
- MIDI file player play button – starts the master clock and any MIDI file which has been imported into Reaktor's MIDI file player. Not applicable when using Reaktor as a VST Instrument within a host sequencing application.
- Tempo selector – allows the setting of the tempo of the internal master clock in bpm.
- MIDI activity LED – registers the presence of incoming MIDI data at one of the MIDI input ports.
- MIDI learn button – allows the assigning of MIDI controller messages to panel controls. To assign a controller, select the panel control, activate the MIDI learn button and then move the chosen MIDI controller.
- Lock button – when activated, prevents the accidental moving of any panel controls. When de-activated, panel controls can be moved around within the display but cannot be used to adjust any settings (i.e. a panel must be locked in order to be able to tweak the parameter controls).

- Show hints button – when the Show hints button is activated, pop-up information windows open automatically when you pass the mouse over the control. Helpful information can be entered for every parameter providing a way of remembering or clarifying the functions of a synthesizer.

Instrument toolbar

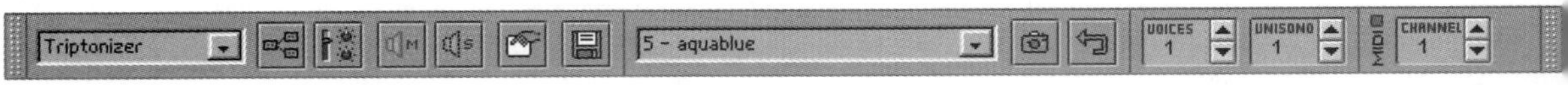

Figure 5.25

The instrument toolbar is concerned with the control and adjustment of the currently selected instrument. The instrument is chosen by selecting its icon in the Ensemble window, by selecting its structure window, its panel window or one of its Macro structure windows. It is also selected by using the Instrument selection menu in the toolbar itself. It features the following buttons and controls (from left to right):

- Instrument selection menu – allows the selection of the Instrument which is to be controlled by the toolbar.
- Structure button – opens the structure for an instrument in a structure window.
- Panel button – opens the control panel for an instrument in a panel window.
- Mute button – mutes the currently selected instrument.
- Solo button – solos the currently selected instrument where all instruments which come before in the signal path are muted and all those which come afterwards remain active.
- Properties button – opens a dialogue where a number of parameters can be set for the instrument.
- Save button – allows the saving of the instrument to disk.
- Snapshot menu – recalls snapshots (preset patches) for the instrument. Comparable to conventional programs or presets.
- Snapshot store button – opens a dialogue for the storage and management of snapshots. Here you can label, store and overwrite snapshots.
- Compare button – compares the settings of the current panel with that which is stored in the compare buffer.
- Voices selector – governs the number of voices allocated to the selected instrument.
- Unison selector – governs the maximum number of unison voices allocated per note.
- MIDI activity LED – registers the presence of MIDI data arriving on the MIDI channel of the currently selected instrument.
- Channel button – sets the MIDI channel for the currently selected instrument.

Using the supplied Ensembles in Reaktor

This section features the brief exploration of two of Reaktor's supplied ensembles, 'Junatik' and 'Random Pitch Shifter'.

Junatik is similar in design to the classic Roland Juno 106 synthesizer, still one of the most popular analogue synthesizers ever produced. It features pulse, sawtooth, and noise waveforms with a sub-bass oscillator and an additional detunable threefold sawtooth wave. Pulse wave modu-

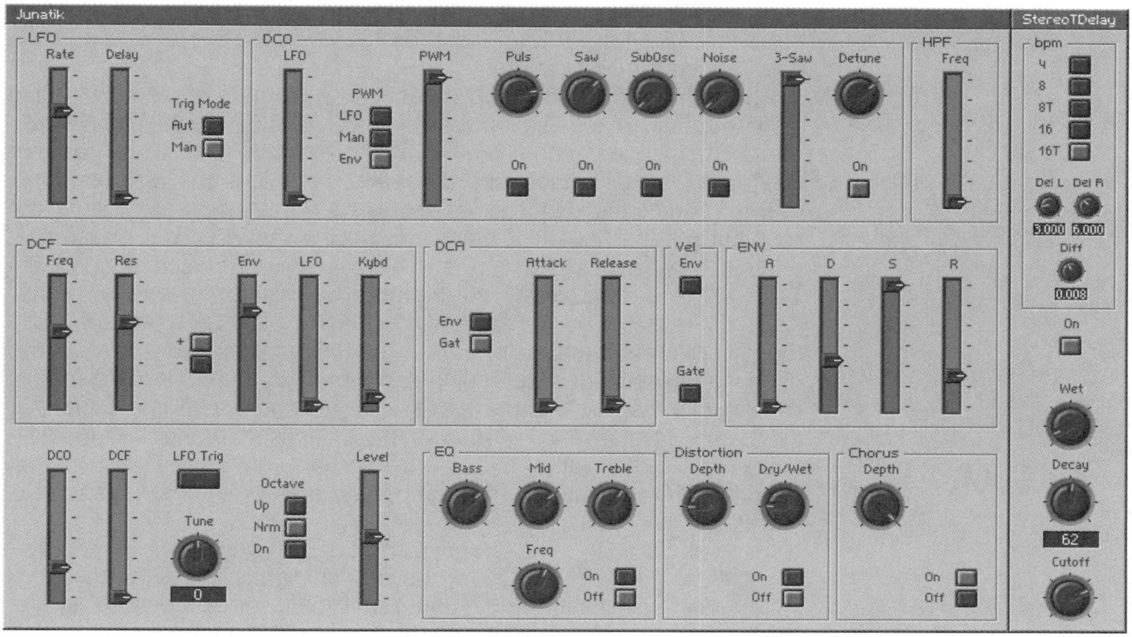

Figure 5.26
The control panel of Junatik (supplied Reaktor ensemble)

lation is supplied via a dedicated, switchable LFO and a separate LFO can be applied to the sound automatically or via the modulation wheel for vibrato effects. The low-pass filter section closely matches the design and behaviour of the original. The ADSR envelope can be set to modulate either (or both) the loudness contour and the filter cut-off. Alternatively, the loudness contour can follow the settings of a simple AR envelope. The filter can also be modulated by the LFO or keyboard pitch. Optional velocity sensitivity has been implemented. The core parameters are supplemented by a 3-band EQ section, a distortion unit, a chorus unit and a tempo-based stereo delay with a built-in filter.

Junatik can produce particularly rich and fat analogue-style sounds due to its additional threefold sawtooth wave with detuning. Just like the original, sounds can be set up in the control panel quite quickly but, of course, in Reaktor you can save your patches using the Snapshot store button. The addition of EQ and distortion considerably increase the sound-sculpting possibilities. The distortion section is good for adding mild saturation and dirt to the signal. The chorus matches the chorus found on the original unit but without the noise. The repeats of the stereo delay can be synchronised to the tempo of your host VST 2.0 application.

Junatik is a comparatively simple subtractive synthesis Ensemble but amply demonstrates Reaktor's virtual analogue synthesis capabilities in an elegant and ergonomic control interface. Junatik is excellent for bass synths, pads and lead sounds. It is found in Reaktor's Premium library.

Random Step Shifter, found in Reaktor's Premium library, is a sampled drum loop re-processing unit where new sample loops are generated from existing sample loops loaded into its sample map. It functions by applying a randomly-generated re-ordering of the contents of the target sample loop at sixteenth note intervals. The blue bars in the display show which sixteenth note division of the sample is played at which position in the bar. The unit is activated by activating playback in the host sequencing application.

The main parameters which govern the generation of the new sample loop are found in the Sequence section (SEQ). Clicking on the New button creates a new random sequence. The PRB dial (probability parameter) modifies the random function which regulates the distribution of events. A different sequence is produced each time you click on the New button and, in conjunction with moving the PRB dial, is the main method by which you can search for a successful new sample loop The T/2 and T/4 buttons divide the tempo of the random sequence by two and four, respectively. When you select either of these buttons you see the blue bars roll by at a slower rate resulting in a thinned-out sequence of sound events. Quantize, tuning and mute parameters are provided in the sampler section and the resulting new sample loop can be further processed with low and high-pass filter sections featuring LFO modulation of the cut-off, an amplifier drive section and a delay section with optional LFO modulation of the delay time for chorus and special effects.

Random Step Shifter is designed to work with one bar drum and percussion loops in 4/4 time which have been tightly edited so that they loop perfectly. Once inside the unit, the sample can be mangled and reshaped in a surprisingly wide variety of ways. If you are seeking to produce a number of loop variations for a one bar drum loop the Random Step Shifter might be the answer. Check out the Snapshots as used with the default sample loop which is present when you first load Random

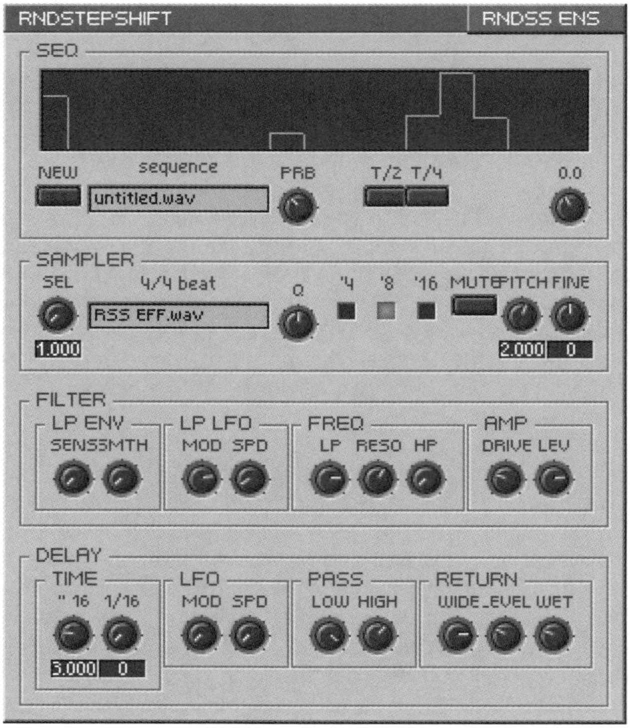

Figure 5.27
The control panel of Random Step Shifter sample loop creation tool (supplied Reaktor ensemble)

Step Shifter. These show some of the possibilities of the unit. To change the sample loaded into the unit double-click on the sample section's grey sample field to open the sample map dialogue.

When you have created a successful patch for these and other Reaktor instruments it can be stored using the Snapshot store button. Each instrument has a capacity for up to 128 snapshots which can be recalled at any time from the Snapshot menu (see the Instrument toolbar above).

The above preset Ensemble descriptions show how Reaktor can change its identity to accommodate both classic subtractive synthesis and sample loop manipulation. However, the possibilities outlined here represent only a tiny fraction of the range and depth encompassed by Reaktor. It supports almost all of the major synthesis techniques and allows the manipulation of samples in ways which are impossible to achieve in most other units. Rhythmic sample manipulation is one of Reaktor's strongest features, as implemented in 6-Pack, Beat Breaker, Cyclane and Gonzzo. It is also capable of producing truly other-wordly atmospheres with instruments like Matrix Modular, Plasma, and Triptonizer. A whole lot of other hybrid synthesis and sampling techniques can be explored with instruments like Cube X, Formantor, InHumanLogic and so on. Readers are strongly advised to explore the Premium and Essentials libraries which are packed full of several hundred ready-to-play Ensembles and Instruments. (See also the Plasma tutorial in Chapter 6).

Building your own instruments in Reaktor

The Reaktor construction process takes place in what are known as structure windows and these exist at various different levels. The different levels are arranged in an overall hierarchy. The aforementioned Ensembles are the highest level within Reaktor. Ensembles usually contain Instruments, Instruments are usually comprised of Macros and Macros are usually made up of Modules. The structure of Ensembles, Instruments and Macros are viewed within Structure windows. Instruments and Ensembles can also be viewed in Panel windows which provide a regular user interface for the synthesizer. You do not necessarily have to stick to the hierarchical approach since nothing prevents you from working with modules directly in the Ensemble window. However, for maintaining clarity in your sound synthesis experiments the hierarchical approach is recommended. Figure 5.28 clarifies Reaktor's hierarchical arrangement.

It is not obvious to know where to start with the building of your own Reaktor structures. So why not start with a simple sine wave?, rather like we did at the beginning of chapter 2. Proceed as follows to build your first extremely simple Reaktor structure:

- Click on the new button to open empty Ensemble structure and Ensemble panel windows.
- Right-click (PC)/ctrl-click (Mac) in empty space in the Ensemble structure window and select Modules/Oscillator/Sine from the pop-up menu. A sine wave module appears in the window.
- Click on the output terminal (Out) of the sine wave module and drag the resulting virtual cable (wire) to input 1 of the Audio Out module. Click on the output terminal of the sine wave module a second time and drag the second resulting virtual cable (wire) to input 2 of the

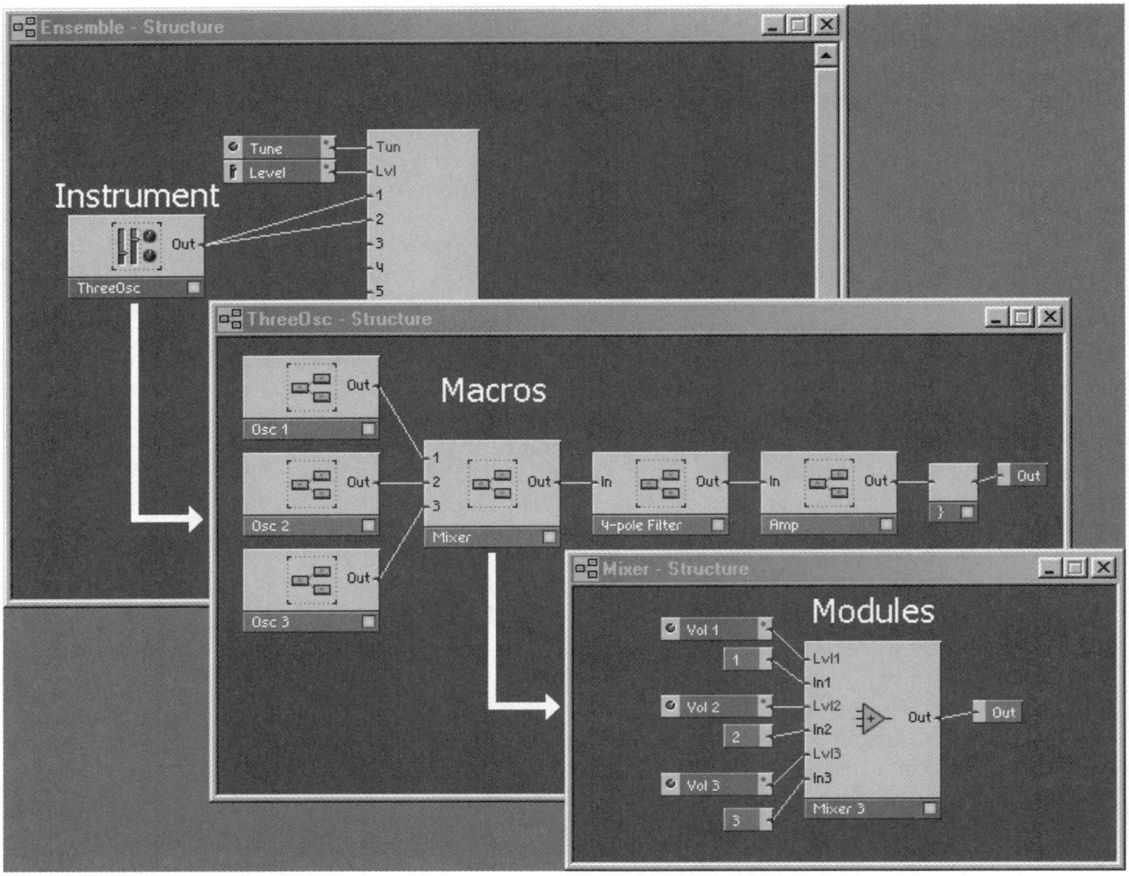

Figure 5.28
Reaktor's hierarchy shown within the structure of the supplied 3-oSC subtractive synthesizer. The ThreeOsc instrument sits inside the ensemble structure window. It is made up of a number of Macros as shown in the ThreeOsc structure window. Each of these Macros is made up of a number of Modules. The Modules for the Mixer Macro are shown in the Mixer structure window.

Audio Out module. The Audio In and Audio Out modules appear in all Reaktor ensembles. They provide the audio link between Reaktor and the outside world. The sine wave oscillator is now connected to the output of Reaktor but we do not yet have a way of triggering it (see Figure 5.29).

- Right-click (PC)/ctrl-click (Mac) in the Ensemble structure window and select Modules/MIDI/Note Pitch from the pop-up menu. A Note Pitch module appears in the window. The Note Pitch module registers the pitch of incoming MIDI notes and transmits this pitch information via its output.
- Right-click (PC)/ctrl-click (Mac) in the Ensemble structure window and select Modules/MIDI/Gate from the pop-up menu. A Gate module appears in the window. The Gate module registers the key on and key off events from your MIDI keyboard and transmits this information via its output.
- Connect the output of the Note Pitch module to the pitch input (P) of the sine module. Connect the output of the Gate module to the gate input (A) of the sine module (see Figure 5.30).

You can now play the sine wave using your MIDI keyboard. If you have managed to trigger the sound then congratulations, you have just built a very simple structure in Reaktor. This has demonstrated a num-

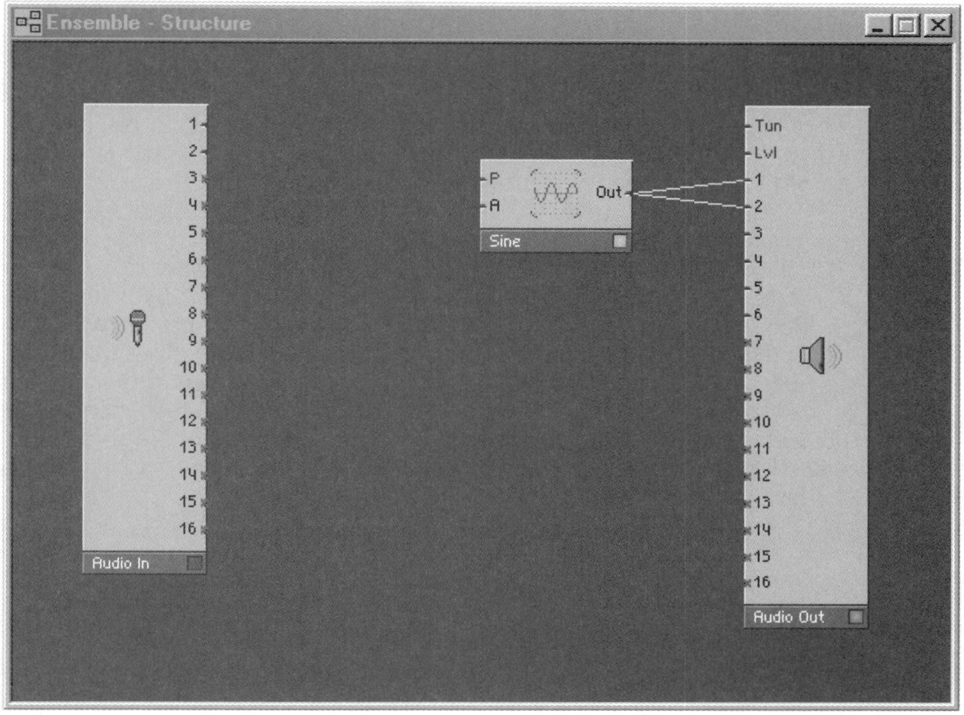

Figure 5.29
A sine wave oscillator module connected to Reaktor's audio output

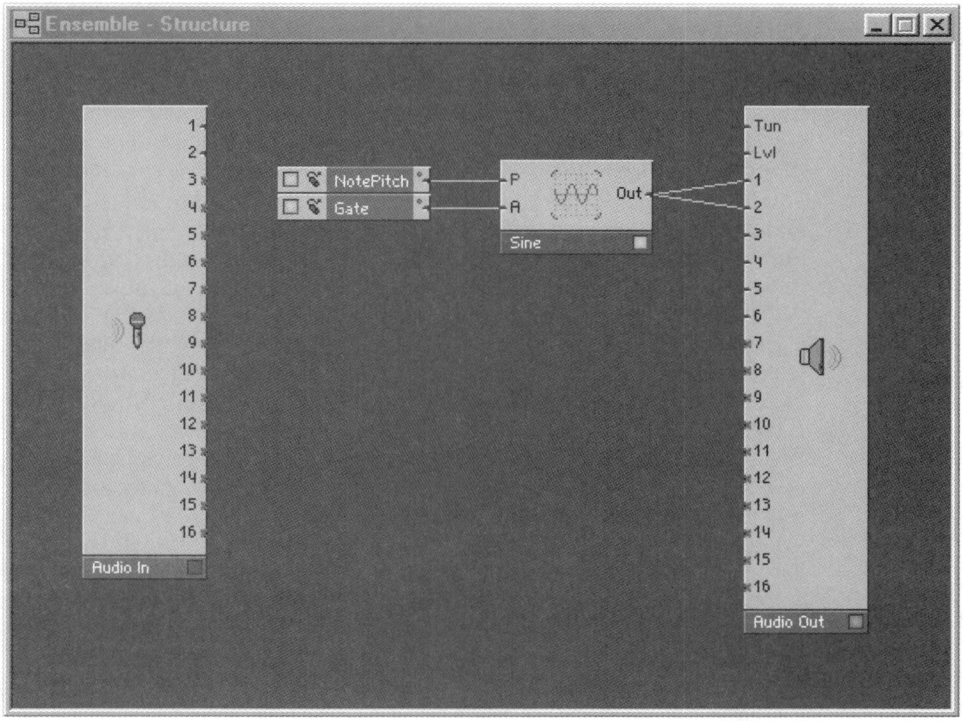

Figure 5.30
Note Pitch and Gate modules provide a way of triggering the sine wave oscillator module using a MIDI keyboard.

ber of the basics of Reaktor structure programming. However, modules are not normally connected together directly in the Ensemble window and we might normally expect to be able to interact with the instrument via a control panel. This particular structure has no control parameters so we cannot create a control panel for it. It produces a bland sound which suffers from an abrupt 'clicky' note onset when it is triggered.

Your first task to improve this structure might be to implement an ADSR envelope generator to control the amplitude envelope of the sound. Refer back to Figure 3.2 to see a diagram of what you are attempting to achieve. Next you could try adding a filter to the structure. This would follow the diagram shown in Figure 3.3. You could follow a more structured approach in Reaktor by moving the interconnected Modules into an Instrument. Various Modules might also be grouped into Macros. The outputs of the Instrument are connected to the Audio Out module in the same way as the sine wave module was connected at the beginning of this tutorial. To build a more sophisticated instrument, we would invariably work in this hierarchical manner to avoid confusion and maximise the logic and clarity of the structure (as in Figure 5.28, above).

It is worth exploring and experimenting with the structures of the supplied Ensembles, Instruments and Macros which you may find rather more complicated than the simple example outlined here. To learn how to start programming structures at a deeper level see 'Building your own subtractive synthesizer in Reaktor' in chapter 6.

Summary and applications

Reaktor provides a particularly powerful modular synthesis environment which is probably unequalled by any other unit. The price you pay for all this is a fairly steep learning curve when you first start using the program. Once you become familiar, you realise that its power is harnessed within a surprisingly compact and ergonomic graphical user interface which is very streamlined. One major advantage is that you can listen to the effects of changes to an instrument's structure while still remaining in the structure windows. This encourages experimentation and helps make the testing and refinement of new instruments an easier task. Reaktor is not particularly greedy with CPU power and appears to have been optimised for the latest processors and operating systems.

Reaktor is a true chameleon and manages to be applicable to an extremely wide range of musical styles. It is particularly at home in the electronic and dance floor musical arenas. Each synthesizer has a character of its own and just about any imaginable synthesizer sound is possible. From fat bass and warm pads to sumptuous strings and sparkling FM electric pianos, from biting lead synths to other-wordly special effects, Reaktor has an awful lot to offer. It is also particularly useful for unique drum loop manipulation and special effects creation. Rhythmic sample manipulation is one of its strongest features. Subtractive, granular, FM, waveset (wavetable) and hybrid synthesis techniques are all supported. Sampled sounds can be warped, treated, modulated and re-synthesized to create a wide variety of timbres or they can simply be mapped and played as desired. Most ensembles also include high quality built-in effects modules which provide extra enlivenment when required.

Bitheadz Retro AS-1

Instrument type:	virtual analogue synthesizer
Polyphony:	up to 64
Number of outputs:	1 stereo
Number of program slots:	16 (each allocated to a separate MIDI channel)
Supported interfaces:	VST 2.0, DXi
Platform:	PC, Mac

Description

Bitheadz Retro AS-1 is a multi-timbral virtual analogue synthesizer (Figure 5.31). It benefits from a substantial period of development as a stand-alone software synthesizer before arriving as a VST Instrument.

Control interface

The interface contains three windows named Main, Mod and FX which are accessible via the tabs in the top right corner of the window.

Figure 5.31
Bitheadz Retro AS-1 VST Main display

Miscellaneous controls

The central part of the display is surrounded by what is known as the 'Frame' which contains a number of parameters and displays which are always visible. These include the following:

- Main, Mod and FX tabs – outlined below
- CPU load display and number of voices display.
- MIDI channel selector menu – to display the program settings for each MIDI channel.
- Default button – returns the currently displayed Retro AS-1 program to the default settings.
- Reload button – reloads the program's last saved state.
- No FX button – disables the Retro AS-1 effects.
- Edited LED – illuminates when the current program has been edited.
- Load button – opens the standard file dialogue in order to load a program.
- Save button – saves the current program.
- Setup button – opens the Retro AS-1 setup dialogue.
- All notes off button – turns off all sound.
- Program display – shows the name of the currently displayed program

Main window

The Main window contains the oscillators, filters and global parameters and features the following:

Three oscillators each with:

- Enable button – enables/disables the oscillator.
- Key tracking button – enables/disables key tracking.
- Oscillator type menu – determines the waveform shape of the oscillator. There is a choice of 13 wave shapes including sawtooth, triangle, pulse and various kinds of sine and noise waveforms.
- Oscillator sync menu – determines which source the oscillator uses to synchronise the start of its waveform.
- FM menu – determines which source is chosen to modulate the frequency of the oscillator.
- Coarse dial – tunes the frequency of the oscillator in coarse steps over a range of +/- 4 octaves.
- Fine dial – tunes the frequency of the oscillator in fine steps over a range of +/- 50 cents.
- Random dial – allows the user to introduce a random amount of detuning into the oscillator.
- Symmetry dial – allows the pulse width to be adjusted when pulse is the chosen waveform and also allows adjustment of the symmetry of the sawtooth, asymmetric sine and glottal waveforms.
- FM amount dial – regulates the amount of frequency modulation if an FM source has been chosen.
- Volume dial – determines the volume for the oscillator.

Two filters each with:

- Enable button – enables/disables the filter.
- Source selectors – indicate which sources are selected for filtering.
- Filter type menu – determines the filter type from a choice of 16

including low pass, high pass, band pass, band reject, comb and others.

- CM menu – determines the filter's CM (cut-off modulation) source.
- Cut-off dial – determines the frequency cut-off point .
- Spread dial – determines the frequency range that is affected around the resonant frequency (not available for all filter types).
- CM amount dial – regulates the amount of cut-off modulation (if a source has been chosen in the CM menu).
- Resonance dial – emphasises the frequencies around the cut-off point.
- Overdrive dial – adds distortion to the output of the filter.

Global section featuring:

- Number of voices menu – determines the maximum number of voices available to the currently displayed program.
- Pitch bend range – sets the range of the pitch wheel in semitones.
- Legato selector – activates/deactivates monophonic response for the Retro AS-1.
- Portamento selector – activates/deactivates glissando (slide) characteristics for the Retro AS-1 when legato is activated.
- Portamento speed dial – governs the speed of the portamento effect.
- Transpose dial – provides global transposition for the Retro AS-1 over a range of +/- 4 octaves (in semitone steps).
- Pan dial – pans the sound in the stereo image.
- Volume dial – controls the overall volume of the Retro AS-1.

Mod window

The Mod window is divided into two sections, one for the routings and the other for the modulators (see Figure 5.32).

The features of the Mod display include the following:

Routings section

- Edit buttons – when selected (illuminated), an edit button displays a routing configuration allowing the parameters to be edited.
- Text display – provides the details of each routing expressed in plain text.
- Add button – adds a routing configuration to the current list.
- Delete button – deletes the currently selected routing configuration.
- Source menu – determines the source that will modulate the destination.
- Destination menu – determines the destination that will be modulated by the source.
- Amount dial – determines the amount by which the destination will be modulated.
- Delay dial – sets a delay time before the modulation starts to take effect.

Modulators section

- Edit buttons – when selected (illuminated), an edit button displays the parameters of the chosen modulator ready for editing.
- Text display – provides the details of each modulator expressed in plain text.

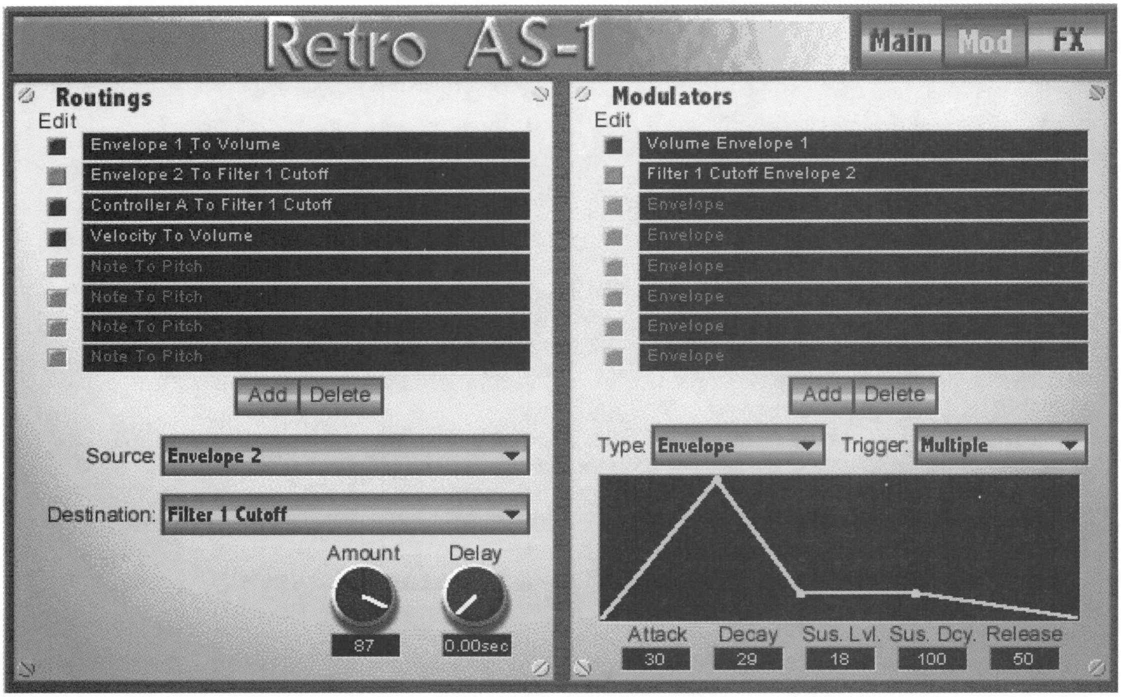

Figure 5.32
Retro AS-1 Mod display

- Add button – adds a modulator to the current list.
- Delete button – deletes the currently selected modulator.
- Type menu – provides a choice of four modulators: envelope, LFO, random or ramp.
- Trigger menu – determines how the modulator is activated.

The display in the lower half of the modulators section changes according to which type of modulator has been chosen. The Envelope display includes a graphic ADSR style envelope which can be manipulated directly by dragging with the mouse. The LFO display provides sine, triangle, square, sawtooth up, sawtooth down and random waveforms and, if desired, the speed can be synchronised to the host application's tempo.

FX window

The FX window (Figure 5.33) features two effects modules which include parametric EQ, shelf EQ, flange, chorus, phaser, delay, overdrive and distortion.

The available controls change according to which type of effect has been chosen.

User guide

Retro AS-1 is 16 part multi-timbral and each channel is accessed by selecting the required MIDI channel in the MIDI channel selection menu (Main window). In order to avoid confusion when using several channels simultaneously make sure that the MIDI channel of the Track you are currently using in the host application corresponds to the currently displayed Retro MIDI channel number (Main window). The audio signal of all channels is routed through the same stereo output.

Figure 5.33
Retro AS-1 FX display

Programs are loaded into the currently displayed channel by clicking on the load button and selecting a Retro AS-1 file. Programs are saved by clicking on the save button. Retro AS-1 program files are given a '.ras' extension. To load or save a whole multi-timbral setup use the standard VST 2.0 program load or save effect files (.fxp extension). Note that VST 2.0 bank files ('.fxb' files) serve no purpose within Retro AS-1. It is also possible to access the supplied preset programs using bank and program change messages via MIDI or from the host VST program.

The Retro AS-1 features a vast range of routing and configuration parameters and a full outline of all the possibilities is beyond the scope of this text. The best approach when learning to program new sounds is to begin with a simple configuration and then experiment with a few carefully chosen controls. For example, to get to know the basics try clicking on the default button to load the default settings. This activates a single oscillator with a sawtooth waveform which passes through a single 1 pole low-pass filter. In 1 pole mode there are only the cut-off and overdrive dials available for tweaking. Try changing the filter to a 4 pole resonant low-pass type which allows access to the spread and resonant dials. This should already open up a wider range of tone colour. Now go into the Mod window and select the filter 1 cut-off envelope and try adjusting the attack in the graphic display so that the filter sweeps in slowly. Try also adjusting the volume envelope. To complete your first experiments try activating the insert effects (FX window) one by one which should already be set to chorus and delay effect types. You may have already produced a tone which is more interesting than what you began with. If not, perhaps go back to the Main window and activate oscillator 2, change the waveform of oscillator 1 to a pulse waveform and set a value of 8 on oscillator 1's random dial. Activate oscillator 2 in the filter 1 display.

Summary and applications

Conveniently, the Retro AS-1 has its own CPU load indicator and the maximum amount of CPU percentage allocated to the instrument can be set in the Setup dialogue. The Setup dialogue also provides a master tuning control, master output level and sets the maximum number of allowable voices.

The Retro AS-1 is supplied with a superb library of over 1400 sounds arranged into 18 categories. These give a good idea of the range of tone colour available and make good starting points for creating your own patches. This instrument can produce an enormously wide range of sounds and the variations are multiplied still further with the addition of its built-in high quality insert effects. It is excellent for rich analogue pads and strings, sumptuous bass and classic synth tones, and just about any other synth sound you may care to imagine. Due to its sophisticated routing and modulation facilities it can also be used to create unusual special effects which go beyond the usual confines of traditional analogue synthesis.

Applied Acoustics Systems Tassman

Instrument type:	modular software synthesizer based on physical modelling
Polyphony:	up to 24 (depending on complexity of patch and CPU power)
Number of outputs:	1
Number of program slots:	100 program (instrument) slots
Supported interfaces:	VST 2.0, DXi
Platform:	PC

Description

Tassman is a sophisticated modular software synthesizer based upon physical modelling techniques. Physical modelling involves the re-creation of real-world phenomena in the virtual world of computers using mathematical equations and computer algorithms (see the physical modelling section in chapter 3). Tassman uses physical modelling to create a wide range of known acoustic and electronic instruments, and also innovative new hybrid instruments. For the construction of these instruments, it features an environment where modules representing the different working parts of musical instruments can be linked together. Each module or object is endowed with behaviour which matches its real-world counterpart. This behaviour is programmed into the modules as mathematical equations which follow the laws of physics. Tassman solves these equations in real-time as you play the instrument.

Info

Comfortable operation of Tassman requires a computer with a very fast CPU.

Control interface

Tassman is comprised of two applications; the Tassman Builder and the Tassman Player. The Builder is where you link modules together to form the interacting components of a musical instrument. When your instrument is built you launch the Tassman Player which automatically creates a custom user interface for your new instrument.

Tassman Builder

When used as a VSTi, the Builder is launched from the Builder launch icon (the third icon in from the right on the TassPlayer toolbar). Alternatively, it can be launched using the TassBuilder icon on the Windows desktop or from the Windows Program menu.

The Builder features a graphic environment into which you can drag and drop modules from the Tassman Library. The modules are organised into categories and shown as icons in the module library to the left of the display. Categories include generators, resonators, filters, envelopes, effects, in/out and sub patch objects. Each module is equipped with a number of inputs and/or outputs and connections are made by dragging virtual cables between modules. In the case of subtractive and similar synthesis instruments, modules are linked together according to standard synthesis principles (see the subtractive synthesis section in chapter 3 for a description of how standard synthesis building blocks are linked together). The difference with Tassman is that, as well as conventional analogue-style synthesis modules, virtual acoustic modules like beams, bowed objects, flute, hammers, mallets, membranes, plates, pickups, plectrums, strings and tubes are also supplied.

TassBuilder example 1

For most users, it is appropriate to start with a simple setup in the Builder. Consider Figure 5.34, below, which shows a simple subtractive synthesis arrangement (similar to Figure 3.4 in Chapter 3). The construction begins with a keyboard module whose function is to receive MIDI input from an external MIDI keyboard or via a recorded MIDI Track in your host sequencing software. This particular keyboard object has two outputs and is not velocity sensitive. The top output is a gate signal which is routed to the ADSR module. This triggers a standard ADSR envelope. The single envelope generator output of the ADSR module is

Figure 5.34
The construction of a simple subtractive synthesizer in TassBuilder

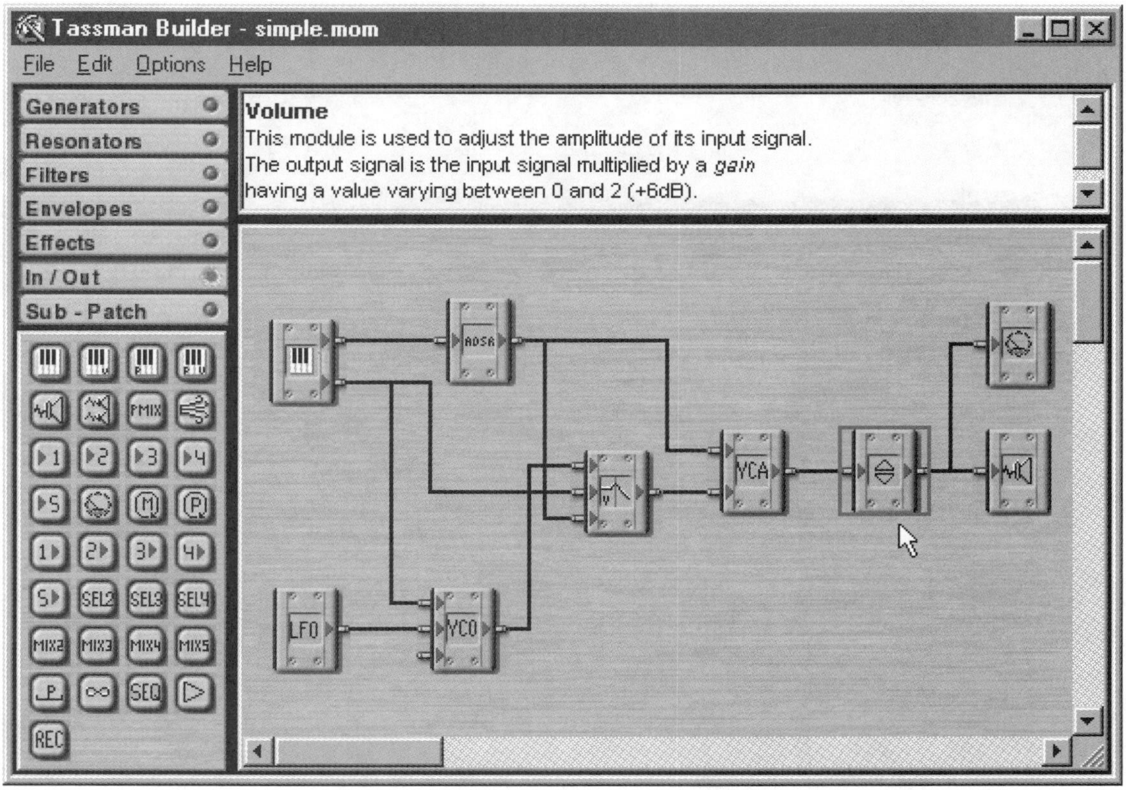

routed simultaneously to both the filter module's cut-off modulation input and the VCA module amplitude modulation input, thereby controlling the spectral evolution and loudness contour of the sound over time in standard analogue synthesis fashion. The second output of the keyboard module is the pitch control signal. This is routed simultaneously to the frequency input of the VCO and the pitch tracking input of the filter. The VCO is modulated by an LFO. The output signal of the VCO passes through the filter and the output of the filter module is routed to the signal input of the VCA. A final volume module, level meter module and a DAC module (digital-to-analogue converter) complete the picture.

Although there are no overt labels on the inputs and outputs of the modules and the function of each module is not always obvious, clicking on a module shows some text in the small window just above the display which gives full information about the module concerned. In addition, holding the mouse close to any of the inputs or outputs displays their function in a small pop-up window.

TassBuilder example 2

You may now be wondering how we might typically build an instrument based on the virtual acoustic modules. Let's consider how we might approach the construction of a mallet striking a plate as shown in Figure 5.35. The network begins with a keyboard object, as before, which registers MIDI input information. This time the keyboard object is velocity sensitive and features three output signals. The upper gate signal is routed to the trigger input signal of the 'noise mallet' module. The noise mallet is a special mallet object which behaves in a similar manner to a real-world mallet but with the addition of white noise in the impact signal. When it receives the gate signal from the keyboard object it sends its output signal. The second output of the keyboard object is the pitch signal. This is connected to the pitch input of the plate module, thereby controlling the pitch of the instrument. The third output of the keyboard

Figure 5.35
The construction of a simple instrument modelling the striking of a plate with a mallet

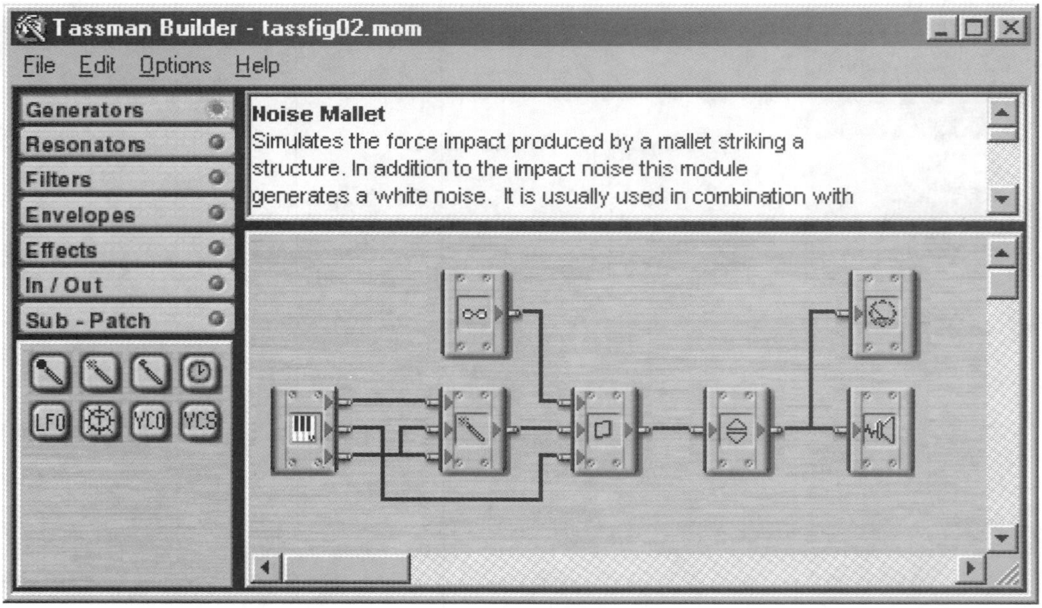

object is the velocity signal. This is connected simultaneously to the stiffness and strength modulation inputs of the noise mallet. This allows the control of the stiffness and the strength of the impact of the mallet according to the velocity of incoming MIDI notes. The output of the mallet is connected to the force signal input of the plate. The first input of the plate is a damper control which is used to regulate the decay characteristics of the plate. In this case, a constant module is connected to this input. The constant module supplies a constant value (1) which ensures that the plate is not dampened for this particular instrument. The output of the plate is routed to a volume module. A level meter module and a DAC module (digital-to-analogue converter) complete the construction.

Tassman provides an extremely wide range of modules covering the design of electronic musical instruments such as subtractive synthesizers, organs and electric pianos and known acoustic instruments such as drums and percussion, plucked and bowed string, and flute instruments. The advantage of this environment is that all modules can be freely connected for the creation of imaginary new instruments and sound-making objects which could only exist in the virtual world. Please refer to the Tassman documentation for a full explanation of all the available modules.

Tip

When building an instrument in Tassman Builder, try starting with a simple construction first and then add to it gradually, testing the instrument at each stage in Tassman Player. Save each version of the instrument methodically so that you can revert to previous versions if things go wrong.

Tassman Player

When Tassman is launched as a VST Instrument it first appears with the Tassman Player on screen with one of the programs loaded by default (similar to Figure 5.36). The Player features the interface for the loaded program (instrument) in the central display of the window with a simple toolbar and buttons above and below the display. The toolbar features the name of the program on the left and the currently loaded preset on the right. Programs and presets can be selected using the up/down arrows next to the names or by clicking on the downward-pointing arrows. Collections of programs and their respective presets can be saved in banks. Bank load and save icons are provided in the left segment of the toolbar and program load and save icons are found just next to them. Buttons in the toolbar below the main display allow the loading and saving of presets. The numbered buttons show/hide the corresponding rack level in the display. Bank files are saved with the standard VST 2.0 .fxb file extension, programs are saved with the .fxp extension and presets are saved with Tassman's own .dxt extension.

Most of Tassman's modules use a graphical user interface which appear as modular units within the Player. Some of these are familiar from the world of subtractive synthesis such as the ADSR, VCA, VCO, LFO, lowpass, highpass and bandpass modules. Equally familiar are the various effects such as the delay, flanger, phaser, reverb and stereo chorus modules. Others are not so familiar, such as the beam, hammer, mallet, noise mallet, membrane, marimba, pickup, plate, plectrum, string, tonewheel and tube modules. These are largely for the modelling of acoustic-style musical instruments. There are also a number of less specific modules whose function is to capture MIDI input, such as notes played on a MIDI keyboard or MIDI controller data from a breath controller or modulation wheel. In addition, a DAC module sends the output of the instrument to the digital-to-analogue converters of the audio hardware. However, these types of modules do not appear within the

Figure 5.36
Tassman Player

control interface of the Player and function invisibly 'inside' the instrument.

In the Player, you interact with each module in terms of how it appears on the screen and the function of each of its control parameters. Depending on how it has been connected in the Builder some parameters may have no function. The following descriptions outline some of Tassman's modules in typical setups within the Tassman Player.

Instrument interface example 1

Let's start with looking at the interface produced from the mallet and plate construction shown in Figure 5.35, above. When you launch the Player with this construction the graphical user interface appears as in Figure 5.37. This features a 'noise mallet' module and a plate module.

Noise mallet module

The noise mallet is a special mallet object which behaves in a similar manner to a real-world mallet but with the addition of white noise in the impact signal. The interface features stiffness, strength, modulation and trigger controls which function as follows:

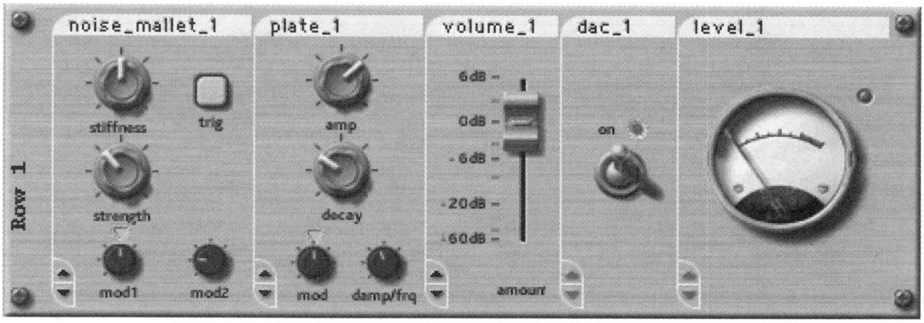

Figure 5.37 A simple instrument interface for a mallet striking a plate

- stiffness – determines the stiffness of the material used in the construction of the mallet where lower values produce a soft mallet (e.g. made of cotton) and higher values produce a hard mallet (e.g. made of wood).
- strength – determines the force of the impact of the mallet where lower values produce less force.
- mod 1 – this parameter is most often connected to the incoming pitch signal at the construction stage. In this case, the level of the mod 1 parameter determines how much the pitch of incoming MIDI notes modulates the stiffness of the mallet (relative to the stiffness parameter setting). If, instead, a velocity signal were connected to mod 1 at the construction stage, the parameter would control how much the stiffness of the mallet is affected by the velocity of incoming MIDI notes (relative to the stiffness parameter setting).
- mod 2 – this parameter is most often connected to the incoming velocity signal at the construction stage. In this case, the level of the mod 2 parameter determines how much the velocity of incoming MIDI notes affects the strength of the impact of the mallet (relative to the strength parameter setting).
- trigger – provides a way of triggering the sound other than from a MIDI keyboard.

Plate module

The plate module simulates the acoustical behaviour of rectangular plates of different materials and sizes. The plate is endowed with various properties such as the length, width, number of modes, point of impact and listening point at the time of construction. The control interface for the plate is a generic front-end known as the 'multimode' module. The multimode module also provides the control interface for other modules such as the beam, marimba, membrane, and string modules which share common behavioural characteristics. The front panel controls include the following:

- amp – determines the amplitude of the output signal of the plate.
- decay – determines the decay time of the sound produced by the plate where low values result in a short decay time (greater damping of the signal) and high values result in longer decay times (less damping of the signal).
- mod – determines how much the pitch input signal arriving at the pitch modulation input of the object affects the pitch variation in the output of the sound. When in the centre position (when the green

LED is illuminated) the pitch variation is equal to 1 which means that the plate plays according to an equal tempered scale.

- damp/freq – varies the decay time or damping factor relative to the frequency. Low values produce shorter decay times in the lower frequencies and longer decay times in the upper frequencies. High values produce the opposite effect. Use low settings for metal and glass plates and high settings for wood.

You might be tempted to set up the parameters of this simple instrument to create the sound of, (you guessed it!), a mallet striking a plate. However, Tassman offers the exciting prospect of creating virtual instruments which could not exist in the real world. You can already start to explore these possibilities within the Tassman user interface by setting up the parameters in unusual ways. For example, try setting up the controls as shown in Figure 5.38 to create a hybrid percussion instrument.

Figure 5.38 Change the parameters of the mallet and plate to produce a hybrid percussion instrument

Instrument interface example 2

The second interface example is a plectrum which plays a string (Figure 5.39). This features the plectrum and string modules. This is an incomplete instrument since a string normally needs to be attached to some kind of resonant structure. You could later add other modules to the interface shown here to create an authentic string instrument.

Plectrum module

The plectrum module simulates the plucking action of a string by a pick or a finger. The output of the module supplies the impulse energy a string needs in order to start vibrating. The front panel controls of the plectrum module include the following:

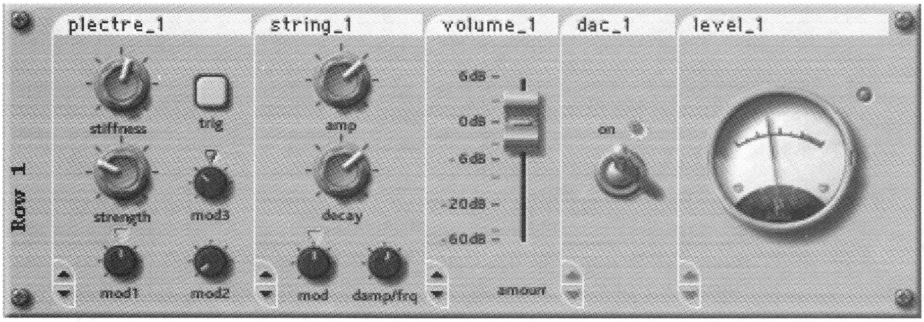

Figure 5.39 A simple instrument interface for a plectrum plucking a string

- stiffness – determines the stiffness of the plectrum where low values produce a softer pick and high values produce a harder pick. The harder the pick the sharper and shorter the impulse attack of the sound.
- strength – determines the amount of energy or force applied to the plectrum thereby affecting the amplitude and timbre of the module's output signal.
- mod 1 – this parameter is most often connected to the incoming pitch signal at the construction stage. In this case, the level of the mod 1 parameter determines how much the pitch of incoming MIDI notes affects the stiffness of the plectrum (relative to the stiffness parameter setting). When adjusted to its centre position the stiffness of the plectrum is modulated by the pitch in such a way as to ensure that the timbre of the plectrum's impulse signal remains uniform across the whole range of the piano keyboard.
- mod 2 – this parameter is most often connected to the incoming velocity signal at the construction stage. In this case, the level of the mod 2 parameter determines how much the velocity of incoming MIDI notes affect the stiffness of the plectrum, where greater velocities decrease the stiffness and smaller velocities increase the stiffness (relative to the stiffness parameter setting). This models the action of the softening of the plectrum as the velocity increases. The effect of mod 2 works in conjunction with that of mod 1.
- mod 3 – this parameter is also most often connected to the incoming velocity signal at the construction stage. In this case, the value of the mod 3 parameter determines how much the velocity of incoming MIDI notes affect the force signal of the plectrum (relative to the strength parameter setting).
- trigger – provides a way of triggering the sound other than from a MIDI keyboard.

String module

The string module simulates the acoustical behaviour of strings of different materials and sizes. The string is endowed with various properties such as the length, inharmonicity, number of modes, point of excitation and listening point at the time of construction. The control interface for the string is a generic front-end known as the 'multimode' module. The multimode module also provides the control interface for other modules such as the beam, marimba, membrane, and plate modules which share common behavioural characteristics. The front panel controls include the following:

- amp – determines the amplitude of the output signal of the string.
- decay – determines the decay time of the sound produced by the string where low values result in a short decay time (greater damping of the signal) and high values result in longer decay times (less damping of the signal).
- mod – determines how much the pitch input signal arriving at the pitch modulation input of the object affects the pitch variation in the output of the sound. When in the centre position (when the green LED is illuminated) the pitch variation is equal to 1 which means that the string plays according to an equal tempered scale.
- damp/freq – varies the decay time or damping factor relative to the

Tip

Before moving onto the construction of complex acoustic musical instruments in Tassman, first try building the 'noise mallet and plate' and 'plectrum and string' instruments outlined in this section. Thoroughly exploring the functions of the parameters in these simple instruments reveals both the expected sonic possibilities of the modules concerned and also some of the more unusual and exciting aspects of sound creation in Tassman.

frequency. Low values produce shorter decay times in the lower frequencies and longer decay times in the upper frequencies. High values produce the opposite effect. Mid and high settings are generally suitable for string sounds.

For more elaborate use of the plectrum and string modules see 'Building an electric guitar in Tassman' in Chapter 6.

Summary and applications

Tassman has great potential for producing inspirational and previously unheard sounds. The price to pay for this is a rather steep learning curve. This is, in part, due to the difficulty of bringing physical modelling techniques within the reach of sound synthesists. There is not an established common control interface. The absence of real-time operation in Tassman Builder does not encourage intuitive use of the software during the building stage since you cannot quickly listen to any changes you have made to the structure of your instrument while remaining in the Builder environment. Tassman also lacks some of the performance playability we have come to expect from synthesizer instruments. For example, at the time of writing, the pitch bend function for acoustic instruments allows pitch changes in semitone steps but does not appear to provide smooth bends. This is good for slides but limiting if you are attempting to create the kind of smooth note bending you might use for a guitar or similar string instrument. However, Tassman features a very comprehensive MIDI implementation where virtually any controller can be linked to any parameter. At the time of writing, Tassman was undergoing a major update so we can expect to see any shortcomings addressed in the new version (version 3.0).

Tassman is to be commended for doing things differently. No other VST Instrument/software synthesizer has attempted to bring us a modular environment where you can create both acoustic and electronic musical instruments using physical modelled building blocks. It is sometimes difficult to tease out a usable patch on some of the acoustically modelled instruments but, with perseverance, there are great rewards to be reaped. The difference with programming sounds on the acoustic instruments is that even very small changes in the parameters can produce drastic differences in the timbre. When you tweak the controls of an acoustic model you are often modifying the actual design of the instrument and not just the sound. This means that you may suddenly need a slightly different technique to play it, and it may perform well in one part of the keyboard range but not in another. When producing instruments of the acoustic kind, keep in mind the context of how you might actually play a real-world version (if a real-world version of your design actually exists). For example, a real-world conga cannot be played across the entire pitch range of a musical keyboard so the physical modelled variety should not necessarily be expected to do so either.

A variety of soundbanks are supplied with Tassman organised into 6 categories according to instrument type. Each bank features, on average, around ten instruments each with its own presets. Categories include acoustic, miscellaneous, monophonic, polyphonic, simple and standalone. Tassman's acoustic models tend to work best with percussive and dampened pitched instruments. Some of the acoustic instruments which come supplied with the program can produce remarkably realistic results, notably african xylo, epiano (Rhodes electric piano), finger bass, harp and kalimba. However, the acoustic presets often need tweaking to be successful. Tassman produces excellent results in the synthesizer category and is supplied with the usual favourites like Juno 106, Prophet and Moog emulations. Its 'generic poly' instrument is good for synth brass and clav sounds, and the 'ensemble' instrument produces attractive synthesized string patches. The synthesizer category also includes a Hammond organ instrument which can turn out some very authentic organ tones.

The miscellaneous instruments include such things as 'airlock' and 'doctor frankentass' which are good for sound effects and experimentation. The standalone section includes a range of instruments which use Tassman's standalone capabilities and 16-step sequencer module to create TB303-style sequencing instruments. At the time of writing, Tassman did not support synchronisation to the tempo of the host software.

Tassman, like other modular software synthesis instruments, is very open-ended. It is endowed with a wide timbral range and is particularly suited to advanced sound design tasks and experimentation. Building complex musical instruments with Tassman is not for the faint-hearted and can be very time-consuming but, for those with the necessary perseverance and patience, new sonic possibilities are waiting to be discovered. Note that, more than most VST Instruments, Tassman requires a host computer with a very powerful CPU in order to function comfortably. (For an in-depth tutorial of instrument construction in Tassman see 'Building an electric guitar in Tassman' in Chapter 6).

Tip

While Tassman's onboard effects are adequate for many patches, certain instruments benefit from the plug-in effects of your host sequencing application. This is particularly true for reverberation and amplifier/speaker simulation. Cubase Reverb 32, Logic Audio PlatinumVerb and Waves TrueVerb are recommended for reverberation. Cubase Overdrive or Logic Overdrive are recommended for amplifier and distortion effects.

Muon Tau Pro

Instrument type:	virtual analogue synthesizer
Polyphony:	monophonic
Number of outputs:	1
Number of program slots:	32
Supported interfaces:	VST 2.0
Platform:	PC, Mac

Description

The Tau Pro is a software synthesizer created in the tradition of Roland's TB303 synthesizer (Figure 5.40). It features a 64-bit audio engine and a switchable 18dB/24dB/36dB-per-octave resonant low-pass filter.

Control interface

The graphical user interface is divided into four main sections, the oscillator section, the articulation section, the master section and the effects section.

The oscillator section

The oscillator section includes two identical VCOs each with the following control parameters:

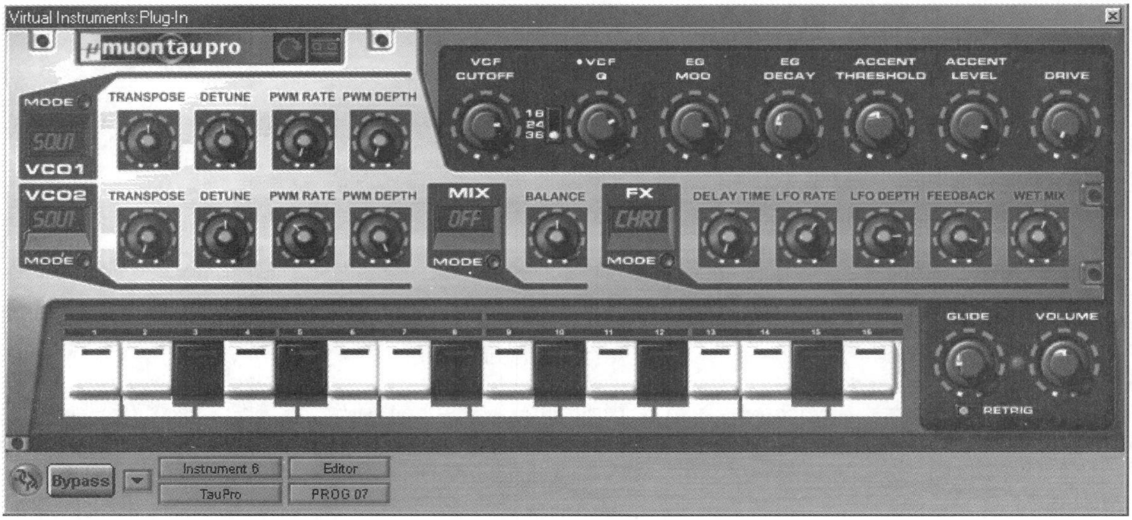

Figure 5.40
Muon Tau Pro virtual analogue synth

- mode – selects the waveform for the oscillator from a choice of five sawtooth waves, five square waves and a sine wave.
- transpose – provides pitch transposition of the oscillator between -12 and +12 semitones.
- detune – detunes the oscillator between -100 and +100 cents.
- PWM rate – adjusts the pulse width modulation rate between 0Hz and 5Hz.
- PWM depth – adjusts the pulse width modulation depth between 0 and 100%.

The mix of the VCOs is controlled in the oscillator mix section which features the following:

- mode – provides three ways of mixing the oscillators. Off mixes the oscillator outputs according to the balance setting in standard fashion. Sync synchronises the onset of VCO1's waveform to that of VCO2 which causes a distortion effect which can be controlled by the transpose and detune settings of VCO1. The Ring setting multiplies the outputs of the two oscillators for ring modulation effects.
- balance – when mix mode is in the Off position balance regulates the mix between VCOs 1 and 2 where fully left is VCO1 only and fully right is VCO2 only. When mix mode is in the Ring position balance regulates the strength of the ring modulation where fully left = no ring modulation and fully right = maximum ring modulation.

The articulation section

The articulation section features filter, envelope shaping and accenting controls as follows:

- VCF cutoff – determines the cut-off frequency of the low pass filter between 0 and 100%.
- VCF Q – determines the resonance of the filter between 0 and 100%. Higher values may cause self-oscillation effects.
- EG mod – regulates how much the filter cut-off frequency is

modulated each time it is triggered by an incoming MIDI note (between 0 and 100%).

- EG decay – regulates the length of time for which the filter is opened each time it is triggered by an incoming MIDI note (between 50 and 5000ms).
- Accent threshold – sets the threshold relative to the velocity of incoming MIDI notes above which the filter's cut-off frequency is opened up a little more according to the accent level.
- Accent level – determines the additional amount by which the modulation of the cut-off frequency is increased each time the incoming velocity rises above the accent threshold setting.
- Drive – adds an amount of saturation to the output signal.

The master section

The master section features the mini virtual keyboard and the following control parameters:

- glide – determines the amount of glissando effect when the retrigger switch is off and you play in a legato style.
- retrig – when the retrigger switch is on (switched to the right) the EG Mod control always retriggers the opening up of the filter regardless of how you play the notes and the glide control has no effect. When the retrigger switch is off (switched to the left) and you play in a legato style the EG Mod control does not retrigger the opening up of the filter so the sound remains slightly dampened.
- volume – regulates the level of the output signal.

The effects section

Tau Pro features a comprehensive onboard stereo effects unit capable of a wide range of delay, chorus and flange effects. The controls include the following:

- FX mode – switches the effects section between chorus, flange, delay and mono chorus/delay and mono flange/delay effects.

delay time – sets the delay time between 1 and 1000ms.

- LFO rate – determines the chorus or flange LFO rate between 0.01 and 2.5Hz. This control has no function with the delay effects.
- LFO depth – determines the chorus or flange LFO depth between 0 and 100%. This control has no function with the delay effects.
- Feedback – determines the amount of delay or flange/chorus signal which is fed back to the input for increasing the decay time of delay repeats and adding richness to the chorus/flange effects.
- Wet mix – determines the amount of effect signal which is mixed with the output signal and in the mixed effects modes determines the amount of delay only.

User guide

Tau Pro is a classic case of 'less is more'. There are no complex envelope shapes to program here since the synth has a preset loudness contour. The gate opens as soon as you press a key and it closes when you release it. Most of the expressive dynamics of the sound are provided by the filter. The EG Mod control regulates how much the filter opens up each time it is triggered and the EG Decay control regulates the length of time for which the filter is opened. Low EG Mod settings provide a more 'rounded' attack to the sound while high settings provide more 'bite'. Low EG Decay settings are good for percussive and plucked attacks while high settings are good for filter sweeps. The 18dB filter setting gives a grainy sound which is good for adding 'dirt' and the 36dB setting is clean and clinical. The 24dB setting is a good all-rounder. Once you have set up the accent controls to suit the velocity of the incoming MIDI notes, the other way of changing the expression of the Tau Pro is to adjust the retrigger and glide controls. When the retrigger switch is on the EG Mod control always retriggers the opening up of the filter regardless of how you play the notes and the glide control has no effect. When the retrigger switch is off and you play in a legato style the EG Mod control does not retrigger the opening up of the filter so the sound remains dampened. It opens up again when you retrigger notes by playing in a more staccato style. If you also add some glide control you can simulate the effect of sliding between notes (glissando). Combining legato and glissando effects significantly adds to Tau Pro's expressive capabilities. Further movement can be added to the sound when you are using a square wave by using the VCO's pulse width modulation controls. If you need to add warmth or aggression to your sound try using the drive parameter which adds saturation to the output signal.

Tip

Tau Pro features two small buttons to the right of the Tau Pro logo. The first button changes the dial manipulation mode between circular and vertical mode. The second button activates a dial position pop-up each time you move a control parameter which is useful for working in fine detail.

If you want to produce the stylised bass lines which made this kind of unit so distinctive try limiting yourself to step input in the piano-roll or drum style editor of your host sequencing application (Cubase: Key or Drum edit, Logic: Matrix edit). Use 1/16th or 1/8th note lengths tightly quantised to 1/16th note divisions of the bar over a one or two bar pattern. Use the host application's step input functions to regulate the velocity of the notes for the triggering of Tau Pro's accenting system. Set the accent level of Tau Pro accordingly. Try overlapping certain of the notes if you have activated retrigger and glide. Once you've entered your bass (or lead) part leave it cycling and tweak the front panel controls of the Tau Pro. Instant bleepy bass lines!

Summary and applications

This synth manages to fill a gap in the VSTi market by doing things differently. Its control parameters are arranged according to its own unique design imperative, i.e. it is monophonic, it does not respond to pitch bend or modulation wheel data, it does not feature an ADSR envelope and it does not respond to velocity in the normal way. Instead, it relies on its lively filter, its retrigger and glide settings and its accent parameters for performance interest and the interface encourages the user to interact with it in an alternative way. It is supplied with a bank of 32 bass and lead sounds which demonstrate the instrument's capabilities. This VSTi is very good for bass synth sounds. It can produce drippingly squelchy effects and ultra deep sub-bass patches. It is particularly suited to rave, trance, techno and ambient dance floor styles.

Steinberg The Grand

Instrument type:	Grand piano VST instrument
Polyphony:	up to 64
Number of outputs:	1 stereo
Number of program slots:	16
Supported interfaces:	VST 2.0
Platform:	PC, Mac

Description

The Grand is a grand piano VST instrument featuring unrivalled authenticity in capturing the sonic nuances and feel of a real-world grand piano (Figure 5.41).

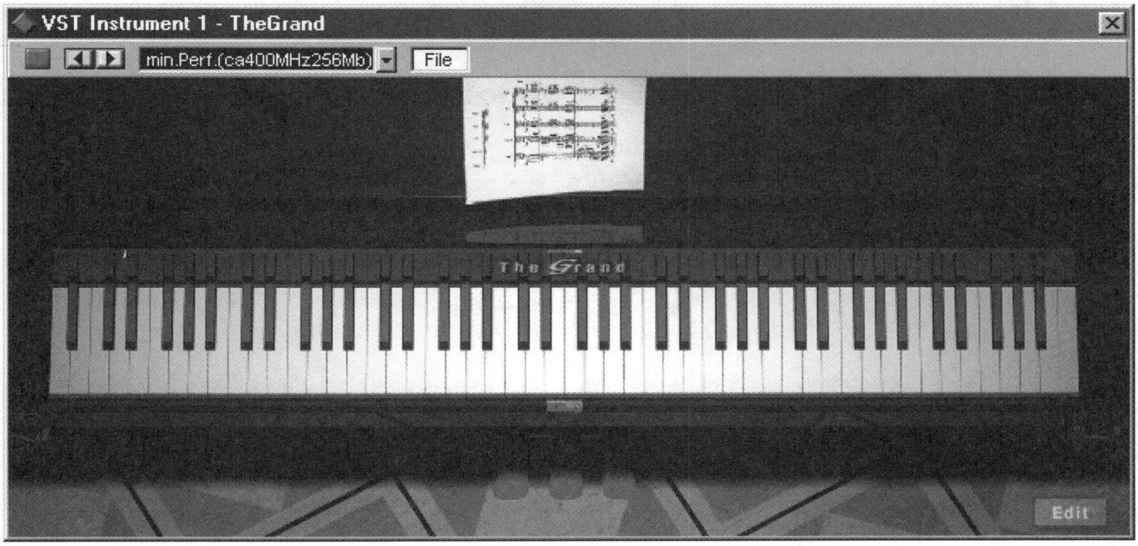

Figure 5.41
Steinberg The Grand VST instrument

Control interface

The Grand features two interface windows: the virtual keyboard window (as shown above) and the Edit window (Figure 5.42). The virtual keyboard can be used to audition the sounds of the Grand using the mouse on the computer screen. The display also includes virtual sustain, sostenuto and soft pedals.

The Edit window is opened by clicking on the Edit button of the main window. The Edit window is divided into three sections; Keyboard settings, Sound settings and Global settings.

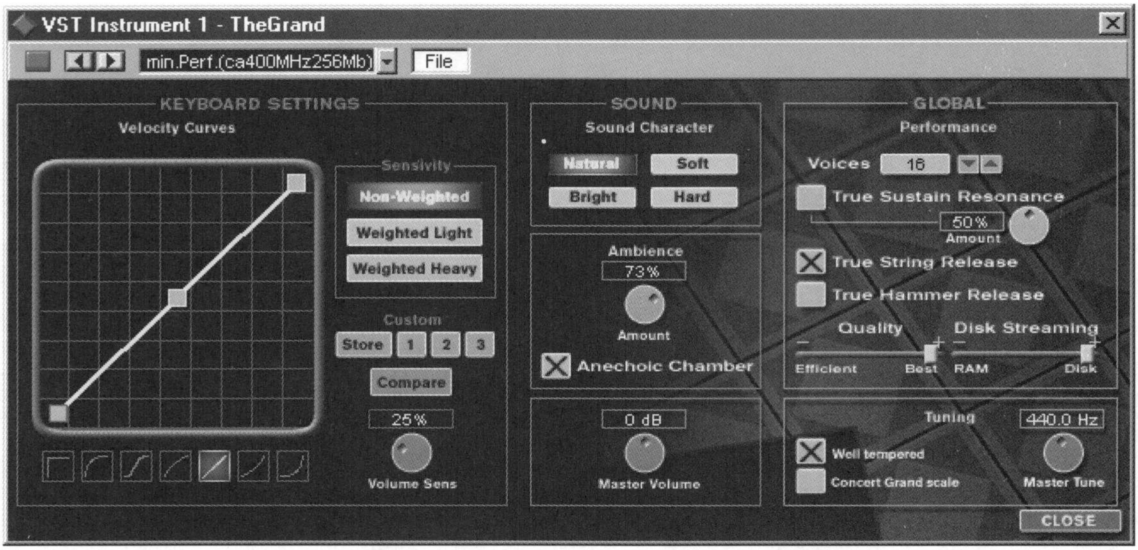

Figure 5.42
The Grand edit window

Keyboard settings

The Keyboard settings section allows you to calibrate the response of The Grand to your own keyboard and playing style. The settings include the following:

- sensitivity – used to calibrate The Grand's response for non-weighted, light-weighted or heavy-weighted keys. Most users are probably triggering The Grand with a standard MIDI synthesizer and this requires the default non-weighted setting.
- velocity curve – determines the velocity response. This can be adjusted to suit your personal preference, playing style and the velocity sensitivity of your MIDI keyboard. The keys of some MIDI keyboards need to be struck very hard in order to produce the full velocity range and this means that without adjusting the curve some users may be missing out on the highest velocity range of The Grand's sampled sounds.
- volume sensitivity – governs how much the velocity affects volume where 100% gives full velocity sensitivity (suitable for classical and jazz) and lesser percentages progressively compress the instrument's dynamic range.

Sound settings

The sound settings determine the tone of the piano and include the following:

- natural – the default setting for the unmodified acoustic piano as recorded.
- soft – dampens the tone while maintaining dynamic response.
- bright – provides added punch and a brighter tone.
- hard – compresses the dynamic response while still providing a brighter tone.
- ambience – adds an amount of room sound to the otherwise dry sound of the piano. De-activate the anechoic chamber parameter and

add the desired ambience using the amount control. (Alternatively, add your own reverberation with an external unit or by playing The Grand in your favourite acoustic space).

- anechoic chamber – The Grand's samples were recorded from a Kawai grand piano in an anechoic chamber. When activated, the anechoic chamber parameter delivers the original dry sound in its pure form, exactly as recorded in the anechoic chamber.

Global settings

The Global section includes the following:

- voices – determines the polyphony of The Grand up to a maximum of 64 voices.
- true sustain resonance – produces natural body resonances and sympathetic string overtones when you strike a key.
- true string release – recreates the subtle effect of the felt damper falling upon the string when each piano key is released.
- true hammer release – matches the manner in which the hammer returns to its original position when each piano key is released. This sound is generally only heard clearly by the pianist seated at the piano.
- quality – determines the playback quality of The Grand.
- disk streaming – governs how much sample data is pre-loaded into RAM rather than being streamed off hard disk.

User guide

Unlike most of the virtual instruments presented in this chapter The Grand is not designed for the creation of a vast range of different sounds. All the adjustments of the controls are directed towards the refinement of one single sound to suit your own particular 'piano purpose'.

The Natural setting is good for classical and jazz music. The Soft setting suits ambient textures and slow ballads. The Bright setting is good for solos and electronic arrangements. The Hard setting suits dance and pop music. The true settings can be adjusted to match all the subtle nuances of a concert grand. True sustain resonance is excellent for other-wordly effects when used in conjunction with the sustain pedal. Although each of the true settings in isolation is rather subtle in its effect, used together these controls add significantly to the realism of a piano performance.

If your hard disk has difficulty coping with the Grand's disk streaming, try moving the disk streaming fader towards the left (towards the RAM setting). This means that more of the first part of each sample is stored in RAM which helps with the playback of large numbers of simultaneous notes. If your system cannot cope with real-time performance regardless of your disk streaming setting then you could lower the playback quality of the Grand using the Quality fader. You can later record the instrument onto an audio track of your host VST sequencing application at full resolution.

Summary and applications

The Grand performs its main task, the creation of an authentic grand piano, to the very highest of standards. Designed to be different, it does more than simply play multi-sampled piano sounds like an ordinary sampler. It features an intelligent VSTi engine which uses hard disk streaming to read sound data from a special sample bank optimised for the nuances and feel of a real piano. The implementation of full sustain, sostenuto and soft pedal functionality increases the instrument's expressive potential. The Grand is supplied with eight preset programs which configure the unit for various different applications. These include three general performance programs designed for different computer resources and various combinations of bright, soft, hard and natural settings.

Due to its authenticity it fulfils any musical function normally assigned to a grand piano and is particularly good for solo performance and musical arrangements where the piano is the main feature. To be played in real-time to its fullest potential requires a particularly powerful CPU and plenty of RAM memory.

VSTi Quick views

This section gives quick descriptions of a range of other VST instruments which were not included in the VSTi close-up section above.

Native Instruments Absynth

Instrument type:	semi-modular synthesizer combining multiple synthesis techniques
Polyphony:	up to 64
Number of outputs:	unlimited (according to CPU power)
Number of program slots:	128
Supported interfaces:	VST 2.0, DXi, MAS, DirectConnect
Platform:	PC, Mac

Absynth is a semi-modular synthesizer which uses subtractive, FM and AM synthesis techniques to create truly inspiring, organic sounds. The design is a joint effort by the original developers Rhizomatic Software and Native Instruments. It features six oscillators with preset waveforms, three ring modulators, a waveshaper, a waveform editor (where you can draw in your own waveshapes for use as an oscillator, LFO or waveshaping function), 4 filters (with low-pass, high-pass, band-pass, notch and comb types), graphical envelopes with up to 68 breakpoints, three LFOs, a delay effects processor (with LFO or MIDI controller modulation) and an 86-note virtual keyboard. The interface is page driven. You set up the basic synthesis structure by linking modules in the Patch window, decide how the amplitude of the sound evolves over time in the Graphical envelope editor, manage envelope-based rhythms and percussive patterns in the Envelope function generator, control the harmonics of the sound in the Spectral Waveform editor, modulate effects, filters, FM parameters and oscillators in any combination using the LFOs, draw your own waveform in the Waveform editor and modify waveforms using fractalize, filtering, FM and other techniques in the Waveform transformations window.

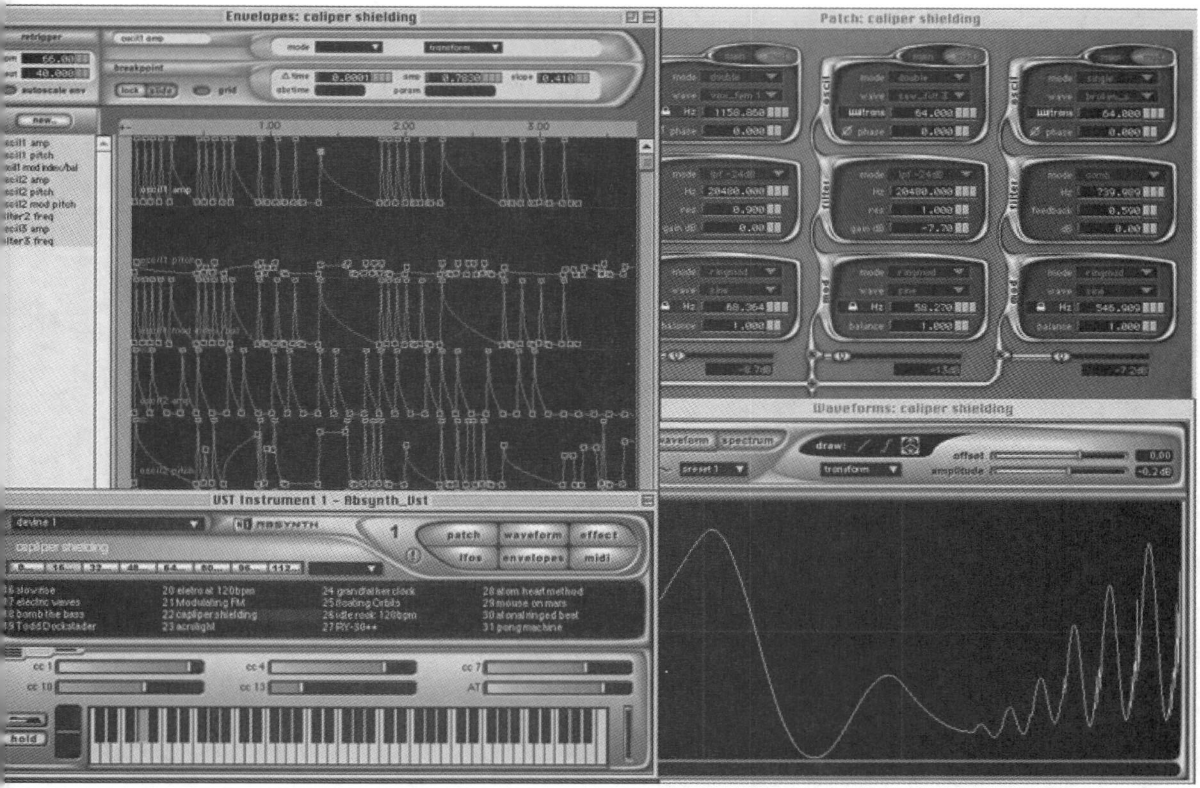

Figure 5.43
Native Instruments Absynth

Absynth is supplied with an extensive sound library of 11 soundbanks, each with 128 presets. It is excellent for ambient textures, lush pads, soundscapes and rhythmic effects and is particularly good for sculpting and morphing sounds over time. This VSTi already has a reputation among users for its outstanding sound quality and exceptional sound library.

Native Instruments Battery

Instrument type:	drum and percussion sampler module
Polyphony:	dynamic resource allocation typically allowing up to 128 stereo voices (features 54 polyphonically playable cells with up to 128 velocity layers per cell)
Number of outputs:	32 (8 stereo, 16 mono)
Number of program slots:	1
Supported interfaces:	VST 2.0, DXi, MAS, DirectConnect
Platform:	Mac, PC

Battery is an advanced percussion sample player, drum module and cell-based sample programming tool. It features internal 32-bit resolution, 54 cells, each with 128 velocity layers, tuning, amplitude envelope, pitch envelope, bit reduction, shaper and looping facilities. There

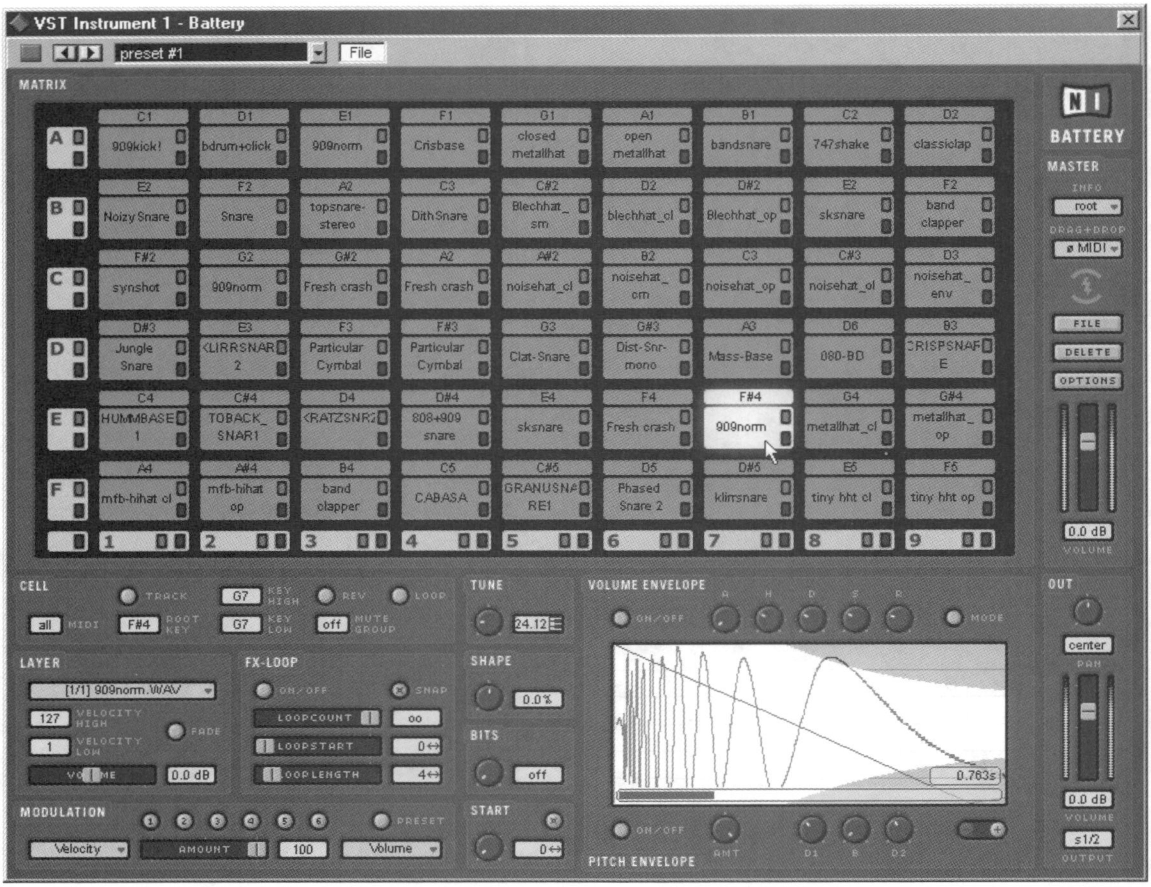

Figure 5.44
Native Instruments Battery

are six modulation inputs for each kit (for changing the volume, pan etc. according to incoming velocity, modulation, pitchbend, aftertouch and so on). It benefits from a total of up to 8 stereo and 16 mono outputs which are invaluable for routing sounds separately in a complex mix. The interface features an easy-to-use one page control surface with clearly laid out parameters and a useful wave display. Full drag and drop functionality is supported where audio files (such as WAV or AIFF) can be dragged directly into any cell and sounds can be dragged between cells. Cell functionality is extremely comprehensive and can display (and be individually adjusted for) volume, pan, output, MIDI channel, mute group, root key and a whole range of other parameters. Notably, a cell can be set to trigger over a key range rather than a single note which is useful for pitched samples. Very long samples and loops can be loaded and, for monitoring purposes, the cells light up when they are triggered. Battery can read samples in several formats including AKAI S-1000, SF2, Reaktor map, LM4, AIFF and WAV (from 8 to 32 bits). It is supplied with an extremely good library of kits including those designed for specific musical styles such as 60's garage, 70's funk, reggae, jazz, hip-hop, rock, soul, dub, dance, drum and bass and so on. The library also features some highly creative kits with such names as 'earth', 'french', 'harsh' and 'wicked' which are well worth checking out. Battery can handle a large number of samples simultaneously and provides an intuitive user interface for quickly tweaking existing kits and also developing your own. It is designed principally to handle drum and percussion samples but also works well with loops and pitched sounds.

Fxpansion DR-008

Instrument type:	advanced rhythm production workstation
Polyphony:	32
Number of outputs:	up to 8 stereo outputs and 8 stereo auxiliary outputs
Number of program slots:	virtually unlimited (drum sound patches are stored in DR-008's Presets folder and are loaded into their respective modules using a generic Preset menu. DR-008 is supplied with 190 presets).
Supported interfaces:	VST 2.0, DXi
Platform:	PC

DR-008 is a modular, open-architecture, drum-based sample playback and drum synthesis instrument. The control interface is based around 96 pads each of which is set to a different note between C0 and B7. The default view when the instrument is opened is the Overview screen where all 96 pads can be viewed simultaneously. Building a kit involves the assignment of sampler or drum synthesis modules to each of the pads. Right-clicking on an empty pad opens the pop-up module selection menu. DR-008 features four modules for handling samples, twelve modules for drum and percussion synthesis and five modules for processing MIDI data. Alternatively, double-clicking on an empty pad opens a file select dialogue where you can select AIFF or WAV audio files or DRS files (DRS files are Fxpansion's own DR-008 format) which are loaded directly into the pad. In this case, DR-008 automatically loads the appropriate module for the pad. Files can be previewed before loading if you have activated 'Enable quick preview' in DR-008's configuration menu. DR-008 also supports drag and drop of samples and DRS files from the file dialogue, from DR-008's own browser and between pads.

The supplied modules include:

- TheEights Bass – an eight parameter synth featuring two-stage pitch and amplitude decay envelopes for synthesizing smooth kick drums.
- HiHat – a hit-hat tone generator featuring mixed tone and noise signals routed through a band-pass filter.
- SnareDrum – a snare drum synth featuring two noise generators routed through bandpass filters and a swept pitch oscillator. Also features drive parameters for adding saturation effects.
- 809 Kick, 809 Snare, 808 Hat – kick, snare and hi-hat generators based on the circuitry used in the classic Roland x0x drum machines.
- HX-Bass, HX-Drum – Similar to TheEights Bass synth but with the addition of distortion parameters. HX-Bass is tuned for bass drums and HX-Drum is tuned for synth toms.
- Tambourine – simple three-parameter synth for generating synthesized tambourines.

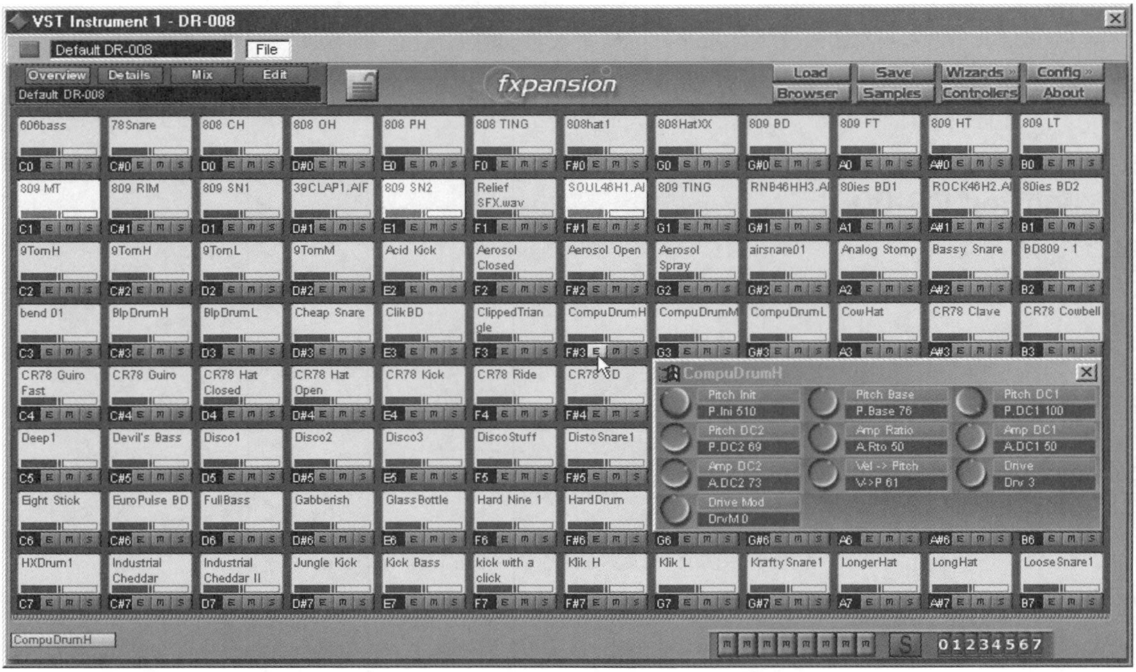

Figure 5.45
Fxpansion DR-008

- Stompin' Kick – bass drum synth producing powerful four-on-the-floor style bass drums by routing a tone through variable-shape envelope, waveshape and distortion parameters followed by a low-pass filter.
- DrumSynth008 – sophisticated drum synth for the creation of a wide variety of drum and percussion sounds using noise and sampled waveforms routed through two band-pass filters, two envelope generators and a tone control.
- Easy Sampler, Ultra Sampler, Quad Sampler, Velo Sampler – modules for the handling and processing of samples. Easy Sampler handles single samples monophonically with minimal control options, Ultra Sampler also handles samples monophonically but allows looping and filtering effects, and Quad Sampler is four Easy Sampler modules in one unit. Velo Sampler allows 128-way velocity switching between multiple samples and triggers samples polyphonically.
- DD Layer, DD Autoflam, DD Alternator, DD Autoroll, DD Sequencer – 'Drum Deploy' modules which produce MIDI output data when they are triggered via MIDI for the creation of layering, flam and drum roll effects. DD Sequencer is a 16-step sequencer which is synchronised to the tempo of the host software.

Once a module has been loaded, presets are selected by right-clicking on the pad and selecting the Presets option from the pop-up menu. The sound of a pad is modified by clicking on the 'E' button just below each pad which opens the editor for the module concerned. Each pad also features solo and mute buttons. Apart from the Overview page (Figure 5.45, above), DR-008 also features three other windows, Details, Mix and Edit. Details shows the pads (48 at a time) with additional auxiliary mini-sliders and hold (one shot) and choke buttons. The auxiliary outputs are used to send audio to effects processors via audio channels in the host software. Mix shows a single horizontal row of 12 pads each with a level fader and mini-sliders for setting up the mix of a kit in fine detail. Edit is similar to the Mix view except that you can access all the module editing parameters via mini-sliders shown above each pad rather than opening up the usual dedicated module editing windows.

DR-008 provides a unique approach to drum and rhythm programming and once you become familiar with its user interface it is intuitive and easy to program. Its open-ended architecture is of particular interest since it allows Fxpansion and other developers to add new modules to the system at any time in the future. It features 32-bit internal processing and you can load samples of up to 32-bit/96kHz resolution. It also supports the import of LM-4 text files. The sound quality is excellent and with its current batch of modules DR-008 produces authentic emulations of all the classic analogue drum machine sounds including the CR78, TR-606, TR-808 and TR-909. It is also capable of producing many of its own highly original drum sounds. DR-008 is produced as PC shareware and is therefore very cost-effective.

Tip

Hold down the computer keyboard Shift key to show the current audio output configuration simultaneously for all pads. Hold down the Control key to show the current auxiliary configuration.

Emagic evp73

Instrument type:	Fender Rhodes electric piano emulation
Polyphony:	73 voices
Number of outputs:	1
Number of program slots:	1
Supported interfaces:	VST 2.0
Platform:	PC, Mac

Figure 5.46
Emagic evp73

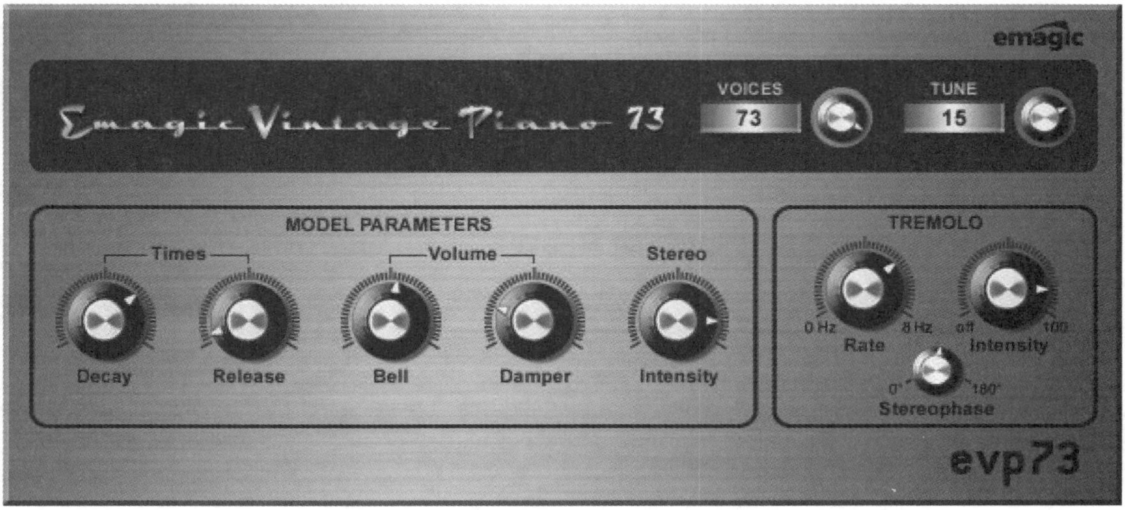

The evp73 is an emulation of the Fender Rhodes Stage Piano Mk II. The Fender Rhodes sound is legendary and has been used on countless numbers of popular music hits. Rhodes pianos were first invented by Harold Rhodes (1910-2000) when he developed the acoustic 'Rhodes Army Air Corps Piano' while serving in the American Army in 1942. Rhodes later set up the Rhodes Piano Corporation and developed his first electric piano the 'Pre-piano' in 1946. The company was bought by Fender in 1959 and in 1965 the classic Fender Rhodes Suitcase piano was released, the company's first real full-size electric piano. This led to the development of the Fender Rhodes Stage Piano Mark I in 1970 and the Fender Rhodes Stage Piano Mark II in 1979. The sound of the Fender Rhodes pianos are characterised by the action of hammers which strike tines (small metal plates) which were then amplified by electro-magnetic pickups.

Tip

To reproduce the Rhodes sounds used on classic recordings try routing the output through stereo pan, chorus or tremolo effects. Wah-wah, phasing or tape-style echo effects also produce good results. The instrument responds well to the kinds of effects which might normally be applied to a guitar. The Rhodes benefits from tube and amplifier simulator plug-ins and works extremely well when passed through the tube amplifier and rotary speaker stages of Native Instrument's B4 (when used as an effects processor).

The evp73 is based upon the Mark II and uses native real-time tone generation to reproduce the timbral characteristics of the real-world instrument. The Mark II was available in 73 and 88-note keyboard versions and the evp73 emulates a 73-key version. It features five controls in the model parameters section. Decay determines the duration of the notes from short at lower settings to long at higher settings, release determines how long the note continues after the key has been released , bell adds the characteristic Fender Rhodes 'tinkly' characteristic to the timbre, damper controls how the bell sound is dampened when the note is released and stereo spread determines how much the keyboard range is spread across the stereo image. It has a tremolo effects section with rate, intensity and stereo phase controls. Tremolo effects are particularly identified as being part of the Fender Rhodes sound. The sound of the evp73 can be further modified with the effects processors of your host software and echo, phasing and wah-wah are particularly recommended.

The evp73 is not supplied with any soundbanks and it has only one program slot in the host software. However, sounds can be set up very quickly and can be saved one at a time when you find sounds you wish to keep. The evp73 uses the same core audio engine as Emagic's evp88, a similar virtual instrument which can be run in Emagic Logic Audio only. It produces the trademark bright, 'tinkly' tones of the original instrument and is suited to a wide range of musical styles from soul to funk and from rock to jazz.

LoftSoft FM Heaven

Instrument type:	FM synthesizer
Polyphony:	64
Number of outputs:	1 stereo
Number of program slots:	384
Supported interfaces:	VST 2.0
Platform:	PC, Mac

FM Heaven is a software FM synthesizer based around the design of the Yamaha DX7 FM synthesizer. The graphical user interface is contained within a single page upon which a deceptively large number of parame-

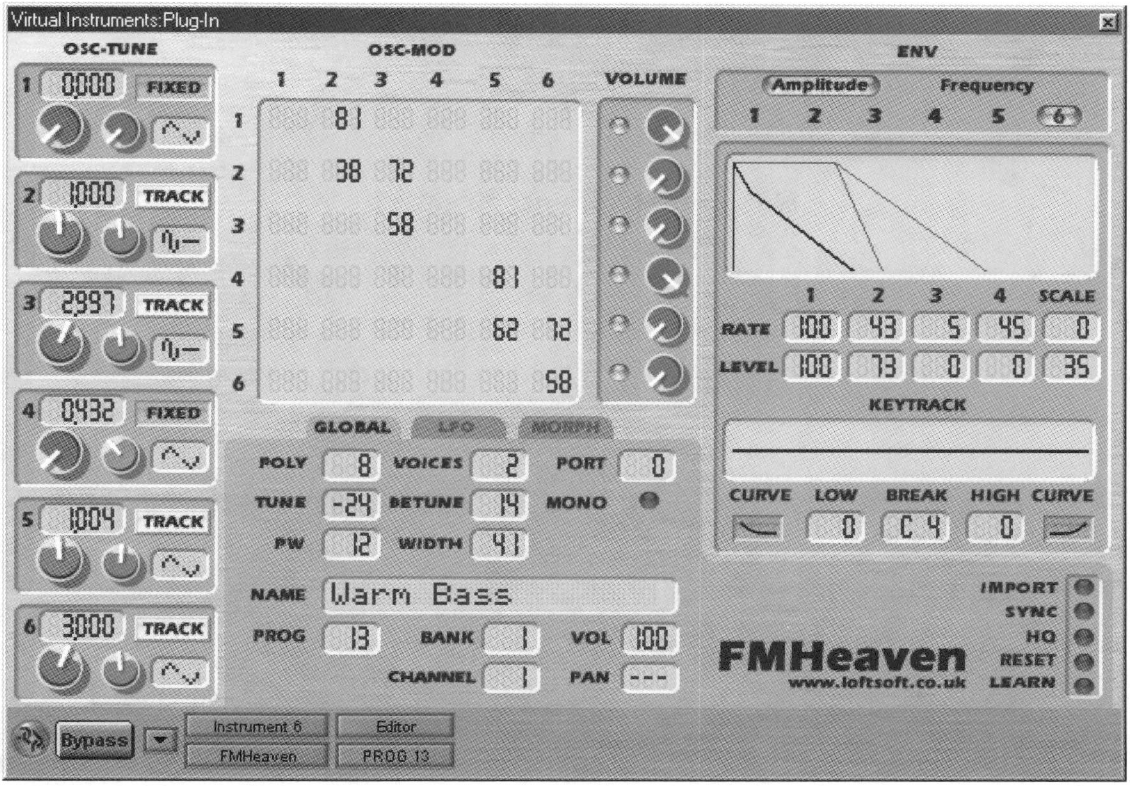

Figure 5.47 FM Heaven

ters can be manipulated. Like the DX7, FM Heaven has six oscillators but, rather than being configured in fixed algorithms, they are freely configurable within a modulation matrix. Any one oscillator can modulate any other, oscillators can be configured to output as carriers while also modulating other oscillators and feedback can be applied. Oscillators can be tuned over eight octaves and set to fixed frequency or pitch tracking mode. Sixteen waveforms are available for each oscillator. Other FM Heaven features include twelve envelope generators for the independent control of amplitude and frequency for each oscillator, voice morphing allowing the real-time control of multiple parameters simultaneously, keyboard scaling for each oscillator, one LFO with sine, square and S&H waveforms, flexible performance controls including portamento, monophonic/polyphonic modes, voice stacking mode (where more than one voice is assigned to each played note), voice detune, stereo width control, and multi-timbral operation on 16 MIDI channels. MIDI controllers can be freely assigned to any of the on-screen controls for the operation of FM Heaven from a remote control surface and complete automation is possible from within the VST host.

FM Heaven is supplied with 12 banks of 32 sounds covering a multitude of musical instrument emulations, pads and abstract timbres. It also supports the import of DX7 and TX81Z System Exclusive files meaning that you can make use of the vast range of FM soundbanks which are available for download on the Internet.

Like the original DX7, FM Heaven is suitable for the creation of bass, bells, brass, electric pianos, organs, pads and sound effects. It has a high-quality sound which, although it is cleaner than the original, avoids becoming too digitally clinical. FM Heaven was among the first FM synthesis VST Instruments. It has a graphically simple but functional user interface and is a cost-effective way in to software-based FM synthesis.

Native Instruments Kontakt

Instrument type:	advanced software sampler
Polyphony:	up to 256
Number of outputs:	32
Number of program slots:	128
Supported interfaces:	VST 2.0, DXi, MAS, DirectConnect
Platform:	PC, Mac

Figure 5.48
Native Instruments Kontakt

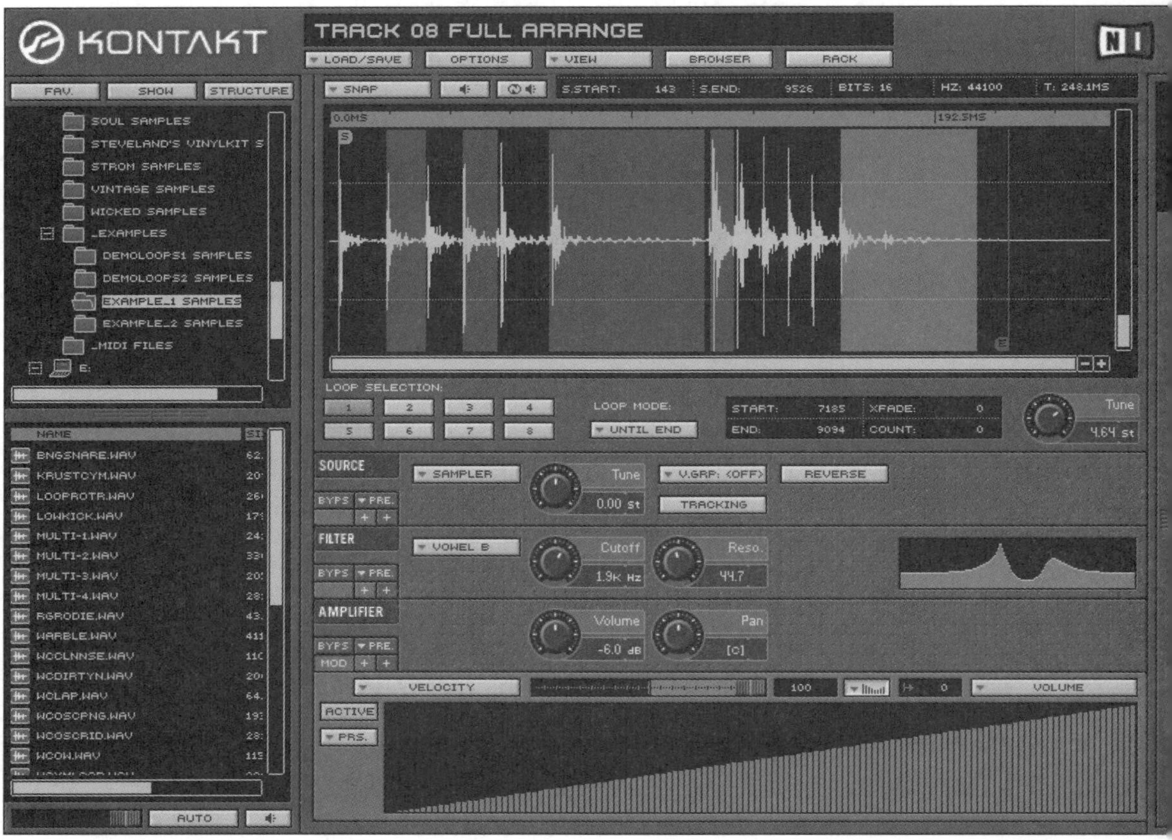

Kontakt is an innovative software sampler designed to be one of the most powerful samplers ever created. 256-voice polyphony, 32 outputs, 128 velocity layers, 17 different analogue-modelled filter types and 16-part multi-timbrality are just some of the reasons why this description might be accurate. Kontakt also features real-time timestretching and resynthesis, integrated loop editing with eight independent loops, graphical multiple-breakpoint envelopes, graphical sample mapping and key range displays, visually displayed modulation, eleven onboard send and insert effects, drag and drop file management, and dynamic resource allocation (where only the currently active parts of the program use any CPU power).

The interface features a number of editing pages which manage different aspects of the sampler. The Mapping editor includes an integrated file browser and sample mapping matrix with drag-and-drop funtionality where keyzones, velocity groups, sample crossfades, velocity crossfades and parameter assignments are managed with ease. The Loop editor displays the waveform of the chosen sample in a number of zoom settings and allows you to draw in up to eight loops. The playback mode, pitch and the number of repeats can be set individually for each loop and the editor supports sophisticated loop crossfade and automated loop find functions. The start point of each loop can be changed according to incoming MIDI control messages or onboard modulators. Kontakt features graphically displayed curves for all filters and includes analogue-modelled low-pass, high-pass, band pass and notch filter types and special sound design and vocal filter types. Almost all parameters within Kontakt can be modulated by LFOs, envelopes, step modulators, envelope followers or controllers and where appropriate modulation can be synchronised to tempo. Kontakt operates in three modes: Classic sampler, Time machine and Tone machine. In Time machine mode, real-time timestretching and pitch shifting are possible. In Tone machine mode, Kontakt imposes the pitch of the currently played note upon the triggered sample, creating pitched instruments out of non-pitched sounds like drums and percussion. The onboard effects include EQ, delay, reverb, waveshaper, lowfi, stereo enhancer, distortion, flanger, phaser, compressor and chorus. Effects can be used as inserts or sends and the order of effects is user-definable.

An outstanding library of over 3Gb of samples is supplied on 5 CDs, organised into separate categories. The samples take advantage of the new sound-sculpting possibilities offered by Kontakt. In addition, the following sample formats are supported: Akai S-1000/S-3000, Gigasampler, SF2, Battery, Reaktor map, LM4, AIFF and WAV (8 to 32 bit sample resolution).

Kontakt offers sonic possibilities far beyond the normal range of ordinary samplers. Above all, it has enormous potential for transforming and sculpting the source samples with its innumerable modulation possibilities and powerful filters. It is extremely versatile and, with its 'what you see is what you use' interface, is comparatively easy to use. Great for all traditional sampling applications but also unrivalled for sound design, special effects and the exploration of new sonic dimensions.

Fxpansion Mysteron

Instrument type:	Theremin emulation
Polyphony:	1
Number of outputs:	1
Number of program slots:	1
Supported interfaces:	VST 2.0, DXi
Platform:	PC

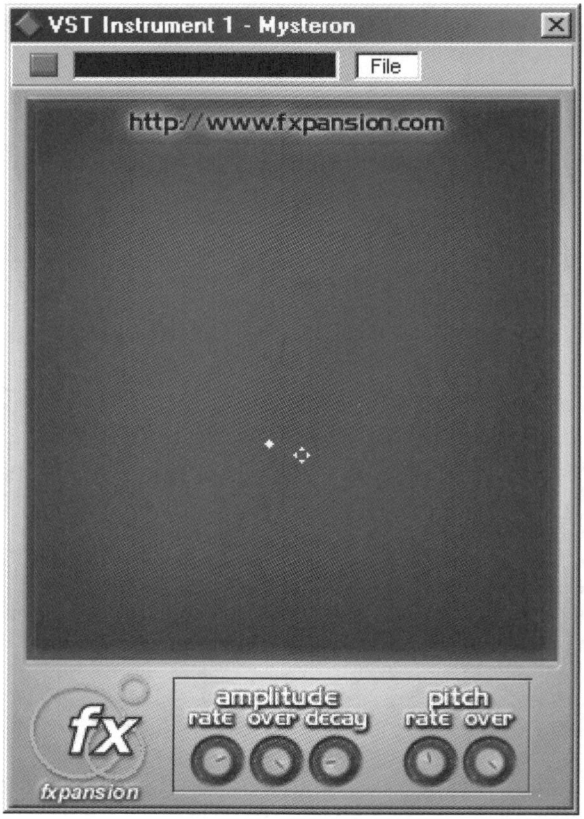

Figure 5.49
Fxpansion Mysteron

Mysteron emulates the behaviour of the Theremin electronic musical instrument. The Theremin was developed and built in 1917 in the USSR by Leon Sergeivitch Termen (1896-1993), a Russian cellist and electronic engineer. The original Theremin sound was produced by a vacuum tube effect known as heterodyning where two high radio frequencies combine to create a lower audible frequency. It was found that the capacitance of the human body in the proximity of the vacuum tubes had an effect on the pitch of the sound and Leon Termen immediately saw the usefulness of this phenomenom for the creation of a unique musical instrument. The eventual Theremin production model (released in 1920) featured a metal antenna for pitch and a metal loop for volume. The pitch and volume were controlled by the movement of the player's hands in relation to the antennae. The sound was a fixed violin-like timbre and featured smooth glissandos between notes during performance. One of its most famous appearances was on the 1960's Beach Boys popular music hit 'Good Vibrations'.

The Mysteron emulates the behaviour of the Theremin by using an X-Y graphical user interface where the vertical Y axis represents pitch (lowest position = highest pitch) and the horizontal X-axis represents amplitude (right side = loudest amplitude). The output signal is a simple sine wave. The current pitch and amplitude is shown by a small cross-hair cursor. The pitch and amplitude is changed by moving the cursor position with the mouse or playing a MIDI keyboard where the cursor responds to the pitch and velocity of incoming MIDI notes. However, the speed of change is regulated according to the position of a small dot which chases the cursor and eventually settles within it. The pitch and amplitude of the output follow the small dot. The speed with which the small dot chases the cursor is set with rate controls for pitch and amplitude. Overshoot parameters regulate how far the small dot overshoots (misses) the target position. At maximum overshoot levels the small dot never finds the target and effectively bounces around the display endlessly (as does the pitch and amplitude). An amplitude decay control regulates the speed with which notes fade to zero level. This interface allows the creation of sounds which accurately emulate the glissandos and volume swells of the Theremin and is also capable of some unique effects of its own.

Mysteron invites experimentation, is great fun to play and, what's more, is available for free download on the Internet. A very good VSTi which is excellent for creating quirky lead lines and specialist sound effects.

Steinberg Neon

Instrument type:	virtual analogue synthesizer
Polyphony:	16
Number of outputs:	1
Number of program slots:	16
Supported interfaces:	VST 2.0

Neon is a simple two oscillator software synthesizer which is included with Cubase VST. Neon's user interface features the following control parameters:

- Range – determines the octave for the oscillators according to the selection of one of the three buttons.
- Waveform – determines the waveform for the oscillators between triangle, sawtooth and square waves.
- LFO Speed – governs the speed of the modulation ('vibrato') which is applied to the signal when Neon receives modulation messages via MIDI.
- Osc 2 Detune – allows the detuning of the second oscillator by ± 7 semitones in order to produce 'chorus' and automatic harmony effects.

Figure 5.50
Steinberg Neon virtual analogue synth

- VCF Cut-off – determines the frequency cut-off point.
- VCF Resonance – emphasises the frequencies around the cut-off point .
- VCF attack, decay, sustain, release envelope.
- VCA attack, decay, sustain, release envelope.

Like many analogue synthesizers, preliminary experimentation with Neon might revolve around the cut-off and resonance controls in conjunction with the filter's ADSR envelope.. To help add some character to sounds try using the detune control for oscillator 2 to create 'chorus' and 'thickening' effects.

The lack of a pulse width control for the square wave setting is a drawback but Neon is still capable of producing a reasonable set of tone colours. It is supplied with sixteen useful presets and is good for bass and brass-like sounds and simple tones for sequencing applications. It also makes a good learning tool for anyone who is new to analogue synthesis.

rgcAudio Pentagon I

Instrument type:	virtual analogue synthesizer
Polyphony:	64
Number of outputs:	1 stereo
Number of program slots:	768
Supported interfaces:	VST 2.0, DXi
Platform:	PC

Pentagon is a powerful analogue-style software synthesizer. It features over 100 virtual control knobs in a single window and includes an extremely comprehensive range of functions. It is among the most complete implementations of subtractive synthesis to be found in any VST Instrument. The specifications are as follows:

- Four oscillators – each with a choice of 13 alias free waveforms and a noise generator including saw, vintage saw, square, vintage square,

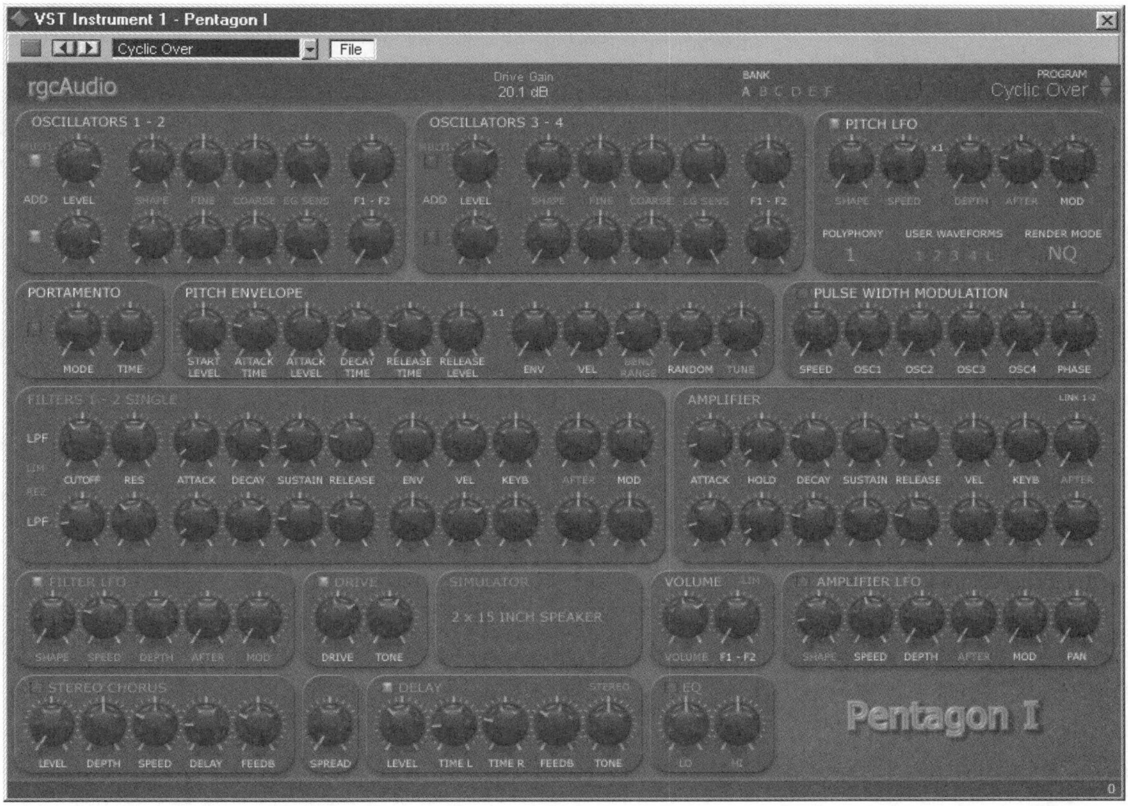

Figure 5.51
rgcAudio Pentagon I

various pulse and harmonic types, pure sine and four user-loadable waveform slots.

- 64 voice polyphonic with polyphony limiter and intelligent voice allocation.
- Legato mode for monophonic operation.
- Portamento with fixed or variable per-key time.
- Individual adjustment of level, waveform, mode, phase, tuning, LFO sensitivity and pitch envelope amount for each oscillator.
- Key sync, inverted, free running or fixed frequency mode for each oscillator.
- Dedicated pitch envelope section, with start level, attack time, attack level, decay time, release level, release time with fully bandlimited operation.
- Random pitch control, with individual generators per oscillator.
- Four operation modes: add (normal), ring modulation, hard sync and frequency modulation. Each group of two oscillators can select any operation mode.
- Pulse width modulation (PWM) with adjustable depth for every oscillator and phase shift control.
- Two resonant multimode filters with low-pass, high-pass, band pass and notch filter types with individual controls for type, cutoff, resonance, ADSR parameters, envelope amount, velocity, keyboard scaling, aftertouch, breath control and modulation.

Tip

To quickly view Pentagon's sounds select one of the bank letters (A-F) at the top of the window and then right-click anywhere on the interface. The 128 sounds of the selected bank appear in a convenient pop-up window. Patches can be copied and pasted between program slots and any slot can be initialised using the Program option in the pop-up menu which appears when you click on the parameter read-out (top centre of window). This helps with the management and arranging of presets.

Tip

All Pentagon parameters named in blue have dual or multiple functions. Select the alternatives by clicking on the name.

- Two amplifier envelope generators with AHDSR parameters, keyboard tracking and velocity control.
- Positive or negative envelope modes.
- Linear/exponential selectable envelopes.
- Dedicated pitch, filter and amplifier LFO's with 13 waveform types including sine, square, pulse types, saw, triangle, step, random, sample and hold.
- Variable offset of all waveforms, delay, fade, speed depth, aftertouch, breath and modulation controls.
- All LFO's individually syncable to the tempo of the host software.
- User-loadable LFO waveforms.
- Five Pitch Bend modes: normal, asymmetric, high note, low note, hold notes.
- Onboard effects section including drive, amp/speaker simulator (19 simulations), chorus (stereo and 4-voice), phaser (stereo and 4-voice), autopan, stereo spread, stereo delay, two band EQ. (Effects can be disabled to save CPU power).

The specifications speak for themselves but the best thing about Pentagon is the way it sounds. This VSTi is the subtractive synthesist's dream come true. The oscillators can be configured for frequency modulation, ring modulation or sync modes and the two filters can be set for single, parallel or serial operation. The filters are particularly smooth and reactive and, with its sophisticated performance parameters and comprehensive MIDI implementation, Pentagon is renowned for its performance playability. The sonic range covers a vast palette of synth timbres from biting synth leads to warm pads to fat bass sounds and inspiring sound effects and textures. It is also comparatively easy to program. Some may not like the idea of all those control knobs but they are practical and allow you to tweak all of the parameters in a single window. For tweaking from an external control surface each parameter can be assigned to a MIDI controller (shift/right-click on the parameter dial). Pentagon has an enormous 768 program slots arranged into six banks and is supplied with 300 factory presets. It is already extremely popular among existing VSTi users.

Also worth checking out in the rgcAudio range is the Triangle II monophonic synthesizer which uses the same audio engine as the Pentagon and is available for free on the Internet.

mda Piano

Instrument type:	sampled piano (Free VSTi)
Polyphony:	32
Number of outputs:	1 stereo
Number of program slots:	8
Supported interfaces:	VST 2.0
Platform:	PC, Mac

The mda Piano is a sampled piano VST Instrument modelled upon 31 piano samples. The control interface is contained within a small but practical window and includes the following parameters:

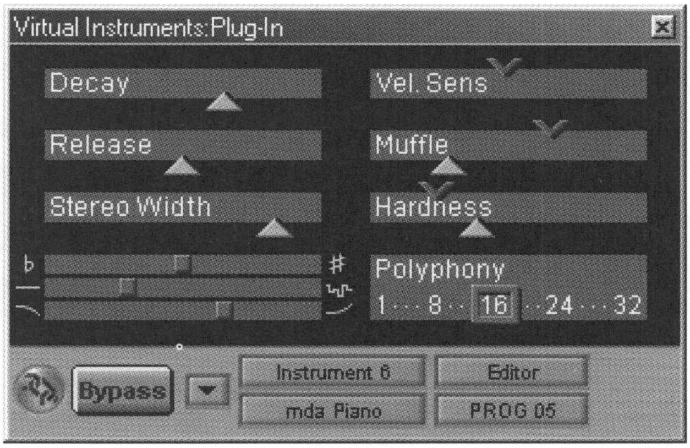

Figure 5.52
mda Piano

- decay and release – determine the loudness contour of the sound.
- stereo width – spreads the notes across the stereo image and at higher settings adds a psychoacoustic widening effect.

velocity sensitivity – determines how much the velocity of incoming MIDI notes affect the loudness.

- muffle – dampens the high frequency content of the attack stage of the note simulating the dampening heard in a real piano.
- hardness – regulates the tonal quality of the sound between rounded and mellow at low settings and sharp and resonant at higher settings.
- polyphony – determines the number of voices available.
- tuning settings – allows the basic tuning of the piano and the setting of special stretched and random tunings.

Considering that it takes up very little CPU the mda Piano achieves very good sound quality. It is supplied with eight presets including such names as Dance piano, Compressed piano, Concert piano and School piano. These presets are very usable and instantly demonstrate the playability and ease-of-use of the instrument. Try the Concert piano sound with a decent reverb plug-in and you are likely to be pleasantly surprised with the result. The mda Piano does not pretend to be a top-flight piano VSTi and is not suitable for solo work. However, it is great for basic chord parts and demos and it may even find its way onto a hit record. The mda Piano is available for free download on the Internet.

Sonic Syndicate Plucked String 2

Instrument type:	physical modelling plucked string synthesizer
Polyphony:	20
Number of outputs:	1 stereo
Number of program slots:	1
Supported interfaces:	VST 2.0
Platform:	PC

The Sonic Syndicate Plucked String 2 module is a plucked string synthesizer based upon physical modelling techniques. It features a simple user interface which includes the following:

Figure 5.53
Sonic Syndicate Plucked String 2

- coarse and fine controls – for adjusting the pitch.
- timbre – varies the timbre from dark at lower settings to bright at higher settings.
- strength – varies the strength of the sound where lower settings simulate the string being plucked closer to the bridge while higher settings simulate the string being plucked further away from the bridge.
- attack, decay and release controls – for shaping the loudness contour of the sound.
- cut-off – sets the frequency at which the high frequency content of the sound starts to decay.
- damp – determines how quickly the high frequency content of the sound decays.
- waveset – the Noise setting produces a thin steel acoustic sound with a hard attack. String produces a rounded, mellow sound with more body and a soft attack. Gourmet adds a more accentuated pluck to the rounded string sound.
- settings button – opens a menu where you can set the polyphony between 1 and 20 voices, change the voice playback mode between single-stereo, dual-stereo and triple-stereo, and set the Pitch Bend range.

Tip

For electric guitar sounds, try routing the output of Plucked String through a distortion or overdrive processor, or through an amplifier simulator. If you are a Cubase VST user, try inserting the supplied 'Overdrive' guitar amplifier simulator into the signal path. Excellent results can also be achieved by adding chorus to Plucked String electric guitar and bass sounds.

Plucked String is not supplied with any soundbanks and it only has one program slot in the host software. This does not detract from the usefulness of this VSTi which is one of the few to use physical modelling techniques effectively and also tackle the synthesis of plucked string instruments. It performs its task rather well and it is possible to create very convincing bass guitar, acoustic guitar, electric guitar, dampened guitar, plucked violin and harp tones. Try adjusting the controls as in Figure 5.53 (with a polyphony of 12, dual-stereo mode and pitch bend at 2 in the settings menu) to produce a Fender Precision style bass guitar.

Waldorf PPG Wave 2.V

Instrument type:	virtual wavetable synthesizer
Polyphony:	up to 64
Number of outputs:	1
Number of program slots:	128
Supported interfaces:	VST 2.0
Platform:	Mac, PC

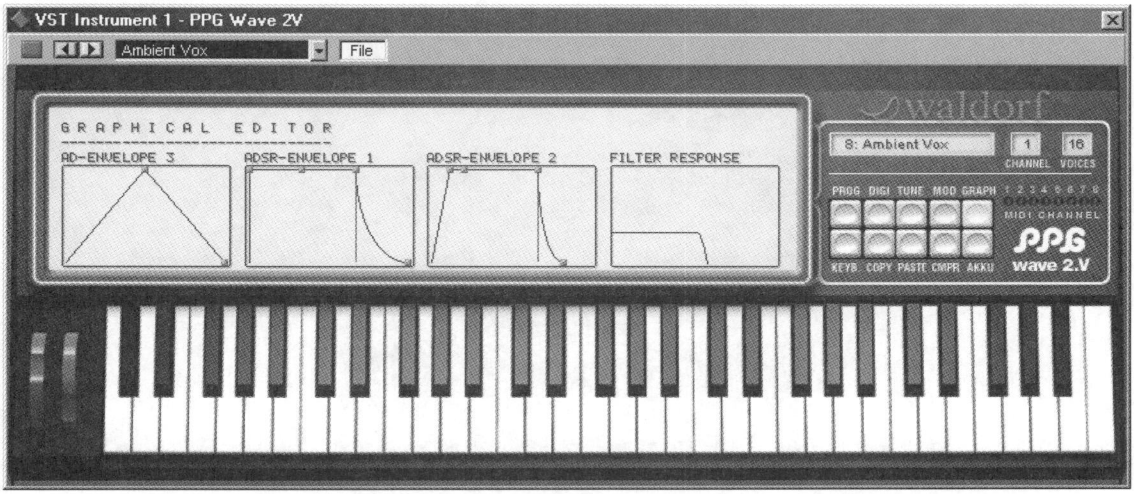

Figure 5.54
Waldorf PPG Wave 2.V virtual wavetable synth

The PPG Wave 2.V is a software emulation of the classic PPG Wave 2.3 wavetable synthesizer. Wavetable synthesis involves reading a number of cyclic waveforms stored in a digital memory. This digital memory is known as the wavetable, which contains a collection of waveforms often referred to as wavecycles. Each wavecycle is a short snippet of digital sound which is played back in a specific sequence. The PPG Wave features 32 such wavetables each of which contains 64 wavecycles. When you press a note on the PPG Wave keyboard, it sweeps through all 64 wavecycles of the chosen wavetable from start to finish. This results in the unmistakeable sound of the original PPG Wave 2.3 and also the PPG Wave 2.V (which is based upon exactly the same wavetables). In addition to the wavetables, the PPG Wave 2.V features 2 oscillators per voice, a low-pass resonant filter, 1 LFO, 3 graphic envelopes (2 ADSR, 1 AD) and a very comprehensive MIDI specification. It is supplied with nine excellent soundbanks each of which contains around 128 sounds. This includes the original Factory presets for the PPG Wave 2.3 and a wide range of other sounds programmed by sound designers and PPG enthusiasts. The PPG Wave 2.V is particularly suited to the creation of glistening, crystalline, bell-like, voice and choir tones, special effects and dreamy, other-wordly timbres. It is also extremely good at producing bass, electric piano and all kinds of pad sounds. Just like the original, it has a particular sound quality which sets it apart from other synthesizers. Great for injecting some originality and inspiration.

Steinberg VB-1

Instrument type:	virtual bass synthesizer
Polyphony:	4
Number of outputs:	1
Number of program slots:	16
Supported interfaces:	VST 2.0

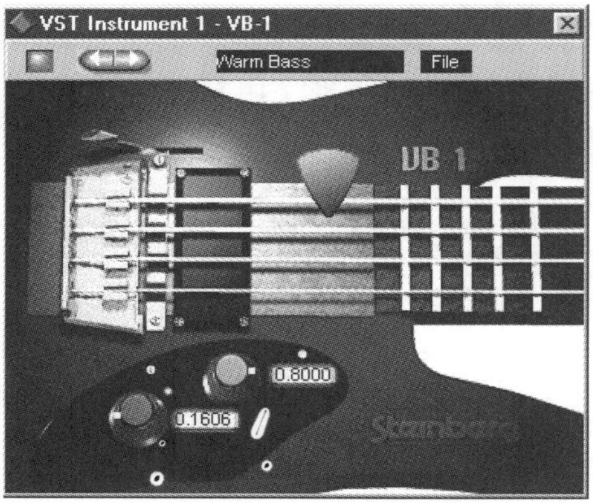

Figure 5.55
The VB-1 virtual bass synth

The VB-1 is a virtual model of a bass guitar and is supplied with Steinberg Cubase VST. The user interface features a graphic representation of the working parts of a bass guitar which can be manipulated with the mouse in order to produce different tones. The five elements which can be manipulated are as follows:

- Dampening control – regulates the characteristics of the sound to simulate the action of dampening the strings of a bass guitar (10 position switch).
- Pickup position – regulates the tone of the sound in conjunction with the pick position.
- Pick position – regulates the attack and tone, assuming a 'mellow' character when positioned far from the bridge and a 'bright' character when positioned close to the bridge. When positioned above the pickup, the sound becomes more 'plucked'.
- Tone control – regulates the overall amount of treble and bass frequencies in the sound.
- Volume control – regulates the output volume.

Updating sounds on the VB-1 involves manipulating the moveable objects of the interface with the mouse. To create bass sounds with very 'sharp' attack characteristics set the dampening control to its most dampened setting and the tone control to its maximum treble setting. Adjust the pickup and pick positions to achieve the required final result. To create more 'synth-like' tones try moderate dampening, with the tone control set towards its bass position and the pick at its furthest position from the bridge.

Although only equipped with five parameters, the VB-1 is capable of producing a wide variety of bass sounds. It is supplied with 16 presets which make useful starting points for creating your own sounds. It is particularly good at producing plucked tones and works well when combined with other VST Instruments to produce composite bass sounds.

Koblo Vibra 1000

Instrument type:	simple virtual analogue synthesizer (Free VSTi)
Polyphony:	1 (monophonic)
Number of outputs:	1
Number of program slots:	unlimited (since patches are saved to your Mac)
Supported interfaces:	VST 2.0
Platform:	Mac

The Koblo Vibra 1000 provides users with a simple entry level VSTi for

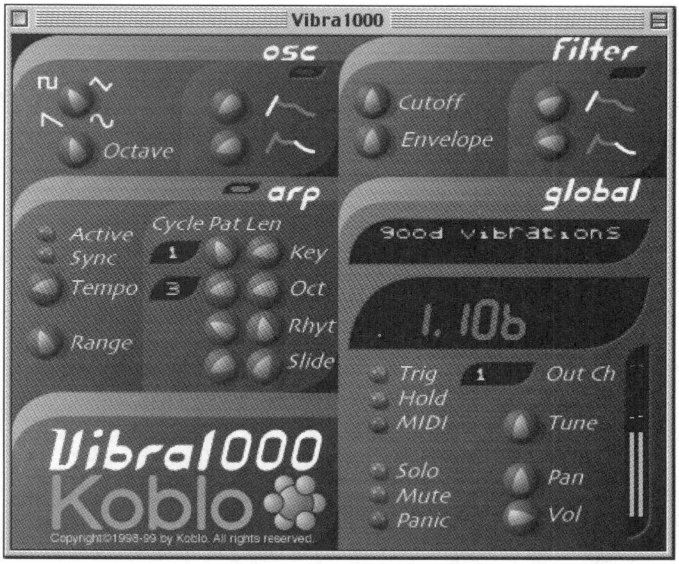

Figure 5.56
Koblo Vibra 1000

gaining an idea of the sound and design of the more powerful synthesizers in the Koblo series, the Vibra 6000 and Vibra 9000. The Vibra 1000 features one oscillator with saw, square or triangle waveforms and an attack, release envelope, a simple filter with cut-off, attack, release and envelope parameters and an onboard arpeggiator. It uses 32-bit internal DSP processing which means that you get the same high quality sound as its big brothers. The Vibra 1000 is useful to have around for simple lead and bass synth sounds. It is available free via the Internet.

Steinberg Virtual Guitarist

Instrument type:	virtual rhythm guitar instrument
Polyphony:	n/a
Number of outputs:	1
Number of program slots:	27 players
Supported interfaces:	VST 2.0
Platform:	PC, Mac

Figure 5.57
Steinberg Virtual Guitarist

Virtual Guitarist is a sample-based rhythm guitar instrument. It specialises in the playing of rhythm guitar in a number of popular styles and features both acoustic and electric sounds. It can't play a solo but what it can do is play a wide range of chords and rhythm styles in any key and tempo. All you have to do is choose a 'player', hold down a chord on your MIDI keyboard and Virtual Guitarist starts strumming away at the current tempo of your host software.

The interface features two instruments, acoustic and electric, and 27 different players. Sounds include spanish, steel string, resonator, clean strat, wah, power chords and ultra metal. Each player has 8 parts with flexible real-time punctuation and variation of the sound. Accents are created by hitting the keys harder, long chords are created by holding down the sustain pedal, vibrato is applied via aftertouch, and fill patterns are activated using the modulation wheel. Authentic fret noises and mute sounds are included and you can humanise your player by adjusting the timing and dynamics controls. Virtual Guitarist can interpret and play 168 different chords and is built upon approximately 30,000 sampled guitar snippets.

Excellent sound quality, intuitive graphical user interface, minimal CPU overhead and convenience are just some of the reasons why this VST Instrument is a popular choice. It is especially useful for recording demos and trying out new ideas in your host software without setting up a guitar rig. It also brings authentic rhythm guitar within the reach of keyboard players who cannot afford to hire the real-life variety.

Summary

VST Instruments provide a convenient means of accessing high quality sound sources within the convenient environment of the host application. All that is required to trigger the sounds is one external keyboard connected to your computer via MIDI and a low latency audio card. This arrangement cuts down on your need to have a large scale MIDI network and therefore saves physical space in your recording studio/working environment. In addition, VST Instruments do not develop electronic faults and are not subject to the usual wear-and-tear suffered by real-world instruments.

The only drawback is that running VST Instruments alongside audio Tracks and plug-ins requires a rather powerful processor. If the CPU load becomes a problem try converting your VST Instrument Tracks into audio Tracks (as explained in chapter 4) since audio Tracks put less strain on the CPU. Unlike regular MIDI Tracks, VST Instrument Tracks can be converted directly into audio data.

At the time of writing there were around 250 VST Instruments available representing a vast array of different instrument types and synthesis techniques. Table 5.1 lists some of the main developers and their products.

Table 5.1
VST Instruments list

Developer	*VST Instrument*	*Description*
Applied Acoustics	Tassman	Modular synthesizer based on physical modelling
Applied Acoustics	Lounge Lizard	Electric piano
Arturia	Storm	Virtual multi-module studio
Big Tick	Angelina	Vocal pad synthesizer (using formant synthesis)
Big Tick	Cheeze Machine	String ensemble synthesizer (Free)
Bitheadz	Retro AS-1	Virtual analogue synthesizer
Bitheadz	Unity AS-1	Virtual analogue synthesizer
Bitheadz	Unity DS-1	Sampler
Bioroid	Turntablist Pro	Turntable emulation and scratch mixer
Bitshift Audio	pHATmatic	REX file player
Bitshift Audio	pHATmatic Pro	Loop player and sample slicer
Bojo	Impulse	Virtual analogue synthesizer
Bojo	Organ One	Organ
Desaster Development	Ruction	Sample sequencer
Edirol	HyperCanvas	GM sound module
Edirol	SuperQuartet	Sample-based sound module
Emagic	EVP73	Electric piano
FXpansion	DR-002	Freeware basic virtual drum machine
FXpansion	DR-008	Modular drum synthesis/sample player
FXpansion	Mysteron	Theremin emulation (Free)
GForce	MTron	Mellotron emulation
Girl	Girl	Sample/loop manipulator and sequencer
Green Oak	Crystal	Modular synthesizer
IK	Sample Tank	Sample player/sound module
Image Line	DX10	FM synthesizer
Image Line	Wasp	Virtual analogue synthesizer
Jorgen Aase	Energy Pro	Step sequencer/synthesizer
Koblo	Gamma 9000	Drum synthesizer
Koblo	Stella 9000	Polyphonic sampler
Koblo	Vibra 1000	Mono virtual analogue synthesizer (Free Mac only)
Koblo	Vibra 6000	Mono virtual analogue synthesizer

Developer	*VST Instrument*	*Description*
Koblo	Vibra 9000	Advanced virtual analogue synthesizer
Lin Plug	Gakstoar Alpha	Virtual analogue synthesizer (2 oscillator version)
Lin Plug	Gakstoar Delta	Virtual analogue synthesizer (4 oscillator version)
Lin Plug	Rupsta Gamma	Virtual drum machine
LoftSoft	FM Heaven	FM synthesizer
mda	DX10	FM synthesizer (Free)
mda	ePiano	Electric piano (Free)
mda	JX10	Virtual analogue synth (Free)
mda	Piano	Piano (Free)
MHC	Space Synthesizer	Ambient texture synthesizer
Muon Software	Atom Pro	Simple but powerful virtual analogue synthesizer
Muon Software	Tau Pro	TB303-style acid bass synth emulation
Muon Software	Electron	Virtual analogue synthesizer
Muon Software	Positron	Virtual analogue synthesizer
Native Instruments	Absynth	Modular synthesizer
Native Instruments	Battery	Sample-based drum and percussion module
Native Instruments	B4	Hammond B3 tonewheel organ emulation
Native Instruments	FM7	FM synthesizer
Native Instruments	Kontakt	Sampler
Native Instruments	Reaktor Session	Reaktor ensemble player
Native Instruments	Reaktor	Powerful modular synthesizer/rhythm processor/software sampler
Native Instruments	Pro-52	Prophet 5 analogue synthesizer emulation
PlugSound	Vol. 1: Keyboards	Sample-based sound module
PlugSound	Vol. 2: Fretted	Sample-based sound module
PlugSound	Vol. 3: Drums	Sample-based sound module
PlugSound	Vol. 4: Hip Hop Toolkit	Sample-based sound module
PlugSound	Vol. 5: Synth	Sample-based sound module
reFX	Quadra SID 6581	C-64 SID chip emulation synthesizer
rgcAudio	Pentagon I	Virtual analogue synthesizer (4 oscillators)
rgcAudio	Square I	Virtual analogue synthesizer (3 oscillators)
rgcAudio	Triangle I	Virtual analogue synthesizer (Free)
rgcAudio	Triangle II	Virtual analogue synthesizer (Free)

Developer	*VST Instrument*	*Description*
Sonic Syndicate	Junglist	Virtual analogue synthesizer
Sonic Syndicate	Plucked String	Plucked string synthesizer based on physical modelling
Sonic Syndicate	Scorpion	Virtual analogue synthesizer
Spectrasonics	Atmosphere	Dream pad sound module based on sampling
Spectrasonics	Stylus	Vinyl remix groove and sample manipulation module
Spectrasonics	Trilogy	Electric, acoustic and synth bass module
SpeedSoft	Virtual Sampler	Software sampler
SpeedSoft	VX 7	FM synthesizer
Steinberg	CS-40	Virtual analogue synthesizer
Steinberg	HALion	Sophisticated software sampler based on hard disk streaming
Steinberg/MDA	JX16	Virtual analogue synthesizer
Steinberg	LM4 MK II	Virtual drum machine (18 drum pad version)
Steinberg	LM9	Virtual drum machine (9 drum pad version)
Steinberg	Model E	Minimoog Model D analogue synthesizer emulation
Steinberg	Neon	Basic virtual analogue synthesizer
Steinberg	Plex	Restructuring synthesizer by Wolfgang Palm
Steinberg	The Grand	Grand piano
Steinberg	VB-1	Virtual bass guitar
Steinberg	Virtual Guitarist	Rhythm Guitar module
TC Works	Mercury-I	Virtual analogue synthesizer
TC Works	Spark Modular	Modular synthesizer
Tobybear	Deconstructor	Sample manipulator
Tobybear	Electric Cowboy	Guitar synthesizer based on physical modelling
Virsyn	Virsyn Tera	High-end modular synthesizer
Waldorf	Attack	Drum and percussion synthesizer
Waldorf	PPG Wave 2.V	PPG Wave 2.2 wavetable synthesizer emulation

VSTi performance table

The VSTi performance table (shown below) provides a detailed summary of the MIDI response and general performance of a number of the most popular VST instruments. When comparing instruments, note that 'more is not necessarily better'. For example, Muon's Tau Pro is monophonic (1-voice) and Steinberg's HALion is 256-voice polyphonic. This does not mean that HALion is always the better of the two. It all depends on your needs. The Tau Pro is a monophonic performance synthesizer designed for the triggering of TB303-style bass and lead synth sounds whereas HALion is a multi-timbral VST sampler. The instruments are designed for very different purposes and both perform their task rather well. You must, therefore, take this kind of difference into consideration when making comparisons.

Table 5.2
VSTi MIDI and general performance table

VSTi	maximum polyphony	multi-timbral	velocity sensitive	modulation controller	main volume controller	pan controller 1	sustain ped. controller 6	sostenuto controller 6	soft ped. controller 67	prog. chnge	aftertouch	pitch bend	automation via sysex	param. control via MIDI CC's	audio outs (Cubase VST)
Atom Pro	12		*									*	*		1
Attack	64		*							*		*	*	*	2s, 4m
B4	91 tones		*	*	*	*	*	*	*	*				*	1s
Battery	128		*	*	*	*					*	*		*	8m, 16s
CS40	8		*	*	*	*	*					*	*		1
DR-008	64		*										*	*	8s
FM Heaven	64	16 part	*	*	*	*	*			*	*	*	*	*	1s
FM7	64		*	*	*	*	*	*	*	*	*	*	*	*	1s
HALion	256	16 part	*	*	*	*	*	*		*	*	*	*	*	4s, 4m
JX16	16		*	*	*		*			*		*	*		1s
Kontakt	256	16 part	*	*	*	*	*	*		*	*	*	*	*	32
LM4 MKII	64		*		*	*				*		*	*		3s,6m
M-Tron	35				*	*							*	*	1
Model E	64	16 part	*	*	*	*	*			*		*	*	*	4s
Mysteron	1		*										*		1m
Neon 16		*	*	*	*	*						*	*		1
Pentagon I	64		*	*			*			*	*	*	*	*	1s
Plucked String	20		*									*	*		1s
PPG Wave 2.V	64	8 part	*	*	*	*	*			*	*	*	*	*	2
Pro-52	32		*	*	*		*	*		*		*		*	1
Reaktor	64	16 part	*	*	*	*	*	*	*	*	*	*		*	1s, 4m
Retro AS-1	64	16 part	*	*	*	*	*	*	*	*	*	*	*	*	1 s
Tassman	24		*	*	*	*	*	*				*		*	1s
Tau Pro	1		*		*								*	*	1
The Grand	64		*		*	*	*	*	*						1s
Triangle II	1		*	*			*			*	*	*	*	*	1s
USM	96	16 part	*	*	*	*	*			*		*			4s
VB-1	4		*		*	*	*						*		1

- The NI B4 MIDI implementation is specialised to suit the performance features of an organ. Modulation (MIDI controller 01) controls rotary speaker speed, volume (MIDI controller 07) controls tube amplifier volume, pan (MIDI controller 10) controls microphone pan position, sostenuto (MIDI controller 66) controls percussion on/off and soft pedal (MIDI controller 67) controls overdrive on/off. The swell pedal of the B4 is controlled by expression (MIDI controller 11).
- NI Reaktor does not feature automation via sysex. Instead, automation is achieved using MIDI controller data. Each Reaktor front panel control can be set to send, as well as receive, MIDI controller data.
- NI Pro-52 and B4 also do not feature automation via sysex and achieve automation similarly to Reaktor (above) except that controller number allocation is preset.

Practical projects with VST Instruments

6

Before proceeding to the practical projects of this chapter let's take a look at some of the global aspects of VST Instruments in the light of the details covered in Chapter 5.

VST Instruments can be divided into two main groups:

1 Instruments whose design features and graphical user interface are pre-determined and fixed.
2 Instruments whose design features and graphical user interface are modular and open-ended.

The majority of VST Instruments fall into the first category and examples include those instruments which are software emulations of existing real-world instruments (such as NI Pro-52 and Steinberg Model E), or fixed-format sampling instruments (such as Steinberg HALion and LM4), and all those instruments which might be described as virtual analogue synthesizers. The advantages of these instruments include high levels of stability and reliability, predictable modes of operation and a user-friendly environment based upon tried-and-tested techniques. They are also likely to benefit from extensive sound libraries, especially if the VSTi is based upon a real-world instrument which already has a history. The possibilities for the creation of known instrument and original new sounds are extensive but not infinite.

The second category includes such instruments as Native Instruments Reaktor and Applied Acoustics Systems Tassman. These are extensive software applications which might best be described as modular sound synthesis environments. Each provides a virtual workshop where you can assemble your own synthesis engine and GUI using the supplied modules (building blocks). The sonic possibilities are considerably expanded since not only can you synthesize your own sounds, you can also re-design or build from scratch the synthesis instrument itself. Since the system is modular, the developers can add new building blocks at any time in the future to further expand the possibilities. In other words, the system is open-ended and the potential for the creation of new sonic textures is almost infinite.

Chapter 5 has already outlined the basic function of a selection of VST Instruments from both categories. Given the exciting sonic possibilities of the modular type of VSTi, this chapter begins with practical projects for the building of software instruments within both Reaktor and Tassman. Both projects concentrate on the construction of known types of instruments (a subtractive synthesizer and a virtual electric guitar) where the emphasis is upon the construction phase alone and not the

Info

If you do not already own the VST Instruments concerned, the projects in this chapter can be carried out using demo versions of the software. Details of where to obtain free downloads are given alongside the individual projects.

subsequent synthesizing of sounds. Readers are encouraged to bear in mind that these first two projects show only a small part of the modular environments concerned, which in both cases is vast. In particular, the strength of such systems is in the domain of the creation of new instruments and completely new and original sounds and textures. The projects outlined here provide the first stepping stones towards more adventurous sonic experiments in these radical new synthesis environments.

This chapter is also concerned with creating a multi-sampled instrument within HALion and the synthesis and manipulation of sounds within other specific VST Instruments.

Building your own subtractive synthesizer in Reaktor

Info

A demo of Reaktor is available as a free download from http://www.native-instruments.com

Native Instruments' Reaktor software synthesizer/VST instrument provides a powerful modular synthesis environment which is ideal for building your own synthesizer. It is assumed here that you have read the subtractive synthesis section in Chapter 3 and the Reaktor description in Chapter 5. Before proceeding with the step-by-step guide below let's become familiar with the essentials of Reaktor's synthesizer construction environment.

Reaktor's environment and hierarchy

When you build a synthesizer in Reaktor you operate in windows known as 'Structure' windows. Viewing a synthesizer as a structure allows you to see how it is put together. When you work with structures it is possible to work at various different hierarchical levels.

The system uses a modular approach. Audio, MIDI and other miscellaneous modules (building blocks) are selected from Reaktor's menus and each module is represented on screen by its own unique icon. Modules are linked together using virtual cables called 'wires' and this allows the building up of sound processing networks. Modules can include such things as oscillators, filters, amplifiers, mixers and many other things. Manipulating the modules themselves is working at the lowest hierarchical level of Reaktor. Modules can be grouped together into convenient groups known as Macros. These can be saved to hard disk and are also represented on screen by their own icons. The Macro level is the next level up in Reaktor's hierarchy. Macros can similarly be grouped together and linked, this time within a window at the Instrument level. Instruments can also be saved to disk. And finally, Instruments (represented once again by their own icons) can be grouped together and linked in an Ensemble window. The whole thing can be saved as an Ensemble file.

You do not necessarily have to stick to the hierarchical approach since nothing prevents you from working with modules directly in the Ensemble window. However, for maintaining clarity in your sound synthesis experiments the hierarchical approach is recommended.

When you need to play your synthesizer and manipulate its controls you open a Panel window. This shows the structure you have built as a regular control interface with the familiar dials, buttons and faders associated with synthesizer interfaces. The controls can be arranged on screen as desired. The Ensemble panel window is what you normally see when you load one of Reaktor's pre-programmed synthesizers from Reaktor's Library.

So, to summarise. The Ensemble level is the highest level within Reaktor. Ensembles contain Instruments, Instruments are comprised of Macros and Macros are made up of Modules. The structure of Ensembles, Instruments, Macros and Modules are viewed within Structure windows. Instruments and Ensembles can also be viewed in Panel windows which provide a regular user interface for the synthesizer.

Step-by-step guide to building a subtractive synthesizer

The subtractive synthesis section in Chapter 3 featured a diagram of classic subtractive synthesis (see Figure 3.4). This guide shows you how to build this classic structure in Reaktor. Here we will be using mainly the existing Macros, which are already available in the Macros menu, and a number of basic modules. The construction of a virtual synthesizer requires patience and attention to detail. Proceed as follows:

1 Preparation

- Launch Reaktor in your host software as a VST Instrument or launch it as a stand alone software synthesizer, if you prefer. Once the user interface is open, load in 'New.ens' from the Reaktor Library (Library/Essentials/Ensembles/New/New.ens).
- Right-click (PC)/ctrl-click (Mac) in the open Ensemble structure window and select Properties from the pop-up menu to open the Properties dialogue. Change the name of the ensemble to 'Ensemble' in the label field.
- Right-click (PC)/ctrl-click (Mac) in the open Ensemble structure window and select an 'Out 1' new instrument from the Instruments submenu (Instruments/New/Out 1). This is an empty instrument (named 'Instrument' by default) into which we can place the modules for our subtractive synthesizer.
- Click on the output terminal (Out) of the empty instrument and drag the resulting virtual cable (wire) to input 1 of the Audio Out module. Click on the output terminal of the empty instrument a second time and drag the second resulting virtual cable (wire) to input 2 of the Audio Out module. The Audio In and Audio Out modules appear in all Reaktor ensembles. They provide the audio link between Reaktor and the outside world. The shell of our virtual instrument is already connected to the outside world but there are not yet any components inside it which produce audio signals.
- Right-click (PC)/ctrl-click (Mac) on the new instrument and select Properties from the pop-up menu to open the Properties dialogue. In the voice allocation section set the number of voices to 16 and in the label field re-name the instrument as 'Subtractive 1'. We are building a 16 voice polyphonic synthesizer called 'Subtractive 1'.
- Right-click (PC)/ctrl-click (Mac) on the instrument icon and select 'Structure' from the pop-up menu to open the Instrument Structure window. The window should already feature two small modules by default, a voice combiner (labelled with }) and an audio output terminal.
- Save your work as an Ensemble under a new name. Select 'Ensemble' (or 'Untitled' if you have not yet re-named it) in the menu below the NI logo and click on the 'Save as' icon. Make sure that the save dialogue

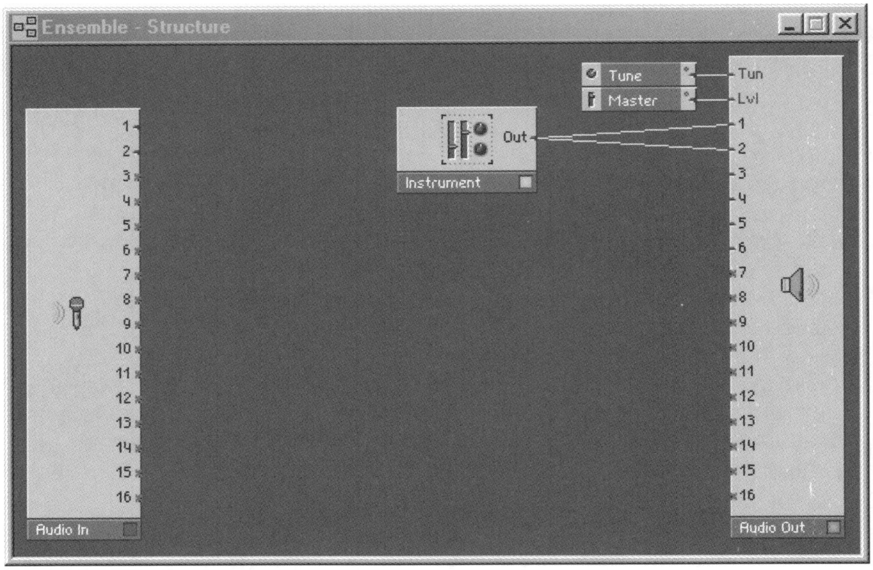

Figure 6.1
A new empty instrument connected to the Audio Out module in the Ensemble structure window

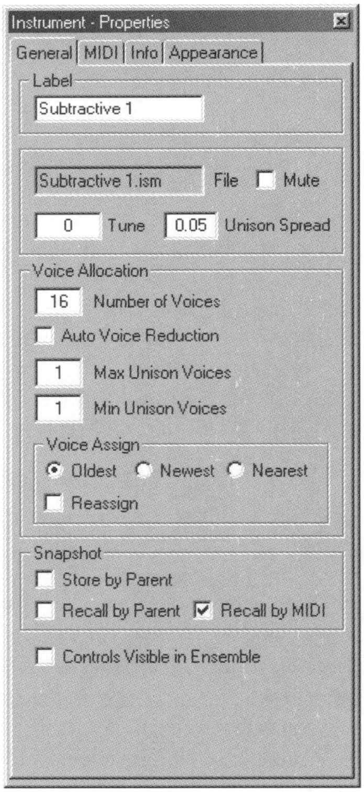

Figure 6.2
Properties dialogue of the Instrument structure window

heading reads 'Save Ensemble as' and then choose a new name and location for your work. Alternatively, right-click (PC)/ctrl-click (Mac) in empty space on the toolbar above the display and select File/Save Ensemble As from the pop-up menu. Ensemble files contain the settings from all of Reaktor's windows and have a '.ens' extension. You can also save the new synthesizer as an instrument. Instrument files contain the instrument alone and have a '.ism' extension. As you continue to work, Reaktor periodically asks if you want to save the ensemble. Choose 'save' only if you are sure that the current settings for the ensemble are correct and thoroughly tested. If this dialogue interferes with your work, de-activate it by selecting 'never save'. You can now save your work manually whenever you are ready.

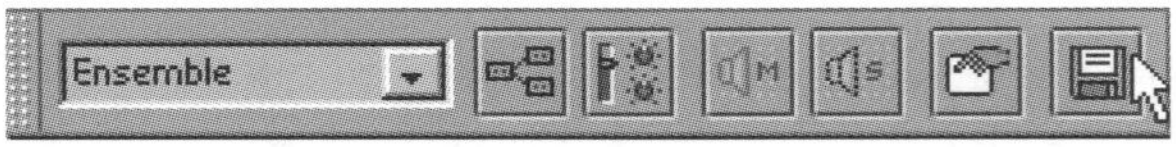

Figure 6.3
Use the 'save as' button to save your work as an ensemble

2 Oscillators

• Right-click (PC)/ctrl-click (Mac) in empty space in the Instrument structure window (Subtractive 1 – Structure). Select Macros/Oscillator/Waves/Osc (pls,saw,tri). An oscillator icon appears in the structure window. Right-click (PC)/ctrl-click (Mac) on the new oscillator and select 'copy' to copy the oscillator. Right-click (PC)/ctrl-click (Mac) in empty space and select 'paste' to paste a copy of the oscillator into the window. You now have two oscillators. Re-name the oscillators as 'Oscillator 1' and 'Oscillator 2' (Right-click (PC)/ctrl-click (Mac) on each icon in turn, select properties and rename the macro in the label field).

• Right-click (PC)/ctrl-click (Mac) in empty space in the Instrument structure window. Select Modules/Oscillator/Noise. A noise generator icon appears in the structure window.

• Right-click (PC)/ctrl-click (Mac) in empty space in the Instrument structure window. Select Modules/Constant. A 'Constant' icon (labelled '1') appears in the structure window. This module produces a constant value for any chosen input terminal. Connect the Constant module to oscillator 1 by clicking on the output terminal and dragging the wire to the amplitude input (A). Repeat the same process for oscillator 2 and the noise generator. This means that the amplitude of the oscillators and noise generator is set to a constant maximum level. The relative levels of the oscillators is to be controlled in the mixer section (see below).

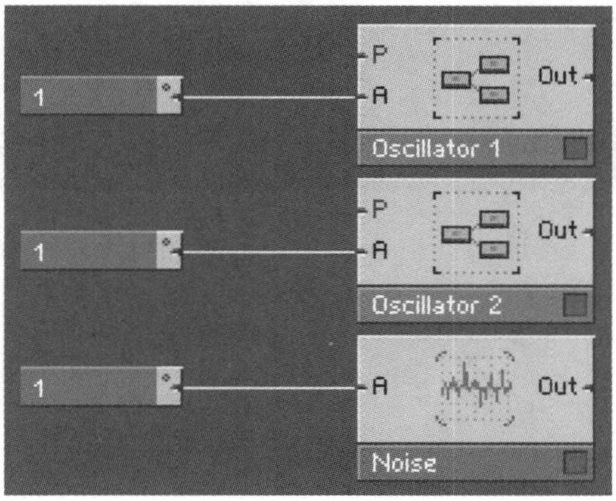

Figure 6.4
Oscillators 1 and 2 and noise generator with constant amplitude modules connected at the amplitude inputs

3 Mixer

• Right-click (PC)/ctrl-click (Mac) in empty space in the Instrument structure window. Select Macros/Mixer/Linear Audio/Mixer (3 In). A mixer icon appears in the structure window. Rename the object as 'Oscillator Mix'.

• Connect oscillator 1 to mixer input 1 by clicking on the output terminal of the oscillator and dragging the wire to input terminal 1 of the mixer. Connect oscillator 2 to mixer input 2 and the noise generator to mixer input 3 in the same way. This provides the method by which the signals are mixed together.

4 Filter and filter envelope

• Right-click (PC)/ctrl-click (Mac) in empty space in the Instrument structure window. Select Macros/Filter/Filter without FM/4-P Filter (BP, BLP, LP). A filter icon appears in the structure window. This macro provides a filter with cut-off frequency, resonance, envelope amount and key tracking with low-pass, band/low pass and band pass modes of operation. Connect the output terminal of the mixer to the input terminal (In) of the filter.

• The filter now needs an envelope generator to determine how it evolves over time. Right-click (PC)/ctrl-click (Mac) in empty space in the

Instrument structure window. Select Macros/Envelope/A...-Envelopes/ADSR – Envelope. An envelope icon appears in the structure window. Rename the object as 'Filter Envelope'. Connect the upper output terminal (Out) of the envelope to the cut-off frequency modulation input (PM) of the filter. This envelope macro provides standard ADSR envelope controls along with keyboard scaling and velocity sensitivity. The structure window now contains nine connected modules.

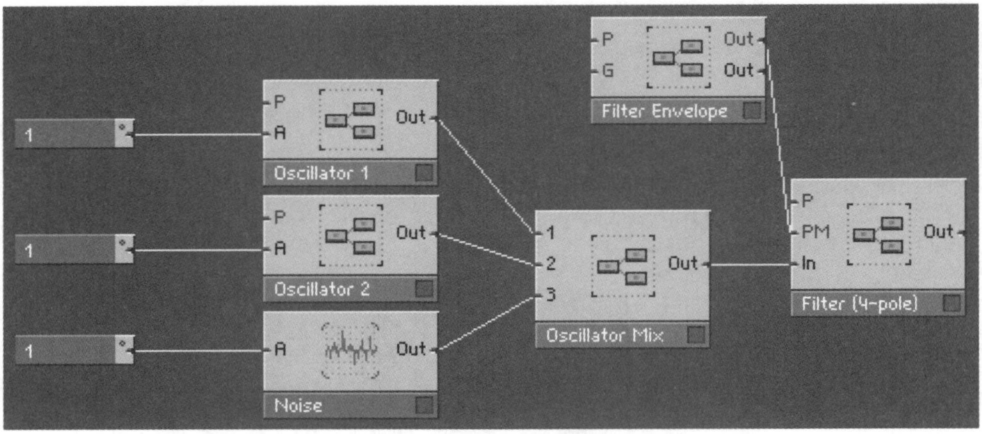

Figure 6.5 Connected oscillator, mixer and filter sections in the instrument structure window

• To take a look at the control panel for the initial structure, Right-click (PC)/ctrl-click (Mac) in empty space in the instrument structure window and select Panel. The controls may need to be re-arranged in the panel window. In order to be able to drag the controls, the padlock button in the instrument toolbar (at the top of Reaktor's main window) must be unlocked (not illuminated). In order to be able to adjust the values of the controls themselves the padlock must be locked (illuminated).

5 Amplitude envelope and volume control

• Right-click (PC)/ctrl-click (Mac) in empty space in the Instrument structure window. Select Macros/Envelope/A...-Envelopes/ADSR – Envelope. An envelope icon appears in the structure window. Rename the object as 'Amp'.

• Unlike the filter envelope. we are going to modify this particular macro to include a master volume control for our virtual synthesizer. Double-click on the Amp icon to open its structure window (see Figure 6.6).

• The Amplifier (ADSR envelope) structure needs an audio input so that we can accept the signal from the output of the filter section. Right-click (PC)/ctrl-click (Mac) in empty space in the Amp structure window. Select Modules/Terminal/Audio In Port. A small module (In) appears on the screen which represents an audio input terminal.

• Next we need to add a volume control. Right-click (PC)/ctrl-click (Mac) in empty space in the Amp structure window. Select Modules/Shaper/Event Expon (A). A small event converter icon (Exp) appears in the instrument structure window. This is a module for converting logarithmic dB amplitude values into linear amplitude values. The values of the volume control (below) can be shown in dBs on the control panel of the synthesizer and are automatically converted into the

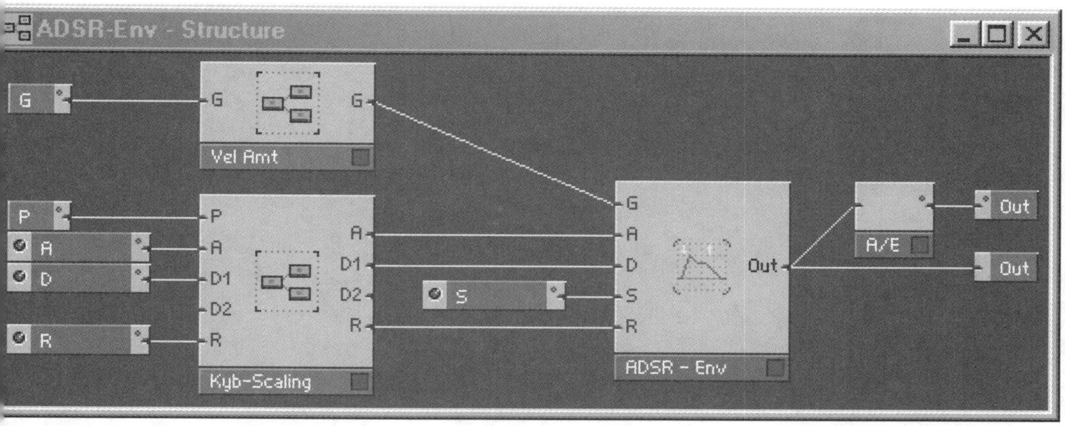

Figure 6.6
The initial structure of the ADSR envelope macro

linear values required by Reaktor. Right-click (PC)/ctrl-click (Mac) on the 'Lvl' input terminal of the Exp object and select 'create control' to automatically create a volume control for the input. Once again, this appears on screen as a small icon, this time labelled 'Level'. Change its name to 'Volume'.

• We now need a manner in which to integrate these new components into the existing envelope structure. This involves the use of an audio multiplier. Right-click (PC)/ctrl-click (Mac) in empty space in the Amp structure window. Select Modules/ +,-,X,/ / Audio Mult 3. A multiplier (X) with three inputs and one output appears in the structure window.

• Connect the components in the following manner:

1 Disconnect the lower output wire of the ADSR envelope module (the wire connected to the lower out terminal).

2 Connect an output wire from the ADSR envelope module to the upper input of the audio multiplier.

3 Connect the Volume control object to the 'Lvl' input of the event exponentiator (Exp). Connect the output (A) of the event exponentiator to the middle input of the audio multiplier.

4 Connect the output of the input terminal (In icon) to the lower input of the audio multiplier.

5 Connect the output of the audio multiplier to the lower output terminal (Out) of the module. The amplifier section now resembles Figure 6.7.

• Close the amplifier envelope structure window to return to the overall instrument structure window (Subtractive 1 – Structure). Connect the output (Out) of the filter to the input (In) of the amp envelope section. Connect the lower output (Out) of the amp envelope section to the input of the voice combiner (}). The voice combiner mixes a polyphonic audio signal into mono and this module is already connected to the output terminal of the instrument. All the operational modules should now be illuminated indicating that the synthesizer is functioning correctly.

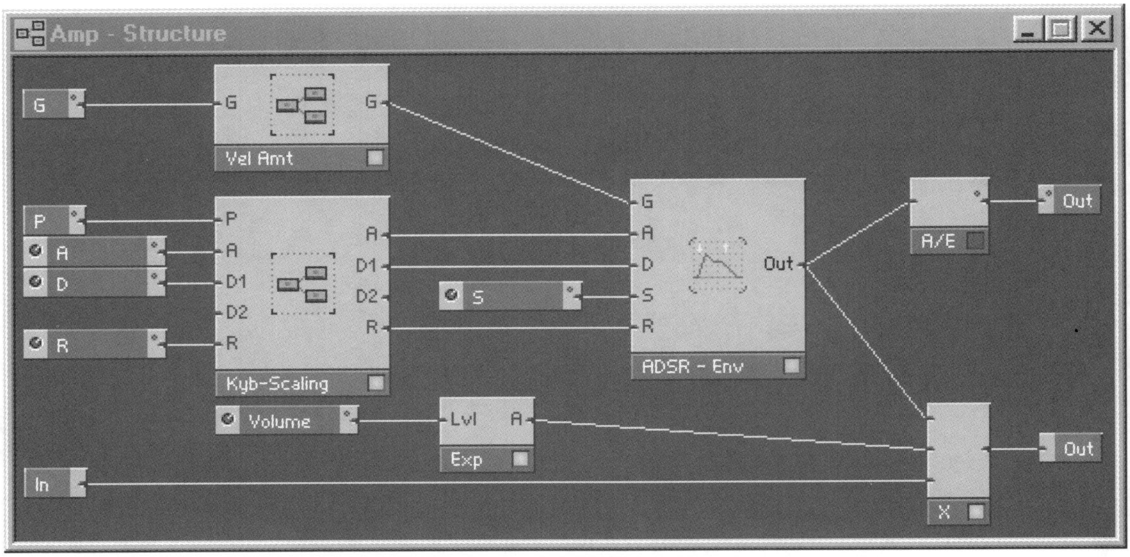

Figure 6.7
New amplifier envelope and volume control structure

6 MIDI note gate and pitch triggering

• Our synthesizer is almost complete but in order to make it function correctly we need a way of interfacing it to the outside world. For this we use MIDI note gate and pitch triggering modules. These are found along with a pitch bend module inside a Macro called 'Pitch Gate'. Right-click (PC)/ctrl-click (Mac) in empty space in the instrument structure window. Select Macros/Pitch, Gate , Event/Sources/Pitch + Gate. A 'Pitch Gate' icon appears in the structure window. The pitch gate macro features pitch (P) and gate (G) control outputs which trigger the pitch and gate inputs of other connected macros (or modules) in the structure according to the MIDI messages received at Reaktor's MIDI input. The pitch is controlled by the pitch of incoming MIDI notes while the gate is controlled by the note on and note off messages which are translated to the key on and key off points for the gate. The pitch gate macro also interprets and transmits incoming pitch bend information.

• Connect the pitch output (P) of the pitch gate macro to all the pitch inputs (P) of the other macros in the instrument structure window. Connect the gate output (G) of the pitch gate macro to the gate inputs of the filter envelope and amp envelope gate inputs (G). If it is connected correctly, the pitch gate object is illuminated. The structure resembles Figure 6.8.

• We have now reached the magical moment when you can actually play your synthesizer! Test the new synthesizer using your MIDI keyboard (or other controller).

• If you have not already done so, you may also like to view the new synthesizer as a control panel. Right-click (PC)/ctrl-click (Mac) in empty space in the structure window and select Panel from the pop-up menu. The panel window for the instrument appears on screen (see Figure 6.10, below). The controls are arranged as desired by dragging them to the required locations within the window. In order to be able to drag the panel controls, the padlock button in the instrument toolbar (at the top of Reaktor's main window) must be unlocked (not illuminated). In order

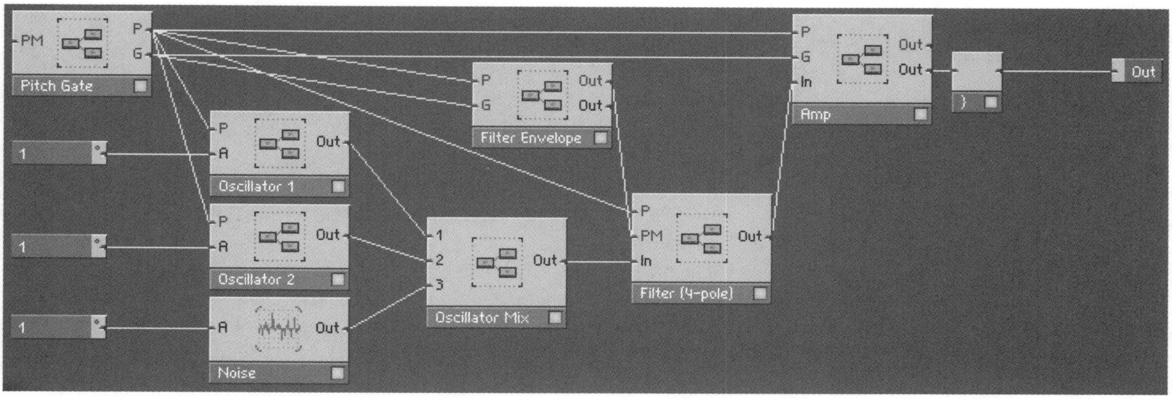

Figure 6.8 The 'almost-complete' synthesizer structure

to be able to adjust the values of the controls themselves the padlock must be locked (illuminated).

7 LFO

• Right-click (PC)/ctrl-click (Mac) in empty space in the Instrument structure window. Select Macros/LFO/Audio/LFO (Audio). An audio LFO icon appears in the structure window. Rename the object as 'LFO' and place it to the left of the pitch gate macro.
• Double-click on the LFO macro to open its structure window. Double-click on the fader object named 'Ampl' (amplitude) to open its properties dialogue. In the function page of the properties dialogue tick the MIDI 'Remote' box and ensure that Controller 1 is selected. This implements control of the amplitude of the LFO from the modulation wheel of your synthesizer for real-time modulation effects such as vibrato. Close the properties dialogue and LFO macro structure window.
• Right-click (PC)/ctrl-click (Mac) in empty space in the Instrument structure window. Select Modules/Auxiliary/A to E. An audio to event converter module (A/E) appears in the structure window. This module is used to convert the output signal of the LFO macro into event data. Place this module in between the LFO and pitch gate macros.
• Connect the output (Out) of the LFO to the input of the audio to event converter module. Connect the output of the audio to event converter module to the pitch modulation input (PM) of the pitch gate macro. The pitch is now modulated according to the amplitude and frequency of the LFO.

8 Oscilloscope

• In order to visualise audio signals Reaktor provides an oscilloscope module. This is not essential for the functioning of our synthesizer but is a welcome feature if you want to reinforce the link between the theory of chapters 2 and 3 and the practice. The oscilloscope allows you to see the waveform of the sound that the synthesizer is producing in real-time.
• Right-click (PC)/ctrl-click (Mac) in empty space in the Instrument structure window. Select Macros/Display/Oscilloscope. An oscilloscope icon (Scope) appears in the structure window. For the purposes of this synthesizer the basic macro needs to be edited.
• Double-click on the Scope macro to open its structure. Double-click

on the audio to event converter (A/E) to open its properties dialogue. Tick the mono option in the Function section.

- Right-click (PC)/ctrl-click (Mac) on the time scale (TS) input control (labelled '200') and select delete to delete this control.
- Right-click (PC)/ctrl-click (Mac) on the amplitude scale (YS) input control (labelled '1') and select delete to delete this control.
- Right-click (PC)/ctrl-click (Mac) on the TS input terminal of the scope module and select 'create control' to create a new controller for the time scale parameter.
- Double click on the new time scale control ('T-scale'). A pop-up properties dialogue appears on screen. Select the function tab and change the range to 1 in the Min. field, 100 in the Max. field and 1 in the stepsize field.
- Right-click (PC)/ctrl-click (Mac) on the YS input terminal of the scope module and select 'create control' to create a new controller for the amplitude scale parameter.
- Double click on the new amplitude scale control ('Y-scale'). A pop-up properties dialogue appears on screen. Select the function tab and change the range to 10 in the Min. field, 0.1 in the Max. field and 0.1 in the stepsize field. Rename the control, if desired.
- Close the oscilloscope structure. In the Instrument structure window connect a second output wire from the output of the voice combiner (}) to the input (In) of the scope macro.

9 Checking the structure and arranging the panel controls

- The overall instrument structure should now resemble Figure 6.9. Two oscillators and a noise generator with unity gain pass through a three channel mixer and 4-pole filter. The filter is modulated by a filter envelope. The output of the filter passes through an amplifier section which determines the loudness contour and the overall level of the signal before it is sent to the audio output. The envelopes are triggered by the gate key on and key off received from the pitch gate macro. The pitch of the oscillators is controlled by the pitch output received from the pitch gate macro which also simultaneously provides the information for the pitch tracking (key tracking) of the filter, filter envelope and amplitude envelope. The pitch gate macro also provides pitch bend information to the structure and is itself modulated according to the settings of the LFO macro. Visual monitoring of the output waveform is provided by an oscilloscope connected just before the main output.

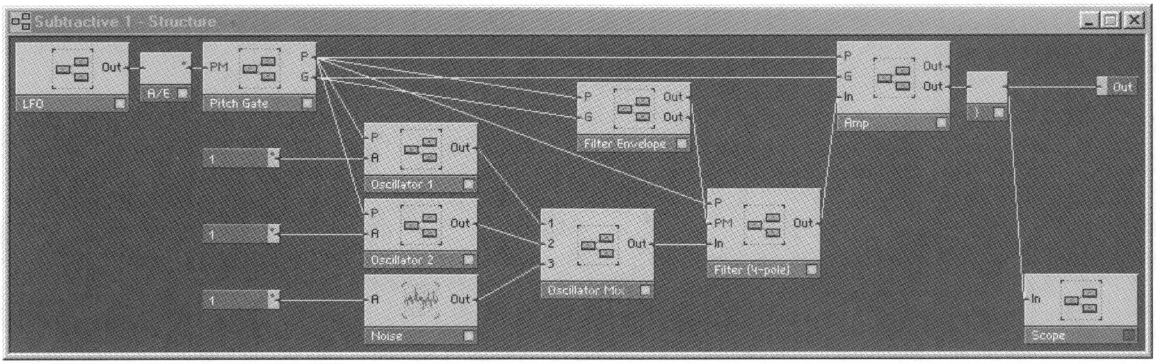

Figure 6.9
Completed subtractive synthesis instrument structure

• Right-click (PC)/ctrl-click (Mac) in empty space in the structure window and select Panel from the pop-up menu. The panel window for the instrument appears on screen. The controls are arranged as desired by dragging them to the required locations within the window. In order to be able to drag the panel controls, the padlock button in the instrument toolbar (at the top of Reaktor's main window) must be unlocked (not illuminated). In order to be able to adjust the values of the controls themselves to create patches for your new synthesizer the padlock must be locked (illuminated).

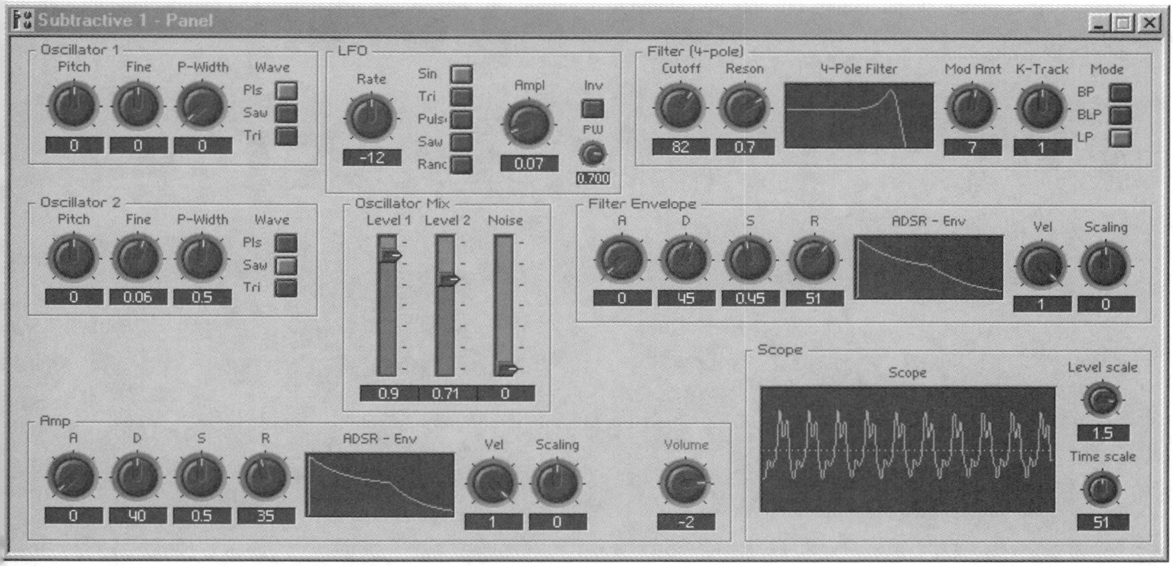

Figure 6.10
Completed subtractive synthesizer instrument panel

10 Displaying the instrument in the Ensemble panel and adding effects

• Select 'Ensemble' in the menu below the NI logo and click on the structure icon to open the Ensemble structure window.

• Right-click (PC)/ctrl-click (Mac) in empty space in the Ensemble structure window to open the Properties dialogue. Tick 'Controls Visible in Ensemble' in the lower section of the dialogue. The subtractive synthesizer can now be viewed in the Ensemble panel.

• Open the Ensemble panel. Note that the Ensemble panel already contains master level and tuning controls which appear in a separate control panel to the synthesizer. Arrange the controls as desired.

• You may also like to spice up the sound of your subtractive synthesizer by adding some effects. This can be achieved in the Ensemble structure window using Reaktor's preset instruments. Try adding a delay effects instrument. Right-click (PC)/ctrl-click (Mac) in empty space in the Ensemble structure window and select Instruments/FX – Delay, Echo/Delay filter A. A delay instrument appears in the Ensemble structure window.

• Disconnect the existing output wires of the subtractive instrument and connect its output to the input of the delay. Connect the left and right outputs of the delay to inputs 1 and 2 of the Audio Out module.

• Right-click (PC)/ctrl-click (Mac) in empty space in the Ensemble structure window to open the Properties dialogue. Tick 'Controls Visible in Ensemble' in the lower section of the dialogue.

• Open the Ensemble panel and arrange the instrument sections as desired. When you are happy with the layout save the final result as an ensemble.

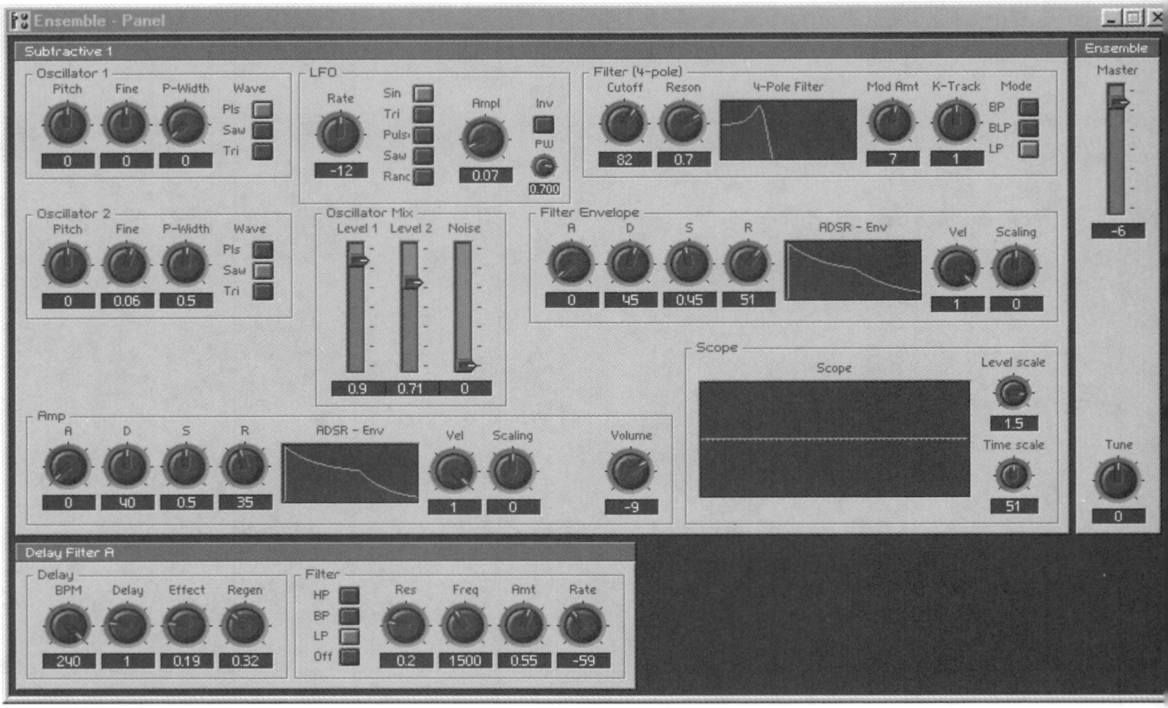

Figure 6.11
Final subtractive synthesizer in the Ensemble panel window, complete with delay effects and master level and tuning controls

Congratulations

Congratulations. You have built a subtractive synthesizer. Although the process is rather detailed, it is invaluable for learning about subtractive and other forms of synthesis. If you feel that your new synthesizer could be improved then it is now up to you to explore and experiment. Reaktor is the ideal environment for this. The construction of a synthesizer invariably takes place alongside the testing of the sound-making possibilities of the design. It is probably during the process of creating new sound patches for this synth that you will discover new ideas for how it could be improved.

Info

A demo of Tassman is available as a free download from http://www.applied-acoustics.com

Building an electric guitar in Tassman

One of the most notoriously difficult instruments to synthesize is the guitar. Vague approximations of either the acoustic or electric guitar are possible using subtractive or FM synthesis but most patches fall well short of an authentic imitation. Sampling techniques can sometimes bring us a little closer but are rarely completely satisfactory. This tutorial explores the possibilities for creating a successful electric guitar using the physical modelling techniques offered by Tassman.

Why is the guitar such a difficult instrument to synthesize?

The following are just some of the reasons why a guitar is so difficult to synthesize by conventional means:

1. The waveform of a vibrating string varies according to the position at which it is plucked along its length. This variation produces an effect similar to that of a comb filter where different frequency components at various harmonic intervals (modes) are enhanced or attenuated according to the plucking position.
2. The angle, shape and apparent hardness of the plectrum or finger on the string varies for each plucking action and this results in a variable spectrum for the initial impulse of each note. This variable impulse also modifies the overall waveform of the vibrating string.
3. Each of the six strings of a guitar has different timbral qualities according to its thickness and elasticity.
4. Vibrating strings reduce their apparent length with increased amplitude and frequency. This phenomenon is known as inharmonicity and results in the sharpening of louder upper harmonics relative to the fundamental the harder and the higher the string is played.
5. A complex system of harmonic interaction takes place between the six strings of a guitar (depending on which strings are being held down on the fretboard, which strings are muted or unmuted and which notes are being played). This produces continuously changing sympathetic resonances and overtones.
6. The sound of the strings is modified by the resonant properties of the body of the guitar and the manner in which the strings are attached.
7. In the case of an electric guitar, the electro-magnetic pickup only responds to the behaviour of the very short segment of the string which is right next to it. This phenomenon produces a comb filtering effect which varies according to the pickup position and which note is being played.
8. A wide range of performance punctuation, musical ornamentation and percussive noise form part of many guitar performances including hammer-on effects, pull-off effects, pitch bend, vibrato, fret noises, percussive hits and dampening effects with the left or right hand. These are difficult to implement in conventional synthesis controller instruments such as MIDI keyboards.
9. The sound of an acoustic guitar is highly influenced by the distance and angle of the listening position. The sound of an electric guitar is highly influenced by its amplification and speaker system.

Step by step guide to building an electric guitar

1 Design plan

Apart from the difficulties outlined in the previous section, the fundamental design of an electric guitar is familiar to most musicians. Six strings are stretched across a neck and body (usually made of wood) and are tuned to various pitches (E2, A2, D3, G3, B3 and E4). Each string is the same length and is attached to a bridge at the body end of the guitar and to tightening pegs (machine heads) on the neck, which are used for tuning purposes. The thickness, density and construction of each string is variable. The strings are plucked using the fingers or a plectrum near the bridge end of the guitar. The pitch is changed by holding fingers down on the strings at various positions on the fretboard of the neck. The vibrations of the strings are modified according to the resonant properties of the body and overall construction of the guitar. The vibrations are captured by an electro-magnetic pickup. The electronic signal of the pickup is routed to the output socket via tone and volume controls on the body of the guitar. The output signal is connected to an external amplifier and speaker system which further modify the characteristics of the signal we finally hear.

Tassman provides most of these components as modular building blocks so 'theoretically' it should be just a matter of connecting them together in the correct order!

2 A plectrum and a string

• Let's start by bringing the plectrum and string parts of the guitar onto our virtual work surface. Unlike a real electric guitar, this guitar comprises only one string and an extremely long fretboard! Launch TassBuilder and click on the Generators section of the module library (to the left of the display). Select the plectrum icon and click within the main display to insert a plectrum object.

• Select a string module from the Resonators section of the module library. Insert the string object in the display to the right of the plectrum object.

• Click and hold on the output of the plectrum object and drag the virtual jack connector which appears to the second input of the string object. The second input is the force signal input of the string. When this input receives an output signal from the plectrum it causes the string to 'vibrate'.

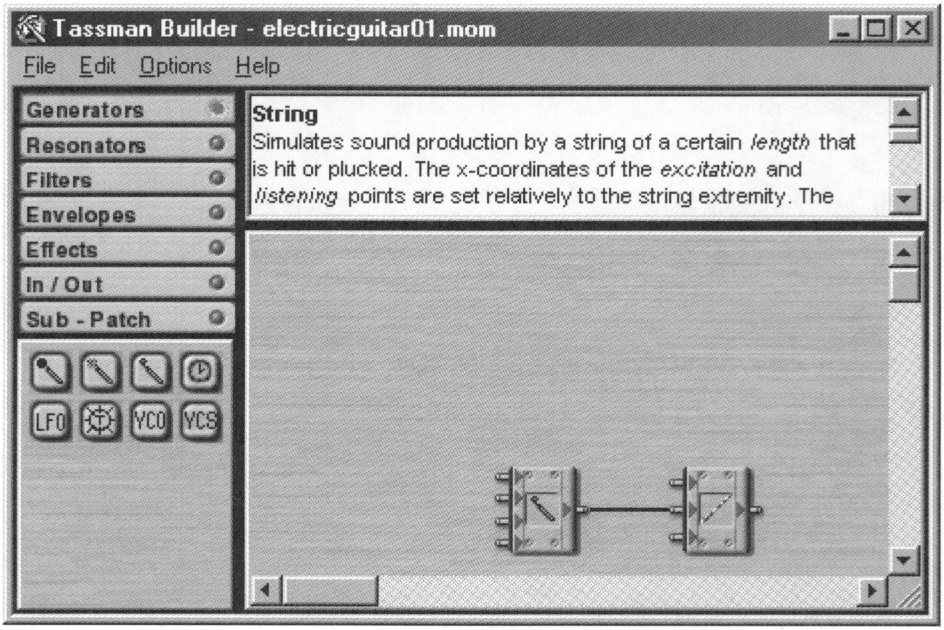

Figure 6.12 Plectrum and string objects in Tassman Builder

3 Plucking the string

• We now need a way of telling the plectrum when it should pluck the string. For this purpose, we use a Tassman keyboard module called 'Polyvkey'. Select the Polyvkey module (the fourth keyboard icon) from the In/Out section of the module library. Insert the object to the left of the plectrum and string objects. The polyvkey module interprets incoming MIDI data and transfers the information to the other modules in the construction. It is polyphonic and velocity sensitive. Our proposed electric guitar is going to be velocity sensitive and will initially feature two-note polyphony.

• The polyvkey module has three outputs. These include a gate signal at the top, a pitch signal in the middle and a velocity signal. Start by connecting the gate output signal of the keyboard to the trigger input of the plectrum and the damper input of the string. This triggers the action of the plectrum and undampens the string each time you press a note on the MIDI keyboard.

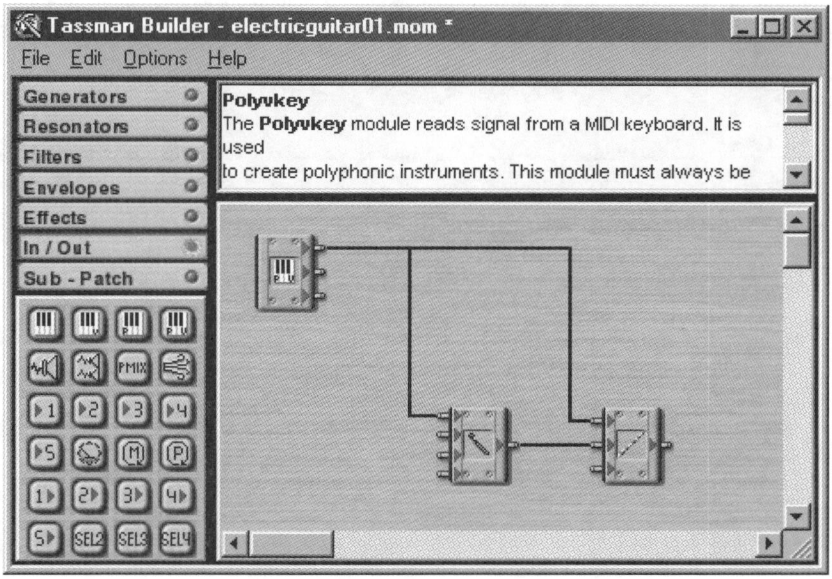

Figure 6.13
Connect the gate signal of the keyboard to the plectrum and string objects

• Now connect the pitch output signal of the keyboard to the pitch input of the string (the third input) and also to the stiffness modulation input of the plectrum (the second input). This implements the changing of pitch for the string and also allows the modulation of the stiffness of the plectrum according to the pitch of incoming MIDI notes.

• Connect the velocity output of the keyboard to the inverse stiffness modulation input of the plectrum (the third input) and also to the strength modulation input (the fourth input). This allows the softening of the apparent stiffness of the plectrum as the velocity increases and it regulates the overall force of the plucking action according to incoming velocity (see 'Instrument interface example 2' in the Tassman section in Chapter 5 for more details of the logic of this configuration).

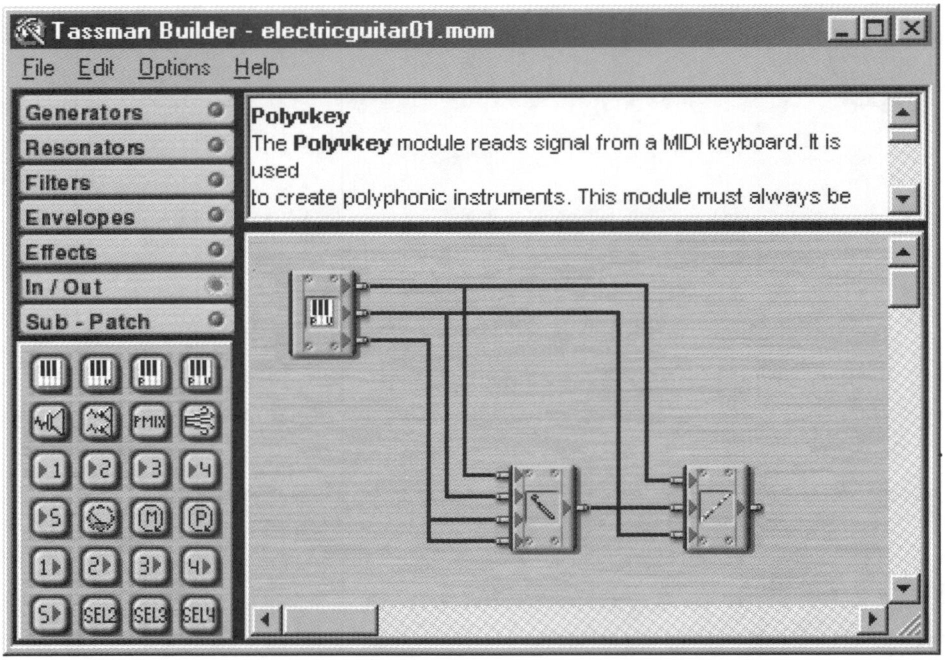

Figure 6.14 Connect the keyboard pitch and velocity signals to the plectrum and string objects

4 Adding the pickup and guitar body

• Select the pickup module from the Effects section of the module library and place it in the display to the right of the string object.

• Select the plate module from the Resonators section of the module library and place it in the display to the right of the pickup object. The plate module simulates the acoustical behaviour of rectangular plates of different materials and sizes and is used to add the resonant behaviour of the body of the guitar. Logic might suggest that the resonator should appear before the pickup in the chain of modules but experimentation with this particular instrument revealed that it worked best just after the pickup.

• Connect the output of the string module to the input of the pickup module. Connect the output of the pickup module to the force signal input (the second input) of the plate module. The main signal now drives the pickup module and the output of the pickup is fed to the plate for the adding of resonance to the system.

• Connect a cable from the pitch output of the keyboard to the pitch input (the third input) of the plate module. Connect a cable from the velocity output of the keyboard to the damper input signal of the plate module. The plate now resonates according to the pitch of incoming MIDI notes and its amplitude is regulated according to incoming velocity.

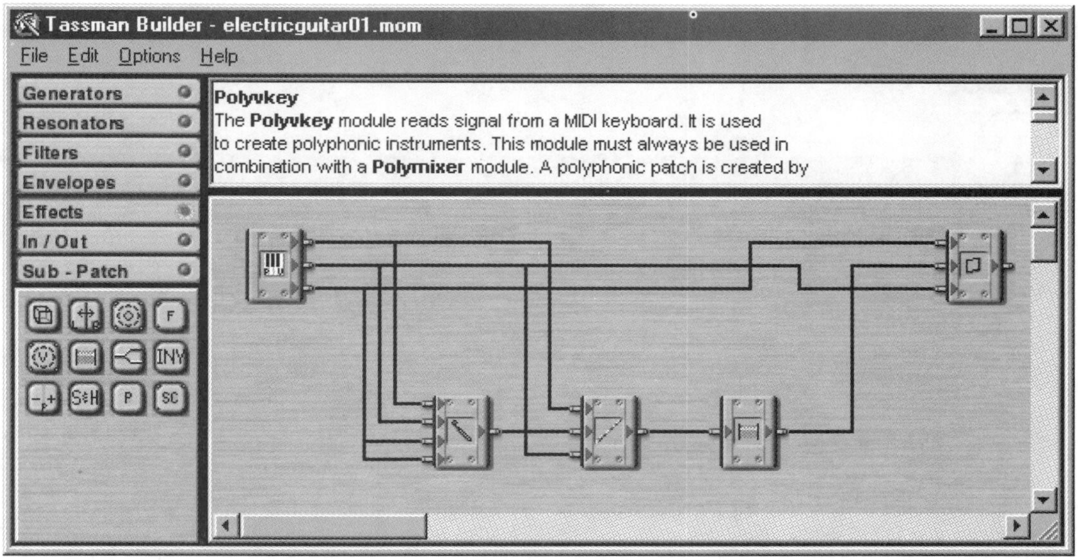

Figure 6.15
Connect the pickups and add the body of the guitar

5 Mixing the polyphonic voices and adding a volume control and level meter

- The voices of a polyphonic patch in Tassman must be mixed together before being sent to the output. This is achieved using the polymixer module. Select a polymixer module from the In/Out section of the module library and place it in the display to the right of the plate module.
- For the control of volume select a volume module from the Envelope section of the module library and place it in the display to the right of the polymixer module.
- Next, select a DAC module (digital-to-analogue converter) from the In/Out section of the module library and place it in the display to the right of the polymixer module.
- Finally, select a level module from the In/Out section of the module library and place it in the display below the DAC module. The level module provides a meter for monitoring the output level.
- Connect the output of the plate module to the input of the polymixer module. Connect the output of the polymixer module to the input of the volume module. Connect the output of the volume to both the input of the DAC and the input of the level meter.

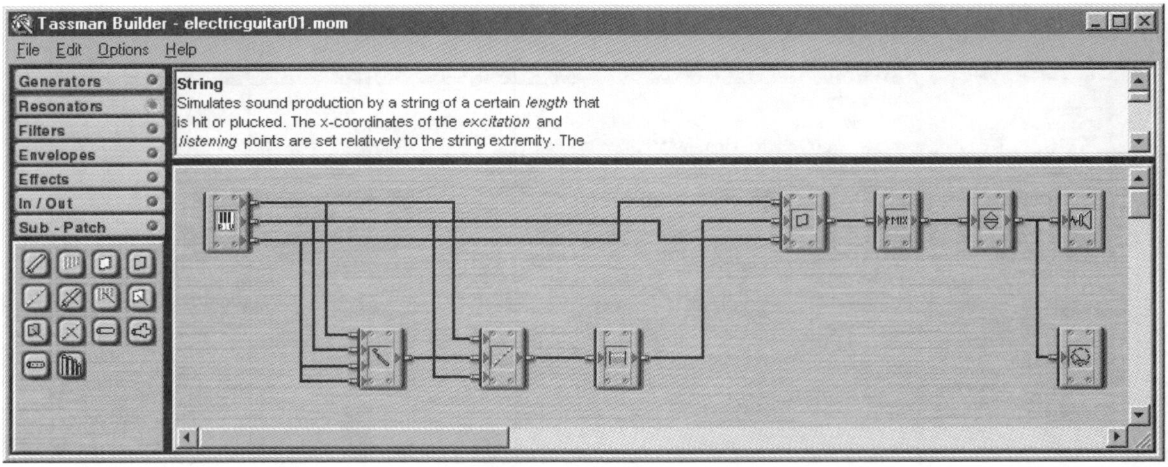

Figure 6.16
Add polyphonic mixing, volume control, level meter and DAC modules

6 Final adjustments

• Double-click on the polyvkey module. In the dialogue window which appears change the pitch wheel range to 0.1666 and change the number of voices to 2. This gives a two semitone bend range and an initial two-note polyphony for the guitar.

• Double-click on the string module. In the dialogue window which appears change the inharmonicity value to 0.0005. This adds a very subtle sharpening of the louder upper harmonics relative to the fundamental the harder and the higher the string is played (a value of 0.000 for this field results in a theoretically 'perfect' vibration for the string).

• Double-click on the plate module. In the dialogue window which appears change the length to 0.6, the width to 0.5, excitation point x to 0.15, excitation point y to 0.125, listening point x to 0.15 and listening point y to 0.125 (see Figure 6.17). Leave all other parameters at their default values. This changes the size of the plate to more closely match the kind of resonances which might be found in an electric guitar.

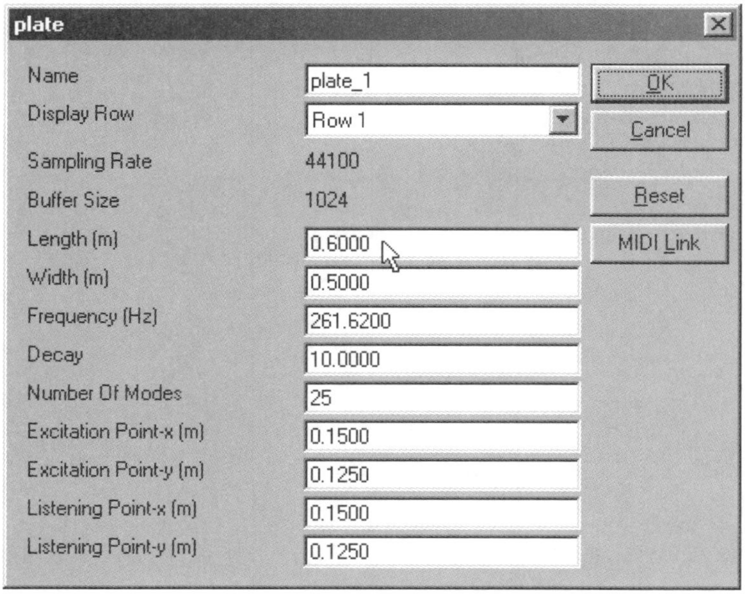

Figure 6.17
Adjust the properties of the plate in its pop-up dialogue window

7 Launch the Tassman Player

Congratulations, you have now completed the construction of the Mark 1 version of the electric guitar. Save your work using the 'save as' option in the File menu. Launch the Player using the Launch Player command in the File menu. This creates the graphical user interface for the new instrument (Figure 6.18).

Figure 6.18
The graphical user interface for the Mark 1 electric guitar in Tassman Player

8 Finding the sound

This virtual electric guitar is capable of producing authentic electric guitar sounds and it is relatively easy to program. However, when you adjust the parameters of an acoustic-style instrument in Tassman you are often changing the design of the instrument itself rather than simply tweaking the sound. This takes some getting used to. Please also bear in mind that it is very difficult to re-create the performance nuances of a real-world guitar using a conventional MIDI keyboard. As well as conventional guitar-like sounds, the instrument is also capable of producing hybrid string tones. If you enjoy experimenting try tweaking the parameters to discover the more unusual sonic possibilities of the instrument.

The lower right corner of Tassman Player features a three digit counter. This changes its value when you click on or adjust any of the Player's parameters. Use this to adjust the parameters according to the following table in order to create a 'clean guitar' patch.

Table 6.1
Clean guitar patch for the Mark 1 electric guitar

patchname	*plectrum*	*string*	*pickup*	*plate*	*volume*
clean guitar	stiffness 80	amp 76	symmetry 81	amp 92	slider value 88
	strength 45	decay 98	distance 93	decay 09	
	mod 1 06	mod 64	ampin 103	mod 00	
	mod 2 20	damp/freq 64	ampout 127	damp/freq 88	
	mod 3 10				

The clean guitar patch is a good all-purpose clean electric guitar sound. It sounds particularly good in the middle range of the keyboard and responds well if you route it through an overdrive, distortion or speaker simulation plug-in within your host software. Keep in mind the normal playing range of an electric guitar which most often covers approximately three octaves between E2 and E5.

9 Improving the design

If you refer back to the section 'Why is the guitar such a difficult instrument to synthesize?', above, you see that we have managed to address some of the difficulties in the design of our electric guitar. Owing to Tassman's physical modelling of the actual behaviour of real acoustic objects, the string vibrates like a real string according to where along its length it is plucked (set at the construction stage), the plectrum features a sophisticated plucking mechanism which is comparable to the real-world version, the inharmonicity effect can be set for the string at the construction stage and some of the resonant behaviour of the body of the guitar can be roughly approximated.

We have, to various degrees, addressed points 1, 2, 4 and 6. But how might we improve matters? The Mark 1 electric guitar does not feature a manner in which to apply vibrato, and the implementation of a comb filter might improve the authenticity of the sound (bearing in mind points 1 and 7). Let's try adding Tassman's comb filter and incorporate an LFO into the design in order to produce vibrato, flanging and other effects. Proceed as follows:

- Select an LFO module from the Generators section of the module library and place it in the display under the plate module. Select a modulation wheel module from the In/Out section and place it in the display under the LFO module. Select a VCA module from the Envelope section and place it in the display to the right of the LFO and modulation modules. Select a portamento module from the Envelopes section and place it to the right of the VCA module. Select a comb filter module from the Filters section and place it to the right of the portamento module.
- Disconnect the cable connecting the output of the plate module to the input of the polymixer module by clicking on the cable (it turns red) and pressing delete on the computer keyboard. Move the right-most four objects further to the right to create more space for the new connections.
- Connect the output of the LFO to the upper input of the VCA. Connect the output of the modulation wheel to the lower input of the VCA. The VCA module multiplies the signals at its inputs. This configuration provides a way for the modulation wheel to regulate the amount of LFO signal which is routed to the comb filter. Connect the output of the VCA module to the signal input (the second input) of the portamento module. Here the portamento module is used to smooth the signal of the LFO and modulation wheel signal rather than its usual function of creating glissandos between notes. This avoids undesirable side-effects in the comb filter when rapidly changing the level of the modulation wheel and creates smooth transitions for vibrato effects. If desired, rename the module to 'smoothing'.
- Connect the output of the plate module to the upper input of the comb filter. This is the input signal of the module to which the comb filter effect is to be applied. Connect the output of the portamento module to the second input of the comb filter. This allows the modulating of the frequency of the comb filtering effect according to the LFO and modulation wheel amount (for vibrato, flanging and other effects).

• Connect the pitch output of the keyboard module to the second modulation input of the comb filter. This allows the modulating of the frequency of the comb filtering effect according to the pitch of incoming MIDI notes. Change the display row field to row 2 for the LFO, portamento and comb filter modules (in the pop-up dialogue which appears when you double-click on the module). The construction of the Mark 2 version of the electric guitar should now resemble Figure 6.19.

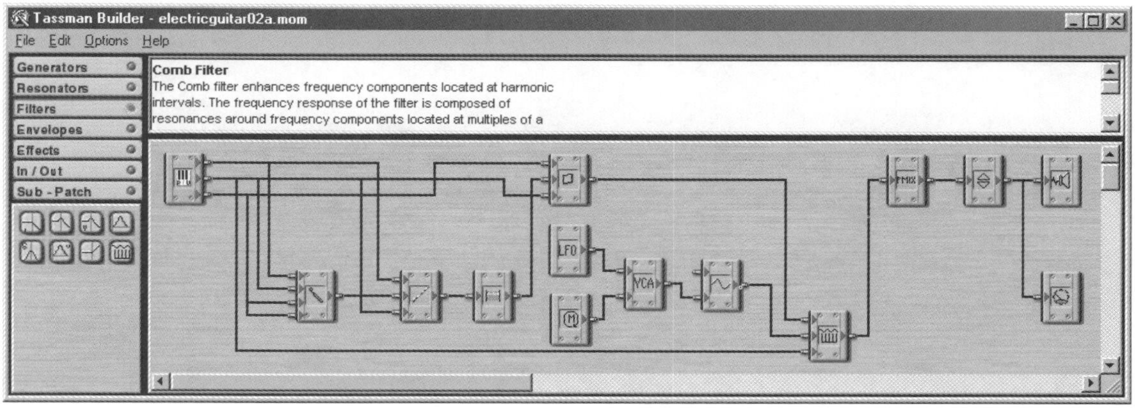

Figure 6.19
The completed Mark 2 electric guitar in Tassman Builder

• Save your work using the 'save as' option in the File menu. Launch the Player using the Launch Player command in the File menu. This creates the graphical user interface for the Mark 2 electric guitar (Figure 6.20).

Figure 6.20
The graphical user interface for the Mark 2 electric guitar in Tassman Player

The Mark 2 electric guitar is capable of producing a wider range of guitar sounds than the Mark 1 but is slightly more difficult to program. The combination of the LFO and comb filter produce some inspiring effects and by using the comb filter in a subtle manner the authenticity of the guitar sounds can be fine tuned and enhanced. For smoothing the output of the LFO and modulation wheel (to produce smooth vibrato and flanging effects) set the smoothing button to 'on' (depressed) and the glide control to its centre position. Try the patches of the following table using the three digit counter in the lower right corner of Tassman Player to adjust the settings (as explained above).

Table 6.2
Guitar patches for the Mark 2 electric guitar

patchname	*plectrum*	*string*	*pickup*	*plate*	*LFO/ smoothing*	*comb filter*	*volume*
bright guitar	stiffness 126	amp 76	symmetry 37	amp 92	wavetype 00	coarse 86	slider 88
	strength 45	decay 100	distance 93	decay 21	frequency 87	fine 59	
	mod 1 39	mod 64	ampin 103	mod 65		range 04	
	mod 2 85	damp/freq 65	ampout 127	damp/freq 127	glide 64	mod 1 64	
	mod 3 16				on/off 01	mod 2 00	
						feedback 01	
jazz guitar	stiffness 81	amp 76	symmetry 99	amp 92	wavetype 00	coarse 84	slider 88
	strength 76	decay 98	distance 88	decay 18	frequency 87	fine 59	
	mod 1 06	mod 64	ampin 103	mod 65		range 08	
	mod 2 20	damp/freq 64	ampout 127	damp/freq 111	glide 64	mod 1 65	
	mod 3 10				on/off 01	mod 2 00	
						feedback 01	
lead guitar 01	stiffness 126	amp 76	symmetry 37	amp 121	wavetype 00	coarse 86	slider 88
	strength 42	decay 100	distance 88	decay 21	frequency 91	fine 59	
	mod 1 30	mod 64	ampin 103	mod 65		range 04	
	mod 2 85	damp/freq 60	ampout 127	damp/freq 127	glide 64	mod 1 16	
	mod 3 12				on/off 01	mod 2 00	
						feedback 01	
neat guitar	stiffness 90	amp 76	symmetry 107	amp 92	wavetype 00	coarse 96	slider 88
	strength 66	decay 98	distance 88	decay 15	frequency 87	fine 59	
	mod 1 44	mod 64	ampin 103	mod 65		range 04	
	mod 2 20	damp/freq 64	ampout 127	damp/freq 115	glide 64	mod 1 65	
	mod 3 18				on/off 01	mod 2 00	
						feedback 01	

To set up a regular vibrato effect, set the wave type of the LFO to a sine wave and the frequency to between 60 and 70 bpm. Set the comb filter frequency to around 300 – 500Hz, the mod 1 parameter to around 50%, the mod 2 parameter to zero and the feedback control to zero. Switch on the smoothing control and set its glide parameter to 50%. Use the modulation wheel of your controlling keyboard to add vibrato.

For flange and special effects increase the feedback level and try different speeds for the LFO and different frequencies for the coarse, fine and range controls.

When modulating the frequency of the comb filter according to the pitch of incoming MIDI notes set the mod 2 parameter to its centre position for the response to match an equal tempered scale.

Further improvements to the design which you may like to consider include the implementation of a tone control for the guitar (the above instruments have no tone controls) or a toggle switch for choosing either the clean sound or the treated signal from the comb filter (the Mark 2 signal passes through the comb filter in series). If you have enough CPU power you could also try increasing the polyphony.

Creating your own sample program in Steinberg's HALion

This project outlines how to create a sample program in HALion using your own samples. It is assumed that you have read the sampling section in chapter 3 and the HALion description in chapter 5.

Recording the samples

A large percentage of the success of any sample program depends upon how the samples have been recorded in the first place. This is notoriously difficult if you are dealing with acoustic musical instruments and sounds from the real world since this involves setting up microphones and recording equipment in acoustically treated environments. This part of the market therefore usually remains the domain of professional sample library suppliers who have the necessary resources to invest in large-scale projects. However, small home-based and semi-professional studios can achieve excellent results with minimal equipment and those using sounds sampled from existing recordings, synthesized sounds or sounds created within a computer can usually produce high-quality samples within a very small set-up (often entirely within software).

If you are recording from the real-world then the minimum requirements are a high-quality professional microphone (most often a large diaphragm, capacitor type) and a microphone pre-amp. A line level signal can be taken from the microphone pre-amp and fed to the line-in of a computer-based recording set-up or other recording device (such as a DAT machine). Popular computer-based set-ups include Steinberg Cubase VST, Cubase SX, Emagic Logic Audio, Steinberg Wavelab, Bias Peak, Cakewalk Sonar and Digidesign ProTools. Recording synthesizers, guitars and other electronic musical instruments is slightly easier since you can often use the line outs on the instruments themselves, bypassing the need for microphones and optimised recording environments. The same is true for samples taken from existing recordings and the media (although here you should ensure that you are not infringing copyright law). It is beyond the scope of this text to describe the details of the recording process itself since this is a whole subject area in its own right. The reader is advised to consult other texts on the subject.

Before recording commences it is essential to have an idea of what the sample program is going to contain. The main possibilities include the following:

- a multi-sampled musical instrument (often with different samples on the same key arranged into velocity zones and with sustain loops for each sample)
- a drum program with drum and percussion hits mapped across the keyboard (often with different samples on the same key arranged into velocity zones)
- drum or music loops mapped across the keyboard (looped and grouped according to tempo)
- miscellaneous sound effects, stabs, hits, and vocals mapped across the keyboard

This project describes the creation of a multi-sampled analogue bass synth program (recorded from a Moog Taurus 1 pedal synthesizer). This tutorial provides most of the information needed to create your own sample programs within HALion.

Of all the variations described above, multi-sampled musical instruments are probably the most difficult from a recording point of view since to get a successful composite instrument each of the samples must be played and recorded in the same manner. Great attention must be paid to the attack, sustain and release segments of each sampled note and each note should have a similar duration. The difficulties are compounded if you intend to include velocity-zoned samples in your program. The success of the samples depends as much on the player of the instrument as it does upon the recording technique and the quality of the instrument itself. If you are recording a synthesizer or keyboard instrument which can be triggered via MIDI then the recording task becomes slightly easier since you can standardise the durations and velocities of each note and pre-arrange the notes you are going to record in a MIDI-based sequencer.

Creating the sample program

1 Choosing the notes to be sampled

One of the most important practical decisions in multi-sampling is which notes you are actually going to record. The following are a number of ways in which you can spread the notes across the keyboard:

- one sample per key (see HALion's 'MiniMoog 3 Osc Bass' default program)
- one sample every three keys – for example, recorded on C, D#, F# and A in each octave (see HALion's 'Nord Disco Bazz' default program)
- one sample every six keys – for example, C and F# in each octave (see HALion's 'Jupiter Euro TekStrynx' default program)
- one sample per octave – for example, C alone in each octave

With a software sampler, the choice is a compromise between sound quality and computer resources. A sample on every key provides very high-quality playback but may put slightly more pressure on your computer's resources. Only one sample in every octave means that the sample is considerably pitch-shifted on some keys and this may result in noticeable audio side-effects during playback. Some sounds are more forgiving than others. A good compromise is one sample for every three notes on the keyboard and this is the resolution chosen for this particular exercise.

The Moog Taurus pedal synthesizer does not have a MIDI interface so it was played manually. One way of ensuring that each sample is of similar length is to play the instrument along with a click. This was precisely the technique employed here and two octaves of sampled notes (C1, D#1, F#1, A1, C2, D#2, F#2, A2, C3) were recorded into Steinberg's Wavelab, giving nine samples in total. The chosen sound from the Taurus was a bass sound and it was therefore not considered necessary to cover the entire range of a conventional keyboard. The samples have a two octave key range but the lower and upper samples are to be stretched across a one octave key zone to give more range. Since the Taurus was a non-velocity-sensitive instrument it was also decided that the program would not require separate velocity-zoned samples so only one set of recordings was needed. All recordings were made in stereo (the Moog Taurus is a mono unit so mono recordings would have been equally acceptable).

2 Editing the samples

When you are satisfied with the recordings, you can move on to naming and editing the samples. This project assumes that you are using a computer-based system to store and edit the samples. The popular audio file formats are AIFF for Mac systems and WAV for PC systems. The Taurus bass samples in this exercise are edited within Steinberg's Wavelab software for PC.

The first task is to name the samples in a logical manner. HALion uses musical letter names for each note so naming the audio files according to this scheme makes life easier when you transfer them to HALion. Name your samples according to the root note at which they are to be placed when imported into HALion. To ensure that they appear in a logical order when viewing the files on your computer system try including the MIDI note number before the note letter name. The Taurus bass samples are named as in Figure 6.21.

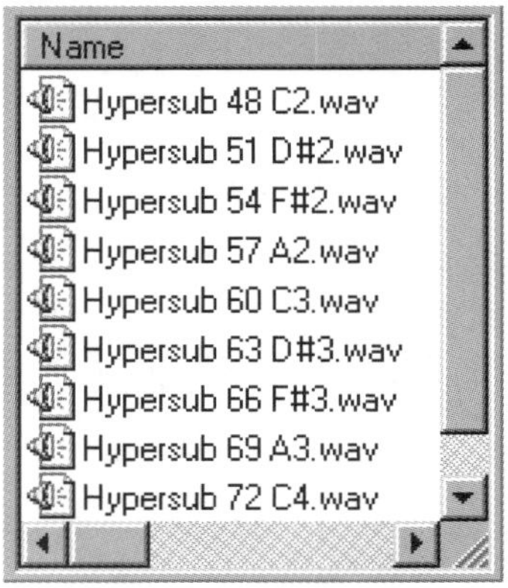

Figure 6.21
Name your samples in a logical manner

Topping and tailing your samples (removing unwanted audio at the start and end) can often be more easily achieved in a dedicated audio editor like Steinberg Wavelab or Bias Peak. A clean sample which begins and ends neatly makes it easier to handle within HALion. You can also use an audio editor for the removal of clicks, the standardising of durations, converting to mono (if desired) or for processing such as compression, gating or creative effects. If you are using Wavelab, you can even set up loops and root note information since the data is embedded in the audio file and recognised by HALion when the file is imported.

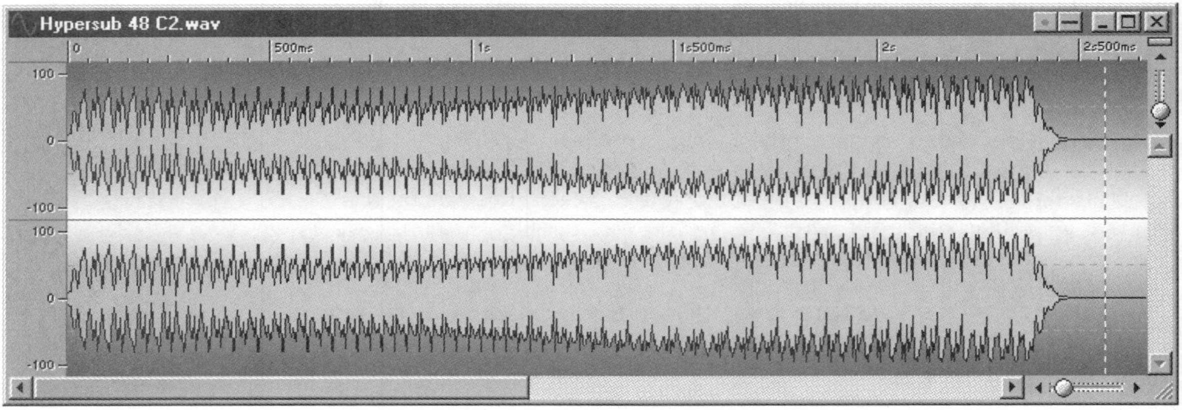

Figure 6.22
Edit your samples in your favourite audio editor (this image shows Steinberg's Wavelab)

3 Importing the samples into HALion

It is assumed here that HALion is installed in the same system where you have stored your audio files. Open HALion within your host software. Right-click (PC)/ctrl-click (Mac) on the generic page frame to open the global commands menu. Select 'Clear All' and confirm in order to clear HALion's contents (ensure that any valuable work has already been saved before doing so). This starts your program creation with a clean sheet in order to avoid confusion.

Click on the first program (Program 1) in the program list to select it for the importing of the audio files. If you have cleared HALion's contents the list should appear in a similar manner to Figure 6.23. The selected program appears in grey with a red outline.

Select a key on the HALion virtual keyboard using the mouse (the selected key is indicated with a small circular blue marker). HALion maps the samples intelligently across the keyboard starting at the key you select (or according to any root note information it finds in the files). Go to the Options page and select 'Import Audio Files'. In the file dialogue which appears select all the relevant audio files (samples) of your multi-sampled instrument and click on 'open'. The loaded samples can be seen in the program list (by opening Program 1) and in the Keyzone page as vertical strips. If you have named your samples in a similar manner to the Taurus bass samples shown above then they should appear in the correct ascending order across the virtual keyboard (see Figure 6.24). If the files contain any root note information each sample is automatically placed at its root note position. If desired, the order of the samples in the program list can be sorted by pitch or alphabetically by right-clicking (PC) / ctrl-clicking (Mac) on the program name and selecting 'Sort' in the pop-up program menu. Similarly, a new name can be entered for the program by selecting 'Rename' from the same menu.

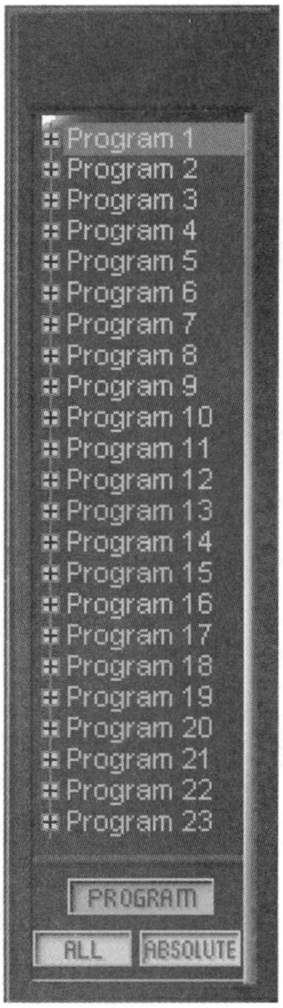

Figure 6.23
The program list after clearing HALion's contents

Figure 6.24
Load the samples into HALion and verify them in the Keyzone page and program list

4 Mapping the samples across key zones

The next stage is to map the samples across the keyboard in the Keyzone page with one sample for every three keys (at least in the central part of the key range). Firstly, place each sample on its root note (not necessary if root note information is contained within the file). The root note is the note at which the sample was originally recorded and, if you have named your samples logically, normally part of its name (see Figure 6.25). The sample strips are dragged to new positions by clicking and holding in the middle of the strip and then dragging when you see the four-way pointer.

When all the samples are in the correct positions right-click (PC)/ctrl-click (Mac) on the program in the program list and select 'Set root key/to low key selected' (Figure 6.26). This adjusts all root keys in the selected program to the current key positions of the samples. This is important for ensuring that the samples play back at the correct pitch.

You can now scale the keyzones of each sample by dragging each of the outer edges by one key below and one key above its root position using the double arrow pointer (which appears when you click near the edge of any sample strip). Each sample is now mapped to three keys each (there should be no empty gaps between samples). The lowest and highest samples of the Taurus bass used to demonstrate this project are

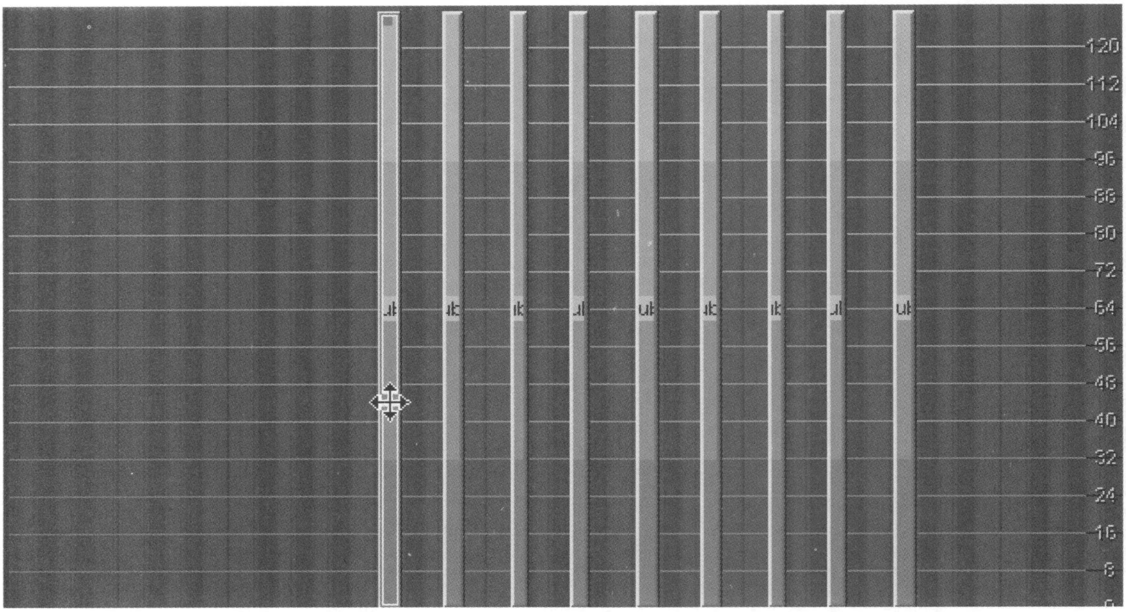

Figure 6.25
Place each sample on its root note

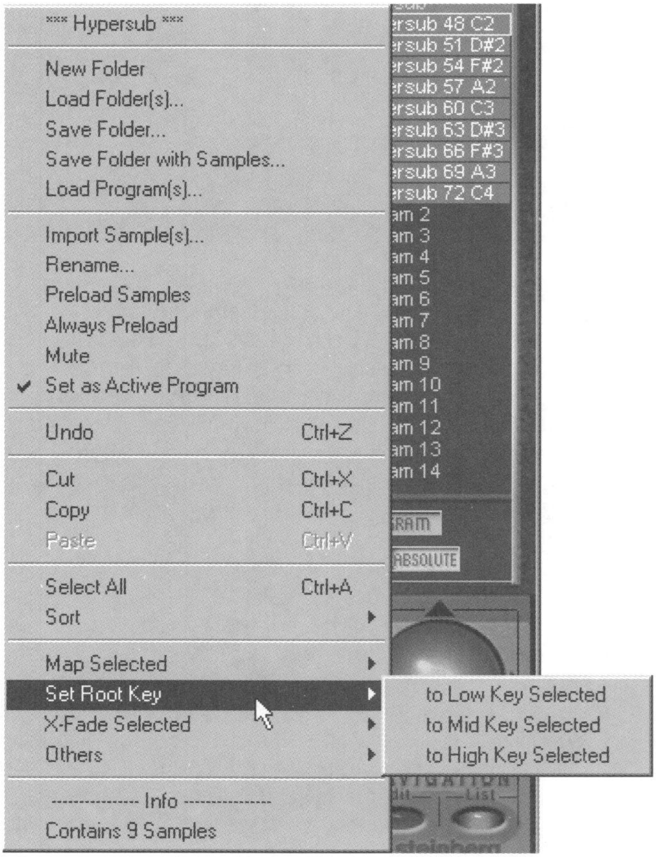

Figure 6.26
Set HALion's root key settings to the current positions of the samples

stretched across a whole octave below and a whole octave above the root positions (see Figure 6.27).

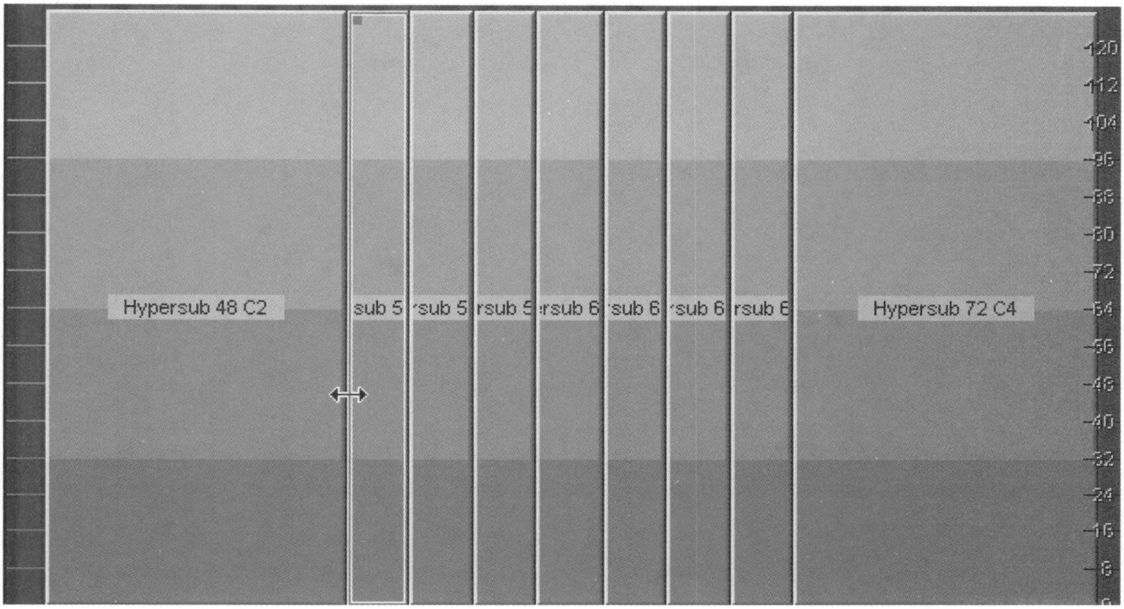

Figure 6.27
Adjust the keyzones of each sample to cover the desired key range

5 Looping the samples

You are now in a position to be able to play the raw samples from your keyboard in the normal manner. This gives an idea of how much work is still to be completed. Some samples play quite well in their raw state while others need an amount of fine tuning and filtering. Almost all samples of musical instruments need to sustain and looping is the most popular solution (although for the highest quality the sustain segment of the notes from acoustic instruments like grand pianos is best streamed off hard disk).

To make loop settings in HALion open the Waveloop page. HALion provides a sustain loop which continues for as long as the key is held and an optional release loop which is triggered when the key is released. Select the sample to be looped in the program list and adjust the thumbnail view so that you can see the whole sample. The start and end points of the sample are shown by handles marked with 'S' and 'E'. Select 'Loop', adjust its mode to 'Loop until release' and then drag with the mouse in the main waveform display in an area which looks likely to provide a suitable loop segment. A light blue shaded area marks the looped segment of the waveform (see Figure 6.28).

Play back the sample and listen for clicks or glitches at the loop point. To adjust the length and position of the loop click near the start or end points and drag the mouse when the double arrow pointer appears. HALion allows real-time loop adjustment while playing back the sample. This helps find the ideal loop point. For detailed work you may need to zoom in to the loop to make fine adjustments or even enter precise values into the loop start and end fields in the Waveloop page (see Figure 6.29).

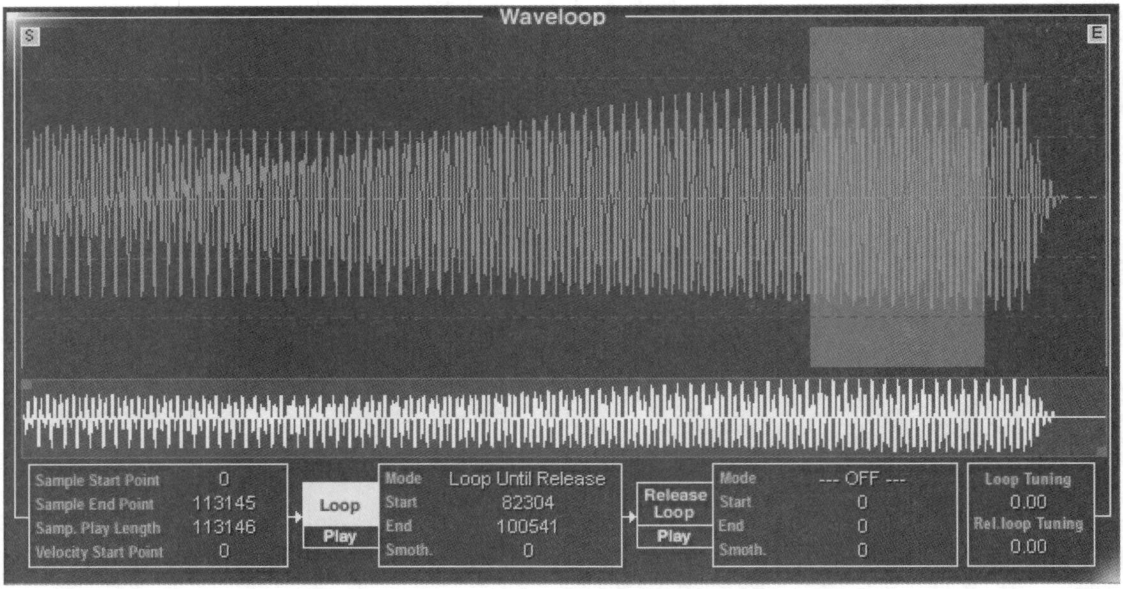

Figure 6.28
Set up a preliminary loop in the Waveloop page

Proceed in a similar manner with the remaining samples so that they are all looped.

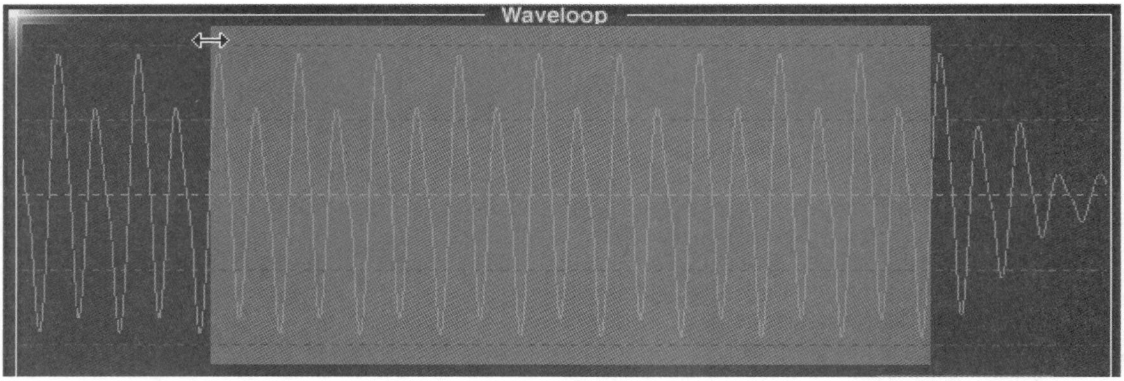

Figure 6.29
Fine tune the loop while listening to the result in real-time

6 Fine tuning

Depending upon the precise nature of your sample program there are probably a number of other elements which need to be edited. It is often the case that samples need re-tuning. To achieve this select the sample concerned in the program list and activate 'select' with the all/select button below the list. Editing is now directed towards the single selected sample. Open the Mod/Tune page and tune the sample as desired. Often a few cents is all that is required. Proceed in a similar manner with any other samples which need re-tuning.

If you intend to use vibrato effects with your sample program you need to set the LFO rate (normally LFO 1) to a suitable setting. HALion's default setting is shown in Figure 6.30.

You may also need to adjust the polyphony to suit the instrument.

Some bass instruments, for example, may benefit from one voice polyphony to avoid dischordant effects with overlapping notes. This is particularly true for the Taurus sub bass program produced for this project and consequently its polyphony is set to '1' in the grouping section of the Mod/Tune page (Figure 6.30).

Other elements which often need attention are the start and end time of some samples (especially the start time). If the sample has not been edited tightly before being imported it can still be adjusted within HALion. Drag the start or end handle to a new position in the Waveloop page.

Finally, adjusting the modulation section in the Mod/Tune page for standard pitch and modulation wheel operation completes the basic sample program (Figure 6.31). Alternative settings might be used for specialist applications.

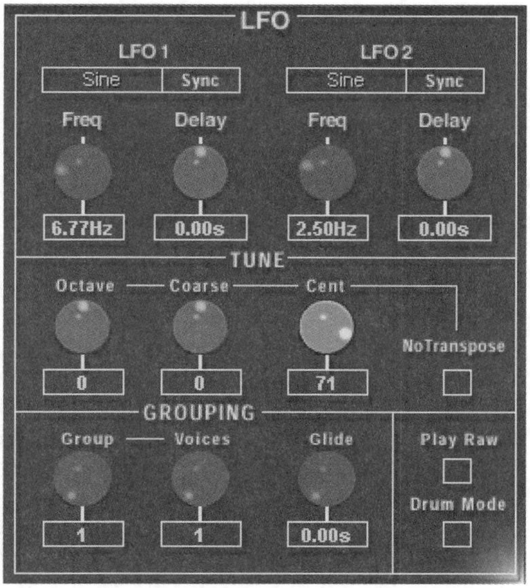

Figure 6.30
Adjust the tuning, polyphony and LFO rate (Mod/Tune page)

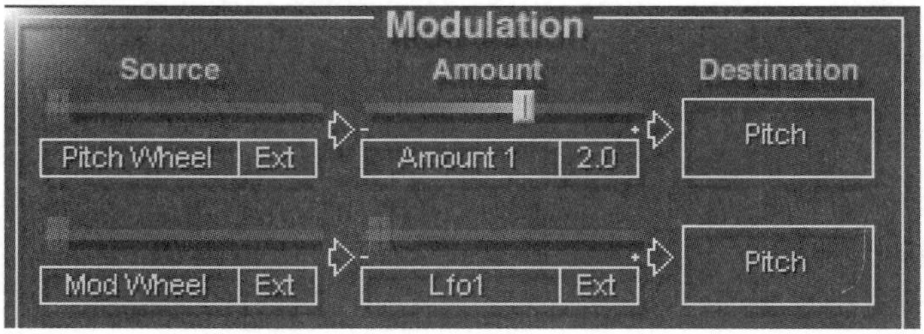

Figure 6.31 Adjust the pitch and modulation wheel to the standard settings (Mod/Tune page)

7 Naming and saving

Right-click (PC)/ctrl-click (Mac) on the program name in the program list and select 'Rename' to name your sample program (if you have not already done so). Alternatively, click on the program name in the main program field. Right-click (PC)/ctrl-click (Mac) on the program name in the program list and select 'Save folder' or 'Save folder with samples' from the pop-up menu to save your sample program to disk. 'Save folder' saves the selected folder as an '.fxp' file (the standard format for HALion sample programs). 'Save folder with samples' saves the .fxp file and also saves all the associated samples into the destination folder you choose in the save dialogue. Alternatively, use the File menu 'Save Instrument' option of your host VST application.

8 Creative techniques

There is a lot more you can do with your samples, mainly for creative purposes. The following are just some of the possibilities:

- Pan a copy of the sample to the right and the original to the left and detune them slightly. Assign each of the detuned pair to the same key range. This produces stereo spread and instant chorusing effects.
- Copy a group of samples two or more times and assign a different velocity zone to each group. Assign different filter settings or other processing to each group for velocity-based effects such as the cut-off filter opening up the harder you hit the keys.
- Apply pitch and velocity crossfading by overlapping the samples on the pitch or velocity axes and using the pitch and velocity crossfade options. This results in automated crossfading between samples according to pitch or velocity which is excellent for effects and smoothing.

FM synthesis: linking the theory to the practice

Info

A demo of FM7 is available as a free download from http://www.native-instruments.com

Chapter 3 outlined the basic principles of FM synthesis in theory and this tutorial links that theory to a series of practical examples using the Native Instruments FM7 VST Instrument/software synthesizer. The FM7 is a superb tool for grasping the fundamentals of FM synthesis. The following tutorial assumes that you have already used the FM7 at the playing level but does not assume any programming knowledge. However, you will get more out of this tutorial if you have read the FM synthesis section in Chapter 3.

Load the FM7 into your host software (or launch the software in stand-alone mode), open the user interface and proceed as follows:

Figure 6.32

Figure 6.33

Figure 6.34

1 Click once on the 'LIB' button (Library) to open the list of available preset sounds for the FM7. (Figure 6.32.)
2 Click on 'INIT EDIT BUFFER' (on the right side of the interface window) to initialise the current sound to the default settings.(Figure 6.33.)
3 Click once on any operator button (the row of green buttons labelled with letters near the top of the editor screen). (Figure 6.34.)
4 Click on 'MATRIX' to open the operator matrix for the FM7. The matrix shows a diagonal line of operators on a connection grid. You should find that Operator F is the only active unit. Operator F is directly connected to the output and is therefore designated as a carrier. (Figure 6.35.)

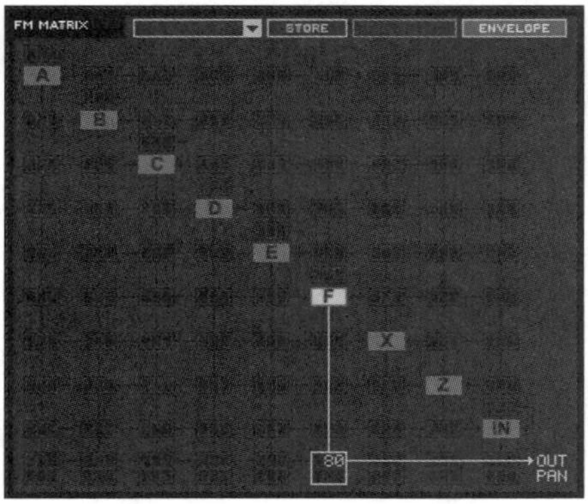

Figure 6.35

5 Click and hold on the output level box and move the mouse vertically to change the level. If you set the level to zero, the output is disconnected. Reset by clicking on the same location and adjusting the level to a value of 80. Note how the level of the frequency component (the carrier frequency) shown in the spectrum display at the top of the screen also changes as you make adjustments. (Figure 6.36.)

Figure 6.36

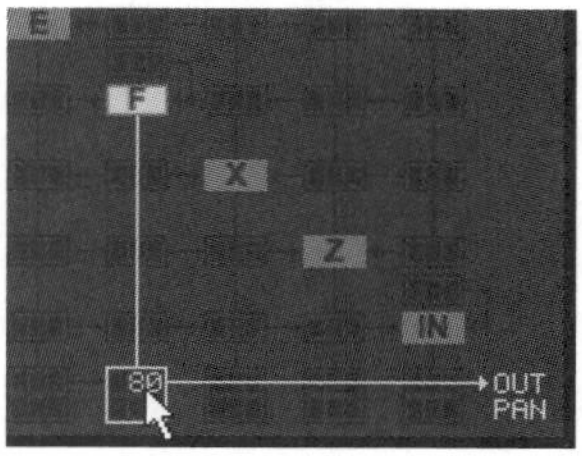

6 To hear the output of the operator F (the carrier) simply play the FM7. You should be able to recognise the sound as a pure sine tone. Looking to the left side of the display reveals that this operator is indeed producing a sine wave. Note also that the frequency ratio is set to 1. (Figure 6.37.)

Figure 6.37

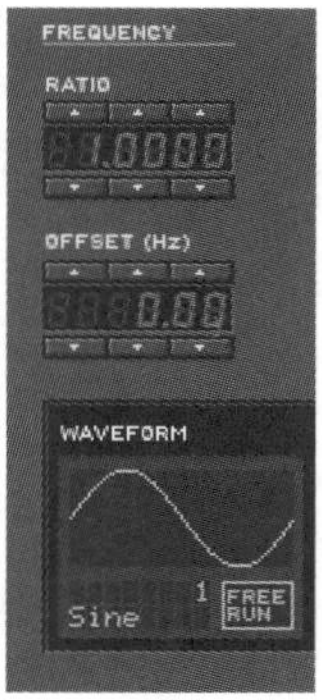

7 Now click on operator E's edit button at the top of the screen. Activate operator E by clicking on its on/off button. The small LED on the button is illuminated in red. (Figure 6.38.)

Figure 6.38

8 Click and hold in the location directly vertically below operator E and parallel to the left of operator F in the matrix display. Adjust the vertical position of the mouse to connect the output of operator E to the input of operator F. Operator E is now modulating operator F. In other words, operator E is the modulator and operator F is the carrier. (Figure 6.39.)

Figure 6.39

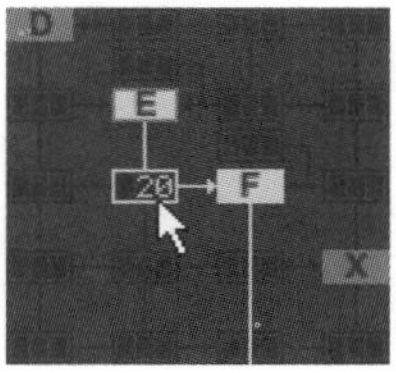

9 Notice that as you change the output value of operator E, the spectrum and waveform displays in the top right corner of the window change accordingly. Increasing the output of the modulator (operator E) increases the modulation index and so more frequency components are added to the signal (as explained in the theory in chapter 3). Enter a value of 20 for the output of operator E. Make sure that the ratio of operator E (the modulator) is set to 1. This sets up the fundamental configuration in FM synthesis where a single carrier (operator F) is modulated by a single modulator (operator E) and the carrier:modulator ratio is 1:1. An output of 20 for operator E equates to a modulation index of around 1. Now play the sound. This setting produces a tone which resembles a sawtooth wave.

Figure 6.40

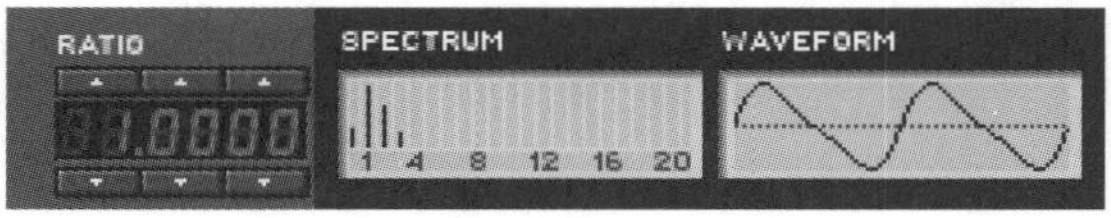

10 Go to the left side of the screen and change the ratio of operator E (the modulator) to 2. Play the tone. This setting produces a tone which resembles a square wave.

Figure 6.41

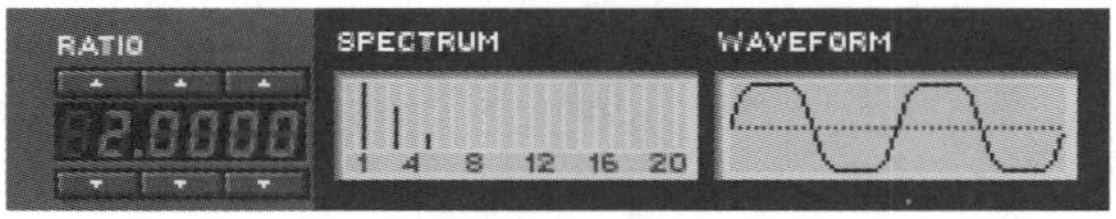

11 Go to the left side of the screen again and change the ratio of operator E (the modulator) to 3. Play the tone. This setting produces a pulse wave.

Figure 6.42

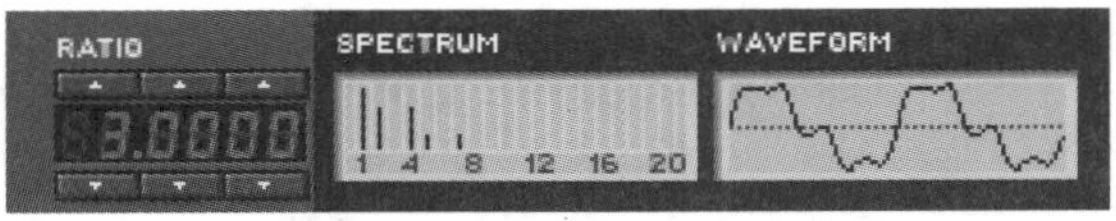

12 Now change the ratio of operator E (the modulator) back to 1 and increase its output to 100 (maximum) in the matrix display. At this level a large number of high frequency components are added to the signal. Click on 'ENVELOPE' (top right of the matrix). In the graphic envelope display which appears, drag the square-shaped handle in the top left of the envelope display to the right to slow down the attack of the modulator. Playing the tone reveals that the high frequency components are now slowly swept in according to the modulator envelope. You are already in FM brass tone territory!

Figure 6.43

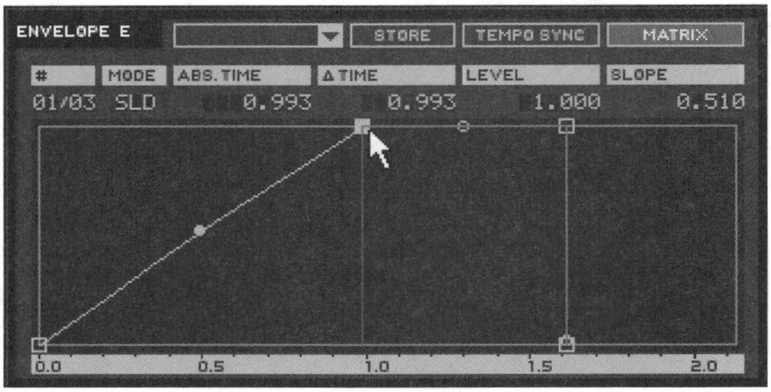

You could now go on to experiment with other ratios, with different modulator output levels and new envelope settings. Always keep an eye on the spectrum and waveform displays in the top right corner of the window as you make adjustments. This is invaluable for providing a visual representation of what is going on within the sound and linking the theory to the audible result. In this way, you can begin to develop a feel for what kinds of results you can expect for each parameter change. The purpose of this tutorial has been simply to link the theory to the practical and not to teach you how to program specific FM sounds. (See chapter 5 for details of the FM7 VST Instrument. See Chapter 3 for the theory of FM synthesis).

Exploring the presets of the NI Pro-52

A good way of getting to know the Pro-52 (and any other synthesizer) is to listen to and experiment with the preset patches. The following points serve as a basic practical tutorial for the exploration of the Pro-52 and may help with other virtual subtractive synthesizers.

Cut-off and resonance

Cut-off and resonance are often the first choices for anybody who enjoys tweaking subtractive synthesizer parameters since they produce among the most predictable influence upon the character of the sound. In the case of a low pass filter the cut-off regulates the high frequency content, ('brightness'), of the sound while the resonance regulates the emphasis at the cut-off point ('sharpness'). Resonance may also go into 'self oscillation' when set at high levels and this is heard as a 'ringing' sound. Balancing the relative levels of the cut-off and resonance controls opens up a rich palette of timbral possibilities. Select any Pro-52 sound and check out the possibilities.

Filter envelope

The filter envelope can be used in conjunction with the cut-off and resonance controls to create sounds which have, for example, a percussive attack. For this you need to set a fast attack time. To listen to an example select default patch 747 ('Night Bells'). For selection purposes, click on the Pro-52's File button (programmer section) and enter the patch number by selecting the corresponding program select buttons. For default patch 747, try switching off the delay effect to hear the attack segment more clearly and try changing the attack parameter of the filter envelope to hear what happens to the sound at different settings. Conversely, slow strings, or instruments where the frequency spectrum needs to swell to a wider range, require a slow attack time. Try default patch 144 ('Squishy Pad') and hold down a note for a long time to hear the full effect of the filter sweep. Listen to the effect of changing any or all of the filter envelope settings. These examples demonstrate how the filter envelope controls the spectral evolution of the sound over time.

Amplifier envelope

The amplifier envelope needs to be set in conjunction with the filter envelope since, for example, a slow release setting in the filter envelope is not audible if the amplifier envelope's release control is set very fast. Overall, the amplifier envelope is the final stage in shaping how the sound's amplitude level changes over time.

Tuning effects

When using both oscillators A and B the sound can be made 'thicker' or 'chorused' by slightly detuning oscillator B using the Fine control. This is often used for electric piano and strings sounds. Try default patch 481 ('Piano Chorus'). Alternatively, the coarse frequency (which changes pitch in semitones) might be used to set oscillator B a pleasing interval apart from oscillator A for automatic harmony effects. Try default patch 428 ('Brass In Fifths'). For other effects the oscillators might also be set to different octaves.

Waveforms

The waveforms provide the starting points for the creation of a new sound and might be applied in any combination. Combinations of pulse and triangle waves tend towards piano and string-like tones, triangle waves tend towards pure, flute-like tones, sawtooth tends to be used for brass-like tones, a combination of pulse and sawtooth tends towards organ-like tones and a perfect square wave produces a 'hollow' tone which resembles a clarinet. Of course, the final characteristics of any sound are also highly dependent on the other active parameters in the patch. Comparisons with known musical instruments help achieve the desired spectral balance when you begin to create a sound, even though you may be aiming for something new and original.

Vibrato

Adding dynamic interest is an effective method of enlivening a static sounding tone. One of the most popular techniques is the application of vibrato. Vibrato can be achieved in the Pro-52 by modulating the pitch of an oscillator with the LFO. Listen to default patch 238 ('Thin'n Cold'). For normal vibrato the shape of the LFO is set to a triangle waveform and the frequency set to around 1 or 2 o'clock. This produces the characteristic 'warbling' effect associated with vibrato. Try changing the waveform and frequency of the LFO for other modulation effects. The modulation wheel is used to regulate the depth of the effect.

Pulse width

If you have selected the pulse waveform, the pulse width control varies the harmonic content of the sound to produce tones which are rich in high frequency energy. At the centre position the characteristic rich, 'hollow' tone of a square wave is produced. Listen to default patch 525 ('Dept. Store Clarinet'). As the pulse width is varied above and below this position, the sound tends to become 'brighter' and more 'reed-like' and, at the extreme positions, more 'buzzy' with a characteristic gain in upper-harmonic energy and a reduction in the fundamental and lower harmonic energy. Try default patch 132 ('Corona'). All this opens up a rich palette of tonal possibilities to the synth programmer.

Pulse width modulation

The application of pulse width modulation, (the automatic variation of the pulse width in a repeated cycle), is excellent for adding dynamic interest to otherwise static tones. It results in the continuous shifting of the harmonic spectrum. To understand this in more detail select default patch 161 ('Big UniBass'). Switch off oscillator B, de-activate the unison switch, set the PW control of oscillator A to the centre position, set the modulation wheel to maximum and set the LFO frequency to its minimum position. Holding down a note on the keyboard clearly reveals the slow cyclic sweeping effect of the changing harmonics as the pulse width is modulated by the LFO.

Synthesizing bass drums in Waldorf Attack, NI Pro-52 and Bitheadz Retro AS-1

This project outlines how to create an 808-style bass drum in three different VST instruments. Before proceeding to the practical details it is worth considering some theory.

Bass drums in theory

The type of bass drum referred to in this project is that which is generally used as part of a drum kit. In the real world, this consists of a beater actioned by a foot pedal which strikes a drum head (known as the batter head) stretched across the circular shell of the bass drum. There is another head on the opposite side of the shell (known as the carry head) which for modern music usually has a hole cut in it. This arrangement produces the distinctive timbre of the modern bass drum. This is characterised by a series of near-harmonic low frequencies mixed with a dense cluster of mid and upper frequencies. The sound usually starts with a short high-frequency click when the beater first hits the batter head. The upper and mid frequency content decays at a faster rate than the low frequencies, which can take some time to fully decay depending on how the drum is tuned and dampened. The pitch of the bass drum falls as the amplitude decays.

The actual spectrum of a bass drum is quite difficult to re-create using subtractive synthesis alone and to get near to the sound of a real bass drum usually requires a mix of both subtractive and FM synthesis. However, few VST instruments or real-world synthesizers have all the parameters in the required configuration, so most practical synthesising of bass drums involves a compromise. The electronically produced bass drum has grown to be a recognisable and much used timbre in its own right. The Roland TR808 kick drum is probably the single most used bass drum in popular music. So how was the original sound synthesized?

The original 808 bass drum sound was made by triggering a special kind of oscillator with a short accented impulse. The oscillator featured a feedback path which controlled the decay rate of the sound. Some of the trigger impulse sound was routed into the audio path after the oscillator to emulate the click of a bass drum. The composite signal was routed to a low-pass filter to remove some of the upper frequencies. Few synthesizers can emulate this precise configuration but two methods can be employed to get very close to an 808-style bass drum.

The first is to assign a sine wave shape to an oscillator with its pitch set at G#1. Apply a small amount of positive pitch modulation using an envelope set to a very short AR envelope shape. This provides a bass drum click (or 'thud') at the beginning of the sound. Another, often better, method of achieving a click is to use a second low-tuned oscillator set to a pulse or some other noisy wave (and preferably frequency modulated) and control its loudness contour with the same envelope used for the pitch modulation of the first oscillator. Pass the composite signal through a low-pass filter and adjust the cut-off frequency to filter out the desired amount of high frequencies. Adjust a second envelope for the fastest attack with a short exponential decay to control the overall loudness contour of the bass drum. The decay of this envelope controls the length of the bass drum.

The second technique is to trigger the sound of a self-oscillating filter (a filter with a very high resonance setting). In these circumstances the cut-off frequency controls the pitch (tone) of the bass drum and the amount of resonance controls its length. An envelope modulating the filter cut-off, to produce a fast sweep down in the pitch, simulates a click for the attack of the bass drum.

Synthesizing an 808-style bass drum in Waldorf Attack

There is already a preset 808 kick and an entire 808 kit in Attack. The supplied 808 kick uses the first of the above methods to synthesize its sound but let's try producing an alternative using the second technique, the self-oscillating filter. Attack is designed specifically for the synthesizing of drum and percussion sounds so achieving results with this particular unit is relatively easy when compared with general purpose synthesizers. Proceed as follows:

- Select a sound button and initialise it using the 'initialise sound' option in the preset menu.
- Set oscillator 1 to its maximum pitch setting (21096.2Hz/E10). Set the waveform type to sine and adjust the envelope amount to 9.83% with envelope 1 selected (Figure 6.44). This part of the patch is for creating a short impulse which triggers the self-oscillating filter and it also provides a click for the attack of the bass drum.
- In the mixer section, set all controls to zero except the oscillator 1 level which should be set to 100% (Figure 6.45).
- In the filter section, select the low-pass filter type. Adjust the cut-off dial to 47.1Hz and the resonance and filter envelope dials to 100% (Figure 6.46).

Figure 6.44
Adjust oscillator 1 to create an impulse click

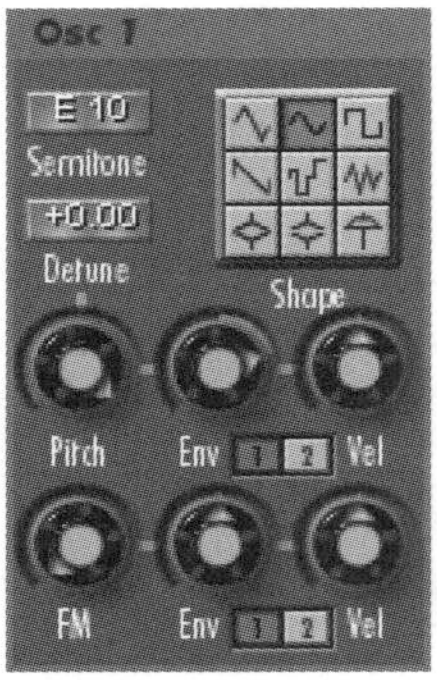

Figure 6.45
Adjust the mix to include the output of oscillator 1 only

Figure 6.46
Set up a low-pass filter

- For envelope 1 set all controls to their minimum values (Figure 6.47). This controls the impulse of oscillator 1 and also sweeps down the cut-off frequency of the filter section very quickly. The impulse of oscillator 1 provides a click for the attack phase and the filter sweep simulates the 'thud' at the onset of the bass drum.
- For envelope 2 set the attack and release dials to their minimum values, set the decay dial to 0.625s and the shape dial to 42% Exp (Figure 6.48). Envelope 2 controls the overall loudness contour of the bass drum.

Figure 6.47
Configure envelope 1 to modulate the cut-off frequency and provide a click

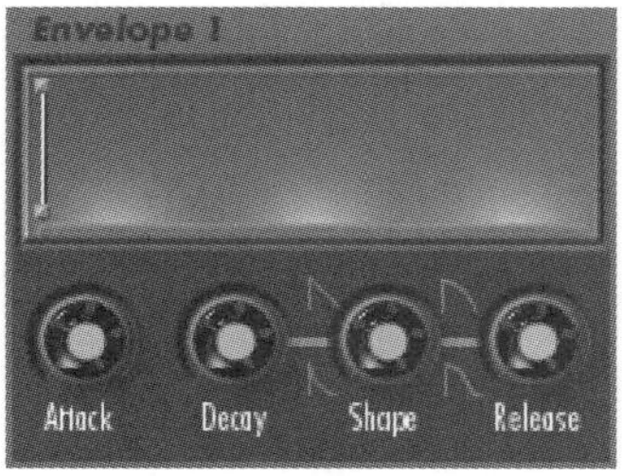

Figure 6.48
Configure envelope 2 for the desired loudness contour

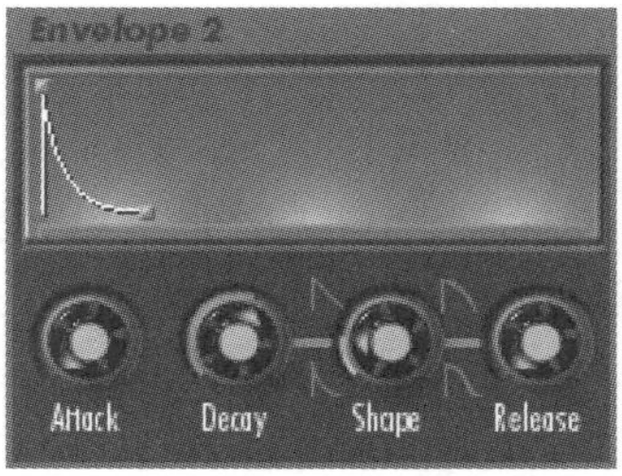

- Set the amplifier volume dial to around -4.44dB and adjust the velocity sensitivity dial to suit your taste for the velocity response of the new bass drum. Try 100% (Figure 6.49).
- Play the new bass drum to hear the result. Note that this configuration includes a longer decay than the original 808 kick. Adjust the filter resonance and envelope 2 decay levels if you wish to change the decay characteristics of the drum. The filter cut-off regulates the pitch of the drum.

Figure 6.49
Adjust the amplifier

Synthesizing an 808-style bass drum in NI Pro-52

The Pro-52 produces a particularly wide range of timbres and drums, and percussive sounds are well within its capabilities. The following technique uses the Pro-52's filter pushed into self-oscillation to synthesize a bass drum. Proceed as follows:

- Load Pro-52 into your host software and select the first patch 'CompSync'.
- Switch off all red illuminated switches in the Poly-Mod, LFO, Wheel-Mod, Oscillator A, Oscillator B and delay effect sections. In the mixer section, reduce all dials to zero. Leave the global velocity and release switches illuminated and set a polyphony of 1 voice (Figure 6.50).

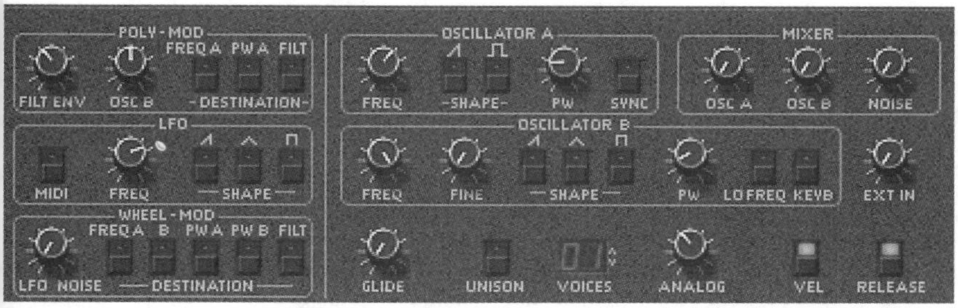

Figure 6.50 Reduce the level of all sources for zero output level

> **Info**
>
> A demo of Pro-52 is available as a free download from http://www.native-instruments.com

- In the filter section, set the cut-off to around 10 o'clock, the envelope amount to 9 o'clock, the resonance to maximum and the keyboard amount to zero. For the filter envelope, set the attack, sustain and release to zero and the decay dial to around 11 o'clock (Figure 6.51). The cut-off frequency controls the pitch of the bass drum and the maximum resonance causes the filter to go into self-oscillation. The filter envelope implements a fast sweep down of the cut-off frequency resulting in a quick sweep down in the pitch of the bass drum. This creates a slight click or 'thud' at the start of the sound. With the Pro-52, the filter is triggered by any MIDI note input and does not require an impulse signal in order to start its activity. However, it may need to be triggered a number of times before it goes into continuous self-oscillation.
- In the amplifier section, set the attack and sustain dials to zero and the decay and release dials to just under 1 o'clock (Figure 6.52). This applies the right kind of loudness contour to the bass drum.

Figure 6.51
Set up the filter for self-oscillation

Figure 6.52
Configure the amplifier envelope for the sound of a bass drum

- Play the bass drum. The result is an 808-style kick. Note that this bass drum is velocity sensitive. As mentioned above, it may need to be triggered several times before the full self-oscillation cycle of the filter commences. You can control the decay characteristics using the decay and release dials of the amplifier envelope and/or the filter resonance control. It plays back at a single pitch but if you wish to experiment with different pitched sounds then increase the keyboard amount dial in the filter section. Try experimenting with the filter and filter envelope controls. A wide range of different drum and electronic percussion effects are possible.

Info

A demo of Bitheadz Retro AS-1 is available as a free download from ftp://68.15.52.55/Downloads/Demos/

Synthesizing an 808-style bass drum in Bitheadz Retro AS-1

The Retro-AS1 is better suited to creating a bass drum using the first of the methods described above, i.e. assigning a sine wave to an oscillator and then somehow adding a click to achieve the desired attack of the kick drum. Luckily the Retro AS-1 has three oscillators and two filters with a very adaptable routing system. Proceed as follows:

- Click on the default button to initialise the Retro AS-1.
- The Retro AS-1 default appears with oscillator 1 and filter 1 switched on. Select a sine wave for oscillator 1 and switch off its keyboard button. Adjust the coarse tuning dial to -28 and turn the volume dial to full. Oscillator 1 is to be used for the lower frequencies of the bass drum (Figure 6.53)

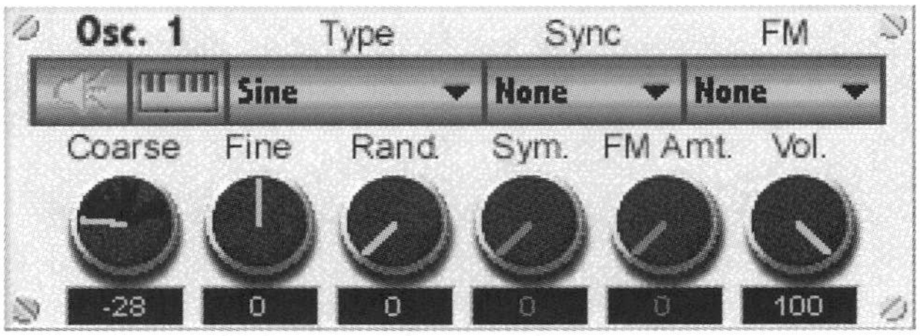

Figure 6.53
Configure Oscillator 1 for the lower frequencies of the bass drum

- Select a 2 pole LP filter type for filter 1 and leave the cut-off frequency at its default 7.8kHz (Figure 6.54). The cut-off frequency is not applicable to the low sine wave of oscillator 1 but filter 1 is later to be used to strengthen the click of the bass drum.

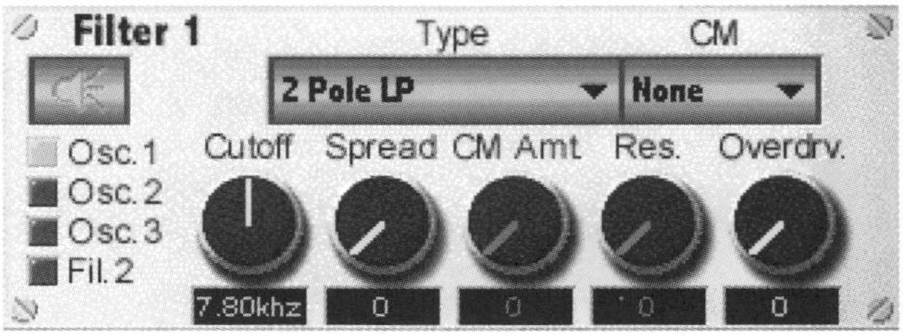

Figure 6.54
Set up Filter 1 ready to strengthen the click of the bass drum

- Select the modulation page (Mod button). In the routings section, leave envelope 1 routed to volume. For the second routing in the list, change the destination of envelope 2 to 'oscillator 1 frequency' and set its amount dial to 100 (Figure 6.55).

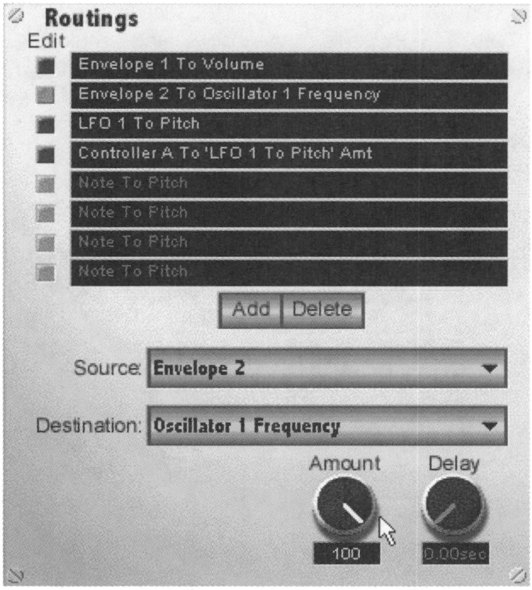

Figure 6.55
Configure the routing of envelopes 1 and 2 in the routings section

- In the modulators section, select the edit button for 'Volume envelope 1' and adjust the envelope as in the screenshot below (Figure 6.56). (If you are using version 1.01 of Retro AS-1, use the envelope display only to make adjustments as there may be a bug when using the number fields which causes irregular operation in some host software). Play the sound to hear the preliminary lower part of the bass drum.

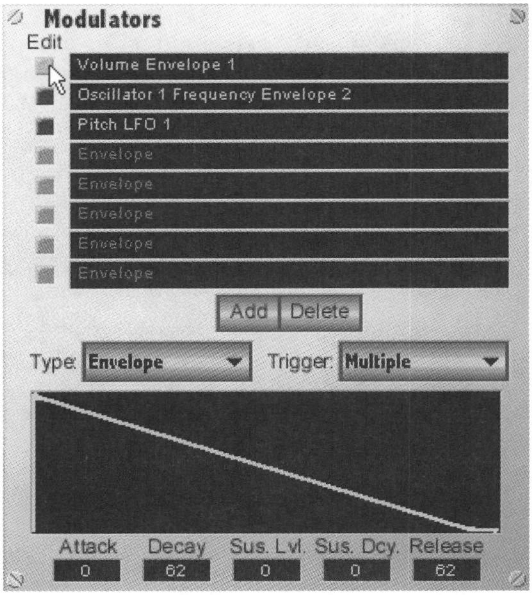

Figure 6.56
Adjust envelope 1

- While still in the modulators section, select the edit button for 'oscillator 1 frequency envelope 2' and adjust the envelope as in the following screenshot (Figure 6.57). Play the sound to hear the lower part of the bass drum with the frequency swept down very quickly according to envelope 2. This adds a slight amount of shape or 'thud' to the front of the kick.

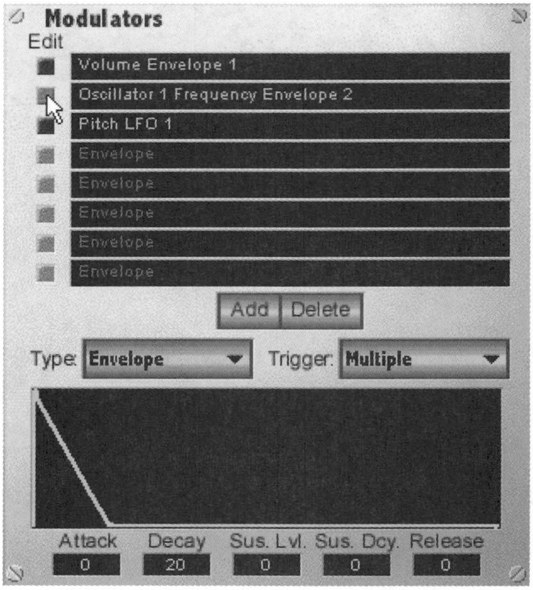

Figure 6.57
Adjust envelope 2

- Select the Main page (Main button). Activate oscillator 2 and switch off its keyboard button. Select the 'glottal' wave type, adjust the coarse tuning dial to -15 and turn the volume dial to full. Select oscillator 2 in the FM modulation source menu and turn up the FM dial to full. Applying frequency modulation helps create a sharper sound. Oscillator 2 is to be used for the click of the bass drum (Figure 6.58).

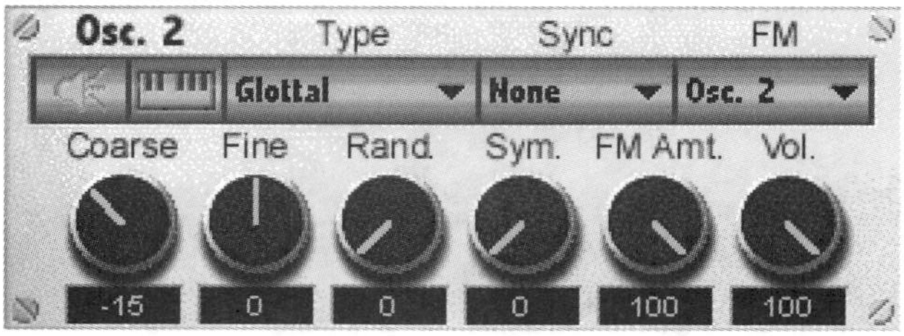

Figure 6.58
Configure Oscillator 2 for the click of the bass drum

- Switch on filter 2 and select a 2 pole LP filter type. Set the cut-off frequency to 10.5kHz and select oscillator 2 as the source to be filtered (Figure 6.59)
- Select the modulation page (Mod button). Click on the add button in the routings section to add another routing. Change the source to 'envelope 2' and the destination to 'oscillator 2 volume'. Set the amount dial to 100 (Figure 6.60). The loudness contour of oscillator

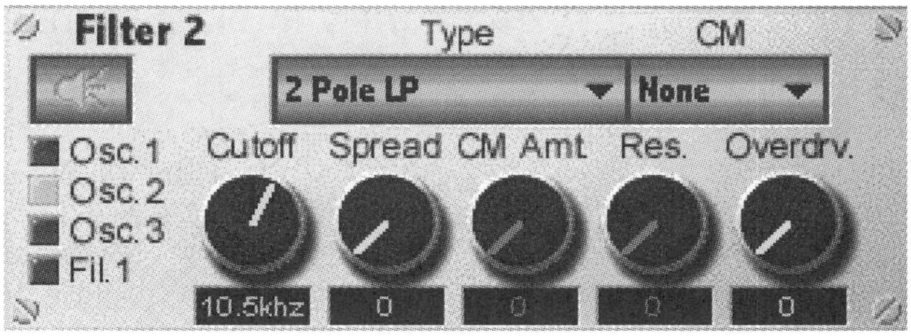

Figure 6.59
Set up Filter 2 to help create the click of the bass drum

2 is now controlled by the fast attack and release of envelope 2. The result is a click at the onset of the bass drum. Play the bass drum to hear the result.

- The level of the bass drum may seem weak. Try routing both oscillators through both filters to increase the level and intensity of the sound. Select oscillators 1 and 2 for both filters on the Main page. Try also selecting one voice in the '# of voices' menu to improve the triggering of the bass drum (Figure 6.61). Experiment with different configurations to attempt to improve the basic model.

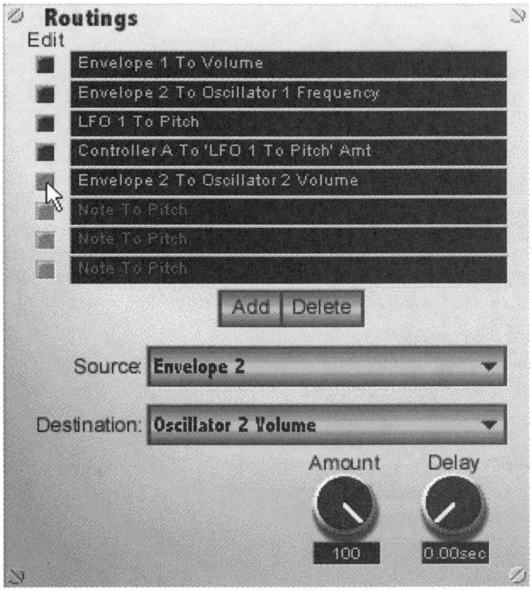

Figure 6.60
Route envelope 2 to control the volume of oscillator 2. This produces the bass drum click.

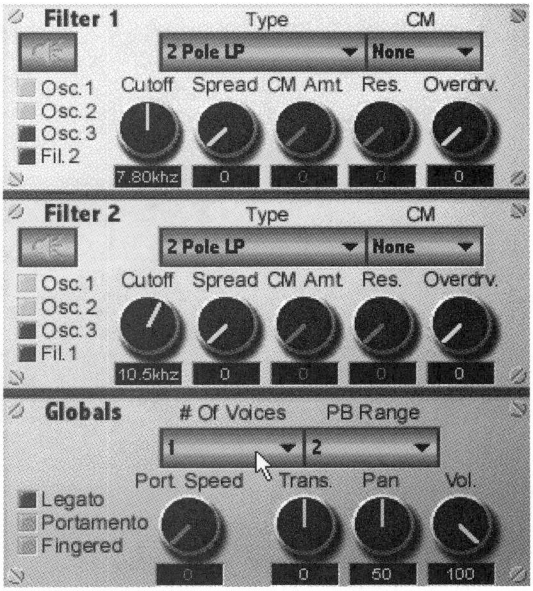

Figure 6.61
Route both oscillators through both filters on the Main page to increase the level

Programming organ tones in Native Instruments B4

Programming organ tones revolves around the drawbar settings, known in organ terminology as registrations, and the percussion, vibrato and rotator settings. The registrations might be viewed as the 'cake' of the sound while the other controls add the 'icing'. Major tonal changes can be implemented in the B4 using the tube amp section which significantly extends the timbral range of the instrument. The tube amp's body and bright controls are particularly significant for regulating the bass and mid frequency ranges of the signal. If you are programming a percussive sound and need more attack, add some 'bite' to the tone using the keyclick parameter. The tone dials of the bass and treble rotators add significant control over the timbre and are worth tweaking when using the speaker rotator.

The following settings produce a wide range of different organ tones. These can be used as found, or modified according to taste.

Info

A demo of B4 is available as a free download from http://www.native-instruments.com

Bright, vibrant jazz sound

Registration: 80 0007 654
Percussion: Off
Vibrato: Mix = C, Depth = 3
Rotator: Fast

Figure 6.62

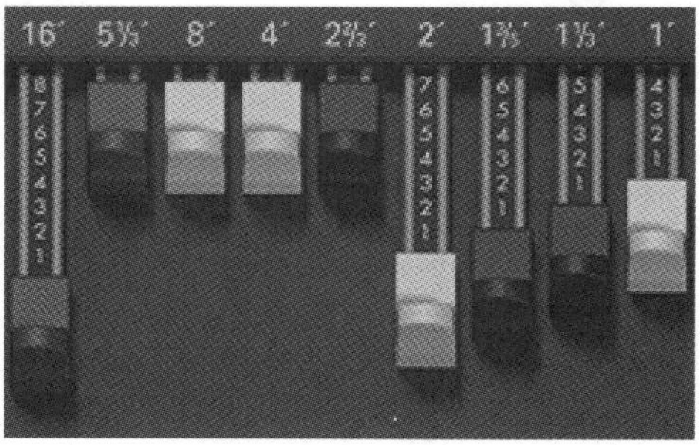

Cool, mellow organ

Registration: 83 6000 000
Percussion: Off
Vibrato: Off
Rotator: Slow

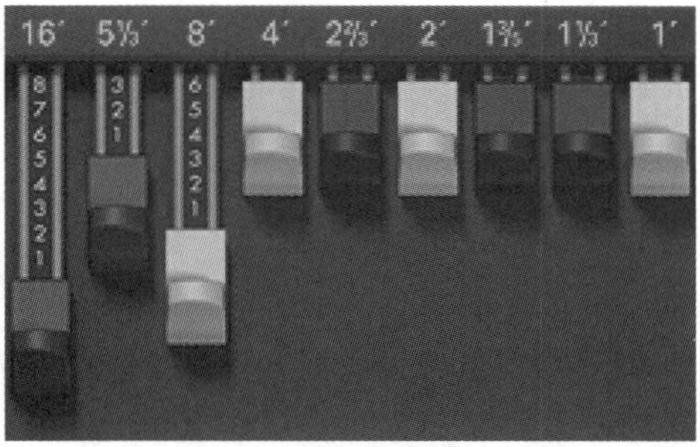

Figure 6.63

Big, theatrical style organ

Registration: 88 8887 765
Percussion: Off
Vibrato: Off
Rotator: Fast

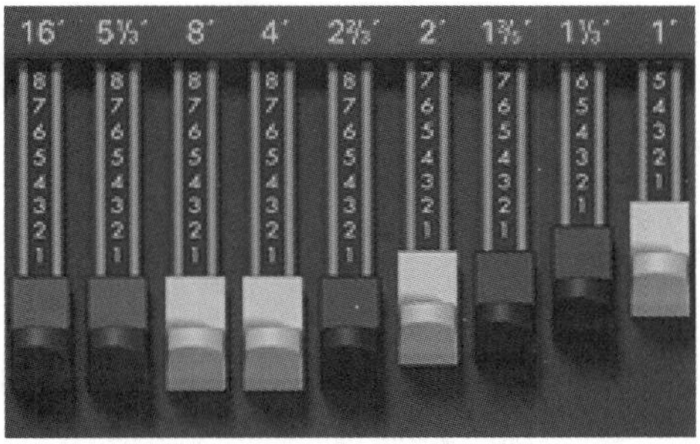

Figure 6.64

Percussive, jazz style (the 'Jimmy Smith sound')

Registration: 88 8000 000
Percussion: Volume = S, Decay = F, Harmonic = 3
Vibrato: Mix = 0, Depth = 3
Rotator: Slow. Treble rotor = max. Bass rotor = 75%.
Comment: Increase the keyclick amount to add more bite.

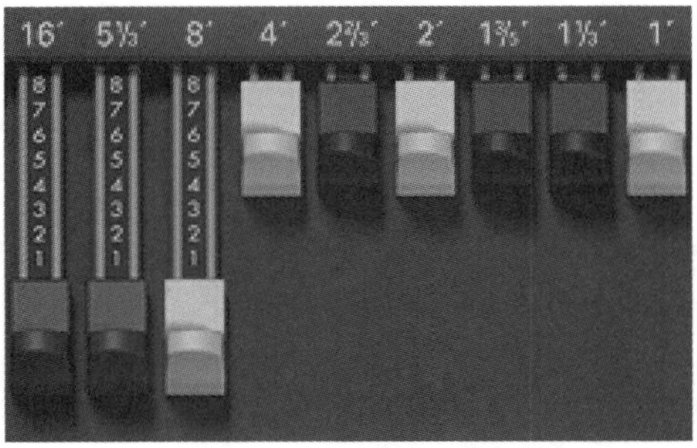

Figure 6.65

Gentle organ for light accompaniment work

Registration: 00 8602 001
Percussion: Off
Vibrato: Off
Rotator: Slow

Figure 6.66

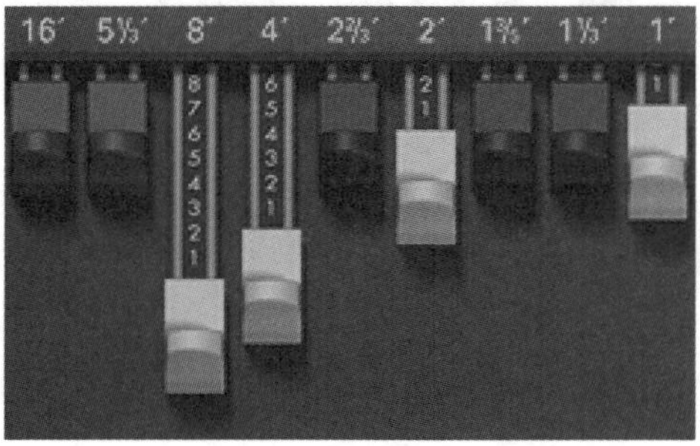

Full church organ

Registration: 42 7866 244
Percussion: Off
Vibrato: Off
Rotator: Slow

Figure 6.67

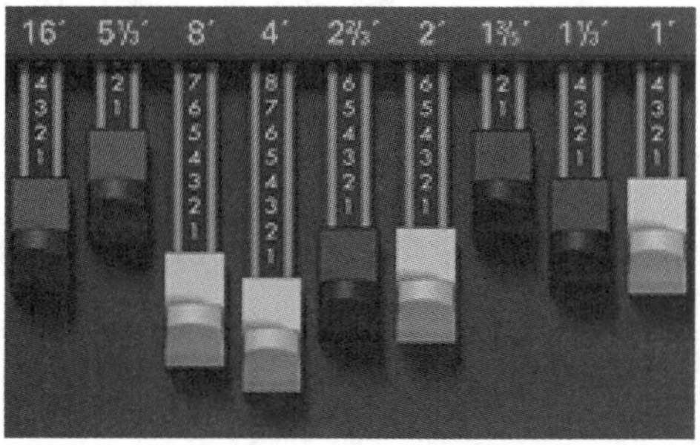

Solo jazz or rock organ.

Registration: 00 8804 885
Percussion: Volume = N, Decay = F, Harmonic = 2
Vibrato: Off
Rotator: Slow or fast
Comment: Add tube amp drive for distortion and keyclick for more 'bite'.

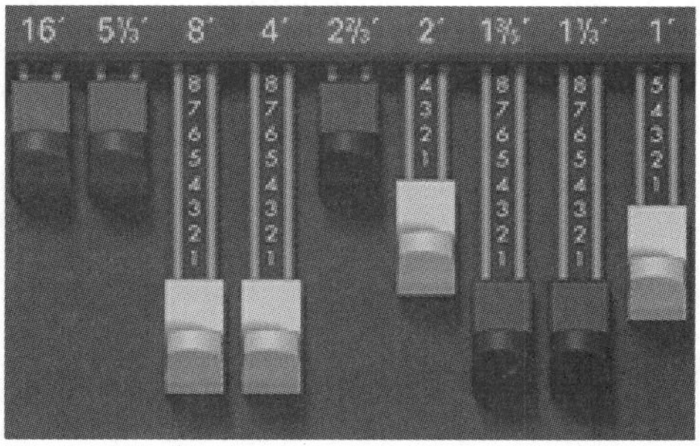

Figure 6.68

Dry theatre organ

Registration: 76 8878 667
Percussion: Off
Vibrato: Off
Rotator: Off

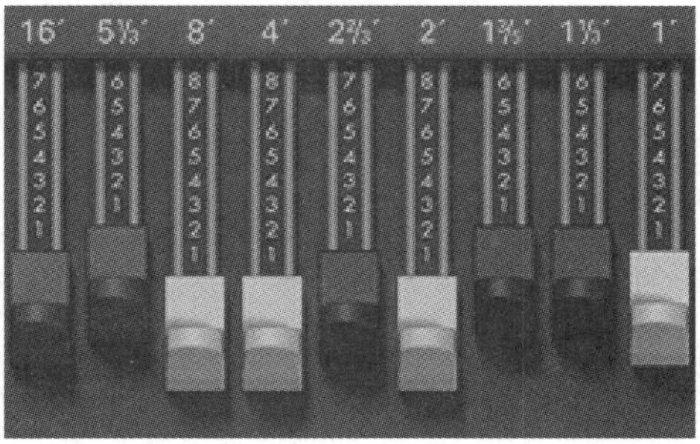

Figure 6.69

Deep sub bass for B4 foot pedals

Registration: 85 8400
Percussion: Off
Vibrato: Off
Rotator: Off or Slow. Treble rotor tone = min. Bass rotor tone = min.
Comment: Turn tube amp 'body' and 'bright' controls fully left.

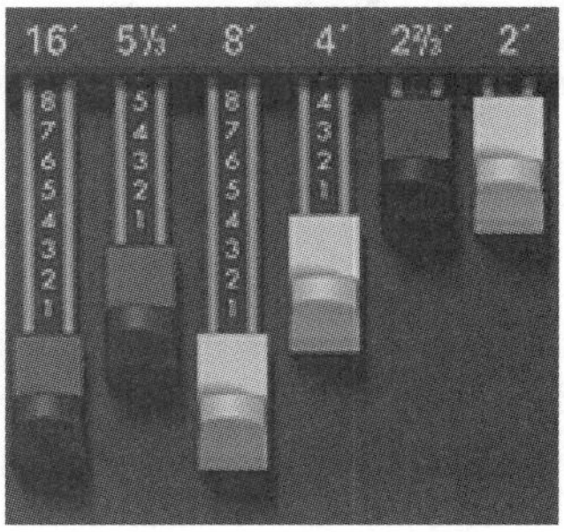

Figure 6.70

Vocal drones and atmospherics with granular synthesis (using Reaktor or Dynamo)

Reaktor is one of the few VST instruments/software synthesizers which makes active use of granular synthesis. Granular synthesis as implemented in Reaktor opens up a whole new palette of sound colours and textures. The possibilities may be unfamiliar to those who are used to more traditional synthesis techniques but if you enjoy experimenting and creating original new sounds then read on.

Info

A demo of Reaktor is available as a free download from http://www.native-instruments.com

Reaktor features several preset instruments which use granular synthesis and these are found in its Premium Library. For this tutorial we will use the 'Plasma' instrument to create vocal drones and a variety of inspiring and extraordinary effects. Load Plasma from the Premium Library (Native Instruments/Reaktor/Library/Premium/Samplers and Transformers/Plasma.ens).

What is Plasma?

Plasma (Figure 6.71) is a steady-state re-synthesizer based on granular synthesis which allows the freezing of samples at an adjustable position within the evolution of the sound. The frozen segments are granularised and the result can be played at different pitches using a MIDI keyboard.

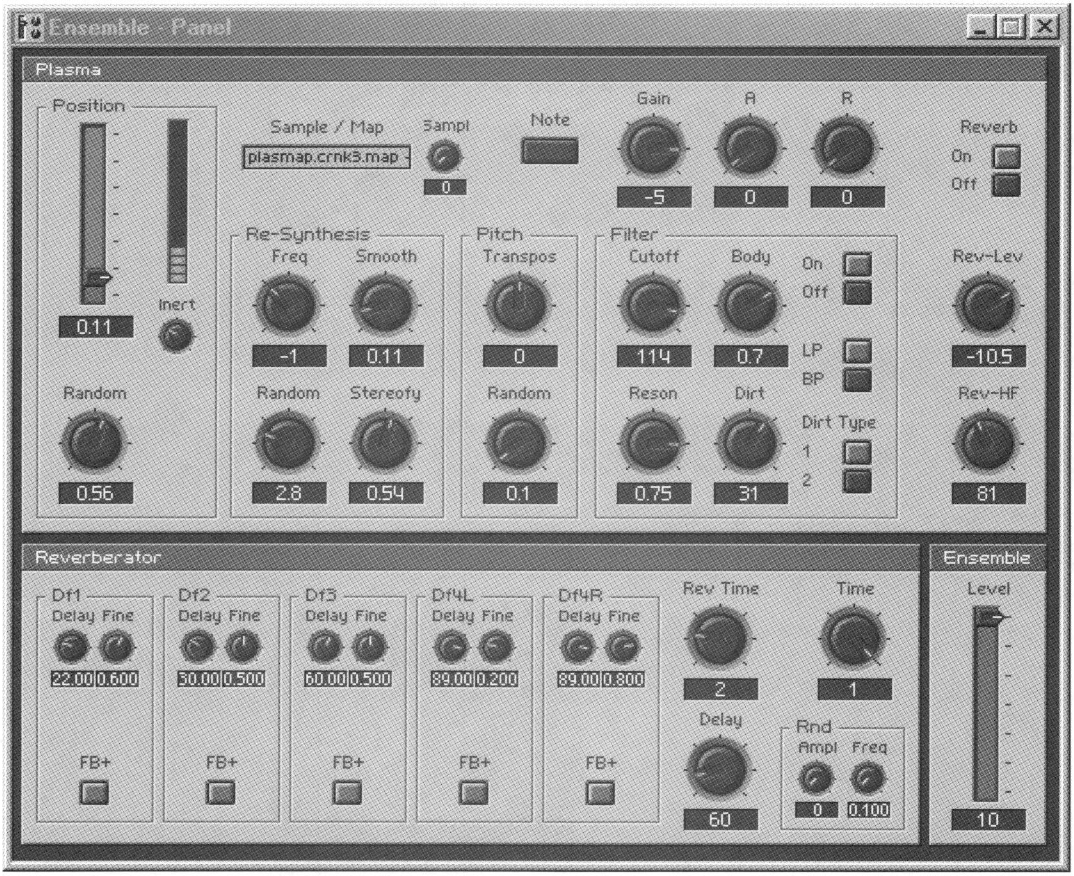

Figure 6.71
Plasma graphical user interface

Samples are loaded into the instrument via the sample map module. Double-click on the grey sample/map name to open the sample map window. For this tutorial leave the sample map in its default state. The sample to be treated is chosen using the sample selector parameter. The essential elements of Plasma are found in the position and re-synthesis sections. The position slider allows you to travel through the sample to choose which point is frozen. Inertia controls the speed with which the sample position follows the slider movements. By default the position slider is assigned to the modulation wheel of your controller keyboard so, if desired, you can tweak the slider remotely rather than using the mouse on the screen. The position section random parameter introduces a randomised playback of the frozen sample position based around the current slider setting. The re-synthesis section controls the main granular synthesis parameters where frequency determines the re-synthesis frequency in semitone steps (lower settings produce longer frozen sound particles and higher settings produce very small sound particles). Smooth adjusts the envelope of each grain (lower settings produce harder more 'grainy' sounds and higher settings produce smoother more 'rounded' effects). The sound particles can be distributed within the stereo soundfield using the stereofy control and the stereo effect can be randomised. The final pitch of the sound can be transposed and randomised using the pitch transpose and random functions. The sound passes through a low-pass/high-pass filter and the amplitude envelope of the result is regulated with the attack (A) and release (R) controls. There is also an overall gain control. Reverb effects can be added in the reverberator section.

Getting to know Plasma

Proceed as follows to get to know the parameters of Plasma:

1 Load Plasma (as outlined above) if you have not already done so.

2 Leave all the settings in their default positions and trigger the sound using your MIDI keyboard or the on-screen note button. The default sound (snapshot 1 – stutter no-no) is a male voice repeating what appears to be non-sensical speech sounds.

3 Set the position slider to 0, the position random dial to 0 and inertia to 0. Set the frequency dial to 40, smooth to 0, random to 0 and stereofy to 0 in the re-synthesis section. Leave all other parameters in their default position (Figure 6.72).

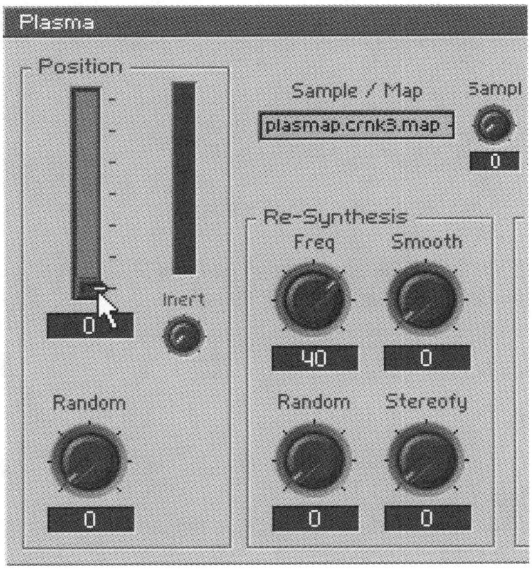

Figure 6.72
Move the position slider with these settings to travel through the original sample

4 Hold down middle C on your MIDI keyboard and slowly sweep the position slider from its lowest position to its highest position either with the mouse on screen or using the modulation wheel. You hear the magic words 'I know you'll die Marcello'. Now you know what the man was trying to tell you ! If you move the position slider back to its lowest position while holding a note on the keyboard you hear the phrase played in reverse. The speed with which you move the position slider controls the speed of the playback.

Creating sustained vocal drones and atmospheric textures

By vocal drone we mean a steady-state voice-like sound texture. To create this kind of effect proceed as follows:

- Following on from the settings outlined above, set the position slider at 0.44.
- Play some notes on your keyboard. Notice that the sound is quite 'grainy'. To create a more rounded sound increase the smooth parameter to 0.82. The sound is now more fluid and you have already created a sound which is suitable for long steady-state voice-like textures.

The above techniques have outlined a basic method for producing a simple vocal drone effect from a sampled speech source. Try changing the position of the slider to obtain other tone colours. Try also adding some random position effect and an amount of the stereofy control to add dynamic movement to the sound. After experimenting for a while you may wonder what happens if you change the source sample. Try this too by choosing a different numbered sample using the sample selector dial. When you have fully explored the possibilities of the above techniques you may like to try changing the sample map to expand the range of available tone colours. To achieve this proceed as follows:

- Double-click on the sample map field.
- In the dialogue which appears click on the load button. This opens a file dialogue.

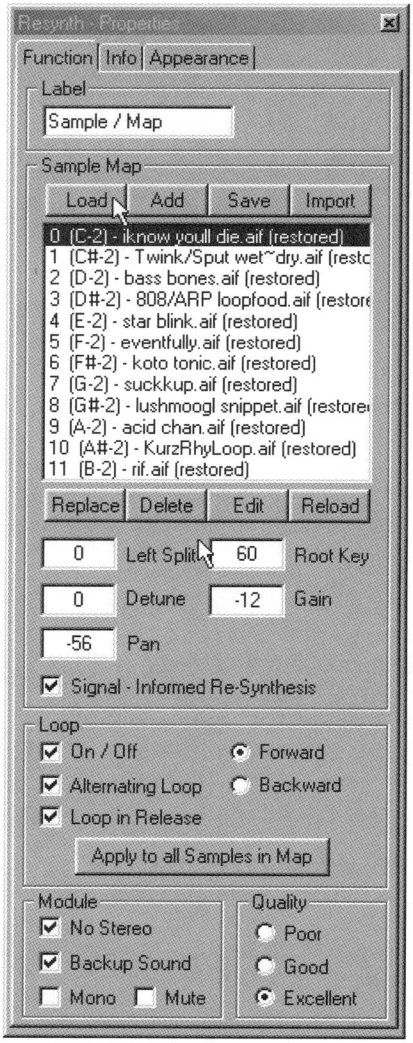

Figure 6.73
Open the sample map dialogue to load in a different sample map

- Open the following directory path: Native Instruments/Reaktor/Library/Wavesets. A file named 'WSM 1.map' is found at this location. This is a comprehensive set of waveforms usually used for waveset (wavetable) synthesis in other instruments within Reaktor (e.g. Vibrator).
- Load the WSM 1 map into the sample map and close the dialogue.
- Reduce the gain using the gain control to around -30 (Be careful with the level as these samples can be rather loud!). Choose sample number 28. Set the position slider to 0.07, the position random dial to 0.58 and inertia to 50%. Set frequency to -2, smooth to 0.58 and both random and stereofy to 0.

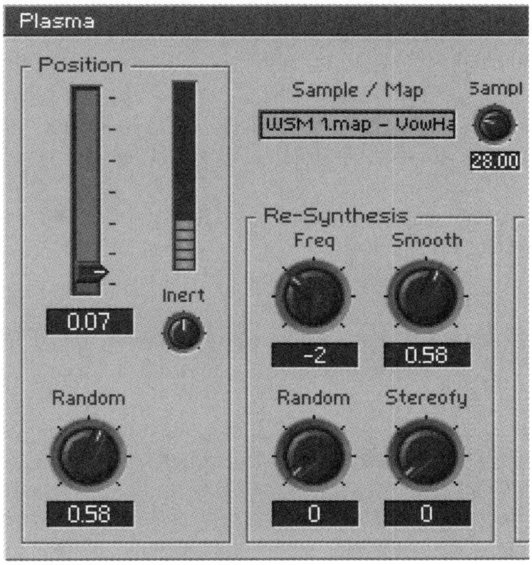

Figure 6.74
Try these settings to explore other atmospheric sound textures

- Play your keyboard to hear the result. You have created an alternative kind of vocal effect. Try changing the position slider as you play (using the modulation wheel for real-time control).
- There are 42 samples available in this sample map so there is plenty of scope for further experimentation. There are an enormous number of combinations of parameter settings and an equally enormous variety of sound textures.

Summary

This tutorial has hopefully brought your attention to the rich source of sound textures offered by granular synthesis. It has been implemented in Plasma in a comparatively simple form. If you would like to explore granular synthesis further, more elaborate implementations are provided in Reaktor's Grain State and Travellizer ensembles (Native Instruments/Reaktor/Library/New in Reaktor 3). There are also a number of other granular synthesis ensembles (and a vast range of other instruments) available on the Internet from the Native Instruments user library (www.native-instruments.com).

7 Recommended reading

Bennett, Stephen 'Making Music With Emagic Logic Audio', (Kent: PC Publishing, 2001), 320pp.

Buick, Peter and Lennard, Vic 'Music Technology Reference Book', (Kent: PC Publishing, 1995), 160pp.

Chowning, John 'The Synthesis of Complex Audio Spectra by Means of Frequency Modulation', (Journal of the Audio Engineering Society Vol.21, no.7, 1973), p.526-534

Chowning, John and Bristow, David 'FM Theory and Applications, by Musicians for Musicians', (Yamaha Music Foundation: Tokyo, 1986), 195pp.

De Furia, Steve and Scacciaferro, Joe 'The Sampling Book', (Omnibus Press, 2002), 152pp.

Dodge, Charles and Jerse, Thomas A. 'Computer music : synthesis, composition, and performance' (Wadsworth Publishing Co. 2nd edition, 1997), 455pp.

Holmes, Thomas B. 'Electronic and Experimental Music', (Routledge, 2nd edition, 2002), 304pp.

Howard, David M. and Angus, James 'Acoustics and Psychoacoustics', (Oxford: Focal Press, 2nd edition, 2001), 416pp.

Kirk, Ross and Hunt, Andy 'Digital Sound Processing for Music and Multimedia', (Oxford: Focal Press, 1999), 352pp.

Lehrman, Paul 'Midi for the Professional', (Music Sales Corp., 1993), 239pp.

Millward, Simon 'Fast Guide to Cubase VST', (Kent: PC Publishing, 3rd edition, 2001), 460pp.

Miranda, Eduardo Reck 'Computer Sound Synthesis for the Electronic Musician', (Oxford: Focal Press, 1998), 224pp.

Roads, Curtis 'The Computer Music Tutorial', (Massachusetts: MIT Press, 1996), 904pp.

Rona, Jeffrey and Wilkinson, Scott (Editor) 'The Midi Companion', (Hal Leonard Publishing Corp., 1994), 96pp.

Russ, Martin and Rumsey, Francis (Editor) 'Sound Synthesis and Sampling', (Oxford: Focal Press, 1996), 400pp.

8 Useful websites

The internet is a very good resource for the latest information about VST Instruments and related products and for general information about sound synthesis, synthesizers and music technology. The following table lists some websites which may be of interest.

VST Instrument developers

Applied Acoustics Systems	www.applied-acoustics.com
Arturia	www.arturia.com
Bioroid	www.bioroid.com
Bitheadz	www.bitheadz.com
Bitshift Audio	www.bitshiftaudio.com
Bojo	www.bojo.dk
Edirol	www.rolanded.com
Fxpansion	www.fxpansion.com
GForce	www.gmediamusic.com
Green Oak	www.greenoak.com
Image Line	www.fruityloops.com
Koblo	www.koblo.com
Lin Plug	www.linplug.com
LoftSoft	www.loftsoft.co.uk
mda	www.mda-vst.com
Muon Software	www.muon-software.com
Native Instruments	www.native-instruments.com
PlugSound	www.plugsound.com
reFX	www.refx.net
rgcAudio	www.rgcaudio.com
Sonic Syndicate	www.sonic-syndicate.com

Spectrasonics	www.spectrasonics.net
SpeedSoft	www.vsampler.com
Steinberg	www.steinberg.net
TC Works	www.tcworks.de
Tobybear	www.tobybear.de
VirSyn	www.virsyn.de
Waldorf	www2.waldorf-gmbh.de

Steinberg Cubase VST / SX and Nuendo

Steinberg main website	www.steinberg.net
Steinberg UK website	www.steinberguk.com
Cubase.net forum and website	www.cubase.net
Cubase FAQ website	www.cubasefaq.com

Emagic Logic Audio

Emagic main website	www.emagic.de

Audio cards/hardware

Aardvark	www.aardvarkaudio.com
Creamware	www.creamware.com
Creative	www.creative.com
Echo	www.echoaudio.com
Edirol	www.edirol.com
Gadget Labs	www.gadgetlabs.com
Guillemot	www.guillemot.com
Korg	www.korg.com
Lexicon	www.lexicon.com
Mark of the Unicorn (MOTU)	www.motu.com
M Audio	www.midiman.com
RME	www.rme-audio.com
Terratec	www.terratec.co.uk
Turtle Beach	www.tbeach.com
Yamaha	www.yamaha.com

Soundbanks, samples and Reaktor ensembles

FM sounds	www.thedx7.co.uk
FM sounds Vol. 1	www.nativeinstruments.de/index.php?Fm7sounds1_us
Groundloops sampled loops	www.groundloops.com
HALion sample CDs	www.biggagiggas.com
HALion samples and info	www.halion.co.uk
kvr VSTi sound libraries	www.kvr-vst.com
PrimeSounds sample library	www.primesounds.com
Reaktor (Martin Brinkmann)	www.martin-brinkmann.de/ens.html
Reaktor (Len Sasso)	www.swiftkick.com/reaktor.html
Reaktor (Paul Swennenhuis)	www.midiworld.org/AuReality
Reaktor (Wave In Head)	www.waveinhead.de
Sizers samples	www.mourningafter.net/sizers
WizooSounds sample library	www.wizoosounds.com

Sound synthesis, synthesizers and music technology

Hammond organ	theatreorgans.com/hammond/faq
Mellotron	members.aol.com/tronpage
Mellotron	www.mellotron.com
Moog synthesizers	moogarchives.com
Sound synthesis	www.creativesynth.com
Sound synthesis	www.sonicspot.com
Synthesizers and synthesis	www.vintagesynth.org
Synthesizer FAQ site	tilt.largo.fl.us/faq/synthfaq.html
Synthesizer history	www.obsolete.com/120_years
Synthesizer information and links	www.synthesizers.com
Synth zone	www.synthzone.com

General interest

Computer Music Magazine	www.computermusic.co.uk
Digital domain	www.digido.com
Electronic music publishing	www.raw42.com
Electronic music website	www.em411.com

Future Music magazine	www.futuremusic.co.uk
kvr VSTi resources	www.kvr-vst.com
Mac audio and music site	www.macmusic.org
MIDI Farm	www.midifarm.com
Millennium Music Software	www.millennium-music.co.uk
Plug-in Spot VSTi resources	www.pluginspot.com
Shareware Music Machine	www.hitsquad.com
Sound on Sound magazine	www.sospubs.co.uk
Tom's PC hardware guide	www.tomshardware.com
Virtual Guitarist website	vg.clubcubase.net
VST central VSTi listings	www.vstcentral.com

Glossary

ADC Analogue-to-digital converter. A device which converts analogue data, such as an audio signal from the real world, into digital data (a sequence of numbers) which can be retained in computer memory or stored on digital media such as hard disks, DAT and CD.

ADSR Attack, Decay, Sustain, Release. A four-breakpoint envelope type used to control how the amplitude of a sound evolves over time. ADSR envelopes are also used to control the spectral evolution of a sound by modulating the cut-off frequency of a filter.

Aftertouch The action of applying pressure to one or more keys of a musical keyboard after the onset of a note or chord. Also referred to as 'Channel Aftertouch' or 'Channel Pressure', it is transmitted via MIDI as Aftertouch messages and affects all notes present on the same MIDI channel by the same amount. It can be used to produce various real-time performance effects such as volume or brightness modulation and vibrato.

Algorithm A clearly defined, step-by-step set of instructions designed to achieve the completion of a specific task. Algorithms are invariably translated into computer programming languages and used as the building blocks for computer programs.

Aliasing A particular type of digital audio distortion which manifests itself as additional frequency components which do not form part of the original audio signal. This occurs when a signal has been sampled at too low a sampling rate to accurately capture the details of the high frequency components.

All-pass filter A filtering device which involves delaying frequency components by varying amounts and mixing the result with the original signal. Unlike conventional filtering, no attenuation in the amplitudes of the frequencies takes place.

AM Amplitude Modulation. A sound synthesis technique (or effect) achieved by modulating the amplitude of one audio signal (the carrier) by another signal (the modulator) where both signals are in the audible range. Using simple sine waves produces a signal containing the carrier and two sidebands which are the sum and difference frequencies of the carrier and modulator. Using more complex signals produces densely packed inharmonic sidebands.

Amplifier A device which increases or decreases the amplitude of a signal which passes through it.

Amplitude A measure of the depth of the compression and rarefaction cycles of a sound signal where the peak amplitude is the point of maximum displacement from the mid-point of the signal's waveform. The amplitude contributes to the perceived loudness of the signal.

Analogue In audio, refers to a sound signal whose waveform has a value at every point in time. There are no steps between each point and the waveform of a recorded analogue signal (such as that recorded onto high-quality analogue tape) closely resembles that of the original. All phenomena found in the natural world are analogue.

Arpeggiator A device for automatically repeating a group of notes in a cyclic pattern, usually by stepping through the notes of a chord which is held down on the musical keyboard.

ASIO Audio Stream Input Output. Computer protocol developed by Steinberg for handling audio recording and playback in digital audio systems.

Attack The shape and duration of the first part of a sound event where the amplitude rises from zero to its peak level (as implemented in an ADSR envelope).

Attenuation The reduction of the amplitude of a sound signal (or of a component within the signal).

Balance i) describes the relative levels of two or more sound elements (for example, when setting up a mix on a mixing console). ii) MIDI Controller 8. Used to adjust the relative levels of two components of a sound.

Band-pass filter A filter which allows a band of frequencies between two cut-off points to pass through with little change while significantly attenuating frequencies both above and below the pass band.

Band-reject filter A filter which significantly attenuates a band of frequencies between two cut-off points while allowing the rest of the signal to pass through with little change.

Bandwidth i) The range between two frequency points within the spectrum of an audio signal. ii) The overall frequency range of the spectrum of an audio signal.

Bank Select A combination of MIDI Controllers 0 and 32. A Bank Select message is usually immediately followed by a Program Change and allows switching to as many as 16384 different Banks.

BIOS Basic Input Output System. A program at the root level of a computer system for controlling its elementary operations.

Bit Acronym for 'binary digit'. The smallest unit of information in a binary number, represented as a 1 or a 0.

Boot A term used to describe starting a computer. This can take the form of a 'cold start', when the computer is booted from its switched off state, and a 'warm start', when the computer is restarted in its switched on state.

BPM Abbreviation for Beats Per Minute. Musical tempo expressed as the number of beats which occur in one minute. For example, at a tempo of 60BPM each beat of the bar has a duration of one second.

Breath Controller A breath operated device connected to a synthesizer used to change the volume or timbre of a sound. It is transmitted via MIDI as Controller 2.

Byte An 8-bit binary number (e.g. 0011 1010), creating the fundamental unit of measurement for computer media. A kilobyte (Kb) is 1,024 bytes, a megabyte (Mb) is 1,024 kilobytes and a gigabyte (Gb) is 1,024 megabytes.

Buffer Temporary storage area used to store data as it flows in, out and through a computer system.

Carrier In frequency modulation, amplitude modulation and ring modulation, the carrier is the audio signal to which modulation is applied. The carrier normally governs the perceived pitch of the resulting tone.

CD ROM Compact Disk Read Only Memory. A read-only CD containing data which can only be read by a computer CD drive and not an audio CD player.

Cent One hundredth of a semitone. A unit in musical instrument tuning systems used for fine adjustments of pitch.

Centre frequency The centre point of the passband or stopband in a band-pass or band-reject filter.

Chorus An effect produced by passing a signal through one or more delay lines and modulating the delay time(s) with an LFO. The result is mixed with the original signal. The modulation of the delay times produces changes in the perceived pitch and timing, creating the illusion of an ensemble of sound sources.

Comb filter A filter comprised of multiple amplitude response curves (or resonances) located at harmonic intervals relative to a chosen fundamental frequency. Passing a signal through such a filter emphasises the chosen harmonics in the source sound and can often change its perceived pitch.

Compressor An automatic level adjustment device which normally results in loud parts of the signal becoming quieter and quiet parts becoming louder. Compression converts a large dynamic range into a smaller dynamic range.

Control Change A type of MIDI message used to control various parameters other than the musical notes. Control Change messages contain information about the Controller number (0–127) and its value (0–127). Each Controller number has a specific function and the more commonly used Controllers include modulation (01), breath control (02), main volume (07), pan (10), expression (11) and sustain pedal (64).

CPU Central Processing Unit. The main processor or chip controlling the operations of a computer, usually found on the main circuit board (motherboard).

Cross modulation The interconnection of the outputs of two oscillators to eachother's frequency inputs resulting in a complex frequency-modulated signal.

Cut-off The frequency at which the response of a filter passes from the pass band to the stop band (or vice versa), i.e. the frequency at which the filter starts to have an effect.

DAC Digital-to-analogue converter. A device which converts digital data into analogue data. For example, before we can hear the music on an audio CD, the digital information picked up by the read head of the CD player must first be converted into analogue form which can be processed by an amplifier and speaker system and, finally, sensed by the ear as sound vibrations in air. The conversion process is carried out by a digital-to-analogue converter.

Decay i) As part of an envelope (e.g. ADSR), describes the shape and duration of a second part of a sound event where the amplitude falls from its peak level to its sustain level. ii) In general terms, describes how a sound fades away to silence.

Decibel (dB) A unit of relative measurement of sound pressure level between audio signals on a logarithmic scale. For example, increasing the level of an input signal by 6dB results in an output which is double the amplitude (voltage) of the original. Attenuating the level by 6dB results in an output which is half the amplitude (voltage).

Delay A replication of a signal which occurs at a set time after the original. Used in audio for delay, echo, chorus, flanging and other effects.

Digital Digital systems handle information as numerical data. A digital waveform is made up of discrete steps each of which is represented by a number. The quantity of these steps (samples) within a given time frame forms the sampling rate of a digital recording. The audio on a CD is recorded at a sampling rate of 44.1kHz, i.e. 44,100 samples per second.

Distortion A non-linear audio process which adds extra frequencies to the signal, thereby changing its waveform.

Download The process of loading a file from another system, such as from the internet or other network, into one's own computer.

Driver Software which provides the communication protocol between a hardware device and the operating system of the host computer. The hardware is usually set up and initialised via the driver software.

DSP i) Digital Signal Processing. The processing of signals using digital microprocessors. ii) Digital Signal Processor. A special computer chip which has been optimised for the high-speed numerical computations required for the processing of audio signals.

Echo A particular kind of delay where the delayed signal is clearly distinguishable from the original, often involving repeating echos. Delay effects may be classed as echo when the delay time is increased to around 30ms or more, (i.e. when the ear begins to clearly differentiate the delayed and original signals).

Emphasis See Resonance.

Envelope The shape of a sound's amplitude variations over time (usually plotted on a graph of amplitude against time with break-points for each stage in the sound's evolution). One of the most common envelope shapes is the ADSR envelope.

Envelope Generator (EG) A device which generates a time-varying control signal (envelope) used to modulate the amplitude of a sound (usually based upon a set of values entered by the user). Envelope generators are also commonly used to modulate the frequency of the cut-off point of a filter.

Equalisation (EQ) Increase/attenuation of the levels of different frequency bands (e.g. bass, mid and treble) within a signal for corrective or creative purposes.

Expression MIDI Controller 11. Used to change the volume of a note while it is sustaining.

Feedback Circuit which allows the connection of the output signal back to the input, producing additional frequency components within the signal, (when used for overdrive and saturation effects), or for creating echo repeats, (when used for delay effects).

FFT Abbreviation for Fast Fourier Transform. An optimised version of the Fourier Transform (Joseph Fourier), a mathematical procedure for calculating the frequency components of a sound from the waveform.

Filter A device which attenuates one or more chosen frequency bands within a sound while allowing the others to pass through unchanged.

Flanging An audio effect created by mixing a delayed version of a signal with the original and modulating the delay time with an LFO while also applying an amount of feedback.

FM Frequency Modulation. A sound synthesis technique (or effect) where the frequency of one signal (the carrier) is modulated by another (the modulator). In the sound synthesis sense, FM implies that both frequencies are within the audible range and when this is the case multiple frequencies known as sidebands are added to the signal.

Frequency The number of times a periodic sound wave oscillates per second, measured in hertz (Hz).

Frequency domain The representation of a sound signal on a graph of amplitude versus frequency. This shows the spectrum of the signal.

Fundamental The lowest frequency component within a periodic soundwave and normally that which gives the tone its perceived pitch.

Gain A measure of the increase in relative amplitude level between the input and output of an amplifier.

Gate i) An audio device which radically attenuates the level of an input signal when it falls below a certain threshold. Used especially to filter out unwanted background noise and interference in the inactive parts of speech or musical performance. ii) The time between the moment a note is triggered by pressing a key on a musical keyboard (key on) and when the note is ended by releasing the key (key off).

General MIDI (GM) An addition to the MIDI protocol, (not formally a part of the MIDI

Specification), providing a standard set of rules for patch mapping, drum and percussion note mapping, multi-timbrality, polyphony and various other elements. Roland introduced an enhanced version of the GM standard known as GS (General Standard) and Yamaha introduced similar enhancements known as XG (Extended General MIDI).

Harmonic Component within a sound whose frequency is a whole integer multiple of the fundamental.

Headroom The difference between the current level of a recorded signal and the maximum output level of the recording medium.

Hertz (Hz) A unit for measuring frequency. It expresses the number of oscillations per second of a periodic soundwave. The greater the number of hertz, the higher the perceived pitch of the sound.

Hexadecimal A base sixteen numbering system often used by computer programmers as an alternative to decimal or binary systems. The decimal numbers 0–9 are expressed as 0–9 in hexadecimal and decimal 10–15 are expressed as the letters A–F. Hexadecimal numbers have much more in common with the way that computers actually work than decimal numbers and they are less cumbersome than binary numbers. Thus they have proved extremely efficient for the analysis and understanding of computer data.

Hold pedal Middle foot pedal featured on acoustic pianos which, when pressed down, sustains the concurrently played note(s) but allows any subsequent notes to be played normally for as long as the pedal is held down. A similar foot pedal is featured on some electronic musical keyboards to create a similar effect. In MIDI-based applications the pedal action is transmitted using MIDI controller 66, (also referred to as sostenuto).

High-pass filter (HPF) A filter which significantly attenuates the frequencies below a chosen cut-off point while allowing those above to pass through with little change.

Latency The delay between the user input and the time it takes for a real-time digital audio system to respond and process the data through its hardware and software.

Level A measure of the amplitude of an audio signal.

LFO Abbreviation for low frequency oscillator. A type of oscillator which operates below the normal hearing range, often used for modulating a second oscillator to produce vibrato, tremolo and other modulation effects.

Limiter A peak level control device used to reduce the gain of the input signal when the input level exceeds the chosen threshold. A limiter is usually characterised by a very fast attack time and gain reduction which acts upon only the loudest peaks in the signal.

Logarithmic A manner in which to manage scales involving very large numbers and helpful in music and acoustics for understanding the human perception of sound intensity and frequency. The ear's response to these phenomena is logarithmic and not linear. For example, plotting frequency on a graph logarithmically shows equal pitch intervals (an equal distance between successive octaves) rather than a linear plot which shows equal frequency intervals (a doubling of the distance between successive octaves).

Loudness The subjective response of the ear to the amplitude of a sound signal.

Loudness contour The shape of the amplitude of a sound as it evolves over time. The same meaning as envelope shape (see envelope, above).

Low-pass filter (LPF) A filter which significantly attenuates the frequencies above a chosen cut-off point while allowing those below to pass through with little change.

Internet Global network of computers interconnected via telephone lines. The internet is now the largest information resource in the world and provides a wide range of services and entertainment.

Master keyboard A MIDI equipped keyboard (often with no sound generating circuitry) used to control a network of MIDI modules and devices. Sometimes referred to as a 'mother keyboard'.

MIDI Musical Instrument Digital Interface. A data communication standard, first established in 1983, for the exchange of musical information between electronic musical instruments and, subsequently, computers. This involves the serial transfer of digital information, (MIDI Messages), via 5 pin DIN connectors. MIDI Messages are governed by a pre-defined set of rules and syntax known as the MIDI Specification.

MIDI Channel A channel for the sending and receiving of MIDI messages between devices. MIDI specifies 16 separate channels and each MIDI device can be set to be receptive to messages on one of these channels or, in the case of a multi-timbral instrument, on several specified channels at the same time.

MIDI Clock A timing related MIDI Message embedded in the MIDI data stream. MIDI Timing Clocks are sent 24 times per quarter note and along with Song Position Pointer, Start, Stop and Continue messages are used to synchronize MIDI-based sequencers, drum machines and other MIDI devices. Unlike SMPTE/EBU Time Code, MIDI Timing Clock is tempo-dependent.

MIDI Controller A type of MIDI Message used to control various musical parameters other than the notes themselves, such as Modulation, Volume and Pan. Controllers are also referred to as 'Continuous Controllers' and 'Control Change messages'.

MIDI Event MIDI data once it has been recorded into a MIDI-based sequencer. This is in contrast to 'MIDI Message' which refers to the same data as it is being sent down the MIDI cable.

MIDI File A standardised file format providing a way of transferring MIDI data between different software sequencers, hardware sequencers and computer platforms. There are three types of MIDI File: Type 0 stores the data as a single stream of events, Type 1 contains multiple parallel tracks and Type 2 allows sets of independent sequences to be stored in a single file. Type 1 is the most popular format.

MIDI In 5 pin DIN socket found on all MIDI-equipped devices used to receive MIDI data.

MIDI interface A hardware interface which provides a link between a computer and external MIDI devices, normally providing at least one MIDI input and one MIDI output with more advanced units providing multiple MIDI sockets and synchronization facilities.

MIDI Machine Control (MMC) An addition to the MIDI Specification to facilitate the control of tape transports and other devices.

MIDI Message A short sequence of MIDI data which passes a discrete instruction or command to the receiving device. MIDI Messages include such things as Note On, Note Off, Polyphonic Pressure, Control Change, Program Change, Aftertouch, and System Exclusive messages.

MIDI Mode An operational mode governing how a MIDI device manages data on different MIDI Channels and whether it performs polyphonically or monophonically. There are four modes including Mode 1 (Omni On/Poly); response to messages on all MIDI channels and polyphonic, Mode 2 (Omni On/Mono); response to messages on all MIDI channels and monophonic, Mode 3 (Omni Off/Poly); response to messages on chosen MIDI channel(s) and polyphonic, Mode 4 (Omni Off/Mono); response to messages on chosen MIDI channel(s) and monophonic. Most units power up in Mode 3.

MIDI Out 5 pin DIN socket found on all MIDI equipped instruments used to send MIDI data.

MIDI Thru 5 pin DIN socket found on most MIDI equipped instruments providing a copy of the MIDI data received at the MIDI In. In other words, the data passes through the unit on to a further destination, such as another module.

MIDI Time Code (MTC) A type of time code which is sent via MIDI, used to synchronize MIDI-based sequencers and other MIDI devices. Similar to SMPTE/EBU time code, MTC is an absolute timing reference measured in hours, minutes, seconds and fractions of a second and so does not vary with tempo.

Modulation i) The modification of one signal by another to produce effects (e.g. vibrato and tremolo). For real-time performance, the intensity of the modulation effect is controlled by the modulation wheel found on the control panel of electronic musical keyboards. Modulation is transmitted via MIDI as MIDI Controller 1. ii) The basis for FM and AM sound synthesis techniques.

Modulator i) The control signal which applies a modulating effect to a second signal. ii) The modulating part of a carrier:modulator pair of oscillators in FM synthesis.

MROS MIDI Real Time Operating System. Operating system developed by Steinberg to manage complex audio and MIDI software systems where timing considerations are a priority.

Multi-timbral The ability of a synthesizer or module to produce several different sounds at the same time controlled on different MIDI Channels.

Native processing Digital audio processing involving the computer's own processor and other resources rather than external digital signal processing hardware.

Noise A sound comprised of randomly distributed and inharmonic frequency components.

Notch filter A specialised type of band-reject filter which significantly attenuates a very narrow band of frequencies between two cut-off points while allowing the rest of the signal to pass through with little change.

Note On A MIDI message produced by pressing a key on a musical keyboard (or by the onset of a pre-recorded MIDI event). A Note On message starts the sounding of a musical event. It contains information about the Pitch and the Velocity of the note.

Note Off A MIDI message produced by releasing a key on a musical keyboard (or by the termination of a pre-recorded MIDI event). A Note Off message starts the release phase of a musical event. It contains information about the Pitch of the note to be switched off and the Velocity with which the key was released.

Octave An interval in pitch between two tones corresponding with a doubling (or halving) of the frequency. In Western music there are 12 notes in each octave.

Operating system An organised collection of software at the next level up from BIOS which enables the user to communicate with the computer. The operating system provides the interface between BIOS and the applications running on the computer.

Oscillator A device which produces a periodic, alternating signal. Oscillators are used for generating periodic waveforms of a given amplitude and frequency.

Overtone Spectral component in a composite sound signal located at a higher frequency than the fundamental.

Pan The panoramic position of a sound within the stereo image. Most devices with two or more audio outputs feature a pan control. Pan data is transmitted via MIDI as Controller 10.

Parametric EQ Flexible signal filtering arrangement based upon a centre frequency selector, a Q control and a gain control. The centre frequency selector allows you to tune in to the frequency band you wish to process, the Q control regulates the width (filter slope characteristics) of this band and the gain control provides the means to boost or cut the chosen frequencies.

Patch A configuration of the controls of an electronic or software synthesizer which creates a specific sound. Also referred to as program, voice, sound or preset. Each patch can usually be stored in the instrument's library for later recall.

PCI Peripheral Component Interconnect. A PCI bus is a standard computer slot for cards and extension boards and is widely used for connecting audio cards.

PCM Pulse Code Modulation. Coding scheme involving the conversion of binary numbers into electronic pulses and fundamental to the conversion of analogue signals into digital form during the sampling process.

Phase The relationship between two or more components of a waveform (or of separate signals) in terms of the relative position of the compression and rarefaction parts of their waveforms. Phase is expressed in degrees.

Phasing An audio effect created by mixing a phase-shifted version of a signal with the original and modulating the phase shifting with an LFO while also applying an amount of feedback.

Pitch The subjective response of the ear to the frequency of a sound signal.

Pitch Bend Variation of the pitch of a sounding note (e.g. the bending of a note on a guitar). It is transmitted via MIDI as Pitch Bend data and on electronic keyboards is usually applied in real-time using a pitch wheel on the control surface of the instrument.

Pole An element in filter design responsible for the characteristics of the filter slope between the pass band and the stop band where a 1-pole filter results in a filter slope of 6dB per octave, a 2-pole filter gives a slope of 12dB per octave, a 4-pole filter gives a slope of 24dB per octave and so on.

Polyphonic Having the capacity to play more than one note simultaneously.

Portamento A sliding of pitch between consecutively played notes (similar to glissando).

Program Change A type of MIDI message used to remotely change the Program number or patch in a MIDI device. There are 128 available program numbers but when used in conjunction with Bank Select messages the number of possible program slots is significantly expanded.

Pulse wave A periodic sound wave containing odd-numbered harmonics similar to a square wave but with certain harmonics in the series missing. Pulse waves are characterised by their pulse width which is the proportion of one complete cycle for which the waveform remains in the compression (or positive) part of its waveform. A pulse wave with a pulse width of 1/n lacks each nth harmonic.

PWM Pulse Width Modulation. The cyclic modulation of the pulse width of a pulse wave using an LFO as the modulator.

Q A measure of the selectivity and filter slope characteristics of a filter. Also referred to as resonance and emphasis.

Quantization The process of transforming a continuous analogue signal into a series of discrete values during analogue-to-digital conversion.

Quantization noise A noise produced when converting very low level audio signals, due to insufficient bit depth (lack of resolution). The noise results from the rounding up or down of some of the least significant bits used to express the signal and is heard as a 'graininess' in the sound reproduction.

Quantize A term used in hardware and software sequencers to describe the action of automatically moving recorded notes onto the nearest fraction of a bar according to a quantize value. For example, using a quantize value of 16 (meaning 1/16 notes) shifts all inaccurately played notes onto the nearest 1/16 division of the bar. While this is useful for correcting inaccurate playing it can also produce undesirably robotic music. The more advanced sequencers provide several different methods of quantizing material. These include the ability to move notes 'towards' a quantize value according to a percentage and moving notes according to a pre-recorded 'feel' template (groove quantize).

RAM Random Access Memory. Volatile memory for the temporary storage of data.

Real-time Instantaneous output (or result) from an input. Real-time digital audio processing refers to processing where there is virtually no delay between the input signal and the processed output signal. Recording music into a sequencer in real-time means that the performance is recorded instantaneously as it is played, much like recording onto a tape recorder.

Release The shape and duration of the final part of a sound event where the amplitude falls from its sustain level to zero.

Resonance The frequency or frequencies at which a device or object vibrates in sympathy with itself. Many filters are endowed with resonant behaviour normally characterised by a boost in the frequencies around the cut-off point. The shape and intensity of this boost in frequencies is regulated by a resonance control (often also referred to as Q or emphasis).

Resynthesis Analysis-synthesis technique where an existing sample is analysed and arranged into a set of parameters and values (e.g. pitch, amplitude and phase for each harmonic) which are used as the basis for synthesizing a new sound.

Reverberation Multiple series of reflections occuring after the original sound in an acoustic space. Also known as reverb, reverberation is characterised by three phases: the original sound which arrives directly from the source to the listener's ear, after a short pause the early reflections from nearby surfaces and finally a complex mass of multiple reflections which fade to silence (known as the reverb tail).

Ring modulation Amplitude modulation technique where two oscillator signals are multiplied to produce the sum and difference of their frequencies in the output. The original frequency of the source signal is not present in the output.

ROM Read Only Memory. Memory with fixed contents which cannot be overwritten.

Sample i) A snapshot of a digital audio signal at one moment in time. ii) A recorded segment of digital audio.

Sampler Computer musical instrument which allows the recording, editing, modifying and playback of segments of digitally recorded sound.

Sampling rate Also referred to as sampling frequency. In the recording of digital audio the sampling rate is the number of times an analogue signal is measured per second during the process of analogue-to-digital conversion. For example, the audio on a CD is recorded at a sampling rate of 44.1kHz, i.e.: 44,100 samples per second.

Sample resolution The number of levels of measurement available in a digital audio system. For example, a 16-bit system features 65536 possible discrete values which can be used to measure the amplitude of an audio signal. The sample resolution, together with the sampling rate, determines the accuracy and quality of the sound recording and reproduction of a digital audio system.

Sawtooth wave A periodic sound wave containing all the harmonics in the natural harmonic series with the level of each harmonic at 1/n that of the fundamental (where n = the harmonic number). A sawtooth wave has a saw-shaped waveform, hence its name.

SCSI Small Computer System Interface. A communication bus system available in several standards which allows very fast data transfer times and the connection of several devices (usually hard drives) on the same bus.

Semitone A shift in pitch of half a tone. In mathematical terms, a change in pitch of one semitone is achieved by multiplying or dividing the frequency by 1.0595. The keys on a piano keyboard are arranged in one semitone steps.

Signal-to-noise (S/N) ratio The ratio of the signal level to the noise level in a system, usually expressed in decibels (dB's). The larger the value of the S/N ratio the lower the level of the background noise.

Sine wave A pure, periodic sound wave based upon the mathematical sine function containing a single component at the fundamental. A sine wave has a sinusoidal waveform.

Song Position Pointer A MIDI message often included when synchronizing MIDI devices using MIDI Timing Clocks. It allows the slaved instrument to be synchronized to the same position in the music as the master instrument after fast forward and rewind operations.

S/PDIF Sony Philips Digital Interface. A digital signal interface standard often found on audio cards, DAT machines and other devices. S/PDIF sockets take the form of RCA phonos.

Spectrum A representation of a sound in terms of its constituent components at one point in time or averaged over a chosen time frame. Expressed graphically in the frequency domain as vertical lines (or peaks) where each line represents a component at a different frequency and amplitude. A spectrum gives a good idea of a sound's timbral quality.

Square wave A periodic sound wave containing all the odd-numbered harmonics in the natural harmonic series with the level of each harmonic at 1/n that of the fundamental (where n = the harmonic number). A square wave has a square-shaped waveform, hence its name.

Steady-state The segment within the envelope of a sound event where the timbre and amplitude is relatively constant. It is within this part of the sound where a loop can be applied using sampling techniques for the artificial sustaining of a note.

Step-time A method of entering notes into a sequencer one step at a time (also referred to as Step input). The pitch, position and duration for each entry is pre-determined and after input is complete the music can be played back at any tempo. Step-time provides a useful method of entering notes into a sequencer when real-time performance is either too fast or too complicated.

Sustain The part in the evolution of a sound event which determines the amplitude level which sustains for as long as the note is held.

Sustain Pedal A foot pedal on acoustic and electronic pianos used to produce a sustaining of all played notes for as long as the pedal is held down. MIDI Controller 64 (also known as the Damper pedal).

Synthesizer An electronic or software-based musical instrument specialised in the creation of a wide range of tones and sound textures beyond those encountered in conventional musical instruments. A synthesizer is normally endowed with a performance interface (a musical keyboard), a control interface (GUI or front panel controls) and a synthesis engine (sound processing circuitry).

System Exclusive A type of MIDI Message allowing non-standardised communication between MIDI devices. Used for the transfer of Manufacturer Specific System Exclusive and also Universal System Exclusive data. Manufacturer Specific System Exclusive includes a unique ID for each manufacturing company and might be used to change or control almost any parameter in the receiving device as deemed appropriate by the manufacturer. Universal System Exclusive data includes MIDI Machine Control, MIDI Show Control, Sample Dump Standard, MIDI File Dump, General MIDI On and General MIDI Off.

Timbre Tone colour, or harmonic structure which gives a sound its sonic identity.

Time domain The representation of a sound signal on a graph of amplitude versus time. This shows the waveform of the signal.

Tremolo A periodic variation in the loudness of a tone produced by modulating its amplitude with a low frequency oscillator (LFO), usually set in the range between 1 and 10Hz.

Triangle wave A periodic sound wave containing all the odd-numbered harmonics in the natural harmonic series with the level of each harmonic at $1/n^2$ that of the fundamental (where n = the harmonic number). A triangle wave has a triangle-shaped waveform, hence its name.

Trigger A short pulse which instructs a synthesizer to start a process like the sounding of a note or the generating of an envelope.

USB Universal Serial Bus. High speed expansion interface allowing the convenient connection of up to 127 external peripherals to a computer (including MIDI and audio devices).

VCA Voltage Controlled Amplifier. Type of amplifier used in analogue synthesis where the gain is regulated by a control voltage.

VCF Voltage Controlled Filter. Type of filter used in analogue synthesis where the cut-off frequency is regulated by a control voltage.

VCO Voltage Controlled Oscillator. Type of oscillator used in analogue synthesis where the frequency is regulated by a control voltage.

Velocity The speed (or force) with which a key is pressed or released on an electronic keyboard instrument. Normally, the harder a key is struck the louder the resulting note and the higher the velocity value. Velocity might also be used to affect the brightness, vibrato, sustain or some other expressive element within the sound. It forms part of the actual MIDI note data, (the third byte of Note On and Note Off messages), and does not assume a separate MIDI data category like many other parameters.

Vibrato A periodic variation in the pitch of a tone produced by modulating its frequency with a low frequency oscillator (LFO), usually set in the range between 1 and 10Hz. Vibrato produces a characteristic 'warbling' effect and is usually applied during the sustain part of the sound.

Virtual analogue Simulated analogue synthesis using digital signal processing techniques in software synthesis instruments.

Volume i) Generic term for loudness, amplitude or level. ii) MIDI Controller 7. Used to regulate the volume of notes in a MIDI recording. Also referred to as Main Volume.

VSTi Abbreviation for VST Instrument (Virtual Studio Instrument).

Waveform The shape of a sound wave when represented on a graph of time versus amplitude. Typical periodic waveforms include sawtooth, square, triangle and pulse.

White noise A sound signal with the same amount of acoustical energy at all frequencies. White noise produces a 'hissing' sound.

Index

More music technology

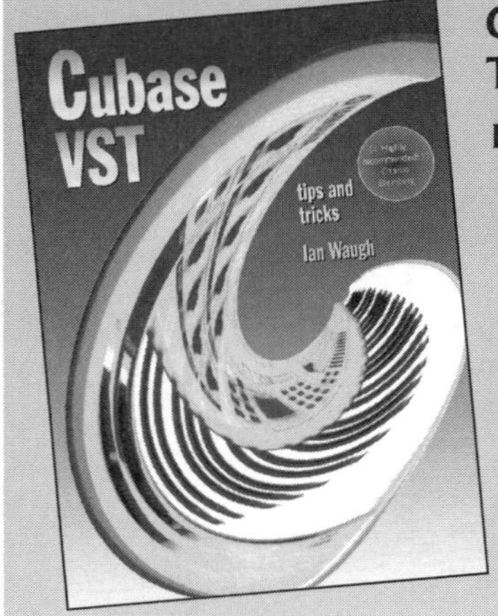

Cubase VST Tips and Tricks

Ian Waugh

154 pp • ISBN 1870775 63 5
£10.95

'Highly recommended' says Cubase creator Charlie Steinberg

There's not much you can't do with Cubase VST – but how many users really achieve full mastery over the program? In this highly practical and creative book you will discover a wealth of tips and tricks to help you become more creative and more productive. The manual explains how VST works but this book shows you how to use it! You'll find tips on optimising your computer system, improving your grooves, audio and MIDI quantisation, using dynamic events, arranging, recording, synchronisation, using the editors, mixing, fader automation, audio processing, using audio effects, EQ, troubleshooting, and much, much more...

One to look out for

Sound Synthesis with VST Instruments

Simon Millward

coming soon!

Making Music with Emagic Logic Audio

Stephen Bennett

314 pp • ISBN 1870775 651
£19.95

This book introduces all the features of Emagic Logic Audio, but never loses sight of your objective – using the program to make great music. Describes the installation of the program on Macs and PCs, gives a practical introduction to setting up and using Logic, and it leads you through your first recording. It describes how to use the Arrange page, the Event list editor, the Matrix, Audio and Hyper editors, and how to use the Score editor to print out your music. Plus Audio and MIDI recording and editing, mixing, virtual instruments, mastering, plug-ins and audio processing. There is an invaluable overview of all the the menus in Logic, choosing and using a computer and audio interface for Logic, as well as lists of key commands and shortcuts.

Quick Guide to Analogue Synthesis

Ian Waugh
64 pp • ISBN 1870775 70 8
£6.95

Even though music production has moved into the digital domain, modern synthesisers invariably use analogue synthesis techniques. The reason is simple – analogue synthesis is flexible and versatile, and it's relatively easy for us to understand. The basics are the same for all analogue synths, and you'll quickly be able to adapt the principles to any instrument, to edit existing sounds and create exciting new ones. If you want to take your synthesiser – of the hardware or software variety – past the presets, and program your own sounds and effects, this practical and well-illustrated book tells you what you need to know.

books from PC Publishing

Quick Guide to Digital Audio Recording

Ian Waugh

64 pp • ISBN 1870775 68 6
£6.95

All modern music recordings use digital audio technology. Now everyone with a computer can produce CD-quality recordings and this book shows you how. Written in a clear and straightforward style, it explains what digital audio recording is, how to use it, the equipment you need, what sort of software is available, and how to achieve professional results. Computer-based recording is the future of music and this book shows how you can join the revolution now.

Quick Guide to Dance Music

Ian Waugh

64 pp • ISBN 1870775 69 4
£6.95

Dance – it's the music of the new Millennium. It's in the charts, played in clubs, you hear it on movie soundtracks and even in restaurants. Its variety and cross-influences mean Dance covers a multitude of styles. It seems to be dominated by a select few – influential producers, DJs and programmers – but everyone with a computer can create Dance music and this book shows you how. In clear and simple language. If you want to create Dance music, this highly practical book explains everything from how to create your own drum and bass lines to putting your music on the Web.

Quick Guide to MP3 and Digital Music

Ian Waugh

64 pp • ISBN 1870775 67 8
£6.95

MP3 files, the latest digital music format, have taken the music industry by storm. What are they? Where do you get them? How do you use them? Why have they thrown record companies into a panic? Will they make music easier to buy? And cheaper? Is this the future of music? All these questions and more are answered in this concise and practical book which explains everything you need to know about MP3s in a simple and easy-to-understand manner. Whether you want to stay bang up to date with the latest music or create your own MP3s and join the on-line digital music revolution, this book will show you how.

Check our website!
www.pc-publishing.co.uk

PC Publishing
Export House
130 Vale Road
Tonbridge
Kent TN9 1SP
UK

tel 01732 770893
fax 01732 770268
email
info@pc-publishing.co.uk
Web
http://www.pc-publishing.co.uk

Fast Guide to Cubase VST

Simon Millward

464 pp • 244 x 172 mm
ISBN 1870775 71 6 • £22.95

- VST Version 5
- For PC and Mac
- Includes VST instruments
- Installing and setting up on PC and Mac
- MIDI and audio features of Cubase VST
- Hands on projects
- Third party plug-ins
- Time saving short cuts

This third edition of the Fast Guide to Cubase VST includes new features introduced with Cubase VST Version 5. It covers the changes to the Arrange window, the Marker Track, the Inspector for MIDI and audio Tracks. It explains the new tools, how to create crossfades and fades in the Audio editor, the new EQ section, True Tape and Apogee UV22 dithering, as well as Window Sets, Keyboard Layouts and Preferences.

Installation and setting up of the program on PC and Macintosh computers are explained. and detailed information on how to record, edit, process and mix digital audio and how to use EQ and effects are all featured. A number of third party plug-ins are explored, and the book shows how to get the best from processing techniques such as compression, expansion and limiting. The software is tested with a range of PC audio cards and with a number of PC hardware configurations.

Projects throughout the book describe Cubase VST in a number of recording situations, providing a valuable practical insight into how best to use the program for specific tasks. The Fast Guide to Cubase VST is the ideal companion for all users of the software, from the home sound recordist/ musician to the audio professional.

Topics covered include: Installing and setting up, the Arrange window, Key, List and Drum edit, Quantise, Synchronisation, The Master Track, the MIDI Effect Processor, Score and Logical Edit, the Audio editor, the Wave editor, the Audio pool, EQ and effects, mixing, plug-ins, audio processing techniques and choosing a PC audio card.

"Excellent ... well written, packed with practical tips"
Personal Computer World
"Projects and tutorials describe valuable insights into how best to use Cubase VST for specific tasks, with plenty of time saving shortcuts"
Sound on Sound

PC Publishing
Export House, 130 Vale Road, Tonbridge, Kent TN9 1SP, UK
Tel 01732 770893 • Fax 01732 770268 • e-mail info@pc-publishing.com
Website http://www.pc-publishing.com

Check our website!
www.pc-publishing.com